Strategic Reward Systems

We work with leading authors to develop the
strongest educational materials in business and
management, bringing cutting-edge thinking and
best learning practice to a global market.

Under a range of well-known imprints, including
Financial Times Prentice Hall, we craft high quality
print and electronic publications which help
readers to understand and apply their content,
whether studying or at work.

To find out more about the complete range of our
publishing please visit us on the World Wide Web at:
www.pearsoneduc.com

Strategic Reward Systems

Edited by
Richard Thorpe and Gill Homan

FINANCIAL TIMES
Prentice Hall

An imprint of **Pearson Education**

Harlow, England · London · New York · Reading, Massachusetts · San Francisco · Toronto · Don Mills, Ontario · Sydney ·
Tokyo · Singapore · Hong Kong · Seoul · Taipei · Cape Town · Madrid · Mexico City · Amsterdam · Munich · Paris · Milan

Pearson Education Limited

Edinburgh Gate
Harlow
Essex CM20 2JE
England

and Associated Companies around the world

Visit us on the World Wide Web at:

http://www.pearsoned.co.uk

First published 2000

ISBN: 978-0-273-63084-5

British Library Cataloguing in Publication Data
A CIP catalogue record for this book can be obtained from the British Library.

10 9 8 7 6 5 4 3

08 07

Typeset by 35 in 10/12.5pt Sabon
Printed and bound by 4edge Ltd, Hockley. www.4edge.co.uk

Contents

Part I · STRATEGIC REWARD – THE CONTEXT OF REWARD

22 Flexible plans for pay and benefits
Ian Smith

Introduction · Flexible plans · Determining the mix · User–chooser issues ·
Overseas experience · For Uncle Sam but not for Britannia ·
Reward management and all that · Simple but glamorous origins ·
Difficulties and complexity · A strategic perspective · Fitting a flexible
approach into the organisation · Overcoming obstacles and resistance ·
Conclusion · Notes · References · Further reading · Learning activities

About the authors

Phil Beaumont, is Professor of Employee Relations in the Department of Social and Economic Research at the University of Glasgow. His publications include *Human Resource Management: Key concepts and skills* (1993) and *The Future of Employment Relations* (1995). His current research interests include changing customer–supplier relationships and the diffusion of employee relations changes.

Emma Bell is a Lecturer in Organisational Behaviour at the University of Warwick. Her research has focused on aspects of strategic reward and the links between payment system design and human resource strategy in the chemical industry sector. Other research projects have concentrated on Investors in People as an approach to the management of cultural change, and the use of employee development programmes to develop extra-functional norms. She has published in International Journal of Human Resource Management, International Journal of Social Research Methodology and Management Learning, and has worked in the National Health Service.

Angela Bowey is currently Director of Organisation Advice and Research (New Zealand). In her long career specialising in pay and pay-related issues, she has worked at Manchester Business School and Strathclyde University and advised many employing organisation and government departments in the UK and most recently in New Zealand. Her specialisms include motivation and remuneration policy. Dr Bowey has written numerous books in the field on pay.

Mary Clark is a partner in the law firm Dibb Lupton Alsop. She is based in Manchester where she is head of the Employment Department. Her major clients include a number of blue chip organisations as well as larger private companies and she regularly presents seminars on all aspects of employment law and practice to major organisations and with Dibb Lupton Alsop Business and Law Training.

Robert Elliott is a Professor of Economics at the University of Aberdeen. He has also been a visiting Professor at a number of universities overseas including Cornell, Stanford and New York. He is currently Director of the Scottish Doctoral Programme in Economics and has directed a large number of research projects in the area of labour economics, the most recent of which were funded by the Leverhulme Trust, HM Treasury, and the Office for National Statistics. He has published extensively in the field of labour economics, his most recent being *Public Sector Pay within the European Union*, Macmillan.

Steve Flather is Managing Director of the Reward Group an Organisation he joined after ten years as a Personnel Manager with Plessey, The Nottingham Manufacturing Group and Josiah Wedgwood & Sons. For eight years he headed up the survey Division which publishes over 60 salary surveys each year. He also developed the Research Division to provide specialist pay advice and in 1991 he assumed responsibility for the Consultancy Division. In 1992 he was appointed Managing Director of The Reward Group, and in 1995 led the five strong Management Team in a Management buy-out. He writes and talks frequently on pay and related issues and broadcasts regularly on radio and television.

Mark Goodridge is Chief Executive of ER Consultants, the leading specialist organisation development and change management practice. A graduate of Cambridge University, Mark has worked in line, project and personnel management and advises boards in both the private and public sectors on transformational change. His research and writing on management includes studies on pay system effectiveness in supporting changes in organisational behaviour. He is co author of Managing Technological Change for Competitive Advantage and has written widely on pay and business management.

Jim Harrington is currently Human Resources Manager for Center Parcs UK. His previous experience includes human resource consultancy across a range of industry sectors and operational and personnel management in the health service. His consultancy expertise includes reward and recognition and employee relations. His interest in team pay grew from observing how teams posed the most challenges for conventional management practices such as 'job' evaluation, appraisal, reward, employee relations and management development. He authored *Pay and Reward Systems for Improved Business Performance* and has written several articles on team reward and other employee relations issues.

Gill Homan is a Senior Lecturer in Human Resource Management at Manchester Metropolitan University. As a practitioner she worked for ten years first in retailing before moving into automotive engineering sectors and then moving into higher education. She teaches and supervises widely on both University and consortia Masters programmes and is currently the course leader of the Human Resource Management programmes within the Department of Management. Her research interests centre on both the reward and development aspects of performance. Other interests include the role of partnerships in enabling organisational and individual learning and change and the development of managerial skills.

Laurie Hunter is Professor of Applied Economics and was Head of the Department of Social and Economic Research before being appointed Director of the University of Glasgow Business School. He has held visiting appointments at a number of universities including Chicago and Cornell. He has been a member of the Secretary of State for Scotland's Economic Advisers' Panel and was a founder member of the ACAS Council. His research interests are principally labour markets, industrial relations and human resource development and management, on which he has written extensively. Professor Hunter was elected a Fellow of the Royal Society of Edinburgh in 1986, awarded a CBE in 1987 and Knighted for services to the Police in 1995.

Catherine Kavanagh is Lecturer in Economics at University College Cork, Ireland. She has published on such topics as the impact of public capital expenditures, unemployment, basic income policies, the distribution of income, active labour market policies, measures of economic progress and the political economy of European Monetary Union. Together with Professor Charles Clark of St John's University, New York, she has recently edited a book entitled *Unemployment in Ireland – Alternative perspectives*, published by Ashgate Publishing Ltd. She has recently spent a period of time at the University of Aberdeen where her research interests have included compensating wage differentials.

Peter Lawson has worked as a senior consultant with ER Consultants, a business consultancy based in Cambridge providing specialised services in organisation design and development, including the development of recognition and reward systems, since 1990. His recent work has included the development of executive incentive arrangements and the development of performance-related rewards in highly innovative and creative settings. Prior to 1990 he held several senior management positions in manufacturing industry. He is a regular contributor to the ER Consultants' management journal *TOPICS* and contributed to the *IDP Performance Management Handbook* (1995).

Tom Lupton retired from the Directorship of the Manchester Business School in 1987 after 25 years. Previously, he had research jobs at Liverpool and Manchester and was, in succession, Senior Lecturer in Social Anthropology at Manchester, Head of Department of Industrial Administration at Birmingham C.A.T. and Montague Burton Professor of Industrial Relations at Leeds. Latterly he has been involved in Management Education in Spain and with the development of doctoral work in management at Manchester Metropolitan University. His main, but not exclusive research interests throughout his academic career has been in the field of work-place behaviour and payment system design. He is an honorary D.Sc. of Aston and honorary D.B.A. of the Manchester Metropolitan University and has a Diploma Honórifico of the Escuela de Alta Dirección y Administración (EADA) in Barcelona. All of these were conferred in recognition of his contribution to management education over many years in the UK and Spain.

Philip Lynch is a co-founder of Philip Lynch Associates a consultancy specialising in strategic working time. After an early career in market research he moved into the field of HR in industry and consultancy, spending ten years working in the Imperial Group, he ended in a senior personnel role in the paper and board division where he was the architect of the first annual hours scheme in the British paper and board industry. He has led a number of projects in a variety of sectors, industry, service, public and private. He has written papers on annual hours and related topics and his firm is widely acknowledged as the leading working time consultancy in Europe.

Colin Massey is a Director of Whitmuir, a consultancy assisting organisations to achieve measurable improvements in business preformance by focusing on people management issues. Accomplished in the management of change, he has held senior and director level appointments in manufacturing, management consulting, and with a major employer's organisation. His consulting clients include many blue chip companies and large public-sector organisations. Colin is a frequent contributor to public seminars and conferences and is the author of several management texts on payment systems, performance improvement and employee relations.

Hamish Mathieson is Senior Lecturer in Industrial Relations in the Department of Management at Manchester Metropolitan University. He teaches industrial relations across the Department's postgraduate courses, including the MA in Industrial Relations with Employment Law of which he is course leader. His research interests centre around the Industrial Relations implications of privatisation in public enterprises. He is currently engaged in a comparison of the implementation of HRM in the UK and Sweden in collaboration with the University of Upsala in Sweden.

Geoff Nethersell is a Director of the Hay Group. He graduated in Economics from the University of Warwick and worked as an economist for 10 years, initially with the Ford Motor Company and in local government. In 20 years of practical consulting, he has developed leading expertise in the areas of management job evaluation and reward. He has provided strategic advice and support to a wide range of organisations across all sectors of the economy, with particular emphasis on large manufacturing and utility plc's. Within the Hay Group he has a leading role in the development of job evaluation expertise and the adoption of consistent quality standards worldwide.

Andrew Pendleton is Professor of Human Resource Management at Manchester Metropolitan University. He has also taught human resource management and industrial relations at the universities of Bath, Bradford and Kent. In 1997–8 he was Visiting Research Fellow in the Department of Industrial Relations at the University of Sydney, Australia. His research interests include employee share ownership and profit sharing, industrial relations in privatised and state-owned firms and the relationship between corporate governance and human resource management.

Sue Shaw is a Senior Lecturer in Personnel Management in the Department of Management at Manchester Metropolitan University and currently acting Head of Department. She contributes to a wide range of Masters and Postgraduate Diploma programmes and leads the MA and Postgraduate Diploma in HRM courses. She is a Fellow of the Institute of Personnel and Development and formerly Chair of its Manchester Branch.

Ian Smith is a Senior Lecturer in Management in the Human Resource Management Unit at Cardiff Business School. After working in Canadian and American industry he entered academia to research and teach in the area of corporate and employee performance and the links with remuneration. He has written extensively on the subjects of Human Resource Management, Pay and Incentive Schemes and advises many private and public-sector organisations. He is Past Chairman of the Faculty of Compensation at Management Centre Europe and writes and edits for many well-known publications on human resource management and pay.

Peter Smith is a Director of the Hay Group. He has ten years consulting experience, advising organisations on reward, performance improvement and management development. His clients include NHS Trusts, local authorities, police forces, universities, government departments and agencies within the public sector, and several major international companies in the consumer sector and in engineering. This consultancy work includes extensive use and development of job evaluation, and advice on best practice. He also worked for ten years in central government, advising on pay, training and employment legislation. He is responsible for expertise and knowledgement in Hay UK.

Stephen Taylor has taught personnel management and industrial relations at Manchester Metropolitan University and at the Manchester School of Management (UMIST) since 1994. Prior to these appointments he held a number of personnel management posts in the hotel industry and the national health service. His research focuses principally on the objectives and effectiveness of remuneration policies, with particular reference to occupational pension schemes.

Richard Thorpe is Professor in Management in the Department of Management at Manchester Metropolitan University and Director of the Graduate Business School. After some years in industry, he joined the Pay and Reward Centre at Strathclyde University Business School, where he researched aspects of pay and performance improvement with a large team of researchers. He has worked as a lecturer at Glasgow University before joining Manchester Metropolitan University in 1986. Although researching in the field of small business and change he has retained his interest in the area of remuneration and reward and is regularly involved in lecturing, consulting and supervising on the subject.

Acknowledgements

This book aims to bring together the recent results of research in the field of pay and make it accessible to practitioners. To achieve this, we have accessed our network of academic colleagues, consultants and professionals who share our belief that pay and remuneration issues ought to have a higher place in the organisational agenda than they currently do. Many have given us a great deal of advice and encouragement and their ideas, we hope are reflected in this book. Of those that have given us help in the later stages we would like to pay a special thanks to Stephen Taylor and Andrew Pendleton both of whom have read the whole manuscript and made many valuable and detailed comments.

The bulk of the secretarial work for the production of this book has fallen to Pat Walker who helped in the initial stages and later to Christine Czechowicz who has had the unenviable task of pulling all the material together. To these two individuals we are most grateful.

We are grateful to the following for permission to reproduce copyright material:

Macmillan Press for their kind permission to use material originally printed in A.M. Bowey and R. Thorpe, with P. Hellier (1986) *Payment Systems and Productivity*, particularly chapter 2, 'Payment Systems and Performance Improvement'; chapter 4, 'Payment Scheme Decision Choices'; chapter 6, 'Payment Scheme Processes'; especially chapter 7, 'Degeneration of Payment Systems' the National Coal Board Study conducted by Geoff Nichols and chapter 8 'Conclusions'.

Whilst every effort has been made to trace the owners of copyright material, in a few cases this has proved impossible and we take this opportunity to offer our apologies to any copyright holders whose rights we may have unwittingly infringed.

Foreword

Tom Lupton

As the Millennium is almost upon us it seems appropriate in this foreword briefly to trace the history of management ideas and practices in the last hundred years with special reference to the issues with which this book deals – issues that I have spent much of my academic career grappling with.

The systematic study of manual work began about 100 years ago and it is rightly associated with such names as Taylor and Gilbreth amongst others. 'Taylorism' is still with us, manifest in elaborate systems to control work and improve performance.

The emergence of Taylorism can be accounted for by reference to three economic and social developments of that period: (a) the realisation that managers of that time were in general ill-equipped to cope with the challenges posed by technological advance and the growth in the size of enterprises, (b) the fact that competition was exerting pressure to use resources more efficiently and effectively and (c) the organised restrictive control of output levels by groups of workers commonly referred to as 'systematic soldiering'.

The practice of Taylorism includes methods of measuring work, the precise design of tools and equipment, systematic attention to workshop layouts and workflows and the rigorous recording and control of labour costs. In the techniques of work study (in the general sense of that term) much of what Taylor and his contemporaries invented is, in more elaborate and extended forms, still commonplace 100 years on. Not only that, but the beliefs and philosophies that lie behind Taylorism persist. This book highlights how these beliefs have been translated into payment system design and the consequences that have followed.

In the attempt put an end to 'systematic soldiering' it seemed logical to simplify work, to treat each worker as an individual, to prescribe in detail the work required and the pay for doing it to the satisfaction of the management. To offer more pay for more effort, for paying attention to detail, and for quality or quantity also seemed to make sense. Payment by the piece (piecework) for repetitive work was as old as work itself but more complex tasks required more complex ways of relating effort and cash reward. This accounted for the early emergence of different designs of incentive-bonus schemes, such as those devised by Taylor himself and by others such as Gantt, Rowan and Bedeaux. These designs are, in various forms, still in current use. All of them are based on the idea that the overriding motive for working harder, or better, or both, is that employees have above all a desire to earn more money. A view which finds later reflection in the emergence of group incentives and company wide gainsharing schemes such as the Scanlon and Rucker plans. All these approaches to reward are reflected in the later chapters of this book.

A century or more later despite the widespread application of scientific management the systematic manipulation by groups of workers of payment schemes of all kinds persists. This could reflect defects in the design of the schemes themselves and/or the existence of motives other than the desire for more money (the desire for social contact for example and for some control of the working environment in ways different from those imposed from above). It could also be an expression of more deep-rooted social divisions. More of this later.

The Hawthorne experiments

The Hawthorne experiments of the 1920s and 1930s have been almost as powerful an element in the development of management thought and folklore as has Taylorism. Following leads from the work of British psychologists who had studied the relationship between working conditions and worker performance during the First World War the researchers studied the effects of lighting, ventilation, length of the working day, the effects of rest pauses, etc. on the productive performance of women workers. It turned out that these factors were less influential on their behaviour than the interest shown in them by the investigators. In another workshop in the same factory, this time employing men, they discovered the self-same control over the work place, the pay scheme and worker behaviour that had been so much deplored by Taylor and others earlier and was central to their efforts to regain management control which in their scheme of things was where it properly belonged.

The suggestions for improvement made by the Hawthorne researchers sprang from their conviction that the answer to the apparently 'negative' behaviour that had been observed, as well as the positive response to attention shown, lay in the nature of the relationship between management and workers. They thought that if managers were to spend more time listening to complaints and suggestions, the level of trust and confidence would improve. Having nothing to fear, and in an atmosphere of openness and transparency, workers would be more co-operative and helpful.

This view was described by some critics as 'cow sociology'. More sympathetic readers of the reports of the Hawthorne work spoke of the human relations approach to management; the emphasis being less about tight formal control than on communication and understanding. Later manifestations and elaborations of this approach are to be found in the work of Rensis Lickert and Douglas McGregor amongst others. When readers consider the chapters which make up this book, they might like to consider to what extent the current best-practice solutions contained in the later chapters of the book fit one or other of these approaches.

The Swedish way

In the 1950s and 1960s new solutions were sought to the problems that the Taylorists and the Human Relations School had failed to solve. Some employers in Sweden reasoned that if groups could work effectively in opposition to management there must be ways of arranging matters so that they could work effectively for themselves and for management at the same time and still be highly productive and concerned with quality. To them the answer seemed to be to re-design production technology so as to create more interesting and responsible jobs. They also thought that work groups should negotiate production targets and work out for themselves the methods by which they might achieve them. Workers they thought should be trained to do more than one job in the group and be paid not for their performance but for their competencies. The economic and status incentives therefore were to increase their competencies in order to move into a higher pay bracket. The overall result would be a multi-skilled and flexible work force motivated to improve their skills.

When implemented, these ideas were impressive to see and were very different from a traditional assembly line. However, as informed observers were quick to point out, the Swedes tended to produce low-volume, high-value products for market niches. The new production systems worked well for these markets but were thought to be uneconomic for competitive markets. In these circumstances the best solution seemed to be to retain the conventional assembly line which used unskilled workers on lower pay.

Of course some of the Swedish ideas and experiences have been taken up elsewhere but their influence was never widespread. By contrast the adoption of Japanese methods of production has in advanced economies been almost universal. Some of the reasons for this and the effects it has had on management, work organisation and worker behaviour are set out below. But first let me reflect on the reasons for the uneasy relationships at the 'frontier of control' which some Swedish organisations faced up to with ingenuity but which are still in Europe and North America quite pervasive.

Where is the 'frontier of control'?

I venture to suggest that there may well be another interpretation for the behaviour of workers than that of the scientific managers and the human relations school. It begins not inside but outside the work place. This approach starts by asking where the employees come from and what view of society and what ideas about their life chances they might bring with them. If one compares the career of a worker with someone who starts a career in junior management it is an unfavourable one. In the great majority of cases starting on the shop floor means ending on the shop floor. For young managers a directorship might be the upper limit of their aspirations. For the young worker the upper limit may well be much more constrained. Of course exceptions can always be cited to this rule. Talented and ambitious workers could move out or up. The sons and daughters of workers might go to university and begin their careers as management professionals but it would be unusual for a manager once having started a career to move down to the shop floor.

Any explanation for all this must take account of social origins. Opportunities are not equal. For a boy or girl born into a working-class family, many potential life chances are simply not perceived as possible or, if they are, there are many obstacles along the way. Children of professional middle-class families, however, experience fewer obstacles in their engagement in education and their preparation for professional work is much easier as a consequence. As Lloyd Warner noted many years ago there is a 'break in the skill hierarchy' the origins of which lie not only in the structure of organisational hierarchies but also in the structure of social classes and their distribution in cities and neighbourhoods. Income differences originating in the place of work thus complete a cycle which makes any kind of structural change difficult. There may be significant movement of people (mostly up but rarely down), but structures persist. To my mind these structural rigidities, which shape attitudes predispositions, perceptions and ideologies, do far more to explain the conflicts that exist between managers and shop-floor workers than do the failures of communication, lack of trust and so on. Indeed they may well be the origin of these conflicts. If this is indeed the case then, short of drastic action and structural change, managers will have to live with the reality of the differences in attitude and expectations that derive from these different social backgrounds and modes of socialisation. This is well illustrated in the work of Paul Willis on the education of working-class boys and is still relevant as a way of explaining the response of workers to payment systems and of arrangements at work.

Those who do manual work and those doing routine clerical work are arguably the greatest risk-takers in modern society. Managers faced with severe price competition, with pressure to reduce costs may decide to reduce labour cost by lay-offs. As they make their decision the problem is transferred to those who then have been laid off and are suddenly confronted with the difficulty of allocating a small fluctuating income over the same set of financial commitments as before, often with the prospect of a long period of unemployment.

Job evaluation

The practice of arranging jobs in rank order according to their level of responsibility in order to determine pay relativities has had a long history. Job evaluation in its more modern and formal sense must have arisen for much the same reasons as Taylorism – that was as a way of formalising the influence of management over the processes by which pay relativities are established and maintained and through this to exercise control over labour costs. The systematic processes for describing jobs and putting them in rank order for the purpose of the pay relativities that exist are fairly recent and have taken off, but, in the eyes of some observers, they lack objectivity. The attempts to find alternative methods of job evaluation that rely less on defining and measuring many factors and assigning each a weighting (a time-consuming process when hundreds of jobs might be involved) have been a preoccupation since the end of the Second World War.

Elliott Jacques, for example, observed that it was a general characteristic of all jobs that they were made up of both required and discretionary elements. The amount of discretion being higher at the apex of organisations and lower as one descends the organisational hierarchy until, at the very bottom, jobs contain few if any discretionary components. He also observed that the exercise of discretion could result in either long-term or short-term outcomes and that, in those jobs where there was a need for high level of discretion, decisions tended to have long-term outcomes. He called this the 'time span of discretion' and proposed that this was intuitively recognised by everyone (therefore felt to be fair) and he used it as the basis on which pay relativities should be based. Although on the face of it this seemed to be the nearest thing possible to an objective evaluation of jobs (presumably the amount of discretion in a job could be measured and the time elapsed to a result could be reasonably stated), the evidence is that Jacques's method was used very little.

The same is also true of the method proposed by T.T. Patterson – the decision band method. This approach also relied on a single variable, in this case the quality of the decision. The basis was that jobs with similar quality of decisions ought to be grouped into 'decision bands' for the purpose of establishing pay relativities.

Job evaluation then, by using factors and weights, is seen by many managers and trade unionists as a way of avoiding conflict by establishing relativities in a participatively systematic way and according to transparent and understood processes so they are 'felt to be fair'. By others they are regarded as the very source of conflict that is inevitably inherent in the subjective judgements that lurk behind the facade of equity. Yet others warn of 'decay' as a consequence of technical change and distortions that will arise as a result of labour market changes. Yet, notwithstanding, they can and do give surface legitimacy to job and pay hierarchies.

Job evaluation in its dominant form emerged in the 1920s and was much used in the 1930s and through the Second World War period, especially in North America where it originated. In the UK its popularity has if anything increased in the last few decades and is seen by many (especially women) as a method of establishing equal pay for equal work.

The 'Taylorisation' of management

'Scientific' managers regard the detailed study of manual work as the initial step in increasing managerial control over that work. Fifty years later the detailed study of managerial work began and was conducted, not by industrial engineers, but by academics. The first study of managerial work recorded was published in Sweden in 1951 and was followed by other studies in the UK and the USA. These showed that at least for middle managers their work was far from being just a matter of planning, decision-making and directing, but was much more 'messy' involving trouble-shooting, negotiating and much 'political' activity. The connection between these studies and the subsequent emergence of techniques for the recording and control of the work of subordinate managers by their superiors – techniques such as management by objectives, management appraisal systems and pay for performance – is a matter for conjecture, but there does seem to be little doubt that practices such as 'downsizing' and 'delayering' and other cost reduction measures expose the jobs of lower-level managers to the risks that stem from the organisation's response to market pressure. Like the shop floor workers, they are seen (depending on one's viewpoint) either as dispensable or more euphemistically as moving into a flexible labour market where their skills will be available to other employers or, as Marx might have said, they join the 'reserve army of labour' while those who remain are, as some have put it, the secure 'permanent core'. Flexible labour markets are, I realise, the new orthodoxy – if everything else is flexible and dynamic in the new world of fierce global competition then why not also labour markets? The question remains: who is carrying the economic, social and psychological cost of the reserve army?

Contingency theory and systems of payment

In the 1950s and 1960s came the realisation, through careful research, that the great generalisations and universal principles previously at the heart of both the theory and practice of management did not hold true for every case. Structure, process and behaviour were instead found to be largely the product of particular circumstances. For example the organisation structure of chemical plants turned out to be very different from that of other manufacturing organisations, such as car assembly plants. Payment systems that worked well for repetitive shop-floor work were found to be unsuitable for more complex longer-cycle assembly operations, for supervisory and managerial work and so on. The practical implications of this discovery led to the idea of a 'best fit' approach. This meant that whatever is being designed – an organisation structure, an appraisal procedure, a job, a payment system it – should be congruent with such variables as the technology, the product market and so forth and should be subject to modification if these variables significantly change. If this does not happen, the structures, systems, processes, pay systems or whatever is being designed will be inappropriate or 'decay'. This approach is congruent with the socio-technical mode of analysis developed at the same time. It is true to say that although some practical procedures for organisational development, for the design of payment systems, organisation structures, and the management of change, have grown from this perspective, it is also true that the habits of thought of some managers, that have developed over the twentieth century, have been deeply ingrained and not changed much as a result of these largely academic outputs.

The influence of Japan

The influence of the simple and yet ingenious production methods developed by Japanese engineers have been profound. The question that intrigues me has been why they have been so easily exportable and been able to take root so straightforwardly in completely different cultural settings. As far as we can tell, European and North American managers and workers adapt easily to Japanese management methods, although it is reported that this is not the case in some of the Eastern and Central European countries. There may well be in existence research findings that describe the relationships between Japanese managers and local managers in Japanese enterprises outside of Japan and their relations with local workers, but I do not know of them. However the superficial 'Cooks Tours' of car assembly and electronics factories in Japan give the impression of tight management and technological control of worker behaviour tempered by worker participation in quality circles and the like and by hands-on management. If in the system there are manifestations of unease in management–worker relationships of this I am not sure. If there are none, then we might well learn something else from the Japanese.

Taylorism and society

In this foreword, I have shown Taylorism to be a set of techniques designed to control the behaviour of employees in work places. The advancement of production and information technology both promise to diminish the importance of the 'fixed' work place. This in no sense alters the general point made here. Control, and its avoidance, will take different forms.

The point of this final part of my argument is that Taylorism, for all its undoubted revolutionary impact as a technique for the control of work, is only one active component of a wider philosophy of social control. This philosophy pervades society generally and not only the work place. In the market economy the demand for labour derives from the demand for a product or service and the price (cost) of labour power, like the price of any other commodity, is influenced by supply and demand. Within the enterprise the owners and their agents (the managers) expect that the contract of employment, whether it be implicit or explicit, confers a right to control the behaviour of the contracted individuals in ways that are profitable to the employer (within the prevailing laws of employment). Any interference with the labour market therefore, such as trade union activity, undue legal restraints, or, at the workshop level, 'systematic soldiering', is regarded as a distortion of the operation of the market mechanism.

In a market economy the scarcity of labour puts employers at a cost disadvantage as the price of it is bid upwards. Therefore, to have a pool of unemployed persons, is to the benefit of the operation of the market mechanism (as we have seen). In reality of course there are many other restrictions in the way markets operate, for example monopoly power in product and service markets, trade union influence and minimum wage laws, the geographical immobility of potential employees and so on. Product and service markets are becoming increasingly more globalised while labour markets remain predominantly national and local. As a consequence, enterprises move into countries where labour is relatively cheap or perhaps begin to contract their production there. Competition is undoubtedly becoming more and more international and the impact on the prosperity of nations becomes a major issue for national governments concerned with the health and competitiveness of the whole national economy. As this takes place the issue of control is then raised from the level of the enterprise to the level of the nation. How else can one explain the National Incomes Policies in Britain, or the Thatcherite attempt (largely successful) to reduce the power of trade unions in the labour market. Also of interest here is the tendency of governments to introduce reforms at the level of the enterprise that revive and resonate with the Taylorist management techniques. For example in recent years there has been a revival of the use of systems of pay for performance at every level of organisations. It is even spreading to the professions, such as school teaching, despite the strong research evidence showing the problems that can arise when these systems are applied to complex professional work. This movement when applied to the public sector has been referred to as new managerialism, whereby great store is placed in 'scientific' approaches, such as planning, the measurement of efficiency and effectiveness.

Taylorism rules supreme? – I think not for many of the reasons I have discussed. However it will certainly live on and its techniques will be refined at every level whatever the colour of governments and the personal beliefs of powerful people. Taylorism, whatever other names it may be called is central to the efficient operation of the market economy. To my mind the great pity is that the great and the good are blind to the research evidence which could inform their policies and their implementation at every level. This book should be required reading for them.

Tom Lupton

Introduction

Richard Thorpe and Gill Homan

The objective of this book is to bring together recent research in the field of pay, particularly that research which offers a critical perspective on theory and practice. In seeking contributions from both academics and practitioners, we feel that this book illustrates the theoretical links between reward and other academic fields, such as motivation, labour economics and economic policy, which are central to a deeper understanding of the wider field of reward management.

Over the years this area of human resource management (HRM) has developed a language that describes a range of different approaches to the subject area, such as pay, compensation, remuneration and reward. This language reflects the different practitioner specialisms and academic disciplines that each contributes to the field. In this book we do not attempt to impose a common language and terminology, deciding instead that anyone seeking to learn, teach or practise in the field of pay will need to be able to comprehend the subject from a variety of perspectives – from the point of view of the economist, the strategist and the psychologist, as well as the human resource management professional and even perhaps as a member of the government. All too often when dealing with issues relating to pay, writers and practitioners have tended to focus on their own narrow area of interest and expertise, giving the occasional nod in the direction of other views and perspectives. As editors of this book we have tried, as far as possible, to reflect not only our own particular areas of specialism but also to bring before the reader as many different perspectives on the subject of pay as we feel appropriate. This is achieved through a critique of the underpinning theories and 'theories in use' that influence reward and reward management. In addition, we begin to make explicit the linkages, synergies and contradictions that exist between these different perspectives. In describing the book therefore it is, perhaps, easier to say what the book does not attempt to do before we go on to outline what we have sought to achieve. First, we recognise that the book is fairly ethnocentric. Although we have begun to work and research within Europe and beyond we make no attempt here to draw any comparisons with our European partners or other international competitors. Our objective is to offer a sound understanding of the nature of reward from a UK perspective. Notwithstanding, we suggest that many of the chapters contained in the first section of the book are applicable to all developed economies of the world. We have included at the end of each chapter a number of key texts and articles for further reading which will deal with issues not fully developed in the body of the text. We also pose a number questions which aim to focus the reader on key issues contained within the chapter, in order to assist them to take their learning further. The book has three major sections.

Section one provides the reader with an understanding of the wider context in which a reward strategy can be devised and managed, as well as an appreciation of the constraints and contextual issues that shape an organisation's reward strategy. We begin by focusing attention on the central, current debates in reward management. This is followed by a review of the relationship of reward policy and practice to strategy – a relationship that has not received the attention in British texts that we feel that it deserves. This is in contrast to many other aspects of human resource management, which have for some time emphasised the links that need to be made between the strategic policy of an organisation and strategy. In order to explore the concept of reward strategy we feel that it is important to understand the context in which it operates. A major influence in this context has been the way in which the discipline of human resource management has evolved. Over recent years there have been a number of new approaches and challenges to the concept of corporate strategy. These challenges have changed the focus of human resource strategy from a 'downstream' activity required to be adjusted and adapted to meet the needs of the organisation's corporate strategy to one that is much more central to the development of corporate strategy.

Simultaneously there have been moves by successive governments to de-regulate the labour market and remove previously existing government controls. (Although this approach may be to some degree reversed by the current government). Finally there has been an increasing focus on the individual as the unit of account with the effect (and perhaps the hidden agenda) of the gradual erosion of trade union influence in the work place. Taken together these factors have enabled managers to take a much more strategic view of reward and the ways in which reward strategy can be used within the organisational system to effect a much wider range of workforce strategies and initiatives for change.

The first part also reviews the objectives and strategies for action of a much wider group of stakeholders, such as the trade unions and government, and explores some of the less widely acknowledged purposes of reward systems, such as authority and control. This leads us to look at the role that the values and perceptions that form an organisation's culture play – values and perceptions that are reflected in the organisations reward systems employed and language used.

In the second part of the book the focus moves to the organisational context and raises awareness on some of the strategic decisions that need to be addressed if a reward system is to meet the organisation's objectives, the aspirations of its workforce and the requirements of the law. We would argue that before the required components of a reward strategy can be selected the organisation needs to have a clear understanding of how it wishes to compete within the labour market, which of its required skills and competencies are freely available and which are in scarce supply. Within all organisations there are a number of broad influences and imperatives that will both enable and constrain managers in the design of their systems. Consideration is therefore given to such things as alternative forms of structure, the degree of flexibility that any new pay system must achieve and how equity and equality can be ensured. Once these questions have been answered the process of designing the framework or structure of the reward system can take place. These considerations form the substance of the third section of the book.

Once the answers to the above questions have been determined a more detailed examination of the components of the system can take place. Generally a reward system will consist of some form of base pay and benefits, and it may also have some additional, variable components designed to encourage specific forms of behaviour. There are, of course, some rewards systems which have no base pay and are formed exclusively by variable pay components.

Base pay has traditionally taken the job as its means of determination, however the development of person-based approaches, such as competence- and skills-based pay, have opened up the possibility for new and exciting alternatives for the reward practitioner. Even within the standard approaches to base pay, there have been recent developments to existing practice, perhaps the most radical of these being the introduction of annualised hours. These offer the opportunity to achieve different forms of flexibility, one of the key objectives of reward systems.

The whole area of employee benefits also reflects both the search for flexibility and the focus on the individual. As a consequence many organisations are exploring the options available for flexible benefits to be tailored to individual needs and life cycles. Pensions merit a chapter on their own for a number of reasons. Pensions are probably one of the most complex and least-understood areas of reward by all but pension specialists. However for the reward practitioner it is likely to be an area of increasing significance in years to come as it is an area that remains high on the government agenda, and for organisations the related costs incurred continue to grow. The likelihood is that increasing numbers of organisations will be looking to re-examine their commitment to the traditional pension scheme and explore alternative options.

Variable pay can vary along a whole range of dimensions: the time between effort and reward, the nature of the effort and its measurement, the numbers involved in the unit of calculation and so on. At the same time variable pay can range from total pay to as little as 3 to 5 per cent in different systems. This section examines the different forms of variable pay and the objectives they each seek to achieve. The extent to which the various approaches have been utilised by organisations and the degree to which their objectives have been achieved in practice are also explored.

In keeping with the style of the book the third section of the book retains its critical and theoretical perspective as opposed to a prescriptive approach. Through reviews of the literature and knowledge of current practice, our aim is to inform the reader of the current issues and debates.

Chapter 1 orientates the reader to the key debates in reward management, debates which are pursued at different levels and in different forms throughout the book as a whole. It begins by focusing on the strategic nature of reward management and goes on to critique the contingency versus best-practice approaches. Both of these topics are reviewed in chapter 7 from the perspective of authority and control. Links between expectancy theory and performance-related pay are an issue argued fiercely in the literature. The chapter takes this debate and acts as an introduction to chapter 5, a chapter that develops in detail the concept of motivation and pay. Finally, the perennial question of equity, central to effective reward systems is reviewed.

Chapter 2 begins by dealing with a number of key dimensions of reward strategy. It explores the links between corporate strategy and human resource strategy and how reward strategy might emanate from these. Three aspects of reward strategy within the organisation are highlighted and explored in more detail: the motivational assumptions that exist together with the requirements and understandings of authority and control and the objectives that the organisation sets itself in order to be successful in both the short and the long term. The chapter concludes by pointing to the number of stakeholders that ought to be considered in the design of a payment system and it highlights the importance of process when moving from one payment system to another.

Chapter 3 takes a historical view of labour economics and its relationship to pay. It begins by outlining classical approaches and quickly moves to develop theories of human capital approaches to collective bargaining and efficiency and the development of internal labour markets. These more recent approaches together with theories of labour economics support the changes currently taking place in human resource strategy in general and reward strategy in particular. Human capital theory to some extent underpins the competence/capability approach to performance as well as offering a contribution to the gender–ethnicity debates in relation to pay – a debate that is addressed in detail in the second part of this book. It also offers an explanation for the recent moves to the individualisation of employment, a move that sees individuals taking greater responsibility for themselves. The chapter also offers a rather different perspective on motivation and highlights the importance of concepts, such as equality, equity and fairness in payment systems – a concept that has been long established as one of the key concerns of employees.

Chapter 4 explores the impact of recent government economic policy on pay. It begins by reviewing the steps that have been taken in the last 20 years to encourage greater labour market flexibility. It is argued that low investment in skills, the threat posed by inflation and the perceived power of the large trade unions, all of which combined together to produce poor economic performance, have been the driving force.

The economic strategies for change discussed included a reduction in the public-sector borrowing requirement, the removal of a number of regulatory frameworks (for example, the abolition of Wages Councils) and indirectly through such devices as privatisation and compulsory competitive tendering. In addition, social policies have been enacted that have attempted to make work more attractive financially.

The chapter then looks at the consequences, both positive and negative of these strategies. Less-desirable outcomes have seen increased dispersion in incomes and an increase in both low-paid and the number of temporary workers. In conclusion it argues that when measured against a range of indicators, the UK economy is more buoyant and productive than in former years.

Chapter 5 examines the concept of motivation in all its aspects with the implications for a reward strategy. It takes the perspective that aspects of both motivation and reward have for far too long been dealt with in too simplistic a manner. It is argued that the complexity of the subject, in relationship to reward management, is one that needs to be thoroughly understood by managers and pay practitioners for success to be achieved. The chapter outlines the various schools of thought in relation to motivation, but more crucially it explores those factors that must be taken into account when devising a reward strategy. Highlighted of importance is the fact that what motivates individuals and teams may well change as a consequence of a change in circumstances of the organisation or because of changes in an individual's working life. Human agency is also explored, particularly the way pay is often manipulated by organisational members. As part of a developing theme the chapter highlights the value of a wide involvement when making changes and adjustment to systems. It explores the impact that such processes can have on the effective outcome of reward systems. Finally, the chapter addresses the corporate and cultural dimensions of motivation suggesting that universal views of reward may not always be appropriate and that there may well be a need to adjust a strategy to more closely align with certain key organisational and cultural variables. The chapter concludes with an illustration of how links can be made between assumptions about motivation and different reward strategies.

Chapter 6 draws attention to the cultural context in which payment systems are designed and implemented and which has not received the attention that it merits within the reward literature. This chapter begins with a historical overview of the approaches to the design of payment systems with a focus on the ideologies that underpin them and are made explicit by the language used to present them.

More recent approaches have recognised the interdependence of culture and change and the role of reward systems within this process and these too are critically reviewed. Finally, the chapter classifies different approaches in terms of the language each uses, both at the level of shopfloor and in the boardroom, and the form of control exercised using Etzioni's framework.

Chapter 7 examines a number of the process issues that ought to be considered when managers consider making changes to reward and remuneration systems. The chapter begins by examining a number of ways of thinking about how change within organisations can be managed before outlining in some detail, and with reference to various research studies, the way in which a process-based approach can successfully surface the motivations and priorities of a wider group of stakeholders. The chapter offers check lists of factors thought important in payment system design and concludes with lessons for management and a blue print for practitioners.

Chapter 8 begins the part of the book with an exploration of the different kinds of pay structures that an organisation might adopt and illustrates the ways in which flexible pay systems can be designed to support organisational requirements. This chapter outlines the decision choices and alternatives that are available to managers in the context of the strategy/structure debate in relation to pay.

Chapter 9 focuses on issues relating to flexibility and suggests that those concerned with the management of pay systems need to consider, at an early stage, both the level and nature of the flexibility required from a system, rather than to attempt to design flexibility into a payment system at a later stage. Flexibility has become an important consideration in recent years, given the speed of change experienced by most organisations. Such changes have affected such things as the range and nature of the skills required and the process and operations involved. These are all features that are very difficult to design into payment systems once a system has been installed, yet are ones that can affect significantly the ability an organisation has to alter the volume or scope of its operation should the need arise. This chapter also has close links to chapter 1 in that it re-states the need for organisations to link their pay systems to the strategic priorities of the organisation.

Chapter 10 discusses the role of trade unions in relation to pay. The chapter begins with a consideration of the role and importance pay plays in the present day role of trade unions and is often the most significant employment issue for those individuals who hold union membership. The chapter then considers the changes that have taken place in recent years, both in terms of the influence of trade unions in the determination of pay but also in respect of the decentralisation of bargaining arrangements. The chapter concludes with a review of the emergent strategies being adopted by trade unions and their likely effectiveness.

Chapter 11 tackles the difficult but important concept of equity and equality. Equity and equality within pay has been an important issue within the literature for the last half century or more. The European Union has renewed the debate by raising questions as to the equality of various groups, women, part-time workers and ethnic minorities. The Equal Opportunities Commission has also been influential, suggesting that, as inequality is more often than not designed into pay systems, it is the responsibility of the architects of payment systems to carefully consider issues of equality at the design stage rather than attempt to justify a system, *post hoc*. Given the long history of concern around matters relating to equality, the chapter can only highlight the slow progress made in addressing this important issue.

Chapter 12 examines job evaluation systems. In recent years job evaluation has received a bad press. Notwithstanding, there are substantial numbers of employees who still have their pay, fringe benefit levels and grading determined through such methods. Any self-respecting book on payment systems would be wanting if it did not include a review of past and current practice, and how recent schemes have attempted to encompass organisational requirements for flexibility and mobility within such systems. This chapter is written by a member of a consultancy organisation that is well known for its job evaluation expertise; as a consequence it offers a contemporary account of current thinking on job evaluation.

Chapter 13 explores the ways in which salary levels are determined through the practice of inter-firm comparisons and the importance of having high-quality practitioner research input into the design process. The chapter illustrates how data (from competitors, both local and national) can be utilised so as to ensure a firm's market compatibility and viability. Of course at one level inter-firm comparisons are not new and in some ways the approach fits into the current interest in benchmarking. In respect of pay this means that organisations should not only seek to compare the levels and forms of pay, but also the structure and character of the jobs and processes that are adopted as well as the whole benefits package offered.

Chapter 14 concludes this second section with an examination of the way in which payment systems inevitably degenerate and decay. The message the chapter gives is that all systems should be regularly and systematically reviewed (audited) – to ascertain whether they are continuing to operate in the ways they were designed. It has long been the view that payment systems, once designed and implemented, have been simply forgotten and allowed to run themselves. Under these circumstances degeneration and decay takes place slowly but inevitably, and the cost, when detected, invariably means that replacement of the system is the only option available. The chapter highlights the responsibility of pay practitioners to develop systems for auditing their pay systems as part of an on-going activity and offers a variety of methods and measures as to how this can be achieved.

Chapter 15 examines how the purchase of time can be negotiated and how the value of time can be differentiated by day of the week and by part of the day. It also examines the way in which flexibility in time-based pay can be achieved and compensated – ways which include additional hours, overtime, shift working and the practise of annualising hours. Annualised hours is one of the most recent and exciting developments, but it is also one of the most complex ways of addressing the question of flexibility yet devised.

Chapter 16 explores the development of pay systems based on the skills and competencies of employees. These systems focus on the individual and their capabilities rather than simply on the job the individual undertakes. Competency-based pay systems bring a new concept to the arena of reward, a concept that offers the potential for new solutions to organisational problems. They also, as might be expected, bring with them new problems and these are discussed. The chapter concludes by showing how competency-based pay systems are constructed, the extent of their use, the advantages and disadvantages that they offer and points to those aspects where further research may prove useful.

Chapter 17 examines the rise of performance-related pay and charts its use from the shopfloor to the highest levels within the organisation. The chapter illustrates the significance of performance-related pay through its widespread use during the 1980s and 1990s. It also highlights the conditions under which it has been seen to be most successful and the range of complex problems the use of such systems bring with them. This is particularly the case when in conflict with other important organisation objectives, such as team working and co-operative working across internal boundaries. The chapter also engages in the debate as to why, when research evidence has yet to show any overwhelming or definitive link between performance and pay, these schemes retain their popularity with organisations.

Chapter 18 explores one of the newer forms of variable pay, team-based pay. Team-based pay is used relatively rarely despite the prevalence of team-working in organisations and this chapter explores the possibility that the approach offers the rewarding of an individual's performance whilst at the same time preserving the ethos of a team. The chapter offers examples of how team-based pay systems can be designed, developed and incorporated into existing reward strategies and systems. The evidence of its use as a reward system is also present both in terms of its context and degree.

Chapter 19 discusses how gainsharing as a payment system has had a low take up within the United Kingdom in comparison to countries such as the USA. It also has a low profile within the literature on reward. As a consequence gainsharing is a concept less familiar to managers than the majority of other concepts covered in the book. In addition to outlining the various forms of gainsharing practised, this chapter puts forward a convincing case for its benefits. It also highlights its relevance for the 'not-for-profit' sector of the economy, which has assiduously sought to try to introduce pay-for-performance systems against much resistance and with variable success.

Chapter 20 explores the heavily regulated area of profit-related pay and share owner-ship schemes. It begins by explaining the various types of schemes in use and the extent to which each attracts tax relief for both employees and employers. It then goes on to review the research evidence relating to the impact of these schemes on levels of both commitment to the organisation and productivity, and their prevalence in 'blue chip' and high-performing organisations. It also highlights the range of objectives and the agendas, not always explicit, that organisations pursue in introducing profit-related pay and share option schemes.

Chapter 21 having explored the options available for base pay and variable pay the final two chapters focus on employee benefits. These form a significant part of an organ-isations labour costs and yet have until recently attracted little attention from remu-neration managers in organisations. This is now changing as the concept of flexibility enters managers' thinking on benefits. The change in focus from the collective to the individual in organisations has developed concurrently with the realisation that indi-vidual employees have individual needs and these might be subject to change during their working life. Blanket benefits may not therefore serve their intended purpose for either employer or employee. This chapter addresses flexible benefits and explores the options available in their design and the advantages and problems that organisations introducing them might need to address.

Chapter 22 concentrates on one single employee benefit, namely pension schemes. Pension schemes, we feel, deserve special consideration for a number of reasons. First, because of the extent to which they are subject to legislative regulation as well as their signi-ficance in the financial markets. Second, because of their substantial costs to both the employer and, over a lifetime of employment, the employee as well. Finally, pension schemes have great social significance, a significance which is currently adjusting to new demographic, political and financial realities and which will raise difficult ques-tions for organisations in the years ahead.

PART I

Strategic reward – the context of reward

1 Debates in reward management

Stephen Taylor

Interest on the part of managers, consultants and academic writers in the use of reward systems as a means of achieving organisational objectives has increased steadily since the 1960s. The opportunity for new thinking in the field has resulted from the retreat from collective bargaining as the dominant method of pay determination in the UK, first at the national level and latterly within organisations generally. This has coincided with the rise of an approach to the management of people, often labelled HRM (human resource management), which gives employment practices a central role in the achievement of competitive advantage. The result has been substantially greater variety in the approaches used to determine the level and form of pay packets, a proliferation of books and articles exploring the relative merits of different types of payment system from a management perspective, and the evolution of several vigorous debates on different aspects of reward management.

FUNDAMENTAL CHOICES

At base there are two key questions which an organisation has to ask when formulating reward strategies and policies:

1 How much should be paid to each employee?
2 What form should that payment take?

A range of alternative payment systems and methods of determining pay levels are available to help managers answer these questions in the best interests of their organisations. In answering the first there is a need to consider the relative merits of paying at or above market levels, using some form of job evaluation scheme, and bargaining with recognised trade unions. These three basic approaches are not necessarily mutually exclusive, but will in some combination determine pay levels within the constraints of the regulatory environment. In answering the second question there is a greater number of alternative systems to consider ranging from traditional time-based rates, through the various output-based incentive schemes to systems which link pay to skills and qualifications. On top of these, managers can add a variety of benefits such as company cars, occupational pensions, private health insurance and discounts on the employer's own products and services. The other fundamental choice, often not properly acknowledged in texts on reward management, is the proportion of the total pay package which is variable. It is not simply a question of deciding that performance-related pay or profit-sharing is appropriate, there is also a need to decide whether it will account for 5 per cent or 25 per cent of an individual's overall remuneration. There is a world of difference between the two sums, a distinction which is likely to be more significant in determining a successful outcome than that about which form of incentive to use in the first place.

In making choices in this area, the principal determining factors are the objectives organisations have for their human resource (HR) policies, and reward systems in particular. A number of distinct objectives can be identified:

1 To minimise expenditure on wages and salaries over the long term.
2 To attract and retain staff of the desired calibre, experience and qualifications.
3 To motivate the workforce so as to maximise organisational performance.
4 To direct effort and enthusiasm in specific directions and to encourage particular types of employee behaviour.
5 To underpin and facilitate the management of organisational change.

It is the diversity of these objectives, relating to competition in both product and labour markets, that makes reward management such a complex and fascinating area of practice. There is no one payment system or form of incentive that can achieve all the above for all groups of staff in an organisation, so managers are necessarily required to weigh up the advantages and disadvantages of any system before making judgements based on a balanced assessment of all likely outcomes. Moreover, it is not an area in which doing nothing is an option, simply because all employers have to have some form of mechanism, however *ad hoc* in nature, in order to pay their employees.

This inevitable dilemma, which when combined with the wide range of objectives and influences which help determine reward policy, has led to the development of several vehemently contested debates among academics, consultants, trade unionists and managers of reward systems. In the following section four of the more prominent debates are summarised. At no other point in the book are they addressed directly, but they form the backdrop to a number of the chapters and have naturally influenced the assumptions behind the arguments that are put forward.

THE REWARD MANAGEMENT DEBATE

This debate concerns the extent to which organisations in the UK have developed new practices in the management of reward over the past two or three decades. Specifically it concerns how far managers have moved away from essentially 'reactive' or '*ad hoc*' approaches towards those which can be described as having a strategic character. Although now primarily associated with developments since the early 1980s, the key themes were clearly in the minds of leading writers several years earlier as the following quotation illustrates:

We have asked ourselves four questions about payment systems; and our method of selecting a scheme has evolved from trying to answer them. They are:

1 What should the objectives of a firm be when installing or modifying a payment scheme?
2 What payment schemes are available to choose from?
3 How should a firm go about deciding which of the available schemes is best suited to its circumstances?
4 Which of the available schemes satisfies its objectives?

These questions seem the simple and obvious ones to ask. Yet they are not questions that are usually asked. In our experience it is rare for a firm to state clearly and fully what its objectives are when installing a scheme; nor is it usual to scan the whole range of known schemes. Although a firm may have it in mind to look for something suitable to its own circumstances, it is also rare for these circumstances to be sharply and fully defined, let alone measured. (Lupton and Gowler, 1969: 8)

Since the above passage was written by Tom Lupton and Dan Gowler there have been substantial changes in industrial structure and competitive conditions, and consequently in the practice of personnel management. Much has also changed in the field of employee remuneration, with a decline in the spread of collective bargaining and a growth in the amount of regulation covering pay issues. Furthermore, remuneration specialists generally agree that the 1980s and 1990s have seen major developments in the payment policies of many UK employers. It is clear, for example, that there has been extension in pay-for-performance schemes of one kind or another (see, Casey, Lakey and White, 1992; Cannell and Wood, 1992) as well as an on-going increase in the proportion of the working population covered by profit-related pay schemes (IDS, 1994). There has also been a growth in the use of analytical job evaluation schemes as a means of establishing internal differentials (IRS, 1993). These trends are consistent with the broad principles of a human resource management approach. They involve a shift away from a focus on fixed, collective, job-based remuneration systems towards the adoption of more flexible practices designed to reward individual or group effort and performance while adhering to broad objectives of equity in establishing individual pay levels.

There is disagreement, however, between both academic writers and practitioners concerning the extent to which these developments can be interpreted as being evidence of a new-found strategic approach to reward management. It is thus unclear whether or not the deficiencies in remuneration management identified as common by Lupton and Gowler have been rectified to any great extent in the period since 1969. The debate has been characterised by a wide divergence of views among its most prominent protagonists. In a series of articles and books, for example, Murlis, Armstrong and Wright have put forward the view that the management of employee rewards has undergone fundamental change. They claim that practice in the field has developed from its previous reactive nature to become a significant tool in the practice of human resource management. The change in approach is dated as having taken place in the mid and late 1980s, following an initial 'sense of inertia and unwillingness to move towards a more strategic view of remuneration policy and development' (Murlis and Wright, 1993: 7). A similar view is put forward by Clive Wright (1996: 58–9) with the election of the Thatcher government being seen as the turning point.

Despite criticisms of these claims, the most recent edition of *Reward Management* by Michael Armstrong and Helen Murlis (1998: 12) firmly and unequivocally re-states such views while further claiming that major recent developments in the field include the adoption of a much more strategic approach to reward and of a widespread acceptance of 'the new pay philosophy' by which 'pay policies and practices must flow from the overall strategy' (pp. 12–14). These claims do not appear to be based on published evidence but are, it is assumed, a reflection of the authors' own experiences as consultants. No one disputes that there has been increased interest in new methods of payment or that the rhetoric of people working in this field has evolved to embrace the language of strategic HRM. What is questioned is the extent to which any kind of fundamental shift has occurred in practice.

The major critic of the position described above is Ian Smith (see 1992: 172, 1993: 45 and chapter 22 of this book). First, he expresses the view that the underlying principles behind these modern incentive schemes are no different from those of traditional payment-by-results schemes long used in the management of shop-floor workers. Second, he argues that there is no evidence to support the notion that these developments are the outcome of a new-found strategic approach on the part of British managers. In his view, the increased interest in incentive schemes has occurred in response to short-term recruitment and retention problems or cost-cutting pressures, and thus must be characterised as being reactive. Far from developing appropriate long-term reward strategies, therefore, the practice of remuneration management in the UK remains a process which is characterised by managers 'muddling through' (Smith, 1992: 183). Crowe (1992: 117) gives a measure of support to Smith in his analysis of the reasons for the failure of many payment systems to motivate employees. In his view, this occurs due to a lack of strategic considerations in the management of remuneration. His experience as a consultant has led him to conclude that traditional payment systems remain in place and that they tend to frustrate managers who find that they interfere with attempts to plan for strategic change.

Kessler (1995) also addresses the question of the extent to which recent developments in payment practice can be described as strategic. His rather more cautious conclusion, based primarily on an impressive analysis of case-study evidence, finds merit in both the positions outlined above. While he accepts that, in many cases, moves towards the establishment of new performance or output-based payment systems amount to little more than a further 'shuffling of the pack' in reaction to familiar management problems, he also points out that:

> the use of reward systems, sometimes in combination with other human resource management techniques, to facilitate or support the process of organisational transformation and culture change is an important departure from past practice. There are examples of rewards being used in qualitatively different ways to restructure and develop certain attitudes, values and skills. (Kessler, 1995: 274)

The most recent academic contribution to this debate is that of Poole and Jenkins (1998). Their conclusion, based on a questionnaire survey of 909 senior managers, found substantial endorsement of 'new pay and human resource management approaches to rewards' but considerably less evidence of their translation into 'actual reward practices':

> in contrast with the policies of companies, many elements of the 'new pay' do not appear to have been widely adopted in practice in British companies. (p. 239)

Like Smith, they thus identify something of a gap between the rhetoric and the reality. However, significantly they also found substantial variation between practices in different kinds of organisation, with larger private-sector organisations being a good deal more original in the reward area than the others they studied. They also found evidence of a particularly strong attachment to strategic reward policies in expanding firms and a tendency for a minority of companies to introduce a bundle of different innovative reward practices.

BEST PRACTICE VERSUS BEST FIT

While the 'reward management debate is primarily concerned with what is happening, the emphasis in the best-practice versus best-fit debate is on what should be happening. Here the division of opinion is between those who take the view that different HR policies are appropriate in different circumstances (the contingency or best-fit school), and those who believe it is possible to identify approaches which have universal value in terms of their capacity to induce the achievement of competitive advantage (the best-practice school). The former stress the significance of strategic alignment of HR policy and of ensuring that it 'fits' the business objectives of the organisation. The latter focus on what is best in terms of attracting, retaining and motivating human beings, developing from such analyses generally applicable policy prescriptions. While for the most part this is a generalist HR debate, writers such as Jeffery Pfeffer have recently sought to apply best-practice principles to the field of reward, an area which has for many years been dominated by 'best-fit' thinking.

A division of opinion in normative HRM literature over the merits of contingency or 'best-fit' models has existed for a number of years. It has emerged, in one shape or form, in the context of debates about the meaning of the term HRM (Marchington, 1992: 9–16) and in those concerning the model of the flexible firm (Hunter *et al.*, 1993), hard and soft approaches (Legge, 1995: 66–7), and in the role of HRM in change management (Storey, 1992: 118–22). There is nothing new about challenges to the contingency perspective from those arguing that some form of 'best-practice' approach to HRM is more likely to lead to performance improvements at organisational level in most or all circumstances (e.g., Walton, 1985; Guest, 1987). However, what has emerged relatively recently is a body of published literature which for the first time gives empirical support to the hitherto theoretical argument in favour of best-practice approaches.

The most emphatic assault on the validity of contingency prescriptions in HRM is contained in the work of Huselid (1995). His analysis of questionnaire data collected from senior HR managers in 968 private, US-owned firms has led him to conclude that the installation of 'high performance work practices' is correlated positively with lower employee turnover, higher productivity and higher corporate financial performance irrespective of which of Porter's (1985) three generic business strategies is being pursued. Huselid then goes on to press home the case for the adoption of his parcel of best-practice HRM policies with estimates of the advantages of doing so in terms of dollars accrued per employee (Huselid, 1995: 658–9).

A similar conclusion is implicitly suggested in work undertaken by Fernie and Metcalf using data provided by 1,500 British organisations for the 1990 Workplace Industrial Relations Survey (Fernie and Metcalf, 1996). Their research is similar to that of Huselid in that it seeks to measure quantitatively the relative effect on various measures of organisational performance of different approaches to the management of employees. In this case three forms of 'workplace governance' are compared: authoritarian, collective bargaining and employee involvement. While their findings were less clear cut than those of Huselid, Fernie and Metcalf were able to conclude that, in terms of promoting productivity and productivity growth, the 'employee involvement' form of governance was quantifiably more successful than the other forms also identified as 'typical' work places.

This study, unlike that of Huselid, is not specifically concerned with testing the validity of the contingency perspective and does not therefore consider distinctions between the effect of each of the forms of governance in organisations pursuing different business strategies. The implication, however, is similar – namely that the presence of a particular set of practices correlates with improved economic performance across a wide range of organisations operating in different industrial sectors and competitive environments.

Wood (1995) and Wood and Albanese (1995) reach similar conclusions in reporting their empirical work on 'high commitment management'. The results of their questionnaire survey of 135 UK manufacturing plants suggested that the adoption of high commitment HR policies (i.e., those which emphasise employee commitment, flexibility and trainability as well as status harmonisation) was not related to observable external environmental factors (Wood and Albanese, 1995: 242–3). In practice, therefore, it would appear that the adoption of such management practices does not result either from conscious or subconscious attempts on the part of managers to align HR policy with business strategy as is recommended in the normative contingency literature.

In a second article discussing the same research data, Wood (1995) goes further in deriving the additional conclusion that high commitment management is 'universally applicable' and that the results lend support to the best-practice approaches suggested in the work of Guest (1987) and Walton (1985). It could of course be counter-argued from a contingency perspective that evidence indicating a failure on the part of managers to apply 'best-fit' principles to the development of HR practices does not obviate the fact that they should do so. Arguably, therefore, further evidence is required on firm performance and the presence of high commitment practices before it can be said with any certainty that empirical data like that collected in Wood and Albanese's study truly undermines the validity of the contingency model.

A further fundamental criticism that can be levelled at each of the studies described above is the implicit assumption that the presence of a correlation between 'best-practice' HRM practices and effective financial performance indicates the existence of a causal relationship. In practice, of course, other factors, such as effective long-term investment or inspirational leadership, may be the fundamental reasons for the existence of both sets of results. Alternatively, it could be the case that financial success permits firms to introduce best-practice HR initiatives rather than the other way round. It nevertheless remains significant that Wood and Albanese, as well as the other authorities, have sought to make an inference in favour of a best-practice approach and that this has led them explicitly to question the validity of best-fit models.

Furthermore, their general conclusions are supported by Pfeffer (1994). Using a qualitative research methodology, he puts the case for a 'best-practice' approach with reference to research which analysed HR practice within a large number of 'effective firms' (i.e., those which have sustained long-term competitive advantage in particular product markets). Using this less-scientific approach he has identified 16 HR practices which are common in effective firms but which are less likely to be present to any marked degree in typical US companies. The 16 practices are not dissimilar from those applied in the questionnaire studies described above with a heavy focus on training, flexible working, generous reward systems, internal promotion and employee participation. His studies, like the others, have led him to conclude that:

> Contrary to some academic writing and to popular belief, there is little evidence that effect-ive management practices are (1) particularly faddish (although their implementation may well be), (2) difficult to understand or to comprehend why they work, or 3) necessarily contingent on an organisation's particular competitive strategy. (Pfeffer, 1994: 27)

The application of best-practice thinking to the more specialised field of reward practice poses particular difficulties for two reasons. The first obstacle is the sheer extent to which alternative best-fit assumptions have dominated the output of writers and consultants working in the field, with leading authorities such as Kanter (1989), Lawler (1990) and Gomez-Mejia and Balkin (1992) all firmly advocating contingency approaches. Indeed, in recent years their perspective has been re-styled 'the new pay' and has been positioned firmly in opposition to best-practice prescriptions, as the following definition of the term makes clear:

> The new pay doesn't necessarily mean implementing new reward practices or abandoning traditional ones; it means identifying pay practices that enhance the organisation's strategic effectiveness . . . it is not skills-based pay, gainsharing or any of the specific pay practices that have cropped up in recent years. Indeed, the new pay is not a set of compensation practices at all, but rather a way of thinking about the role of reward systems in a complex organisa-tion. The new pay argues in favour of a design process that starts with business strategy and organisational design. It argues against an assumption that certain best practices must be incor-porated into a company's approach to pay. (Lawler, 1995: 14)

The second problem in applying best practice to the reward field is how to avoid simply equating best practice in reward management with higher levels of pay and bene-fits. It may well be the case that greater generosity leads to a more satisfied, loyal and creative staff, but in many business environments this is likely to lead to lower overall competitiveness as higher costs of production are passed on to consumers. Moreover, there is a good amount of anecdotal evidence which suggests that high levels of reward are in fact often associated with poor practice in other areas of HRM. The implica-tion is that a corporation can intensify work, offer little job security and sustain a fairly brutal management style, while maintaining acceptable levels of commitment and employee retention, provided it pays above market rates. According to Neil (1996: 184 and 192), such an approach is used at News International, allowing the company to buy acceptance from its employees with a range of 'low-commitment / high-control' HR practices. There are thus grounds for arguing that while best-practice ideas have a good deal to offer in other areas of HR practice, their significance for reward specialists is rather more limited. In the face of such criticism, two types of argument are advanced in favour of best-practice reward prescriptions. First, it is pointed out that high pay need not lead to lower competitiveness and that the opposite is often the case. Second, it is argued that even if best practice has only a limited role to play in setting the level of rewards, it still has plenty to offer in determining the form rewards take.

Of late, Jeffery Pfeffer (1998 a and b) has been the most prominent advocate of the first argument. He argues that, while it is counter-intuitive to many, organisations which pay higher wages are often more productive than direct competitors who pay considerably less. This, he argues, is because high pay rates attract and retain the most motivated, experienced and capable staff. Not only are such employees more productive, their presence also provides the basis for competitive strategies based on innovation and quality as well as price. The commonly held belief that labour rates equate to labour costs, is cited by Pfeffer as 'myth number one' – head of his list of 'six dangerous myths about pay' (1998a: 110–11). In making these points of course, Pfeffer is not breaking new ground, as they have all been developed at length by efficiency wages theorists and have long formed the subject of debate among labour market economists (see Tarling and Wilkinson, 1987). He is however very effectively popularising important ideas about pay policy, establishing their place in the normative management literature and backing them up with new case-study evidence.

The second argument in favour of best practice in reward is concerned with the type of incentive payments that employers make, with wage structures and with methods of wage determination. While to date, there is relatively little hard evidence supporting the view that particular reward practices are generally applicable across all business situations, all the surveys have included reward policy prescriptions in the more general 'bundles' of HR philosophies, tools and techniques said to constitute best practice. While a number of prescriptions could be cited in this context, the following three underlying principles can be distilled from the work of Huselid and Pfeffer, referred to above, and Wood (1996), as well as from other publications focusing on specific aspects of reward policy (including later chapters of this book):

1 an emphasis on incentive payment systems which are based on group rather than individual performance (profit-based pay, gainsharing, share ownership plans, etc.);
2 the presence of extensive and genuine employee participation in the design / re-design of payment systems;
3 a high level of concern for internal pay equity (minimising the differentials between the highest and lowest paid, as well as effective usage of analytical job evaluation schemes).

It must be stressed, however, that the extent to which these principles can be said to have some kind of universal applicability as a means of promoting competitive advantage is unknown. Indeed, what robust evidence does exist, such as that reported by Wood (1996), suggests that no one type of payment system is clearly associated with companies which pursue other forms of best-practice HRM. The best-fit–best-practice debate thus remains undecided either way. One side confidently asserts that there is no one best way of managing reward policy, the other suggests that there might well be. Both sides make reasonably convincing cases, but as yet neither can draw on a sufficient body of empirical research to back up their declared positions. At present we can only conclude that the jury is still out.

EXPECTANCY THEORY AND PERFORMANCE-RELATED PAY

Our third debate has the longest history and is the most fundamental in the field of reward management. While it manifests itself in different ways with each successive wave of fashion in reward systems, it is ever present because at base it simply concerns the extent to which individual workers are motivated by money. Expectancy theory holds that money is a significant motivator for most, and that we will usually alter our behaviour, either by increasing effort or directing it in specific directions, in order to secure a higher base salary or some form of bonus payment. Advocates of the theory's validity argue that money is important, not simply for its own sake, but because it is a means to the achievement of other ends. Pay is instrumental, for example, in the achievement of security, status and autonomy aside from its more general role in providing us with purchasing power. Often associated with the work of Vroom (1964) but with a far longer history, an acceptance of expectancy theory underpins much recent prescriptive literature on reward systems (see Lawler, 1981: 1–27 and Thierry, 1992: 139–40). In short, it is argued, tying pay to specific performance outcomes will both ensure that these are met while at the same time motivating employees in a more general sense, by providing them with desired rewards.

In the past 20 years the practical application of expectancy theory has been seen in the growth of individual performance-related payment (PRP) systems and the maintenance, where appropriate, of piecework and commission-based incentive schemes. The idea of linking a portion of pay directly to formal performance appraisal and to the achievement of specific performance objectives has proved particularly attractive to employers, with such approaches becoming increasingly common in both the private and public sectors (Kessler, 1998: 586–8). This trend is readily understood when the many theoretical advantages of PRP systems are considered:

- attracting and retaining good performers
- improving individual and corporate performance
- improving motivation
- clarifying job roles and duties
- linking effort explicitly to organisation objectives
- improving communication
- reinforcing management control
- identifying developmental opportunities

In addition to all these, PRP may be attractive as a means of reinforcing the individual employment relationship and reducing trade union influence. Moreover, again in theory, PRP can be advanced as being a reasonably fair and objective method of distinguishing the good performer from the bad and of distributing rewards accordingly. It also provides a means of rewarding individuals for their efforts without needing to promote them into better-paid jobs for which they may in fact be unsuited.

The merits of a PRP system, however, have never achieved general acceptance among writers in the reward field. While the leading contingency theorists (e.g., Lawler, 1990: 86–107; Armstrong and Murlis, 1988: 280–97) see it as having a useful role to play where the circumstances are appropriate, others have developed a series of sustained critiques, with the result that the literature in recent years has been dominated by writers attacking it both in principle and in practice. For some the problems are essentially pragmatic, systems simply being judged very difficult to manage effectively. For others PRP, along with the theory of expectancy on which it is based, has more fundamental flaws. Interestingly, this last position encompasses people coming to the debate from very different perspectives. The psychologists question the effectiveness of money as a motivator, sociologists view PRP as a tool aimed at re-enforcing management control and argue that consequently it decreases trust and increases conflict at work, while a third group object to its inherent unfairness and suspect that it is used as a means of perpetuating gender inequality. The most vehement criticisms, however, have come from advocates of TQM (total quality management), for whom PRP represents the opposite of all they believe to be necessary in achieving competitive advantage. W. Edwards Deming sums up this view as follows:

> It leaves people bitter, crushed, bruised, battered, desolate, despondent, dejected, feeling inferior, some even depressed, unfit for work for weeks after receipt of rating, unable to comprehend why they are inferior. It is unfair, as it ascribes to the people in a group differences that may be caused totally by the system they work in. (Deming, 1986: 75)

Unlike the best-fit–best-practice debate, there is a considerable volume of research evidence available to assist in reaching conclusions about expectancy and performance-related rewards. Several major UK-based research studies have been undertaken in recent years looking at the effects of PRP and other individual incentive schemes in action, the most prominent of which include those of Bowey and Thorpe and Hellier (1986), Kinnie and Lowe (1990), Marsden and Richardson (1991), Cannell and Wood (1992), Kessler and Purcell (1992) and Thompson (1993). Without exception, these studies point to a number of significant problems or disadvantages in the way individual incentive schemes operate in practice. Seen strictly from a management perspective, however, these do not necessarily indicate that individual incentive schemes are necessarily flawed. Rather they suggest that PRP is difficult to manage effectively. This is made clear by Cannell and Wood (1992: 66–106) in their report of interviews carried out with 44 HR managers:

1 Interviewees were unsure whether or not PRP positively motivated staff. The motivational effect appeared limited given the relatively small amounts of bonus paid in most UK organisations.
2 Virtually all managers agreed that PRP schemes had a de-motivating effect on some staff. In the case of poorer performers this was not necessarily perceived as a negative effect as it encouraged them to leave.
3 A number of interviewees saw PRP as damaging in so far as it encouraged short termism on the part of employees.
4 Approximately half the managers interviewed perceived PRP to have a negative impact on team working. In some cases this led to lower levels of co-operation between staff, while in others the problem had been addressed by incorporating team-based criteria into individual performance objectives.
5 Opinion was divided among public-sector managers between those who saw PRP as essentially incompatible with the public-service culture, and those who saw it as effectively reinforcing established performance appraisal systems and assisting in the promotion of cultural change.
6 Few organisations carry out formal evaluations of the effect their PRP systems have on organisational performance, with managers being uncertain whether or not there was a significant positive effect.
7 The practical business of setting appropriate performance objectives was found to be problematic. Interviewees reported concern about inconsistency between the approaches taken by different line managers.

8 Problems associated with a conflict between the developmental and evaluative objectives of performance appraisal processes when pay is linked to them were not found to have been insurmountable.

9 Significant difficulties were encountered by some employers when environmental factors out of the control of staff impacted on their ability to achieve performance objectives. Problems in this area were generally overcome by permitting a degree of flexibility in the way schemes operated.

10 PRP was generally agreed not to have raised overall labour costs and to have provided organisations with better value for money. Overall it was usually self-financing.

A second stream of research findings, suggests that the above problems are at base neither practical in nature nor surmountable via more effective design of systems. Instead they are merely symptoms of more fundamental problems associated with the application of expectancy theory to reward management. In short, it is argued that the very idea that incentive payments can positively motivate employees is flawed. The most emphatic recent statement of this point of view is the article published by Alfie Kohn in the *Harvard Business Review* in 1993. Drawing on several academic studies (some laboratory based) to back up his main points, he claims that incentive systems do not and indeed cannot form the basis of long-term improvements in productivity, because pay is in fact a poor motivator. The implication is that any link between incentive payment systems and firm performance is co-incidental, with other factors being responsible for corporate success. In most cases, he argues, individual incentives actually have a negative effect both on motivation and firm performance. The main points made are as follows:

1 Survey evidence backs up Herzberg's (1966) assertion that pay is a 'hygiene factor' in terms of its effect on human motivation. It does not positively motivate or satisfy, but can demotivate or dissatisfy if not perceived as being adequate.

2 Incentive rewards linked to performance objectives are actually a means whereby managers control employees. At root they are manipulative and are 'likely to assume a punitive quality over time' because the failure to be given an expected reward is perceived as a punishment.

3 Performance-related reward focuses effort on short-term individual gain at the expense of longer-term collective gain. The result is competition between team members when co-operation is the true route to the achievement of sustained competitive advantage.

4 The presence of incentive schemes deters managers from addressing underlying causes of poor or inadequate performance such as dissatisfaction with aspects of the work environment. In this respect they discourage supervisors from developing the more effective motivation skills associated with effective leadership.

5 PRP in particular stifles innovative thinking, constructive criticism and creativity. Instead people focus simply on achieving specific tasks in the most unchallenging way they can find.

6 The fact that incentives are first and foremost tools of management control and are perceived as such by staff, undermines the extent to which work is self-directed. This reduces our interest in what we are doing and thus undermines intrinsic motivation.

This third debate, like the first two is characterised by a wide divergence of view-points. Interestingly though, unlike them, the divide is largely between management practitioners and consultants on one side and academic writers on the other. The former retaining a belief in the attractions of individual incentives, while the latter assert that they are wrong to do so. A possible reason for this is that the two groups are actually coming at the issue with different perspectives and see the objectives of schemes such as PRP as being rather different. Reading the literature one is struck in particular by the centrality in the critical works of the idea that effective motivation is a necessary pre-requisite of organisational success. It follows that management inter-vention cannot be appropriate either if it fails to motivate positively or de-motivates in some way. From such a perspective it is easy to condemn PRP outright and argue that its impact is virtually always going to be negative for organisations. It is, however, plausible to argue that managers view these matters through different eyes, and that this explains the continued growth of schemes like PRP in the face of the research findings summarised above.

First, as has been pointed out, payment systems are not the only HR intervention used by managers to achieve performance objectives. Indeed, the evidence suggests that, even judged exclusively in monetary terms, PRP forms a relatively small part of most employees' pay packets. It is thus possible to conclude that it is used in a relatively small way in most organisations, a useful tool for achieving certain objectives, but by no means the major mechanism for achieving motivation. Second, it can be argued that maintaining a fair degree of management control is just as significant in the achievement of long-term organisation objectives as sustaining reasonable levels of motivation. In fact both are equally important and PRP, as both critics and supporters agree, is an effective tool of management control. The continued attraction of incen-tive payment systems may not therefore in fact be due to their supposed motivational qualities but to their role in directing effort towards the achievement of management objectives. The need for positive motivation can be addressed using other interventions. Third, as was pointed out in the introductory paragraphs, employees have to be paid in some way. Managers can not therefore view the individual incentive payment system in a vacuum, as some of the researchers often appear to do. Some form of payment system is necessary and all the major alternatives have some drawbacks when viewed from the organisation's perspective. A further explanation for the continued use of systems like PRP may therefore be very pragmatic, they are straightforward, readily understood and have no more disadvantages than the potential alternative approaches.

COMPETING DEFINITIONS OF EQUITY

Our fourth debate is somewhat less clear cut than the first three, with fewer authorities taking distinct positions on one side or the other. It is nevertheless central to decision making in reward management and underlies a range of other prominent debates, such as those about executive remuneration, equal value/comparable worth and the rights and wrongs of minimum wage legislation. It is fundamental to these because it is basically concerned with establishing what general principles, if any, should be used to determine different pay levels within organisations. Equity theory is chiefly associated with the work of the psychologist J.S. Adams (1963) who argued that the major determinant of satisfaction at work is the extent to which workers judge the 'outputs' that accrue from their work (such as pay levels, pay increases, promotions, etc.) to be distributed equitably. His contention was that we are less interested in how far these 'outputs' equate to our 'inputs' (effort, skill, experience, qualifications, etc.), than we are in the extent to which the ratio between the two compares with that achieved by others. The level of pay per se is thus less important in determining satisfaction or 'consonance' than our perception of its fairness in proportion to the pay that others receive relative to their contribution. It follows that dissatisfaction or 'dissonance' is the likely outcome even of apparently positive occurrences such as pay rises – for example when others are perceived to have been treated more favourably relative to their inputs. From a management point of view, of greater significance, was Adams' further finding that perceived inequity is rarely accepted and that people are consequently motivated to take action aimed at its reduction. Among the methods used to do this are a decrease in personal effort, demands for more equitable treatment and active attempts to find alternative employment. Equity theory thus holds that perceived unfairness in the distribution of rewards is likely to be damaging to the organisation, with lower levels of commitment, higher levels of absence and staff turnover, and either the development or intensification of adversarial industrial relations.

While there is some doubt about Adams' assertion that over-compensation for individual contribution relative to payment is as likely to lead to dissonance as under-compensation, few have found grounds for criticising his basic findings. Moreover, a range of subsequent research projects set up to test the validity of equity theory have found strong evidence to support its principal contention (see Mowday, 1996 for an effective summary of this work). We can thus conclude with some confidence that the achievement of perceived equity in the management of reward systems must be a major objective of those with responsibilities in this area. The difficulties and debates arise over attempts to put the theory into practice, because, while all agree that fairness in pay is desirable, there is no real agreement as to what exactly constitutes equity when it comes to the establishment of systems to determine reward levels.

Runciman (1995: 44–6) argues that there are 'two entirely consistent theoretical positions' concerning who should get how much money but that 'nobody actually holds either of them'. The two are as follows:

1 A basic egalitarian position centred around the notion of need. This is summed up in the phrase 'when anybody is starving it is a crime to have more than enough'.
2 An extreme libertarian position rooted in trust of the free market and the belief that it is invariably harmful to interfere with its workings.

What we have, therefore, is a situation in which people broadly agree that rewards should be distributed unequally, with some, such as those who work hard, possess particular skills, take risks or shoulder heavy responsibilities, receiving more than others, but less agreement about what actual mechanisms should be used to determine these matters or about how great the disparity between the highest and lowest paid should be. The central problem is that those factors which most people would like to be used to determine differentials and relativities (effort, skill, risk, experience, need, etc.) are very difficult to measure in any kind of objective way. We want equity and fair dealing in the distribution of reward, but have yet to develop satisfactory methods of delivering such an outcome.

In practical terms, notwithstanding intervention of the law, collective bargaining processes and ability to pay, there are basically two alternative approaches available to the determination of relative pay levels. The first is to focus on the external labour market and to pay everyone in the organisation at around their market rate. The second is to look first and foremost at internal differentials and to establish a pay structure which distributes rewards according to organisational objectives or some assessment of job worth. Both approaches can be seen as being equitable within the meaning of equity theory, it is just that in the first case the comparisons are made with people employed in other organisations (external equity) and in the second between people employed within the same organisation (internal equity).

In an ideal world, of course, both could be achieved at the same time – and in some situations such is the case. This occurs when an individual's external market rate is roughly equivalent to the rate regarded as fair internally when compared to the wages paid to those higher up and further down the organisational hierarchy. Very often, however, the two rates are not the same and may be substantially different. In such circumstances a decision has to be made as to which approach to take. Is pay to be determined primarily with reference to external or internal equity?

A number of arguments can be advanced in favour of paying the external market rate. First, except in the case of particularly uncommon jobs or of individuals with unusual attributes, it is straightforward in practical terms to establish what the going rate for a particular job is at a particular time. For many jobs the level of hourly rates in particular areas is common knowledge throughout the industry, with figures being quoted in job centres and newspaper advertisements. For others some further research has to be done by making use of published data, salary surveys or through membership of salary clubs. Second, it is argued that paying the market rate is the most economically efficient approach. It helps minimise the extent of staff shortages while also ensuring that profit is not needlessly forgone through over-payment of staff. According to Gomez-Mejia and Balkin (1992: 292–3) the following advantages in HRM terms, can accrue from such an approach:

- a reasonable pool of applicants from which to select new employees
- speedy filling of vacancies following resignations
- low employee turnover and thus a reasonable return on training investment
- well-qualified and experienced staff attracted by good wages

A third argument is based on the notion that markets are simply the most economically efficient means of distributing wealth and that it is in the interests of the economy, and hence society in general, that external rather than internal equity is the principal concern of remuneration managers. In his highly critical analysis of equal value law, Steven Rhoads (1993: 30) puts the case as follows:

> If wages for scarce male-dominated professions, say computer scientists, are fixed at a level below the point where supply and demand are equated, there will be labour shortages. Employers will find it hard to attract the workers needed to meet the demands of consumers. A higher wage would attract more workers to the market and increase output. Thus, as Ronald Ehrenberg and Robert Smith conclude in their popular text on labour economics, 'an increase in the wage level would benefit the people in society in both their consumer and worker roles'.

In addition to these, there is the straightforward argument that in certain labour markets, perhaps where money is the primary motivator, there is no real alternative to paying the market rate. It is simply necessary to do so in order to attract staff with the required qualifications and to ensure that employees do not become so dissatisfied with what they are being paid that they are continually looking for other career opportunities. In short, according to Wallace and Fay (1988: 49), 'an employer that ignores the external market will not survive for long'.

The alternative point of view, in support of internal equity, starts with the assertion that labour markets differ from product markets in important ways. According to Smith (1983: 38), it is common for employees to have imperfect knowledge of the going-rates for potential alternative jobs. Raising or cutting wages does not therefore necessarily lead to an increase or decrease in the supply of labour. Moreover, ignorance may also prevent external inequity from generating the kind of dissatisfaction predicted by Adams's equity theory. Second, different labour markets are very often insulated from one another in terms of the skills and experience required to enter them. This limits the opportunities available for individuals to apply for different jobs even when dissatisfied with the remuneration offered by a particular employer. Third, as was pointed out above, pay is not the only motivator or the only determinant of labour supply. Hence, as is shown by Gomez-Mejia and Balkin (1992: 293–4), it is feasible for some employers to attract, retain and motivate sufficient staff despite 'following the market' in terms of overall levels of remuneration. This occurs because some people at least will trade in a higher rate of base pay for one or more of the following:

- job security
- flexible working arrangements
- benefits such as car-parking, holidays, pensions, health insurance
- career development and training opportunities
- convenience of a work location
- work which is intrinsically satisfying or meaningful
- a pleasant working environment
- friendly and considerate colleagues

Others are prepared to forego high pay now for the possibility of higher pay later. Hence small organisations with growth potential can attract staff by promising a greater share of rewards than would be obtainable elsewhere should the business expand successfully in the future.

Having established that the case for pay based on external equity is not as clear cut as its proponents often assume, a positive case for looking primarily to internal equity can be put. Ultimately this must rest on the belief that dissatisfaction and its negative consequences are more prevalent and extensive when people perceive internal inequity than is the case with external inequity. The case is thus based on the proposition that we are more likely to reduce effort, take unauthorised absence, look for other job opportunities and look to trade unions to improve our position, when we think the distribution of rewards within the organisation is unjust than when we are dissatisfied with the position vis-à-vis other employers. Hence, it is argued that employees will understand that one employer is able to pay higher wages than another. In such circumstances they may seek to secure employment in the higher-paying organisation, but the situation will not necessarily lead to 'dissonance'. However, this will not be the case if the low pay is perceived to be a consequence of unfair distribution, as might be the case where senior managers are paid very handsomely or where individual shareholders are believed to be taking too great a cut of profits. Ultimately it means that we are more concerned with internal differentials (i.e., our rate of pay *vis-à-vis* colleagues) than we are with external relativities (our rate of pay *vis-à-vis* those of employees in other organisations). Interestingly, this is the definition of equity used by the law in determining fairness in equal pay and equal value cases. While the requirements of the external market may be used by an employer to defend their actions, it is fair distribution between groups within the organisation that the courts seek to establish.

While internal equity may be desirable in theory, it is a great deal harder to achieve in practice than external equity. Two basic issues have to be determined:

1 How to measure the worth of jobs and thus assign them a place in the hierarchy.
2 What is an appropriate pay gap between different levels in the hierarchy.

In each case, there is potentially any number of answers, but one or two approaches are worthy of specific mention because they are most common or most frequently cited in the literature. In the case of the first issue some form of job evaluation exercise is necessary (i.e., a formal, reasonably systematic study made of job content and the skills needed to perform it to the expected standard). Job evaluation is well-covered elsewhere in this book, so it is not necessary here to go into great detail about its different forms. The main distinction is between analytical systems (which consider each component part of a job) and non-analytical schemes (which make comparisons between whole jobs). Another is between systems that look at several different factors and those which focus on one or two, such as that suggested by Elliott Jacques (1961) in his work on equitable pay. What is significant is that the fairest systems, and indeed the only ones recognised by Employment Tribunals, are the more sophisticated analytical schemes which take a range of factors into account. Not only, therefore is true internal equity hard to achieve, it is also a costly and bureaucratic process.

The second issue is also a matter of debate, with some commentators (e.g. Pfeffer, 1994) arguing that a low level of pay compression is desirable. According to this view, satisfaction, motivation and commitment are maximised when the difference between the highest and lowest package paid by the organisation is minimised. Too great a disparity, even if jobs are graded fairly relative to one another, will thus lead to dissonance and loss of competitive advantage. While this theory is attractive in principle, there is relatively little evidence available to back it up. The extent of the differential between the highest and lowest paid in organisations varies greatly around the world, with both high and low levels of pay compression being typical in different successful economies (100:1 in the USA compared with 17:1 in Japan).

The major alternative approach cited in the literature is associated with tournament theory (see Lazear, 1998: 223–58). Here it is argued that the difference between the pay awarded to people on each rung of the organisational ladder should be set at the level which maximises motivation and effort amongst those seeking promotion. Hence the organisational hierarchy is likened to a knock-out sports tournament, the prize money increasing with each successive round that the athlete remains in the competition. Just as organisers of tournaments set big differentials between the money awarded to champions, beaten finalists, beaten semi-finalists and people who depart in earlier rounds in order to maximise the effort exerted in each match played, so employers should set high enough differentials to ensure that those competing for promotion accentuate their efforts on behalf of the organisation. Here too however, with the exception of analyses of the achievements of professional sports people, there is as yet relatively little empirical evidence on which to base firm conclusions. The debate between those who argue for high and low levels of pay compression is thus another which remains wide open for further analysis by reward specialists.

It is perhaps best to conclude this review of thinking on equity in remuneration with a discussion of one possible 'solution' to the range of management dilemmas identified above. This is the suggestion that what really matters in determining consonance and dissonance is not the level of reward itself, but the manner in which decisions about it are reached. The key distinction here is between the distributive and procedural forms of justice, the former being concerned with who gets what and the latter with how it is decided who gets what. Research in this field suggests that two different forms of dissatisfaction are identifiable in remuneration matters (see Cropanzano and Folger, 1996: 72–83). On the one hand there is dissatisfaction with pay, while on the other there is dissatisfaction with the organisation from whom payments are received. Studies suggest that unfair distribution of rewards through a system which is perceived as fair leads to the former, while unfair distribution via an unfair mechanism leads to the latter. Of significance for remuneration managers is the further finding that the negative consequences of inequity described above (absence, low effort, hostility, etc.) are primarily associated with organisational dissatisfaction. The inference is that the method used to determine different pay levels in an organisation is in fact relatively unimportant as far as perceptions of equity are concerned. Any method can be used (market rates, job evaluation, collective bargaining, tournament-models, etc.) as long as it is perceived to operate in a just manner. This brings us back to issues identified in the discussion of best practice; namely the importance of employee involvement, of openness and in avoiding decision making which either is or might be seen as being arbitrary. Cropanzano and Folger (1996: 81–2) sum up their contention as follows:

> In a world of finite resources people cannot have all the things they want. Although organizations should strive for the best allocations possible, some perceptions of unfavourable outcomes are inevitable. The existence of fair procedures may be a more realistic goal. If procedures are just, then the negative consequences of unfavourable outcomes are less likely. Procedural fairness should motivate employees away from activities viewed by management as being destructive and should motivate employees toward activities seen as being more constructive.

The problem here, as elsewhere, is a lack of definitive research findings on which to base firm conclusions about the theory. Such evidence as is presented is mainly from laboratory studies in which volunteer subjects are put through various tests which simulate a working environment. A substantial body of research addressing the same issues, but using different methodologies, is therefore needed. We may thus conclude with the observation that equity in reward management may be best defined as 'fair dealing' rather than 'fair distribution', but that as yet it is not possible to make a general assertion to that effect with great confidence.

REFERENCES

Adams, J.S. (1963) 'Toward an Understanding of Inequity', *Journal of Abnormal and Social Psychology*, 67: 422–36.

Armstrong, M. and Murlis, H. (1988) *Reward Management: A handbook of remuneration strategy and practice*. Fourth edition, London: Kogan Page.

Bowey, A. Thorpe, R. and Hellier, P. (1986) *Payment Systems and Productivity*. London: Macmillan.

Cannell, M. and Wood, S. (1992) *Incentive Pay: Impact and evolution*. London: IPM.

Casey, B. Lakey, J. and White, M. (1992) *Payment Systems: A look at current practice*. London: Policy Studies Institute.

Cropanzano, R. and Folger, R. (1996) 'Procedural Justice and Worker Motivation', in R. Steers, L. Porter and G. Bigley (eds), *Motivation and Leadership at Work*. Sixth edition, New York: McGraw Hill.

Crowe, D. (1992) 'A New Approach to Reward Management', in M. Armstrong (ed.), *Strategies for Human Resource Management*. London: Kogan Page.

Deming, W.E. (1986) *Out of the Crisis: Quality, productivity and competitive position*. Cambridge: Cambridge University Press.

Fernie, S. and Metcalf, D. (1996) 'Participation, Contingent Pay, Representation and Workplace Performance: Evidence from Great Britain'. Discussion Paper 232. Centre for Economic Performance, London School of Economics.

Gomez-Mejia, L. and Balkin, D. (1992) *Compensation, Organisational Strategy and Firm Performance*. Cincinnati: South Western.

Guest, D. (1987) 'Human Resource Management and Industrial Relations', *Journal of Management Studies*, 24(5): 503–21.

Herzberg, F. (1966) *Work and the Nature of Man*. Cleveland: World Publishing.

Hunter, L., McGregor, A., Macinnes, J. and Sproull, A. (1993) 'The Flexible Firm: Strategy and segmentation', *British Journal of Industrial Relations*, 31(3): 383–407.

Huselid, M. (1995) 'The Impact of Human Resource Management Practices on Turnover, Productivity and Corporate Financial Performance', *Academy of Management Journal*, 38(3): 635–72.

Incomes Data Services (1994) 'IDS Study 564' (Profit-related pay), London.

Industrial Relations Services (1993) 'Job Evaluation in the 1990s', *IRS Employment Trends*, 546: 4–12.

Jacques, E. (1961) *Equitable Payment*. London: Heineman.

Kanter, R. (1989) *When Giants Learn to Dance*. New York: Simon and Schuster.

Kessler, I. (1995) 'Reward Systems', in J. Storey (ed.), *Human Resource Management: A critical text*. London: Routledge.

Kessler, I. (1998) 'Payment Systems,' in M. Poole and M. Warner (eds), *The Handbook of Human Resource Management*. London: Thomson.

Kessler, I. and Purcell, J. (1992) 'Performance-Related Pay: Objectives and application', *Human Resource Management Journal*, 2(3): 16–33.

Kinnie, N. and Lowe, D. (1990) 'Performance-Related Pay on the Shopfloor', *Personnel Management*, November: 45–9.

Kohn, A. (1993) 'Why Incentive Plans Cannot Work', *Harvard Business Review*, September/October: 54–63.

Lawler, E. (1981) *Pay and Organization Development*. New York: Addison Wesley.

Lawler, E. (1990) *Strategic Pay: Aligning organizational strategies and pay systems*. San Francisco: Jossey-Bass.

Lawler, E. (1995) 'The New Pay: A strategic approach', *Compensation and Benefits Review*, July/August: 14–22.

Lazear, E.P. (1998) *Personnel Economics for Managers*. New York: Wiley.

Legge, K. (1995) *Human Resource Management: Rhetoric and realities*. London: Macmillan.

Lupton, T. and Gowler, D. (1969) *Selecting a Wage Payment System*. London: Kogan Page.

Marchington, M. (1992) *Managing the Team. A guide to successful employee involvement*. Oxford: Blackwell.

Marsden, D. and Richardson, R. (1991) 'Does Performance Pay Motivate? A study of Inland Revenue staff', Inland Revenue Staff Federation, London.

Mowday, R.T. (1996) 'Equity Theory Predictions of Behavior in Organizations', in R. Steers, L. Porter and G. Bigley (eds), *Motivation and Leadership at Work*. Sixth edition, New York: McGraw Hill.

Murlis, H. and Wright, V. (1993) 'Report from the UK', *Benefits and Compensation International*, 22(6): 5–10.

Neil, A. (1996) *Full Disclosure*. London: Macmillan.

Pfeffer, J. (1994) *Competitive Advantage through People*. Boston: Harvard Business School Press.

Pfeffer, J. (1998a) 'Six Dangerous Myths about Pay', *Harvard Business Review*, May/June: 109–19.

Pfeffer, J. (1998b) *The Human Equation*. Boston: Harvard Business School Press.

Poole, M. and Jenkins, G. (1998) 'Human Resource Management and the Theory of Rewards: Evidence from a national survey', *British Journal of Industrial Relations*, 36(2): 227–47.

Porter, M. (1985) *Competitive Advantage: Creating and sustaining superior performance*. New York: Free Press.

Rhoads, S. (1993) *Comparable Worth: Pay equity meets the market*. Cambridge: Cambridge University Press.

Runciman, W.G. (1995) 'Pay as you earn', *Prospect*, November: 44–8.

Smith, I. (1983) *The Management of Remuneration: Paying for effectiveness*. London: IPM.

Smith, I. (1992) 'Reward Management and HRM', in P. Blyton and P. Turnball (eds), *Reassessing Human Resource Management*. London: Sage.

Smith, I. (1993) 'Reward Management: A retrospective assessment', *Employee* Relations, 15(3): 45–59.

Storey, J. (1992) *Developments in the Management of Human Resources*. Oxford: Blackwell.

Tarling, R. and Wilkinson, F. (eds) (1987) *The Level, Structure and Flexibility of Costs*. London: Academic Press.

Thierry, H. (1992) 'Pay and Payment Systems', in J. Hartley and G. Stephenson (eds), *Employment Relations*. Oxford: Blackwell.

Thompson, M. (1993) *Pay for Performance: The employee experience*. Brighton: Institute of Manpower Studies.

Vroom, V.H. (ed.) (1964) *Work and Motivation*. New York: Wiley.

Wallace, M. and Fay, C. (1988) *Compensation Theory and Practice*. Second edition, Boston: PWS-Kent.

Walton, R. (1985) 'From Control to Commitment in the Workplace', *Harvard Business Review*, 63(2): 77–84.

Wood, S. (1995) 'The Four Pillars of HRM: Are they connected?' *Human Resource Management Journal*, 5(5): 49–59.

Wood, S. (1996) 'High Commitment Management and Payment Systems', *Journal of Management Studies*, 33(1): 53–77.

Wood, S. and Albanese, M. (1995) 'Can We Speak of High Commitment Management on the Shop Floor?', *Journal of Management Studies*, 32(2): 215–47.

Wright, C. (1996) 'The State of the Art in the Private Sector', in H. Murlis (ed.), *Pay at the Crossroads*. London: IPD.

2 Reward strategy

Richard Thorpe

INTRODUCTION

There have been major changes in the nature and priorities of organisations over the last decade and it is argued these have to some extent been reflected in the way payment systems have been designed and operated.[1] Walton (1985) offers a broad if somewhat contested view of how increased competition and change have affected organisations – showing the growing importance now being placed on concepts such as teamwork, flexibility and harmonisation. The need to reward groups as opposed to individuals has inevitably led to changes in pay system design, with many features identified a decade ago as likely characteristics of future pay systems (Grayson, 1986) having continued to find their way into common practice (see table 2.1).

Amongst the payment systems that have become more popular are broad-banded ones which ostensibly support cultural change by aligning the contribution and competence of individuals with the requirements of the organisation (Massey, 1996). Various kinds of performance-related pay are also back on the agenda with schemes linked to key organisational priorities.

These schemes are still seen as important ways of improving organisational effectiveness which they see as encouraging performance through increasing the effectiveness of individuals. In Britain about 30 per cent of male employees work under incentive conditions and about 20 per cent of female employees (*New Earnings Survey*, 1997). For individuals, the current trends are in areas such as skill-related progression, and performance appraisal linked to merit pay. For groups, new schemes are being designed that focus on 'team' performance, related to such things as measured day rates or other group outputs. For schemes related to business performance, there has been a big increase more recently in profit-related pay and share option schemes. These types of schemes have been growing at spectacular rates. Purcell (1991) reports that there has been a seven-fold increase in eligibility for such schemes, which now involve two million employees (private sector) or nearly one in eight of the private-sector workforce.

But also, with the re-emergence of economic value added as a way of measuring performance, there is a renewed interest in added-value schemes and other forms of gain sharing. Notwithstanding these innovations, remuneration and reward are still much

Table 2.1 The characteristics of existing and future pay systems

Current payment systems	Future payment systems
Unilaterally designed by management.	Collaboratively designed by management and employee representative.
Limited objectives concerned with recruitment and retention.	Wider objectives linked to business strategy.
Emphasis on levels of output.	Emphasis on levels of overall performance.
Emphasis on incentive payment systems, systems linked to the individual.	Emphasis on the group or company-wide-individual as part of a team.
Emphasis on task and specialisation: individual skills confined to a single type of operation.	Emphasis on competence and flexibility; rewards for multi-skill acquisition.
Emphasis on individual jobs with separate, distinct job identities, details job descriptions.	Emphasis on whole work systems: broad job outlines.
Many grades: multiple in-plant structure.	Few grades: single plant-wide structure.
Heavy emphasis on pay increases linked to annual negotiation.	More emphasis on pay linked to annual company performance, and additional skill acquisition.
Fixed fringe benefit programmes.	Flexible fringe benefits. Cafeteria plans or cash payments in lieu of fringe benefits.
Different conditions of employment for different groups.	Common terms and conditions of employment for all groups.
Multiple occupational job evaluation schemes applied to separate groups.	Single company wide job evaluation schemes.

Source: David Grayson (1986) Work Research Unit Working Paper, Department of Employment.

under-researched and little understood components of organisational and human resource management (HRM) policy. There are, however, still a number of trends that can be discerned from the literature.

KEY TRENDS IN REMUNERATION AND REWARD

Kessler and Purcell (1994) suggest that a whole range of issues related to the selection, design and operation of payment systems is re-emerging after being somewhat in the doldrums. The focus that appears to be of paramount importance is that of strategic context. Singled out are systems that relate pay to individual performance, or, more specifically, where there is an 'attempt to translate and transmit market-based organisational goals into personalised performance objectives or criteria whilst at the same time preserving the integrity of coherent grading structures'.

The rationale for the use of such schemes needs to be viewed in the context of theories of HRM, as well as against the predominant schools of managerial thought, which fundamentally challenge the perspectives of both managers and research academics with regard to issues of pay and performance.

An increasing amount of literature on HRM identifies rising concerns regarding the effects of strategic choice on firm performance, and individuals beginning to be rewarded for the success of the organisation as a whole and their contribution to it (Milkovich and Newman, 1996). However, it has to be said that there is a real sense in which much of this rhetoric lacks detailed empirical research that tests the claims being made (Ehrenberg and Milkovich, 1987).

Research into reward strategy is not new, but it has been rather limited and rarely taken notice of by managers. In a recent paper in the *Harvard Business Review*, (Pfeffer, 1998) laments the fact that managers in the United States are bombarded with advice about pay – unfortunately, he argues, much of it wrong! In Britain (and again this is a point Pfeffer raises), there has been a growing body of evidence that shows how, under various conditions, pay linked to performance does not in fact improve performance at all but often reduces it! Bell (1997), in a review paper, also highlights the very diverse and cross-disciplinary nature of past research in the field of pay, and suggests that there is a continuing and enduring insularity within the perspectives offered in the literature, one that fails to acknowledge the historical context of much of the research in the field, or 'the wider narrative and sweep of events over large tracts of time'. By this Bell means, the changing structure of industry, the very different situation that now exists in work-place relations than in former times, and issues such as the globalisation of industry.

There has also been a dominance of American literature with its universalist perspectives and cultural bias. This alone should serve as a warning to the application of American research ideas with, for example, their strong emphasis on new industrial relations and their absence of an appreciation of Western Europe's forms of capitalism – where there is greater involvement of a much wider number of interest groups and stakeholders. From research conducted in the transforming economies of Central and Eastern Europe, we are able to see the way in which American views of pay and motivation have begun to influence the design of incentive schemes. In some organisations studied (Lupton *et al.*, 1998), the ratio of 'incentive' to basic pay was as high as 3:2. These organisations, it appears, are destined to repeat many of the mistakes made in the UK in earlier years as they embrace schemes in the hope of raising the performance of their employees but instead bringing on themselves a variety of unforeseen problems. Many of the pay system designs owe little to the challenges and insights of writers such as Adler (1986), Hofstede (1983) and Usunier (1998) who have all, from time to time, offered a cultural critique of pay policy.

The point I wish to make here is that managers and researchers need both to recognise and to acknowledge the plurality in payment system design. To 'rediscover' the organisational specific and contingent nature of pay systems, whilst maintaining a healthy regard to the epistemological basis and historical context of research that has been conducted in the past and on which we are, perhaps mistakenly, building our future.

Review of the literature on pay and reward

There are probably many ways to categorise the literature on pay. I have chosen three aspects that appear to be of central importance in the formulation of a remuneration strategy and the design of a remuneration system. The first of these is the motivation system, which includes not only pay but also a whole range of job design characteristics, as well as aspects of the physical and psychological environment. This aspect relates to the organisation's view on how to motivate individuals and groups, and to its management style (autocratic or participative). Second, the organisation's perspective on how best it can control the business, and exercise authority, is important. The third aspect relates to the objectives of the organisation, and the priorities of the business, for its continued success (however that is measured).

Of course, each of these three aspects is subject to detailed examination in subsequent chapters. Motivation, for example, will be examined in more detail in chapter 5 (and authority and control in chapter 6) whilst strategy and design are predominantly dealt with in chapter 7.

MOTIVATION

This aspect of payment scheme design has tended to rely almost exclusively on psychological theories and places great store on rational behaviour. Little (1991) exemplifies this when he comments that motivational views of pay as a reward are all connected by the notion of pay 'as a mechanism which links cause and effect, typically grounded in the meaningful intentional behaviour of individuals'.

So, for example, payment by results is payment for producing results, whereas merit pay is payment for exhibiting the appropriate attitudes and commitment. Profit sharing, on the other hand, is payment for putting the organisation first. From this perspective, managers have believed that they can achieve certain objectives and determine the way people will perform by basing their pay designs on a set of psychological calculations. The expectancy theories of Vroom (1964) and later Porter and Lawler (1968) reflect this approach, albeit in a more sophisticated way, and it forms an implicit part of what has become known as the effort–reward bargain, highlighting as it does the complexities of the link between effort and reward, that is the different kinds of effort organisations might seek on the one hand and the variety of possible rewards on the other. Table 2.2 shows the range of rewards that employers might offer to

Table 2.2

Rewards	*Effort*
Basic pay	Physical effort
Extra pay (Bonus)	Mental effort
Fringe benefits	Flexibility, willingness to work extra hours
Time off	Good attendance
Autonomy	Co-operation with change
Interesting/satisfying work	Commitment
Power and influence	Initiative
Relationship with colleagues	Co-operation with others
Sense of achievement	Enthusiasm
Self-evaluation	

employees in exchange for a range of different kinds of effort. Some years ago, great effort went into measuring the physical and mental effort expended in different kinds of work for which individuals were rewarded by a seemingly scientifically derived salary or salary plus bonus. More recently, with the changing nature of work, aspects of work such as commitment and flexibility have become much more important, and, similarly, employers are recognising that a greater variety of rewards is both sought and possible.

Which of the rewards are seen by individuals as appropriate depends, of course, on which motivation theory or theories are seen as most relevant. In a review paper Guest (1984) has categorised the current motivation theories into needs, goals and orientations, expectancy theory, goal theory and reactance theory. These are all developed further in respect of how they relate to pay design in chapter 5. However, as we shall see later, pay cannot substitute for a working environment high on trust, fun and meaningful work (Pfeffer, 1998) and there is a basic flaw in a manager's assertion view that money is an important motivator.

AUTHORITY AND CONTROL

This aspect of payment scheme design suggests that a major concern of the management of a company ought to be to focus on those management practices that will have the most positive effect on employee behaviour in any particular context. Once these have been identified and fully understood, they should be measured, rewarded and controlled. Pay is only one of the mechanisms that can be used for the purpose of control, but for many organisations it is an appealing one. However, a major dilemma, as the literature has shown over the years, is that the people who are actually in control are not, in fact, always those whom managers believe to be.

Managers seek to use pay for a whole range of control purposes in a business. Pay is used through job evaluation schemes to signal the relative worth of jobs and to introduce a 'felt fair' system into the wages and salary policy. The remuneration system is also used to retain good employees or at least to prevent them from leaving. This is an attraction also of incremental salary scales that encourage loyalty and an interest in promotion. Pay is also used to reward merit more generally and in the case of blue-collar workers, to compensate them for adverse working conditions. These to a greater or lesser degree are 'control' features of any wage and salary system, but many managers also feel it necessary to use pay to motivate employees to achieve higher levels of performance. This additional use of the remuneration system can often serve to distort (and eventually even destroy) its originally carefully worked out principles, leading to disputes and disagreements that undermine the initially inherent logic and equity. Systems frequently highlight the extrinsic features associated with motivation and satisfaction whilst unintentionally devaluing the intrinsic ones (Frey and Osterloh, 1998).

It is not just organisations that try to use pay as a mechanism of control. Governments too have attempted to use pay to control wages at a national level. Over the last three decades, we have experienced various types of income policy all used in an attempt to control inflation. In the 1970s income policies were used in an attempt to control both public- and private-sector pay. In the 1980s and 1990s, however, the controls have become less formal and have operated largely in the public sector, aiming to hold down images through limiting public-sector borrowing, requiring strict adherence to 'cash limits', and the imposing of greater central control on local authority and health service budgets.

However, organisations are often keenest to control costs (particularly of labour), in the belief that, if they can control costs, then they will be able to both control and predict prices, and thus improve competitiveness. One of the problems is that, as firms fix on a measure, it becomes prone to manipulation. In the late 1970s, I conducted a participant observation study in an engineering company. This study revealed from the company's own data that some jobs were taking up to three times longer to complete than they needed to. Here it wasn't the performance measures the workers were complaining about and manipulating, but their pay! And they manipulated their pay by manipulating the measures, whether they were based on profit, standard hours or quality.

There is a view (Bowey and Thorpe, 1986) that the use of pay for all these different purposes is often self-defeating. To achieve any one of the objectives, an employer needs to pay those individuals to whom that particular objective applies more money in relation to other employees. Having multiple objectives cancels out the impact of one differential by superimposing another which may 'pull' the employee in a different direction.

Notwithstanding this, vast sums of money have been spent by British managers in designing, implementing and modifying schemes for some or all of these purposes. The approach is not confined to non-management staff and has been used extensively in recent years to motivate and reward managers through such means as share option or bonus schemes.

The advantage to managers of using the pay system as a method of control is that it appears to place a large amount of responsibility for organisational success on the shoulders of the workforce in the mistaken belief that, if only employees can be controlled to perform in a particular manner and direction, performance will be assured.

The inherent flaw in this perspective is that employees can also, it seems, exert quite powerful influences on the system. It appears that managers remain unaware of, or choose to ignore, the importance of human agency. Indeed, the historically large, and ever-growing literature (Roy, 1952; Dalton, 1948; Ditton, 1979) illustrates that individuals are not the passive agents of production that managers think they are, but are instead quite active in striving to make sense of their environment, in which they are able to reduce uncertainty by controlling various factors, particularly those that influence rewards. Figure 2.1(a) offers an illustration of the rather naive view that many managers have of the way that a pay system might operate as a motivator of staff. They assume, for example, that when a bonus is available, employees will work hard to earn it, which will increase their pay and have positive effects on the performance of the organisation. Figure 2.1(b) attempts to map a similar logic, but this time from the perspective of the employee. It illustrates the complexity of the choices and decisions that may lead to the production of a high bonus for the individuals but not necessarily to high output for the organisation. In pay systems linked to appraisal, which increased in the 1980s, the same types of manipulation can be observed. In this case, however, individuals also ingratiated themselves with their superiors in order to

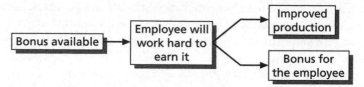

Fig. 2.1a Over-simplified view of incentives schemes

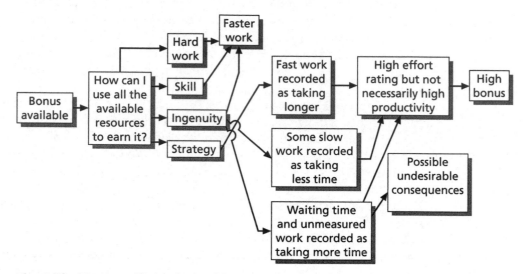

Fig. 2.1b More realistic view of incentives schemes

manipulate the latter's opinion of them in order to obtain the rewards as well as meet the targets set. This is the way in which wage drift takes place, a practice that seems set to continue as new generations of managers make the same old mistakes.

There is a tension and duality at work here. Giddens (1984) suggests, that, although the notion of individual agency implies that employees are sometimes able to use skill to influence the activity and purpose of pay system management, they are, at the same time, constrained by the particular rules of the pay structures and bonus schemes under which they work. Reconciling the tension between 'structure' and 'agency' is a need that managers have both to understand and to resolve.

Of course employees also react against control. It has been suggested that when an individual's freedom and personal control comes under threat, then the potential exists for that person to reassert their control over a situation, in other words to react. If individuals are increasingly expected to control their own work, through organisations adopting strategies such as empowerment, then perhaps we should not be so surprised if they devalue those objectives that are imposed on them by managers. Of interest and importance here is the growing body of research on the way individuals seek to draw meaning from events. These meanings are often socially constructed and serve to provide for individuals a rationale from what they experience and observe. By imposing their own frame of reference over events and so winning back control, individuals can produce a kind of certainty for themselves. This may go some way to explaining why, for example, pay systems are often so very difficult to change.

Another issue which relates to control is that of equity. As Elliot Jacques (1961) once remarked, 'There is no problem with pay that does not have at its root, problems of differentials.' Equity theory research has a contribution to make in this respect and is an important aspect of any serious study of pay. It has, for example, indicated how, and under what circumstances, employees will strive for fairness, and how they will adjust their output or performance to relate to that of colleagues. It appears that some individuals or groups will go to incredible lengths to ensure that they are treated equally – be it in of the distribution of work or in the perceived acceptability of their salaries. Thorpe (1979) and Lawler (1971) showed how employees might consider their satisfaction with a particular level of pay. This idea of satisfaction with pay is the basis of the practice of salary surveys, an area to which we devote the whole of chapter 11. Bell (1997) picks up on a suggestion by Adams (1965) that it may well have been inequitable personal or social situations that lay behind complaints from employees which occurred during the 'Bank Wiring Room Experiments' which made up part of the longitudinal Hawthorne Reseach Studies (Roethlisberger and Dickson, 1939).

BUSINESS OBJECTIVES

This third aspect of pay, and one which links pay to the strategic dimension, arises out of a recognition that developments in the design of pay systems have often had little bearing on the real priorities of, and problems faced by, the organisation. As a consequence, pay systems have frequently been changed as a reaction to isolated and possibly unrelated problems, or used to tackle organisational difficulties which they could never really have much hope of solving. In order to make payment systems relate more closely to the priorities of an organisation, contingency theorists sought to devise pay systems which better linked business strategy with company culture. Viewed in this way, as systems components, pay systems can be seen not only as a means of paying individuals or groups more money, but also as part of a policy instrument, that works to influence organisational change by carrying appropriate messages that reflect and influence behaviour in particular ways.

Contingency theory is now a well-established approach within management decision making, although there is still a great deal of confusion about what exactly it means. There are two conceptually very different theoretical approaches – both labelled 'contingency theory'. Legge (1978) makes a distinction between *structured* or *positive*, and *normative*, contingency theory. Structured or positive contingency theory assumes that the structural characteristics of an organisation are determined by the state of various contingent factors in its environment, such as its technology, its market or its economic environment, and that there is a direct relationship between a number of contingent factors and the characteristics of the organisation. This view of contingency has been strongly criticised (Shreyogg, 1980) on two grounds – first, that there is often a whole range of factors that intervene, for example, the strategic choices made by managers about matters such as organisation structure and the procedures or styles of working that they adopt, and, second, that, as we now know, organisations are able to survive often under a very similar set of contingent constraints. This structured view of contingency theory was based on the empirical findings of the early contingency theorists such as Woodward (1959) and Burns and Stalker (1961), and was consistent with the prevailing developments at the time in disciplines such as sociology.

The second approach to contingency theory Legge terms 'normative contingency theory'. This view suggests that there are 'best-fit' choices available to managers in designing pay policies. But that is not all, the contingency theories of researchers such as Lupton and Gowler (1969a), and Lupton and Bowey (1974) also indicate the dimensions of the variables that ought to *determine* the payment system choice. In this approach, the dependent variable is seen as the effects or outcomes of the structural and procedural arrangements, which in turn is dependent on strategic choices. Management decisions about structure and procedures are viewed as the intervening variables between the contingent constraints within which the organisation operates and the effects these have on organisational performance. The contingent factors over which managers have little or no control may influence their strategic choices, but they do not determine them. This means that there can be all kinds of different dimensions of performance influenced by a payment system choice, and that organisations can survive with a wide range of performance levels on each of these dimensions. It is therefore not the payment system that is contingent on the constraints, but the eventual performance of the organisation. The reason why this model is termed *'normative'* is that it implies that managers *should* act and take decisions about payment systems in order to achieve the maximum impact on the performance of their organisation.

Research work conducted at the Manchester Business School in the 1960s and 1970s produced diagnostic tools to determine the situations suited to the introduction of particular kinds of scheme. These analytical and diagnostic tools were designed to be of practical use to managers, enabling them to use profiling methods to choose the most suitable pay design for a particular pattern of contingent characteristics. Lupton and Gowler (1969) produced some 21 variables thought to be significant. These were later extended to 29 (Lupton and Bowey, 1974), a selection of these variables are shown below.

- Type of effort
- Unit of accountability
- Length of job cycle
- Number of job modifications
- Degree of automation
- Number of product changes
- Number of job stoppages
- Duration of job stoppages
- Per cent job elements specified by management
- Per cent material scrapped
- Per cent products/components rejected
- Time required to fill vacancy
- Labour stability
- Labour turnover
- Disputes about pay

- Man hours lost in pay disputes
- Per cent earnings decided outside plant/company
- Number of trade unions
- Occupational structure
- Absence (per cent normal hours)
- Average age of working force
- Per cent labour cost in unit cost
- Per cent males in working force

Missing from their research, however, was the importance of the process, particularly the handling of implementation.

This approach to pay scheme design certainly did overcome the notion that there could be one type of payment system suitable for all situations and industries, moving the study of pay into the exploration of issues such as the 'relationship between individual motivation and the social system'.

Research in which I was involved at the Pay and Reward Research Centre at Strathclyde University (Bowey and Thorpe, 1986) began by building on the insights developed by the Manchester researchers into the structural and behavioural patterns associated with the success or otherwise of different kinds of payment systems in different organisational circumstances. This research (reported in more detail in chapter 7) began by attempting to find relationships between schemes which varied in their effectiveness. In other words, were managers introducing the kinds of schemes the contingency theorists said they should be doing? Our results were ambiguous and we found it extremely difficult, despite some elaborate measuring indices, to say categorically that one type of scheme was poor whilst another was successful. This was because we found very similar types of systems producing good results in some organisations and poor results in others. Our results, did, however, indicate that some factors influenced success – tightly specified work, variable bonuses and group incentives, to name a few. But by far the most significant finding, however was the importance of a composite variable we labelled *consultation*. With this variable, we were able to correlate and discriminate between systems in terms of their relative success – the greater the degree of consultation, the better the performance and the greater the positive effects on the organisation. Our conclusions were summed up by Lawler and Bullock (1978) in the United States when, following their own research, they commented that 'most approaches to changing payment systems are top-down; they assume that people above will make all the decisions. What about letting the people who will be affected by the plan be a fundamental part of the decision?'

Such a process offers three distinct benefits: management and employees would learn more about exactly what the priorities for the organisation were; they would learn how best these could be measured and the pay system used to support them; and, providing there was a sufficiently large coalition of organisational members involved in the process, there would be a critical mass of individuals committed to change and to the success of whatever was decided. So, just as it had been more in-depth research strategies that had uncovered the importance of consultation, our conclusions were that a more, qualitative 'process-led' approach to pay scheme design is more flexible and productive in terms of information gathering. It is recognised, however, that such a process demands considerable time and effort. Achieving a match between the payment system and the expectations, motivations, patterns of interrelationships, past history and understandings of people in the system, through a process of discussion, negotiation and debate, appears to be far more important than simply matching the payment system to non-social characteristics of the organisation.

This kind of 'action research' approach to data collection and change has been used in change programmes many times but is now also being used in the re-design of performance measurement systems. de Hass (1998) sees such approaches to strategy and design as 'learning rather than planning' – part of an iterative process that places emphasis neither on the system itself nor on matching a payment system to organisational circumstances, but recognises that a good management team can achieve success with many different types of system.

This kind of action research recognises that learning and change amongst organisational members are social processes, in which the experiences of the organisational world are developed and shaped through contact with others. As a consequence, if behavioural change is to be one of the outcomes, solutions need to be found by listening to the views of others. In the context of pay management, an important task for managers will be the recreation of order and clarity in such situations, and, through the resulting debates and a process of fact finding, the establishment of a more determined account of what would otherwise be contested issues in the organisation. The participatory process serves to drive the organisation forward in the direction in which its performance can be maximised.

CONCLUSION

At the beginning of this chapter, I highlighted that the common threads within payment systems practice are beliefs about motivation, aspects of authority and control and organisational objectives. Missing from current research into pay are insights gained in the past into the social context of organisations, particularly the significance of the informal organisation and the extent to which conflict manipulation is still a feature of organisations, and is unlikely to go away. Whilst the diagnostic/prescriptive approach to pay systems development has moved the field forward considerably, more recent literature has focused on payment systems designs that link reward strategy to the achievement of the organisation's strategic objectives. As Gomez-Meija and Balkin (1992) remark, this approach attempts to align organisational strategies with the human resource strategy. With such an approach, planning, strategy and implementation are seen as of seminal importance.

The conclusion of this chapter makes a plea to see the process of strategy determination and pay system design not as sequential and linear but as an iterative learning process carried out with the wide involvement of key employees. One approach to diagnosis that, it is suggested, might lend itself to this kind of method is that of action research. This approach begins with the view that research should lead to change which therefore should be incorporated into the research process itself. It stresses the importance of establishing collaboration between the researchers and the researched, leading to the development of shared understandings. As a consequence of the collaborative features of action research, those involved are likely to learn a lot from the process itself. Their interest may be not simply in what should happen next in the process, as much as in the formal identification of issues relating to management of the pay system.

Remuneration system management perhaps needs to be a discursive, sense-making activity that acknowledges the contingent nature of design, and that fits closely within the broad framework of Learning Organisations, where strategy, learning and change are inextricably linked through a process of negotiation, argumentation and debate, and where language has a central role.

NOTE

1 However, Wood (1996) has shown in a study of British manufacturing between 1986 and 1990 that, although one might think the trends towards new commitment-oriented personnel management ought to lead, as Purcell, (1991) and Storey, (1992) suggest, to an increase in performance-related pay no such relationship could in fact be detected.

LEARNING ACTIVITIES

1 Identify the major changes that your organisation has undergone in the last ten years, classified in terms of its structure, the processes it adopts, its culture and its markets. Analyse the extent to which the reward systems have kept pace with these changes.

2 One of the major changes outlined in this chapter has been the change in focus from the group to the individual. To what extent is this true of your organisation, how appropriate is it and how is it reflected in changes in reward systems?

3 Outline what the broad objectives might be in the design of a reward strategy and justify these choices.

4 To what extent is the integration of reward strategy, human resource strategy and corporate strategy essential to effectiveness?

REFERENCES

Adams, J.S. (1965) 'Inequity in Social Exchange', *Advances in Experimental Social Psychology*, 2: 267–99.

Adler, N.J. (1986) *International Dimensions of Organisational Behaviour*. Boston MA: Kent Publishing Company.

Alderfer, C.P. (1972) *Existence, Relatedness and Growth*. London: Collier Macmillan.

Armstrong, M. and Murlis, H. (1994) *'Reward Management': A handbook of Remuneration strategy and practice*. London: Kogan Page.

Balkin, D.B. and Gomez-Meija, L.R. (1990) 'Matching Compensation and Organisational Strategies', *Strategic Management Journal*, 11: 153–69.

Bell, E. (1997) 'Implications for Control within Strategic Compensation Management: Relating payment to performance, a study within the chemical industry', Manchester Metropolitan University.

Bowey, A.M. and Thorpe, R. with Hellier, P. (1986) *Payment Systems and Productivity*. London: Macmillan.

Burns, T. and Stalker, G.M. (1961) *The Management of Innovation*. London: Tavistock.

Dalton, M. (1948) 'The Industrial Rate Buster: A characterisation', in T. Lupton (ed.), *Payment Systems*. London: Penguin.

de Haas, (1998) 'Business Unit Performance Measurement in the Context of Strategic Change: A design approach', Peformance Measurement: Theory and practice. Univeristy of Cambridge, July.

Ditton, J. (1979) 'Baking Time', *The Sociological Review*, 27: 1.

Ehrenberg, R.G. and Milkovich, G.T. (1987) 'Compensation and Firm Performance', in M.M. Kleiner *et al.* (eds), *Human Resources and the Performance of the Firm*. Madison: Industrial Relations Research Association.

Elliott, J. (1961) *Equitable Payment*. London: Heinemann.

Frey, B. and Osterloh, M. (1998), 'Does Pay for Performance Really Motivate Employees?', in A. Neely and D. Waggoner, *Performance Measurement Theory and Practice*. Centre for Business Performance, Cambridge.

Giddens, A. (1984) *The Constitution of Society: Outline of a theory of structuration*. Cambridge: Policy Press.

Gomez-Meija, L.R. and Balkin, D.B. (1992) *Compensation, Organisational Strategy and Firm Performance*. Cincinnati, Ohio: South Western Publishing.

Goodridge, M. (1986) 'Practical Payment Systems', *Employment Relations*, Cambridge.

Gowler, D. and Legg, K. (1983) 'The Meaning of Management and the Management of Meaning: A view from social anthropology', in M.J. Earl (ed.), *Perspectives on Management: A multidisciplinary analysis*. Oxford: Oxford University Press.

Grayson, D. (1986) 'The Integrated Payment System in Practice', Work Research Unit, Occasional Paper 35, July.

Guest, D. (1984) 'What's New in Motivation', *Human Resource Management and Industrial Relations, Personnel Management*, May: 20–3.

Hertzberg, H.F. (1974) *Work and the Nature of Man*. Granada Publishing.

Hofstede, G. (1984) *Cultures Consequences: International differences in work related values*. Abridged edition, Beverly Hills, CA: Sage Publications.

Hofstede, G. (1991) *Cultures and Organisations: Software of the mind*. Maidenhead: McGraw Hill.

IRS Survey (1995) 'Pay and Benefits Survey', Bulletin 360.

Jacques, E. (1961) *Equitable Pay: A general theory of work, differential payment and individual progress*. Second edition, London: Heinemann Educational.

Kessler, I. (1994) 'Performance Related Pay: Contrasting Approaches', *Industrial Relations Journal*, 25: 122–35.

Kessler, J. and Purcell, J. (1994) 'Performance Related Pay: Objectives and application', *Human Resource Management Journal*, 2: 3.

Kunda, G. (1992) *Engineering Culture: Control and commitment in a high-tech corporation*. Philadelphia: Temple University Press.

Lawler, E.E. and Bullock, R.J. (1978) 'Pay and Organisational Change', *The Personnel Administrator*, May.

Lawler, E.E. (1971) *'Pay and Organisational Effectiveness': A psychological view*. New York.

Legge, K. (1978) *Power, Innovation and Problem Solving in Personnel Management*, London: McGraw Hill.

Little, D. (1991) *Varieties of Social Explanation: An introduction to the philosophy of social science*, Oxford: Westview Press.

Locke, E.A. (1975) 'Personal Attitudes and Motivation', *Annual Review of Psychology*, 26: 457–80.

Lupton, T. and Bowey, A.M. (1974) *Wages and Salaries*. London: Penguin.

Lupton, T. and Gowler, D. (1969) *Contingency Approaches to Setting Wage Payment Systems*.

Lupton, T. and Gowler, D. (1969a) *Selecting a Wage Payment System*. London: Engineering Employers Federation Sage.

Lupton, T. and Gowler, D. (1972) 'Wage Payment Systems: A review of current thinking', *Personnel Management*, 4(11): 25–8.

Lupton, T. and Tanner, I. (1987) *Achieving Change: A systematic approach*. Aldershot: Gower.

Lupton, T. (1963) *On the Shop Floor*. London: Pergamon Press.

Lupton, T. (ed.) (1972) 'Payment Systems', Research Paper, No. 111, London: Engineering Employers Federation, London: Penguin.

Lupton, T. (1975), ' "Best Fit" in the Design of Organisations', *Personnel Review*, 4: 15–31.

Lupton, T., Kauscek, G. Hrabitova, E. and Thorpe, R. (1998). 'Aspects of Transition to the Market Economy in the Czech Republic and Hungary', in F. McDonald and R. Thorpe (eds), *Organisational Strategy and Technological Adaptation to Global Change*.

Maslow, A.H. (1954) *Motivation and Personality*. New York: Harper & Row.

Massey, C. (1996) 'Broad-Banded Pay System', *Topics Issue*, 1: 5–11.

Milkovich, G.T. and Newman, J.M. (1996) *Compensation*. Fifth edition, Chicago: Irwin.

McClelland, D.C. and Burnham, D.H. (1962) 'Power is the Great Motivation', *Harvard Business Review*, 54: 100–10.

New Earnings Survey (1997) Part D. Analysis by Occupation. Office for National Statistics.

Pfeffer, J. (1998) 'Six Dangerous Myths and Pay', *Harvard Business Review*, May–June: 109–19.

Porter, L.W. and Lawler, E.E. (1968) *Managerial Attitudes and Work Performance*. Homewood, Illinois: Irwin.

Purcell, J. (1991) 'The Rediscovery of the Management Prerogative: The management of labour relations in the 1980s', *Oxford Review of Economic Policy*, 9: 33–43; Profit Related Pay (1995).

Roethlisberger, F.J. and Dickson, W.J. (1939) *Management and the Worker*. Cambridge, MA: Harvard University Press.

Roy, D. (1952) 'Quota Restriction and Goldbricking in a Machine Shop', *American Journal of Sociology*, 67: 427–42.

Roy, D. (1954) 'Efficiency and "The Fix": Informal Intergroup Relations in a Piecework Machine Shop', *American Journal of Sociology*, 60: 255–66.

Shotter, J. (1993) *Conversational Realities: Constructing life through language*. London: Sage.

Shreyogg, G. (1980) 'Contingency and Choice in Organisation Theory', *Organisation Studies*, 1: 305–26.

Storey, J. (1992) *Developments in the Management of Human Resources*, Oxford: Blackwell.

Thorpe, R. (1980) 'The Relationship between Payment Systems, Productivity and the Organisation of Work'. Strathclyde University Business School, M.Sc. Thesis.

Usunier, J.C. (1998) *International Cross-Culture Management Research*. London: Sage.

Vroom, V. and Yetton, P. (1973) *Leadership and Decision Making*. University of Pittsburgh Press.

Vroom, V.H. (1964) *Work and Motivation*. New York: John Wiley.

Walton, R. (1985) 'From Control to Commitment in the Workplace', *Harvard Business Review*, 63(2): 77–84.

Whyte, W.F. (1952) 'Economic Incentives and Human Relations', in T. Lupton, *Payment Systems*. London: Penguin.

Wood, S. (1996) 'High Commitment Management and Payments Systems', *Journal of Management Studies*, 33: 53–77.

Woodward, J. (1959) *Management and Technology*. London: HMSO.

Woodward, J. (1965) Industrial Organisation, Oxford University Press.

FURTHER READING

Gomez-Meija, L.R. and Balkin, D.B. (1992) *Compensation, Organisational Strategy and Firm Performance*, Cincinnati, Ohio: South Western Publishing.

Pfeffer, J. (1991) 'Six Dangerous Myths about Pay', *Harvard Business Review*, May–June: 109–19.

Usunier, J.C. (1998) *International Cross Cultural Management Research*, London: Sage.

Wood, S. (1996) 'High Commitment Management and Payment Systems', *Journal of Management Studies*, 33: 53–7.

3 Labour economics, competition and compensation

Phil Beaumont and Laurie Hunter

INTRODUCTION

The aim of this chapter is to review the contribution of economics to the understanding of the remuneration of labour. In much of their work, economists are primarily talking to other economists in a common, technical language which makes it less than easy for non-economists to carry the findings of economics across to their own areas of interest. A key task of the present chapter is to convey an understanding of the economic analysis of remuneration in such a way that it will be helpful to personnel practitioners in resolving the many challenges posed for them by the design and consequences of different approaches to employee compensation.

We begin with a statement of the standard core of the economic theory of pay, based on the neoclassical paradigm which has been much criticised but remains the starting point for most economists. We consider the main lines of criticism and defence: the debate has led to some important amendments and extensions of the theoretical core, but has not replaced it with a new superior theory. Earlier criticisms from institutional economists were perhaps relatively easily shaken off by the defenders of the orthodox theory, but the critique has persisted and more important theoretical objections have been developed and supported by powerful empirical evidence. We go on to discuss four of the most significant developments, relating to efficiency wages, bargaining models, internal labour markets and agency theory which are particularly relevant to the aims of this chapter. In conclusion we focus on two important areas of current concern, executive compensation and profit-sharing schemes, which arguably provide some insights into economic approaches which are capable of making more positive contributions to the problems faced by the practitioner.

Our aim in this chapter is not to try to resolve the differences among the various approaches, but rather to point to ways in which economic analysis may be helpful to practitioners in addressing their own problems. The more a firm or a business sector approaches the conditions of full and effective competition, the more likely it is that the competitive theory will provide useful pointers. But where competition, whether in the product market or in the labour market, is restricted, the greater the departure from competitive theory that is required to explain empirical observations or to analyse the consequences of alternative strategies for remuneration.

THE 'STANDARD' COMPETITIVE APPROACH

For the economist, wage rates are the price of labour services which act as signals to allocate labour resources efficiently among competing alternative employments. As soon as we acknowledge differences in the skills and other attributes of labour we are faced with the need to explain, not just a wage *level* and its movements but also a wages *structure*. Conventional market principles suggest that wages will be determined by the interaction of demand and supply. The demand for labour is derived from the demand for the goods and services that labour will produce, while the supply of labour depends on the willingness of individuals to provide labour to the market at different offer levels of (real) wages. In other words, wages are a form of compensation that will draw labour into the market and persuade individuals to give up leisure which they value positively. If the wage is too low, the potential worker will not achieve his or her reservation wage (the wage required to compensate for the loss of leisure) and no labour will be forthcoming. If the wage is too high, more workers will be attracted into the market than are required by employers and there will be unemployment. In a freely operating market, price changes act as a signal of shortage and surplus by floating up or down to correct imbalances and restore equilibrium.

This standard market approach is encapsulated in neoclassical wage theory in which the demand for labour is dependent on the marginal productivity of the employee (or the unit of labour resource): profit-maximizing employers will hire labour up to the point at which the value of the increment of output to the employer is just equal to the addition to labour costs. With the assumption of homogeneous labour such that one unit of labour is readily substituted for another, and with perfect information flowing freely in the market place, full employment should be a natural condition to which the economic system will tend due to competition among employers (for workers) and competition among workers (for jobs). Under competitive conditions, the law of one price will hold: that is, wages for equivalent workers will not vary among employers. Differences in wages will reflect only short-term friction in the matching process of the market, differences in the risk or unpleasantness attaching to different kinds of work or perhaps the differing tastes of individuals for different kinds of work – reflecting vocational preferences. Subject to these conditions, wages will gravitate to a level at which the net advantages (both pecuniary and non-pecuniary) of different employments are equalised: persistent differences over time are viewed as *compensating differentials*.

The problem is that the real labour market does not fulfil these conditions. The empirical evidence reveals long-term departures from full employment, a tendency for wages to be relatively inflexible downwards, and differentials in pay which are difficult to explain in terms of the standard competitive theory. Economists have responded to this problem in various ways. Strict neoclassical theorists have introduced a number of amendments to get round the difficulties, while others have sought alternative theories. Virtually all these approaches are characterised by the pursuit of an *economically rational explanation* for the apparent discrepancies. Richard Thaler (1989: 181) observes:

Economics can be distinguished from other social sciences by the belief that most (all?) behavior can be explained by assuming that agents have stable, well-defined preferences and make rational choices consistent with those preferences in markets that (eventually) clear.

Within this framework, wages serve to allocate labour across job vacancies and the outcome in terms of the wage structure and the distribution of income is typically assessed in efficiency terms. This is quite different in purpose from the social interpretation of wages as providing a legitimate basis for social stratification and social cohesion, and different again from the management approach to remuneration as a tool capable of motivating and raising the performance of workers. Economics has its own agenda.

But this rationalist economic approach is now coming under question as a result of recent trends in the labour market, particularly the observation of growing inequality in pay and economic opportunity, and in the implications of enhanced 'flexibility' deriving from the deregulation of the labour market. As Rubery (1997: 338) puts it:

> The predominant theories, from the neo-classical to the radical, have overstressed coherence and functionality and underplayed both the persistence of conflict and contradictions and the scope for discretionary, random or opportunistic decisions . . . wage determination decisions have been held partially in check in the past by a series of institutional and social processes which served to link wage determination across sectors and organizations and labour force groups. Many of these processes . . . have disintegrated in the 1980s and 1990s.

If this is a valid critique, it implies that a fully satisfactory theory of the behaviour of wages needs to break out of the straitjacket of rationality and accept that much of the 'noise' in the system, which continues to cause problems for the social scientist, is due to forms of behaviour which are not consistently rational and orderly. If, at the same time, some institutional and social forces operating on the wage mechanism are weakening, the scale of the 'noise' problem may be increasing and the search for a new approach may be more pressing. In the meantime we will focus on the attempts of the economist to bring the theory based on rational principles of allocative efficiency into line with increasingly rich empirical evidence on wage behaviour and structures and seek to assess its value for the manager.

CRITICS, DEFENCE AND DEVELOPMENT

The neoclassical theory based on the marginal productivity theory of demand has long had its critics. For example, Lester (1946) argued that the theory was unrealistic as employers cannot and do not think in terms of marginal revenue calculations. The orthodox response was that this was not necessary, as long as the economic agents behaved *as if* they were profit maximising. If theory based on specific assumptions provided good predictions, it was doing its job even if the assumptions proved to be poor descriptors of reality. The defenders of the orthodox theory (e.g. Rees, 1973: 58) also pointed to the fact that the critics had failed to come up with a convincing alternative and there was no justification for discarding the conventional approach – though a number of developments were introduced in order to cope more satisfactorily with the awkward facts thrown up by new empirical research. A pragmatic defence acceptable to many might run as follows (Reynolds, Masters and Moser, 1986: 135):

Although the economic environment of firms is more uncertain and more complex than the simple marginal productivity theory suggests, the theory is still highly useful. Firms may not be able to maximize profits with a precision in determining their optimal employment levels. The attention of a firm's top executives is a scarce resource, so small differences in wage rates do not always influence important decisions. Nevertheless, large differences in wage rates cannot be ignored without jeopardizing the firm's survival. In this sense, the survival principle appears valid, even in a complex, uncertain and changing economy. Therefore, the conclusions of the marginal productivity theory have wide applicability, even if the reasoning that leads to them may appear oversimplified. Of particular importance, the demand for labour does have a negative slope.

Criticisms of competitive labour market theory continued to grow, particularly in the United States, with the lead in this regard being taken by the 'institutional' labour economists of the 1940s and 1950s. It was contended that competitive theory was useful only for three basic purposes (Pierson, 1957: 18–19):

1 providing a theoretical benchmark for studying the operation of labour markets;
2 as a guide to predicting very general or long-run tendencies in wage relationships;
3 as a reminder that competitive forces place distinct limits or bounds on the administrative discretion of managers, union leaders and government officials.

This judgement was underpinned by a series of 'real-world' surveys and case studies which variously documented (i) the imperfect information and mobility of employees in searching for jobs; (ii) the existence of wage differentials that were inconsistent with the predictions of competitive theory; and (iii) the impact of institutional arrangements, such as collective bargaining, on wage levels. However, the institutionalists made only limited progress in developing an alternative framework of analysis, although some of their work was important in initiating the notion of *internal labour markets*.[1] From the 1960s their work experienced a strong 'counter attack' from advocates of competitive theory, based primarily at the University of Chicago. It is to this group which we now turn.

RATIONAL BEHAVIOUR AND HUMAN CAPITAL

The institutional critics had argued that imperfections in the labour market were widespread, and that the assumptions of competitive theory did not reflect this reality. The advocates of competitive theory responded to this charge in two main ways. First (as noted earlier), they argued that the real test of a theory is not the realism of its assumptions, but rather its predictive value and power. Second, and more importantly, they sought to account for these imperfections in terms of rational behaviour. That is, they sought to *re-define* competitive theory by arguing that (Kaufman, 1994: 175–6):

alleged deviations from reality were themselves the product of rational, economizing behaviour by economic agents. The long-run effect of this argument has been to shift the entire focus of the debate from a test of the predictions of competitive theory *per se* to that of a theory of rational behaviour where rational behaviour means action consistent with maximization of self interest in response to a set of known (or estimated) benefits and costs.

In the extreme case this means that anything done by an economic agent is assumed to be rational and maximising – which may be all very well for explaining events *ex-post* but not very helpful in predicting behaviour.

A second development of much greater significance in the development of the neoclassical thinking also emerged in the 1960s, the introduction of a supply-side approach to the wage problem, embodied in *human capital theory*. Previously the supply of labour had been a necessary but rather neutral ingredient in the neoclassical theory, the main operative factor being demand acting through the marginal productivity principle. The new human capital approach emerged from the finding of T.W. Schultz that the prevalent economic models failed fully to account for US growth. The standard production theory of the day assumed that all units of capital and of labour were identical, but it was increasingly recognised that input quality, especially for labour, could have marked effects on productivity, affecting growth over time or across countries. Unmeasured human capital thus emerged as a factor able to contribute to the explanation of varying growth rates, and the study of investment in human capital began to open up a new vista for the understanding of wages.

Earnings were now seen as a reflection of the human capital embodied in individuals, who invest in education and training so as to maximise the discounted value of lifetime earnings. This investment raised productivity and hence the attractiveness of the worker to the employer who would pay higher wages to acquire it. The basic model is subject to a daunting set of simplifying assumptions. Over time, however, developments and extensions have emerged to provide a much more rounded theory capable of handling problems such as the differences between types of human capital investment, the effects of intermittent labour market participation and variations in attitudes to risk. Applications of the theory have shed light on the existence of the gender and ethnic minority wage gaps, job search behaviour and migration or mobility patterns. (For an excellent account of this development and extension of the basic theory see Polacheck and Siebert, 1993). Yet despite the undoubted strength of human capital theory in providing insights into much labour market and wage structure behaviour, some doubts remain. It is essentially a supply-side theory and it is not clear where the existing wage structure, on which investment decisions are supposed to be made, actually derives from. As Polacheck and Siebert (1993: 272) puts it:

> how the human capital rental rate (w) is determined is completely neglected in human capital literature.

Thus although human capital theory offers a unified explanation of much that we observe in the real world of wages and labour markets, there remain serious concerns that this is not the whole story.

DEPARTURES FROM THE COMPETITIVE MODEL

Many contemporary labour economists still share the basic values and beliefs of the earlier institutional critics of competitive theory. They reject the basic view that labour markets operate along essentially similar lines to commodity markets. What is exchanged in the labour market is inherently embodied in people. As a consequence they argue that, first, one needs to develop a much broader and more complex theory

Exhibit 3.1

Pay and the notion of fairness: two views

1 There is, of course, an established body of economic thought on the determination of rates of pay, which may be found in any contemporary textbook. But orthodox theory, though by no means so otiose as is sometimes suggested, is to my mind deficient in certain major respects. In particular, it fails to take account of the influence of ideas of fairness, especially in the minds of employees. The pattern of pay relativities is powerfully influenced also by normative forces. Of particular importance are pressures to eliminate or reduce various kinds of inequality of pay, pressures by certain comparatively highly paid groups to maintain their relative position, and pressures to ensure that pay relationships reflect authority relationships. Normative pressures of these and other sorts significantly modify the broad framework of relativities between different industries and occupational categories; they have a very large effect on relativities between particular establishments and between particular narrowly defined industries and occupations; and their influence is at its greatest as regards the various types of relativities within particular establishments and industries.

2 recent trends in personnel management . . . have been towards individualized and performance-related pay, delayering of hierarchies, and rapid increases in pay for high-fliers compared with bureaucratic deferred reward structures. Pay is legitimized by market value rather than by internal job descriptions, and redistribution towards higher earners has undermined notions of internal fairness.

Sources adapted from: (1) Wood (1978), pp. 1 and 203; and (2) Rubery (1997), p. 355.

of employee motivation in which social and psychological influences play an important role; in other words, a view of people as simple, rational, maximising agents is inadequate. Equity and fairness matter too. This has long been argued by some labour economists, such as Phelps Brown (1962: 4–6) in Britain, while Thaler (1989: 191) finds 'the pattern of industry wages difficult to understand unless we assume that firms pay attention to perceived equity in setting wages, an assumption that only an economist would find controversial'. Exhibit 3.1 contains a further reflection of this view, though a contemporary comment suggests that some of the traditional equity arguments are under challenge.

Second, this group attaches a great deal of importance to the notion of 'learning' which is seen as all-important in trying to ensure that organisational objectives are achieved via the 'people factor'. To them it is this wider, more complex nature of motivation, together with the notion of learning, that is so important in accounting for many of the observed patterns of behaviour and outcome that do not neatly square with the assumptions and predictions of competitive theory. They also attach a more important, and frequently 'positive', role to the influence of institutional arrangements in the labour market, as is illustrated by the findings of exhibit 3.2.

The link with the earlier institutional critics is underlined by Freeman (1989: 321):

one of the major conclusions which led the (older) generation of labor economists to reject the competitive model of the labor market was the finding of significant wage differences among workers doing seemingly similar work across industries and among plants within an industry in particular local labor markets. For a long time, modern labor economists ignored these results. . . .

Exhibit 3.2

Changes in the wage structure in four OECD countries

1 Educational and occupational wage differentials narrowed in the USA, Britain, Japan and France in the 1970s. But this pattern reversed itself with increases in skill differentials in the USA, Britain and Japan in the early 1980s, with a muted but somewhat similar pattern appearing in France from 1984.

2 Reductions in the rate of growth of the relative supply of college-educated workers in the face of persistent increases in the relative demand for more skilled labour can explain a substantial portion of the increase in educational wage differentials in the USA, Britain and Japan in the 1980s.

3 Similar changes in relative skill demands are likely to have occurred in France, but the effect of such changes on wages has been somewhat offset by a high minimum wage and the ability of French unions to extend contracts even in the face of declining membership.

Source: L. Katz, G. Loreman and D. Blanchflower, 1993.

More recently, younger economists interested in wage determination from a broader perspective have re-examined the role of the industry, establishment and firm in wage determination, with empirical findings totally supportive of the older generation ... While all the modern analysts, like the older generation, have tried to build competitive studies to explain industry and plant differentials, the broad conclusion they have reached also mimics that of the older generation – namely, that competitive theory cannot explain the observed phenomenon.

The modern group of critics confronts the rational school of thought on grounds similar to the earlier institutional economists but employs essentially the same methodology as the neoclassical school (with an emphasis on deductive hypothesis testing using quantitative methods to analyse large bodies of survey data). Specifically, they analyse differentials that are inconsistent with the 'one price' rule for equivalent workers, predicted by competitive theory (reflecting individual productivity). Empirical evidence of sustained wage differentials linked to plant size, firm size and industry (even when measurable labour quality is held constant) is inconsistent with conventional theory. Exhibit 3.3 lists some specific findings from relevant micro-level British studies of this area.

As a consequence of these and similar findings, theories of wage determination departing further from the standard competitive version have developed. Groshen (1991) suggests five versions which progressively distance themselves from standard competitive theory in order to explain inter-firm wage differentials for similar workers: in simplified terms, these are:

1 workers not quite homogeneous due to innate or acquired worker quality, leading to firms sorting applicants by ability;
2 compensating differentials mitigate undesirable terms of employment deriving from management strategy or technological requirements;
3 random variations due to imperfect information, search costs and lags;
4 efficiency wages, where higher pay generates higher productivity;
5 bargaining, where the firm earns rent through its competitive advantage, but stakeholders are able to capture some part of it (or management is altruistic).

Exhibit 3.3

> ## Non-competitive wage model findings: some evidence from Britain
>
> **Study One**
> - Increases in a firm's market share, decreases in important penetration, and increases in the industry concentration ratio all serve to increase wages.
>
> **Study Two**
> - Firm-specific factors influence wages, but these effects are not influenced by union status, firm size or extent of market power.
> - Conditions in the external labour market are a very important influence in company wages, although less so for firms with a high degree of market power.
> - Product market power has a positive impact on wages, which is enhanced in large firms, but is not influenced by union status.
>
> **Study Three**
> - Employees who work in areas of high unemployment earn less, other things constant, than those who are surrounded by low unemployment; Bargaining and efficiency wage models are consistent with this pattern; This pattern is difficult to reconcile with the textbook competitive model of the labour market

Sources: Vainiomaki and Wadhwani (1991) (Study One); Nickell, Vainiomaki and Wadhwani (1992) (Study Two); Blanchflower and Oswald (1994), pp. 360–1 (Study Three).

The first two models are minor variants on the standard theory, while the third allows for random factors to intrude. The fourth and fifth models are more radical departures which require more discussion especially as they focus on management behaviour within the organisation and bear directly on our concerns here.

CURRENT DEBATES

These moves away from standard competitive theory recognise that the level of firm-based compensation will vary considerably, reflecting the existence of discretion or choice available to firms. Once this is accepted a more open-ended approach becomes feasible. There is no problem in accepting that many firms have some monopoly power in their product market, enabling them to earn a 'rent' over and above the competitive level of profits. Once this rent is available the pressure of competition forcing firms to operate on the knife-edge of survival is reduced. Discretionary behaviour by managers, including decisions on pay for managers and workers alike, is possible. The limited effects of competition presumably allow firms paying above the market to survive since they are no longer on the knife-edge. But why should firms pay more for labour than would seem to be necessary?

Efficiency wage theory

The basic belief here is that paying above the market rate will be efficient and profitable to the organisation, as it results in a positive impact on employee productivity. There are four leading versions of efficiency wage theory (Elliott, 1991: 349–51):

1 *The shirking model*: The contention here is that because individual worker productivity is often difficult to measure, this provides workers with the incentive to 'shirk'. However, if firms pay workers more than they can obtain elsewhere, they will be motivated to reduce shirking, because of the risk of being caught and hence losing this wage premium.

2 *The turnover model*: The contention here is that the wage premium is designed to reduce labour turnover which would involve considerable costs to the firm, particularly the loss of employees who have been in receipt of firm-specific training.

3 *The superior job applicant pool*: According to this version, it is not easy for firms to attract, identify and hire workers with high productivity potential. As a consequence, the high wage strategy is designed to attract a superior pool of applicants so that even random hiring produces a more productive workforce.

4 *Fair wages*: According to this version, the 'gift' of higher wages is reciprocated by a 'gift' of higher productivity. This is because these higher wages satisfy individual employee demands for equitable and fair treatment, and thus result in a reciprocal exchange of enhanced effort, reflected in increased morale and performance.

There are varying assessments of the worth and value of this particular body of work, largely due to the difficulties of developing suitable tests able to discriminate between different theories, but the following conclusion is one that might command broad support (Elliott, 1991: 352):

> Recent attempts to explain these industry effects have focused on efficiency wage theory. This has the appeal that it attempts to explain why wage rates may be established and remain above the market clearing level. Some of the variants of efficiency wage theory are merely 'old wine in new bottles'. More novel are the versions that emphasize considerations of morale and fairness. These notions are by their very nature difficult to investigate empirically and it has to be admitted that at this time there is little empirical support for these versions of the theory. Such a remark is not meant to pour cold water on these ideas for they represent one of the more important developments in labour economics in recent years. However until we resolve some of the measurement difficulties standing in the way of empirical evaluation of these theories, our appreciation of the importance of these issues is likely to be severely curtailed.

Bargaining models

Allowing again that firms are able to earn rent above normal profit due to some degree of monopoly power, it is possible for stakeholders in the firm to capture a share of that rent, either through bargaining or through altruism on the part of the employer. Trade unions, for example, may be able to engage in collective bargaining to increase the wage rates of their members by obtaining a mark-up on the market rate, thereby providing an incentive for employees to join the union. Equally, employers may feel disposed to share the benefits of their market position with managers (through executive perks) or employees on a discretionary basis – though this would be difficult to separate from the payment of efficiency wages. A special case arises in relation to senior executive compensation which we discuss below.

Internal labour markets

A further development in labour economics with important implications for the analysis of pay at the firm or plant level has been the focus on *internal labour markets*. The internal labour market concept reflects the observed behaviour of many large organisations in which pay structure is effectively insulated from the forces of (external) labour market competition. Contact with the external labour market is confined to recruitment through limited 'ports of entry', and jobs in the organisation are arranged hierarchically. Employees receive company-specific training and are promoted in the hierarchy as they acquire skill and experience. Being sheltered from competitive forces, companies are not driven to relate wages directly to (marginal) productivity but can organise administrative systems of job allocation, training and career development, with an appropriate pay structure, to suit their own needs. Wages are attached to jobs rather than reflecting individual marginal productivity. The internal labour market thus breaks the link between competition and marginal productivity which is central to the competitive wage theory.

This challenge to conventional theory has been taken seriously, since the evidence indicates widespread use of internal labour market arrangements.[2] Again, however, the defendants of the neoclassical lines have sought to rationalise the challenge by arguing that 'the internal labour market is an efficiency-orientated institutional response to the basic market imperfections arising from specific training and the costs of information' (Addison and Siebert, 1979: 195): in other words, it is an organisational response to a form of market failure.

There is no doubt that internal labour markets have been – and remain – an important type of employment system adopted by employers to contribute to corporate objectives. They involve long-term employment relationships (employee commitment), substantial wage rigidity (reflecting income security and progression), an emphasis on internal promotion and training (human resource development) and a positive association between employee earnings and tenure (effective job matching) enhancing employee loyalty. Many personnel practitioners will recognise these features as design elements in their own organisations' remuneration policy, and their strong link into human resource management practice.

But it is worth noting that there has recently been some questioning about the future of the internal labour market. If the internal labour market was developed to overcome various forms of market failure, might it not be that, as the labour market itself undergoes change, this device will be less important. Cappelli (1995) and Cappelli *et al.* (1997) has observed that the long-term commitment of many employers to their employees, including middle managers, has declined. Downsizing, the adoption of more flexible labour contracts, deregulation of the labour market, the reduction of union power and the shrinking of collective bargaining coverage with its emphasis on the common rate, all seem to be moving away from the employment and income security values imbedded within the internal labour market. As new payment systems dependent on strong links between pay and individual performance multiply, the importance of the pay–productivity relationship (at the heart of the standard theory) might be coming back into play. At least this is an area that requires to be watched.

A fourth area which has attracted a good deal of attention involves the economic theory of *agency*. This theory focuses on those forms of payment by which the principal party (the firm) seeks to motivate the agent (worker) to behave in a manner which is of advantage to the principal. When a principal considers contracting with an agent for the performance of a service, each party has (asymmetrical) information which is private to itself: only the agent knows the true cost of the effort required of him, while the principal knows the (expected) value of the output. In the design of an optimal contract, both face risks – will the agent deliver the required output on time, will the principal pay enough to reward the effort? And what happens if external conditions intervene and frustrate genuine effort on the part of the agent – e.g. weather conditions? This goes to the heart of many compensation problems: how to provide motivation for the agent (for example through incentive payments) or how to ensure that the agent does not shirk or cheat in ways that the principal finds difficult or expensive to monitor: supervision may provide an answer but it too comes at a cost to the principal. One solution for the employer may be to adopt a deferred compensation approach in which employees are paid less than their marginal revenue product in their early years, but more than their marginal revenue product in their later years. Such an approach should reduce both quits and shirking and would be consistent with the observed positive correlation between earnings and tenure. Equally, however, collective incentive schemes such as profit sharing and employee ownership, may improve alignment between employer and employee objectives. As we shall see, the principal–agent analysis also has a bearing on the issue of executive compensation.

A PART OF THE STORY, BUT NOT THE FULL STORY

A distinguished economist once stated that 'economists were people who thought very seriously about small issues'. Is this a fair and accurate summation of the contribution of labour economists to our understanding of firm-level compensation practices? That is, have they focused on the important, strategic questions concerning compensation at the firm level, and produced useful insights into these areas? To assist our overall assessment in this regard we set out in exhibit 3.4 some of the leading strategic issues involved in firm-level compensation.

With exhibit 3.4 as a reference point, our reading of the economists' contribution to the compensation literature inclines us to the following broad conclusions.

1 The body of theoretical literature is considerably greater than the empirical literature.
2 The focus has been much more on the *determinants*, rather than the *consequences* of compensation arrangements.
3 *Efficiency* is the over-riding theme, though more assumed than demonstrated.
4 The level of pay or compensation has been the major research concentration.
5 Research on the structure of compensation, the mix of compensation, the criteria or basis of compensation decisions, and the processes involved (see exhibit 3.4) is growing, but is much less than on the level of compensation.
6 These generalisations from the American literature hold even more strongly for the literature from other countries.

A number of important implications follow from the above conclusions. For instance, compensation practitioners at the firm level essentially ask themselves the following

Exhibit 3.4

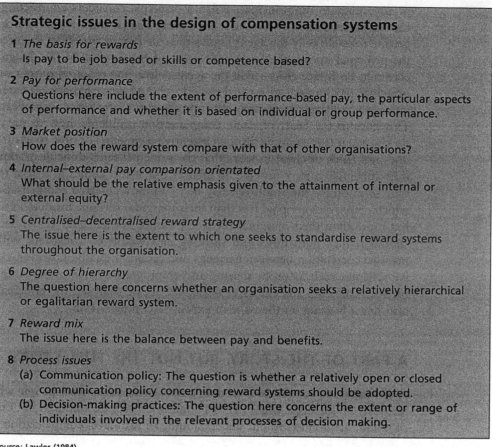

Strategic issues in the design of compensation systems

1 *The basis for rewards*
Is pay to be job based or skills or competence based?

2 *Pay for performance*
Questions here include the extent of performance-based pay, the particular aspects of performance and whether it is based on individual or group performance.

3 *Market position*
How does the reward system compare with that of other organisations?

4 *Internal–external pay comparison orientated*
What should be the relative emphasis given to the attainment of internal or external equity?

5 *Centralised–decentralised reward strategy*
The issue here is the extent to which one seeks to standardise reward systems throughout the organisation.

6 *Degree of hierarchy*
The question here concerns whether an organisation seeks a relatively hierarchical or egalitarian reward system.

7 *Reward mix*
The issue here is the balance between pay and benefits.

8 *Process issues*
(a) Communication policy: The question is whether a relatively open or closed communication policy concerning reward systems should be adopted.
(b) Decision-making practices: The question here concerns the extent or range of individuals involved in the relevant processes of decision making.

Source: Lawler (1984).

questions: What choices do I have to make (see exhibit 3.4); What should influence my choices; and What are the consequences of my choices? Arguably, by concentrating on the determinants, rather than consequences, of compensation decisions, economists run the risk of telling practitioners what they already know. Relatively few practitioners are likely to be surprised by, or find much helpful insight, in studies which tell them that, for example, payment by results systems are more likely when employment contracts are shorter, that the number of supervisors varies inversely with the incidence of payment by results schemes, or that payment by results is more likely to be found in large establishments.[3] Furthermore, because economics takes much less of a contingency-based prescriptive perspective than, for example, the strategic human resource management literature, it is arguably of less interest and relevance in pointing up the factors which shape compensation choices. As a consequence, it is likely to be the economists' contribution to the *consequences* of choices that is of major interest to practitioners. However, as noted earlier, this body of literature is only in its relative infancy. A recent symposium noted the following (Ehrenberg, 1990: 4–5 and 6–9):

1 Little empirical testing by economists has been directed at whether pay structures have incentive effects at the individual employee level.

2 There is very little empirical evidence that firms pursuing high wage strategies actually outperform other firms.

However, as with any generalisations, exceptions exist. Accordingly we note in the next section two such areas of research by economists which have been of considerable interest to compensation practitioners at the firm level. Indeed the approach involved in these two areas is one which we feel can and should be pursued by economists more widely.

TWO EXCEPTIONAL CASES: THE WAY FORWARD?

The first area is that of executive or senior management compensation. Studies of executive compensation in the US in the 1970s and early 1980s frequently documented the lack of a relationship between corporate performance and executive pay (Cappelli *et al.*, 1997: 39). Ehrenberg and Milkovich, (1987: 92). interpreted this as evidence that:

> corporate executives may pursue objectives such as sales maximization, growth maximization, or market-share maximization that are not necessarily in the best interests of shareholders who are concerned with short-run (accounting profits) and long-run (total stock market return) measures of the economic profitability of the corporation.

The result was the development of a number of theoretical models seeking optimal ways to resolve this *principal–agent* problem (Lazear, 1995). If there is a divergence of interests between the owners of companies and the top directors, the problem for the shareholders is to design contracts that will bring the top executives (agents) into line. In practice, this would seem to involve a larger proportion of stock-based, long-term incentives relative to fixed pay. There is a growing body of empirical research on executive compensation designed to examine the implications of agency theory, namely that an increased alignment of shareholder and executive interests increases the performance of the firm.

A number of existing studies reveal that changes in executive compensation are highly and positively correlated with firm measures of economic performance (Ehrenberg and Milkovich, 1987: 93). However, both the definition of compensation and the measures of economic performance vary across the studies. Moreover, the existence of such a correlation is not in itself evidence of the fact that the compensation–performance linkage has led to improved economic performance. As Ehrenberg and Milkovich put it (1987: 94):

> One possibility is that corporations initially don't know what the true productivity of their executives is. However, to the extent that the executives' productivity can be imperfectly *signaled* by corporate performance, relating their compensation to corporate performance is a way of 'paying them what they're worth'. If this is occurring, the compensation–performance nexus could reflect learning about executives' 'true ability' over time, not necessarily any incentive arrangement to stimulate economic performance. Furthermore, even if appropriate incentives *do* exist, it doesn't necessarily follow that they will have their intended effect. Disentangling whether the observed correlation is due to 'incentives' or 'learning' is not an easy task.

Although important issues, such as those outlined in the above quote, remain unresolved, empirical research on executive compensation has already produced some important findings, as indicated in table 3.1.

Table 3.1 Empirical support for propositions concerning predictors and correlates of executive pay

Proposition	Empirical support
Executive pay varies as a function of firm performance.	Very mixed, minimal
The more dispersed the ownership of a firm, the more executives will structure their compensation package so that their pay is flexible to move up as firm performance improves, but will not suffer if firm performance declines.	Strong
The more dispersed the ownership of a firm, the more likely executives will be driven to increase firm size, even if additional growth results in decreased performance.	Strong
The more concentrated the ownership of a firm, the more likely executive decisions will have a long-term horizon.	Moderate
Greater monitoring and incentive alignment of executives result in improved firm performance.	Moderate
Greater monitoring and incentive alignment of executives lead to a greater observed linkage between executive pay and firm performance.	Moderate
Relationship between executive pay and firm performance varies by extent of diversification.	Strong
Extent of division autonomy affects criteria used to reward executives.	Strong
Executive pay is more strongly related to stock-related performance criteria than to accounting measures.	Negative
Executive decisions are very responsive to what incumbents perceive will lead to the greatest financial reward.	Very strong

Source: Gomez-Mejca, Paulin and Grabke (1995).

Research on executive level compensation and its relation to corporate performance has been growing in the UK.[4]

1 The UK evidence points to the existence of very small pay–performance sensitivities, suggesting that the incentive link is not strong; and more recent evidence post-1988 could not detect any relationship between the basic pay of UK executives and the stock market performance of their companies.

2 However, more recent work which separates out executive salary from bonus payments suggests that salary is strongly related to company size, while annual bonus is 'moderately' associated with size and performance (McKnight, 1996: 557–66).

3 There is strong evidence that managerial incentives are not closely aligned to those of shareholders and this leads to significant under-performance in the corporate sector, in particular because of poorly judged acquisitions (Curcio, 1992).

Given the continuing controversy about executive pay levels in Britain we see this as an area that warrants continued research, not least for its implications for corporate governance issues.

The second area of research by economists which we would draw attention to has been in relation to profit-sharing schemes. Economists have taken the lead in arguing that such schemes can enhance organisational performance and, if widespread, can be an important source of overall employment stability at the macro-economic level (Weitzman, 1984). Moreover their empirical research has yielded consistent evidence of significant, positive links between the existence of profit-sharing schemes and organisational performance, usually defined as value added (Weitzman and Kruse, 1996). Admittedly, reservations and criticisms have been expressed about some elements involved in this particular stream of research. For example, important questions have been raised about the appropriateness of the variables used in the studies, the lack of explicit attention given to the precise mechanisms involved and the difficulty of establishing clear-cut lines of causation. Nevertheless we would argue that it is the direction of this research that has been particularly important and worthwhile. Economists in this particular area have focused on the firm level of analysis, been concerned with the consequences of the arrangements and have often broadened their frameworks of analysis to include process variables which have traditionally received little attention in their work. For example, one can now find economists concluding that employee participation and contingent compensation, taken together, produce stronger positive organisational performance gains than each can achieve individually (Levine and Tyson, 1990; Kruse, 1996).

CONCLUSION

The themes treated in this chapter serve to demonstrate that there is no single orthodoxy among economists in their approach to the study of compensation. It is also clear that many of the concerns of economists in this area, notably the focus on overall economic efficiency and the stickiness of wage response to environmental change, are far removed from the concerns of managers and human resource practitioners who view remuneration as a management tool, amongst others, which can help deliver organisational objectives. We have seen that much of the economist's interest focuses on industrial and occupational dimensions, rather than on the inter-firm analysis of compensation policy and practice, though we have noted growing interest in this dimension. Yet the central issues for many companies, their ability to attract and retain suitable labour, their capacity to motivate workers to deliver what the company wants, and the well-recognised social concern within the work place for equity in compensation, are not exactly at the top of the economist's agenda.

This does not mean, though, that we should write off the economists' contributions as irrelevant. In the first place, it is important to be reminded that, even though many firms are able to exercise considerable discretion in their remuneration strategy, both the product market environment and the labour market environment will set limits which cannot be ignored in the formulation of strategy for the business and for the management of the human resource.

Second, the opening up of discretionary decision making, rather than simple acceptance of a ruling market wage rate, still seems to leave considerable scope for analysis at the level of the firm. Human capital theory reminds us that human capital is embodied in individuals who have free will and can move with that capital intact, even if its acquisition has been largely at the expense of an employer. And agency theory returns us to the familiar problem that worker performance is not something that can be guaranteed by the presence of a labour contract. Performance needs to be elicited and refreshed in a variety of ways which leaves considerable discretion in the design of compensation: this applies both to the elimination of shirking (a negative element) and to the encouragement of continued development and application of firm-specific skills and experience in the pursuit of organisational goals (a positive element). Enough has been said in the course of this chapter to illustrate the range of reward systems which have the potential to deliver these goals, but they fall far short of any recipe or 'one best way'. Rather they underline the need for good analysis of goals and an understanding of alternative means of achieving them, whether through the reward mechanism directly or the reward mechanism in association with other management tools. Where economics can make further contributions to this is particularly in the development of research into the effectiveness of different combinations of reward and other management policies at the level of the firm.[5]

Finally, the economic analysis of efficiency wages, internal labour markets and principal–agent relationships for the design of the optimal contract, though they do not constitute a coherent theory, provide a framework for the understanding of pay related to many of the behavioural and organisational variables which are of interest to the practitioner. If these links are to be further developed they would seem to require more of what Thaler (1989: 190) calls 'micro–micro' (nano?) economics:

> Economists would have to get their hands dirty collecting data on the actual operation of organisations. Unless the profession is willing to reward this type of time-consuming research activity, many important questions will remain unresolved.

NOTES

1 See below, p. 54.
2 But see below.
3 See Heywood, Siebert and Wei (1997).
4 For a summary, see M. Conyon, P. Gregg and S. Machin (1995).
5 For a good example, see Kruse (1996).

LEARNING ACTIVITIES

1 Critically evaluate the standard classical approach to the economic theory of pay.

2 Identify the insights into the design and management of reward systems offered by more recent approaches to economic theories of pay.

3 Identify the factors that might impact on the future demand for and supply of labour to the employment market.

4 How might the factors identified in question three impact on organisational reward systems?

REFERENCES

Addison, J. and Siebert, W.S. (1979) *The Market for Labor: An analytical treatment*. Santa Monica: Goodyear.

Blanchflower, D.G. and Oswald, A.J. (1994) *The Wage Curve*. Cambridge, MA: MIT Press.

Cappelli, P. (1995) 'Rethinking Employment', *British Journal of Industrial Relations*, 33(4): 563–602.

Cappelli, P. *et al.* (1997) *Change at Work*. New York: Oxford University Press.

Conyon, M., Gregg, P. and Machin, S. (1995) Taking Care of Business: Executive compensation in the UK, *Economic Journal*, 105(May): 704–14.

Curcio, R. (1992) 'Managerial Ownership of Shares and Corporate Performance: An empirical analysis of UK companies 1972–86', Centre for Economic Performance, LSE, Working Paper No. 290, August.

Ehrenberg, R.G. (1990) 'Introduction: Do compensation policies matter?', *Industrial and Labor Relations Review*, 4(3): 3–5, 10–5.

Ehrenberg, R.G. and Milkovich, G.T. (1987) 'Compensation and Firm Performance', in M.M. Kleiner *et al.* (eds), *Human Resources and the Performance of the Firm*. Industrial Relations Research Association, University of Wisconsin-Madison, pp. 87–122.

Elliott, R.F. (1991) *Labor Economics: A comparative text*. London: McGraw Hill.

Freeman, R.B. (1989) 'Does the New Generation of Labor Economists know more than the Older Generation?', in R.B. Freeman, *Labour Markets in Action*. New York: Harvester Wheatsheaf, pp. 317–42.

Gerhart, B., Milkovich, G.T. and Murray, B. (1992) 'Pay, performance and participation', in D. Lewin *et al.* (eds), *Research Frontiers in Industrial Relations and Human Resources*, Industrial Relations Research Association, University of Wisconsin-Madison, pp. 193–238.

Gomez-Mejca, L.R., Paulin, G. and Graske, A. (1995) 'Executive Compensation: Research and practical implications', in G.R. Ferris, S.M. Rosen and D.T. Barnum (eds), *Handbook of Human Resource Management*. New York: Blackwell, p. 556.

Gregg, P., Machin, S. and Szymanski (1992) 'The Disappearing Relationship between Directors' Pay and Corporate Performance', Centre for Economic Performance, LSE, Working Paper No. 282, September.

Groshen, Erica L. (1991) 'Five Reasons Why Wages Vary Among Employers,' *Industrial Relations*, 30(3): 350–79.

Hammermesh, D.S. and Rees, A. (1993) *The Economics of Work and Pay*. Fifth edition, New York: HarperCollins.

Heywood, J.S., Siebert, W.S. and Wei, X. (1997) 'Payment by Results Systems: British Evidence', *British Journal of Industrial Relations*, 35(1): 1–22.

Katz, L., Loreman, G. and Blanchflower, D. (1993) 'A Comparison of Changes in the Structure of Wages in four OECD Countries', Centre for Economic Performance, LSE Discussion Paper No. 144, May.

Kaufman, B.E. (1994) 'The Evolution of Thought on the Competitive Nature of Labor Markets', in C. Kerr and P.E. Standohar (eds), *Labor Economics and Industrial Relations*. Cambridge, MA: Harvard University Press, pp. 145–88.

Kruse, D.L. (1996) 'Why Do Firms Adopt Profit-sharing and Employee Ownership Plans?', *British Journal of Industrial Relations*, 34(4): 515–38.

Lawler, E. (1984) 'The Strategic Design of Reward Systems', in C. Fombrun, N. Tichy and M.A. Devanna, *Strategic Human Resource Management*. New York: Wiley, pp. 131–46.

Lazear, E. (1995) *Personnel Economics*. Cambridge and London: MIT Press.

Levine, D. and Tyson, L.D. (1990) 'Participation, Productivity and the Firm's Performance', in A.S. Blinder (ed.), *Paying for Productivity*. Washington: Brookings.

Lester, R.A. (1946) 'Shortcomings of Marginal Analysis for Wage–Employment Problems', *American Economic Review*, 36: 63–82.

McKnight, P.J. (1996) An Explanation of Top Executive Pay: A UK study, *British Journal of Industrial Relations*, 34(4): 557–66.

Millward, N. *et al.* (1992) *Workplace Industrial Relations in Transition*. Aldershot: Dartmouth.

Nickell, S., Vainiomaki, J., Wadhwani, S. 'Wages, unions, insiders and product market power', Centre for Economic Performance, LSE, Discussion Paper No. 77, May.

Phelps Brown, E.H. (1962) *The Economics of Labor*. New Haven: Yale University Press.

Pierson, F.C. (957) 'An Evaluation of Wage Theory', in G.T. Taylor and F. Pierson (eds), *New Concepts in Wage Determination*, 3–31.

Polacheck, S.W. and Siebert, S. (1995) *The Economics of Earnings*. Cambridge: Cambridge University Press.

Rees, A. (1973) *The Economics of Work and Pay*. New York: Harper and Row.

Reynolds, L.G., Masters, S.H. and Moser, C.H. (1986) *Labor Economics and Labor Relations*. Ninth edition, Englewood Cliffs: Prentice Hall.

Rubery, J. (1997) 'Wages and the Labour Market', *British Journal of Industrial Relations*, 35(3): 337–66.

Thaler, R.H. (1989) 'Interindustry Wage Differentials', *Journal of Economic Perspectives*, 3(2): 181–93.

Vainiomaki, J. and Wadhwani, S. (1991) 'The Effects of Changes in a Firm's Product Market Power on Wages', Centre for Economic Performance, LSE, Discussion Paper No. 18, February 1991.

Weitzman, M.L. (1984) *The Share Economy*, Cambridge, MA: Harvard University Press.

Weitzman, M. and Kruse, D.L. (1996) 'Profit sharing and productivity', in A.S. Blinder (ed.), *Paying for Productivity*. Washington: Brookings.

Wood, A. (1978) *A Theory of Pay*. Cambridge: Cambridge University Press.

FURTHER READING

Elliott, R.F. (1991) *Labour Economics: A comparative text*. London: McGraw Hill.

Groschen, E.L. (1991) 'Five Reasons Why Wages Vary Among Employers', *Industrial Relations*, 30(3): 350–79.

Hammermesh, D.S. and Wei, X. (1993) *The Economics of Work and Pay*. Fifth edition, New York: HarperCollins.

Rubery, J. (1997) 'Wages and the Labour Market', *British Journal of Industrial Relations*, 33(4): 337–66.

4 Economic policy, the labour market and reward

Catherine Kavanagh and Robert Elliott

INTRODUCTION

For almost two decades now, the thrust of economic policy towards the UK labour market has been to enhance labour market flexibility. This has substantially increased the freedom of companies operating in the UK to construct and implement reward strategies that meet their needs. The change in government that occurred in May 1997 seems unlikely to substantially change these developments (although some greater measure of labour market regulation is encouraged with the introduction of a minimum wage). The policies implemented to achieve this objective have been many and diverse and, thus, this chapter ranges wide.

The substantive change in policy toward the labour market dates from 1979. Most of the reforms were carried out during the 1980s by the Conservative government under the leadership of Margaret Thatcher. Thatcher's fundamentally different economic strategy consisted of two major elements. The first, on the demand side, was to pursue a policy of firm monetary control in order to reduce inflation. The second was to pursue radical market-orientated supply-side policies. The main thrust of these market-orientated supply-side policies was to encourage and reward individual enterprise and initiative, to reduce the role of government, and put more reliance on market forces and competition and less on government intervention and regulation.

In the labour market, the UK programme of reforms focused on promoting flexibility. To attain a more flexible labour market, successive governments sought to reduce as much as possible all restrictions on the deployment of labour, whether from unions, employers' organisations or protective legislation giving workers rights either at work or against its loss. Deregulation and decentralisation replaced incomes policies and, in some cases, collective bargaining agreements. There has been a large drop in union presence and, even in the unionised part of the private sector, national- or industry-level pay agreements have all but disappeared. In the private sector, pay is now more likely to be set within the firm or the work place. The central aim of successive administrations has been to restore the initiative to employers (as opposed to unions or the government itself). In so doing, the concern is to ensure that employers' freedom is strongly structured by market incentives.

Cuts in income tax, designed to restore the incentive to work, were the keystone of consecutive governments' strategy during the 1980s. Chancellor Geoffrey Howe, in the Budget speech of 1979 (*Hansard*), espoused the then government's view that cutting 'income tax at all levels' was the 'only way we can restore incentives and make it worthwhile to work'. In his Budget speech of 1988 (*Hansard*), Nigel Lawson also argued that:

> Excessive rates of income tax destroy enterprise, encourage avoidance, and drive talent to more hospitable shores overseas. As a result, far from raising additional revenue, over time they actually raise less.

As a result, the UK tax and transfer system has been substantially reformed: structure and rates of tax have changed; there has been a shift away from direct taxation and towards indirect taxation; the incidence of means testing has increased; and stricter availability testing is in place.

These reforms continued into the 1990s. In 1992, the Conservative government under the leadership of John Major reaffirmed their belief in the free market and in the need for flexibility of real wages by abolishing wage councils. More recently, the Chancellor of the Exchequer in the new Labour administration, which assumed office on 1 May 1997, outlining a new approach for the twenty-first century, emphasised that the labour market policy of the new government would focus on five key responsibilities. These were:

● to ensure macro-economic stability and growth
● to promote a flexible and adaptable labour market
● to help people from welfare to work
● to encourage investment in skills
● to make work pay.

This policy would continue to focus on many of the same areas as those of previous administrations although the emphasis would be different.

There appears to be little doubt that the reforms have promoted a more flexible labour market. As noted by the OECD (1996: 89), '[t]he UK labour market is now one of the least regulated among OECD countries, as regards restrictions on terms and conditions of employment, working times and hiring and firing rules'. However, increased flexibility has been accompanied by increased earnings dispersion, increased income dispersion, an increase in the number of low-paid jobs, and a rise in the number of temporary jobs.

The purpose of this chapter is to examine how the economic policy of post-1979 administrations has impacted on reward structures; to identify the way in which government economic policy has changed the environment within which firms choose and construct their reward strategy; and to identify the changing opportunities and challenges this presents to firms. In what follows, we explore why labour market policies since 1979 have focused exclusively on promoting greater flexibility and we present some evidence of the impact of these reforms on reward structures.

The chapter is structured as follows. The next section addresses the question: Why have governments favoured supply-side policies? The answer to this question requires both a report of the events leading up to 1979 and a brief description of the theoretical basis for supply-side policies. Section 3 details the supply-side policies which were promoted. The following section then assesses the impact of the policies on both the external and internal environment, in areas such as pay, wage dispersion, labour supply, work organisation and industrial relations. A final section concludes with some comments on the future outlook for reward strategies.

WHY SUPPLY-SIDE POLICIES?

Why did the government of 1979 decide to focus on supply-side policies and abandon the Keynesian demand-management policies popularised in the 1960s and early 1970s? To answer this question, it is important to first set the context in which the reforms were introduced. This requires a review of the economic situation prior to 1979 and an understanding of the theoretical basis for the policies, which motivated the reforms.

Reasons for reform

During the 1970s, the threat to economic stability posed by inflation became acute. A particular problem had been a tendency for wages to rise rapidly in sectors demanding skills during economic recoveries. This had largely been a result of the neglect of training and other elements of skill provision during recessions, leading to skill shortages which firms sought to resolve by bidding up wages. However, a rise in the price of labour is unlikely to lead to an increase in skilled labour supply in the short run and the consequence was wage inflation. The governments' responses to this were to introduce a series of incomes policies. Incomes policies, which were a prominent feature of government policy, were designed to control inflation by limiting pay claims in the public and private sector. Disagreements exist on the effectiveness of such policies. Keynesians and monetarists, while both agreeing that supply-side policies have a role to play in promoting growth, disagree about the role that incomes policies can play as an instrument to achieve this end. Monetarists and indeed new classicists argue that prices and incomes policies merely suppress inflation for a short period while distorting the structure of relative prices and, thus, they should not be used. Over the longer term, they argue that incomes policies reduce aggregate supply by impeding the working of the market. In contrast, many Keynesians argue that incomes policies play an important role in the short run by making rapid and substantial reductions in inflation, while, over the longer run, such policies can be part of a social contract.[1]

Incomes policies in the UK took a variety of forms and were adhered to to varying degrees. Policies were both voluntary (the government either simply asked for unions' and/or firms' support or offered something in exchange) and statutory (backed by law). Policies took the form of a complete freeze on wages, with or without certain limited exceptions, and of ceilings on increases in wages, prices and profits. Most of these varieties were tried in the UK at one time or another between the late 1940s and the late 1970s.[2] The three major attempts to operate an incomes policy were in 1964–70, 1972–4, and 1975–9. In each case, there were initial successes, but then resistance and evasion grew. In 1979, the incoming Conservative government abandoned formal incomes policies and such policies have not been used since. The Thatcher government saw them as, at best, ineffective, and, at worst, distortionary, preventing markets from functioning well. It argued that freezing wages impeded the movement of labour, which, in a market economy, was induced to move as a result of changes in relative wages. Furthermore, because an incomes policy reduces labour market efficiency, it increases unemployment. Aggregate supply and growth are thereby reduced, and, because of the resulting excess of demand over supply, ceteris paribus, demand–pull pressures increase and inflation increases. Incomes policies may also fail to control inflation if: (a) people can evade the policy; (b) the government finds enforcing it difficult; (c) the government feels less constrained to control aggregate demand; or (d) there is a wage/price explosion when the policy ends. For these reasons, incomes policies were deemed ineffective as a tool to fight inflation.

Theoretical basis

The supply-side policies pursued by successive governments since 1979 were regarded as the key to achieving sustainable growth and the associated objectives of reducing unemployment and ensuring sustainable low levels of inflation. Supply-side policies focus on potential income and aim to shift the production possibility curve outwards, thus resulting in growth in the economy (see figure 4.1). While demand-side policies may be effective at increasing the actual rate of economic growth in the short run if there is slack in the economy, in the long run, economic growth can only be achieved by increasing the potential rate of economic growth. Supply-side policies can be used to increase the total quantity of factors of production (e.g. policies to encourage investment in capital) or, alternatively, used to encourage greater productivity of factors of production (e.g. policies to increase the incentives to work).

As well as shifting the production possibilities frontier outwards, supply-side policies aim to shift the aggregate supply curve to the right, that is, to increase the amount that firms wish to supply at any given price. When directed at the labour market, supply-side policies aim to influence labour supply by either (a) making workers more responsive to changes in job opportunities or (b) improving job opportunities by making employers more adaptable and willing to co-operate within existing labour constraints, or both. Hence, supply-side policies are aimed at reducing both equilibrium unemployment (caused by imperfections in the market system which result in insufficiently mobile labour) and disequilibrium unemployment (which may be caused by wage rates being set above

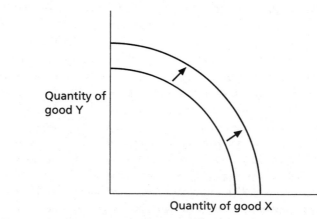

Fig. 4.1 The production possibilities frontier

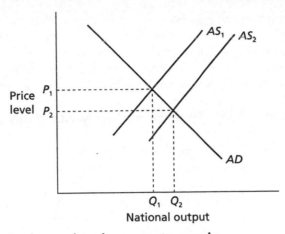

Fig. 4.2 Aggregate demand and aggregate supply

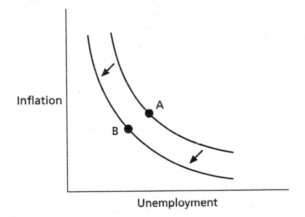

Fig. 4.3 The Phillips curve

the equilibrium level). In the first case, the government can react by, for example, increasing the incentive to work by reducing tax rates, and, in the second case, the government can impose a policy to reduce the power or impact of institutions responsible for setting pay.

Supply-side policies are also aimed at reducing inflation, which may be caused by cost–push pressures, usually due to the exercise of economic power. Effective unions exercise economic power in the supply of labour and drive up wages. Firms with a degree of market power in the supply of goods can drive up prices. Again, supply-side policies, by reducing the power of unions or firms (e.g. anti-monopoly legislation) can reduce cost–push inflation.

Both monetarists and Keynesians see a role for supply-side policies. If successful, such policies could lead to both lower unemployment and lower inflation (see figures 4.2 and 4.3). However, while monetarists favour market-orientated supply-side policies, Keynesians de-emphasise the role of the market and emphasise regulation. This difference stems, no doubt, from the different views that both schools have on the shapes of the aggregate supply curve and the Phillips curve. Monetarists regard both the long-run aggregate supply curve and long-run Phillips curve as vertical. They argue that supply-side policies can shift the aggregate supply curve to the right and if directed at the labour market, can also reduce the natural rate of unemployment, by shifting the vertical long-run Phillips curve to the left. Keynesians argue that the short-run aggregate supply curve is upward sloping and that supply-side policies are therefore most useful when the economy is approaching full employment.

It is important to recognise that supply-side policies often have demand-side effects, and vice versa. For example, supply-side policies of tax cuts designed to increase work incentives will lead to an increase in aggregate demand unless accompanied by a reduction in government expenditure. Similarly, a cut in interest rates may boost investment (demand-side effect) and this increased investment will create increased productive capacity (a supply-side effect). Obviously, it is important that governments take these secondary effects into account when formulating economic strategies.

HOW WERE THE SUPPLY-SIDE POLICIES PROMOTED?

Advocates of the supply-side policies proposed they would 'free up' the labour market, by: encouraging enterprise, risk-taking and competition; increasing work incentives; and reducing the income-supporting and regulatory roles of government. So, how were these labour market policies pursued? They took the form of the following reforms.

- Taxes on earned income were reduced with the objective of increasing work incentives.
- Automatic entitlement to certain welfare benefits was reduced to encourage greater self-reliance and employment take-up.
- Government expenditure as a proportion of GDP (gross domestic product) was reduced in order to release more resources for the private sector.
- Competition in the provision of services was promoted through privatisation, market testing and contracting out.
- Competition in labour markets was promoted through deregulation and reducing the monopoly power of trade unions.

We discuss each of these in turn.

Tax reforms

The impact of any reduction in the marginal rate of income tax on work effort is theoretically ambiguous. In economics, we distinguish between two possible effects of a cut in the income tax rate: the 'income' effect and the 'substitution' effect. The argument that lower tax rates encourage people to work harder draws on the substitution effect: the lower the marginal tax rate, the greater the financial return from working an extra hour (at a given wage rate) and the more likely people are to exchange an hour of leisure for an additional hour of work. Another way of describing the same effect is to say that a tax cut effectively makes leisure more expensive in terms of the income forgone in order to enjoy that leisure, and thus people 'consume' less leisure and work more. The income effect usually acts to offset the substitution effect. Lower tax rates mean more take-home pay for a given number of hours of work. With this higher income level, people may well choose to consume more leisure, i.e. work less hard, while maintaining their pre-tax-cut level of income. There is no theoretical reason to suppose that the substitution effect will outweigh the income effect. Even if it does, people may not be able to work any harder, since they may be constrained by their employer in the number of hours they can work. Thus, it cannot be argued on a priori grounds that tax cuts will lead to more work effort. The impact of any tax change on work effort can only be predicted from empirical evidence.

Governments introduced substantial reforms to the UK tax system during the 1980s. There were three main features to the reforms to income tax: a cut in marginal income tax rates, an increase in the real value of the income thresholds before tax became due, and a shift toward indirect taxation. Changes during the 1980s included the abolition of income tax rates over 40 per cent, the reduction of the basic rate of tax from 33 per cent to 25 per cent, the abolition of both the reduced-rate band and the investment income surcharge (IIS), and the virtual doubling of VAT from a standard rate of 8 per cent and a higher rate of 12.5 per cent to a single rate of 15 per cent. The standard rate of National Insurance Contributions increased from 6.5 per cent to 9 per cent. Other reforms to the tax structure affecting the private sector included the imposition of VAT on domestic fuel, increases in excise duties, notably on petrol and tobacco, and the change in local taxes.

Following the cut in the top marginal income tax rate from 83 per cent to 60 per cent in 1979 and the abolition of the investment income surcharge in 1984, the share of total tax revenue paid by the richest 5 per cent of tax payers increased between 1978/9 and 1985/6. In his Budget speech of 1988, Nigel Lawson cited this as evidence of the incentive effects of cutting taxes: '[t]he top 5 per cent of taxpayers today contribute a third as much again in real terms as they did in 1978–9 . . . while the remaining 95 per cent of tax payers pay about the same in real terms as they did in 1978/9'. Sweeping reforms were also introduced to the structure of UK corporation tax to encourage business and investment. The approach taken was to widen the tax base by reducing or eliminating various allowances, while simultaneously reducing the statutory rate.

Benefit reforms

The UK has consistently devoted a lower proportion of its national output to public spending on social protection than most other EU countries (OECD, 1996). This has been achieved largely by limiting rises in contributory benefits to the rate of price rather than earnings inflation. Nevertheless, the social security programme is the single largest item of government expenditure and is also the government's most powerful redistributive tool. However, reform was encouraged by the publication in 1985 of the White Paper, 'Reform of Social Security' which identified five 'clear and fundamental' defects of the social security system as it then stood. These related to: (a) the complexity of the system, (b) the failure to give effective support to particular needy groups, (c) the problems faced by those 'trapped' in poverty or unemployment because of the tax and benefit system, (d) the effects of the system on individual freedom of choice, and (e) the implications of the then present social security policies for future generations of tax payers. The Social Security Act 1986, which represented the culmination of more than two years of consultation and debate about the future of social security in the UK, introduced major changes to the system of income-related benefits, which were only fully implemented in April 1988.[3]

The government believed that a major disincentive to work existed due to the small difference between the welfare benefits of the unemployed and the take-home pay they would command if in work, and that this was one explanation for growing unemployment. One solution to this problem was to cut benefits, but, in practice, there was a greater concentration on ensuring that claimants were available and actively seeking work. This type of supply-side policy has a very rapid effect, and it shifts the effective labour supply curve to the right. Other steps included the abolition of earnings-related supplements to basic unemployment benefits. Each of these changes increased the incentives to seek and to take up work if offered.

Government expenditure reforms

The scale of public expenditure, it was argued, hindered economic prosperity because the financing of the public sector required high taxation and pushed up interest rates and inflation. The priorities were therefore to (a) cut public expenditure and (b) achieve a more efficient use of resources within the public sector. A consequence of reducing the size of the public sector by cutting employment levels and resource claims would be to increase private investment and consumption with no overall rise in nominal aggregate demand. The supply-side benefits of higher investment could thus be achieved without the demand-side costs of higher inflation.

At the heart of these changes lay a deep-rooted scepticism about the contribution that the public sector could make towards the UK economy and a belief in the superiority of market provision and of the necessity of competition to sharpen performance. These views, which were a hallmark of the Conservative administrations of the 1980s, suggested that the proportion of total expenditure and employment, which was absorbed by the public sector, should be reduced.

In addition to cutting expenditure via grant and subsidy reductions, a number of other measures which directly affected reward structures in the public sector were adopted.

- Cash limits were imposed on various government departments and local authorities.
- Changes in the way public-sector pay was set were introduced.
- The government no longer saw it as necessary to fulfil the role of 'good employer'.
- Public-sector management was substantially strengthened as a new breed of managers was employed to carry out the new functions.
- The civil service was restructured and executive agencies, charged with responsibility for pay and grading, were created.

We discuss each of these below.

Cash limits

The imposition of cash limits broke with the previous system of volume spending, which had allowed policy makers to plan services in volume terms and receive additional resources to meet unanticipated increases in wage costs and prices. In contrast, cash limits were less flexible; they allocated a fixed amount of money for service provision, and required services managers to accept the responsibility for staying within predetermined budgets.

Public-sector pay

Motivated by a search for increased efficiency and flexibility, alternate governments sought to reform the way that they paid their employees. Reforms in central government have generally taken the form of the decentralisation of pay bargaining and the individualisation of pay. Decentralisation recognises that different areas of the public sector need to adopt different approaches to service provision and allows them to construct pay and grading structures that reflect these needs. In turn, this has resulted in both more diverse and more flexible pay arrangements. The link between pay and performance has been forged most closely at senior levels in central government and the health service but some links between pay and performance now exist in most of central government. However, attempts to generalise this principle to local government, education and the health service have been less successful. In these areas, centralised negotiations conducted along sectoral lines still set pay and conditions.

New financial and performance targets have been introduced to increase managerial accountability and to provide criteria against which to judge employee performance. There has been a proliferation of performance indicators and league tables, which compare the relative efficiency of organisations.[4]

The good employer

The government encouraged changes in the nature and style of public-sector management. In consequence, there was less concern with the traditional role of the state as a good employer. Cash limits forced union and employer negotiators to confront the tradeoff between income and employment and required more active management participation in the pay-negotiating process in which the priorities for them were to attract, retain and motivate the employees required.

Management in the public sector

A distinctive feature of the 1980s was that successive Conservative governments intervened more actively to reshape the management and organisation of the public services. Changes accorded managers greater authority over financial issues and personnel policy. The belief was that a more active management style, organised on a decentralised basis and held accountable for performance, would ensure greater control of expenditure and lead to better public services. In all parts of the public sector, this involved major structural changes.[5]

The Civil Service

This decentralised approach originated in a report by Sir Robin Ibbs (1988) entitled *Improving Management in Government: The next steps*, which argued that the civil service was too big and too diverse to manage as a single entity. It proposed that the executive activities of government should be distinguished from those parts of government giving policy advice, and that the former be separated into agencies with specific responsibilities and targets. These agencies, headed by chief executives often recruited from outside the civil services, would be granted greater flexibility over matters such as finance, pay and grading, and personnel policy to enable them to meet the performance targets which would be specified for them.

Successive governments after 1979 instigated major reforms in an attempt to curb government expenditure. However, expenditure reductions were not without their problems. In some sectors, the effect was to cut services rather than increase efficiency. Additionally, there was a sharp decline in capital expenditure on new roads, schools, etc., as it was found much easier to cut this kind of expenditure than it was to cut current expenditure. Furthermore, as unemployment rose through the first half of the 1980s, this led to large increases in expenditure on unemployment and other social security benefits.

Privatisation, market testing and contracting out

This area of policy focused on the public sector and assumed three forms: privatisation (transferring ownership to the private sector), marketisation (the introduction of market relationships into the public sector) and contracting out (the transfer of specific activities on a contractual basis to the private sector). The privatisation programme resulted in the sale of most of the major public corporations. Marketisation involved attempts to introduce competitive pressures and managerial disciplines in the form of 'internal markets', executive agencies and market testing through which public employers are obliged to allow private contractors to bid for the right to carry out specified services. It also involved compulsory competitive tendering in the non-traded public services. The aim of these measures was to force public managers to refocus their attention away from other public-sector actors and towards the more impersonal forces of the market. These measures, it was hoped, would increase competition and lead to greater efficiency.

Privatisation and marketisation

The transfer of ownership from the public to the private sector, privatisation, has gone hand-in-hand with changes in the competitive structure of previously monopolistic industries and, most recently, has meant an end to statutory limits on the activities of privatised companies which are now free to diversify into new sectors and to expand internationally. A logical consequence of diversification has been the reshaping of organisational structures towards more devolved forms of management, such as subsidiaries or divisions organised along business lines.

Marketisation has been a prominent feature of reform in the National Health Service (NHS) where is has been associated with a variety of initiatives, most notably the creation of an internal market (although this is to be dissolved under the new Labour administration). The establishment of NHS Trusts also enhanced managerial control in the name of increased efficiency. This decentralisation of organisational structure may at some time in the future find a reflection in the decentralisation of arrangements for setting pay and conditions of employment, but this has not happened yet. To date, the main impact of the reforms has been felt through competitive tendering, often resulting in contracting out.

Contracting out

Contracting out began in the UK in 1980. Direct labour organisations (DLOs) were required to compete with private firms for most of the construction and maintenance work of local authorities. Following the passage of the 1988 Local Government Act, compulsory competitive tendering was extended to refuse collection, catering, street cleaning and vehicle and ground maintenance in local government. The purpose of competitive tendering was to obtain better value for money.

In the NHS, contracting out also began in the early 1980s and gained momentum in the middle 1980s. Competitive tendering in the NHS focused on hospital catering, cleaning and laundry services. By 1986, 68 per cent of all health support services had been subject to competitive tendering, but the vast majority of contracts had been won by in-house teams. By early 1988, 80 per cent of cleaning contracts, 85 per cent of laundry contracts and 97 per cent of catering services contracts had been won by in-house teams.

In local government, the initial experience was rather different, because local authorities exercise a degree of autonomy. Contracting out was as a result, despite some highly publicised cases, much slower to take off. Few authorities engaged in competitive tendering, and even fewer went the further stage of contracting out. By the end of 1985, only two dozen councils had privatised street cleaning or refuse collection, and only half a dozen had contracted out school cleaning or the provision of school meals. These represented little more than normal changes in the mode of services provision, and, indeed, several councils returned to in-house service provision over the same period. However, the compulsory tendering which began to take effect in late 1989 is estimated to have had a significant impact on the employment of manual workers from early 1989 onwards (Local Government Management Board, 1992 and 1993). Employment was reduced both as a consequence of unsuccessful bids by existing employees and as a result of labour shedding by successful in-house teams in an attempt to contain costs.

Labour market deregulation

Deregulation of the labour market was aimed at reducing labour costs and enhancing labour market flexibility, which, by enhancing profitability, it was assumed would encourage more investment and hence economic growth. If was further argued that if the monopoly power of labour in the form of unions were reduced, then cost–push inflation would also be reduced. The aims of weakening the scope for unions' action and preventing wider solidarity action could be viewed as part of the post-1979 governments' more general aims of weakening and localising collective organisation. The policies were pursued by imposing restrictions on union closed shops and on secondary picketing, by providing financial assistance for union ballots, and through enforced secret ballots on strike proposals. The first two administrations also set an example by resisting strikes in the public sector. Because of these developments and because they no longer consulted union leaders over issues of economic policy as once occurred within the framework of the National Economic Development Council, unions lost a substantial degree of their power and influence during the 1980s.

Governments also sought to deregulate labour markets by abolishing the 'fair wages resolution' and Wages Councils. The 'fair wages resolution' was abolished in 1980. This protected the wages of public-sector workers in low-paid occupations and the wages of workers in any organisation contracted to do work for central or local government. The Wages Councils were independent bodies comprising representatives of employers and workers under an independent chairperson. The purpose of the Wages Councils was originally to set various rates of pay and conditions in low-paying industries, in which there was little or no union representation, or where unions were weak. There were 26 of these Councils remaining in 1993, when the government announced they were to be abolished. As it was, their powers had been considerably reduced in the Wages Act of 1986 (when the number of inspectors was reduced and young workers were taken out of the net), which virtually confined their role to setting a single hourly rate of pay and overtime premium for their respective industries.

Even though eschewing formal incomes policy, governments have still sought to encourage wage restraint. In 1992, with a large rise in the public sector borrowing rate (PSBR) and worries about the contribution of the public-sector pay rises to the size of the borrowing requirement, the government sought to impose a 1.5 per cent pay ceiling throughout the public sector for 1992/3. In the years following this initiative, the government announced it was freezing the public-sector pay bill, thus substantially constraining the wage increases that can be awarded to public-sector workers. The Chancellor of the Exchequer in the new Labour administration that took office in May 1997, in his first pre-Budget statement, emphasised the need for 'wage responsibility', wage moderation, in all sectors of the economy.

Deregulation and marketisation has led to re-organisation of the way work is done in the public-services organisations. First, the creation of a customer culture in response to market pressures has driven management to seek ways of responding more flexibly to market demand. Second, the decentralisation of managerial authority has increased pressures for local adaptations in working practice to suit local circumstances. Third, even when changes are technologically driven, as in telecommunications, privatisation has often shifted the balance of power away from unions towards management. Fourth, the growth of market mechanisms has altered managerial work. Managers key responsibilities and the terms of their employment are now more likely to be explicitly codified in a personal contract, which often provides the basis for setting personal targets through performance appraisal systems.

THE IMPACT OF THE REFORMS ON ORGANISATIONS

These reforms have changed the environment within which firms operate. They can be evaluated in terms of their impact on both the external macro-economic environment and the internal climate, and we look at each below.

The external environment

There seems to be little doubt that supply-side policies have been associated with improvements in economic performance in a number of key areas. Virtually all estimates suggest that the structural rate of unemployment, otherwise known as the natural rate of unemployment, has fallen since the late 1980s and, according to the OECD (1996: 22), '[the] objective has been realised. Inflation is now below 3 per cent and trend unemployment is falling, implying an improving "tradeoff" since the mid-1980s.' Reform of the social security system has also all but eliminated the extreme form of the unemployment trap, although the disincentives to work facing some groups are still pronounced. Nevertheless, the OECD (1996: 82) claim that 'the tax-transfer system in place is basically sound'.

However, the reforms have also had various negative effects. The environment of intensified competition and of enhanced shareholder/customer expectations has resulted in cost cutting and labour shedding, especially in the public services, which has had a direct effect on the employment and pay prospects and the working conditions of large numbers of people. In some areas, unions have been enfeebled and with the agenda of change increasingly dictated by managers, no 'countervailing power' is evident. Wage and income dispersion has increased, long-term unemployment remains a problem while it has been estimated that the NAIRU (non-accelerating inflation rate of unemployment) is still unacceptably high. This section briefly summarises the main macro-economic impacts of the reforms in each area.

Employment

- There have been significant reductions in employment in privatised companies and in the marketised public services.
- There has been an increase in the proportion of staff employed in a managerial capacity in many parts of the public sector at the same time as the private sector was reducing management overhead costs that may be reflected in prices.
- Set against these, total unemployment has fallen since 1993 and job creation has increased employment over the period 1993–5 by about 2.4 per cent (OECD, 1996: 107).

Labour supply

- The extent to which tax cuts have affected behavioural changes, and in particular increased work incentives for the majority of the population, remains unclear. There is evidence of a moderate behavioural response to the reductions in higher rates of income tax in the 1979 Budget (Dilnot and Kell, 1988) but little else.
- Married women are the group that appear to be most responsive to tax reforms but the income effects seem to, in large part, cancel out increased labour supply in response to marginal tax reductions with the result that the net increase in supply from this group may be small (Blundell, 1992).

Market rates of pay

- Compulsory tendering has exerted substantial downward pressure on wages both where private-sector firms have taken over services and where contracts have been retained in-house (Colling and Ferner, 1995) The abolition of the 'fair wages resolution' in 1980 magnified this effect.
- Regulatory and collective bargaining changes have considerably narrowed the scope and influence of wage protection mechanisms in the UK.

Low-paid workers

- The incidence of low-paid jobs in the UK is the third largest in any country in the OECD (OECD, 1996).

Wage dispersion

- The distribution of earnings widened in the UK during the 1980s and 1990s (OECD, 1993, 1996). This has been attributed to:

  Moves away from national- and industry-level wage setting (Leslie and Pu, 1996).

  The elimination of minimum wages as a result of the abolition of wage councils (Machin and Manning, 1994; Machin, 1997).

  Inequality in full-time disposable earnings which increased during the 1980s, chiefly due to the tax and benefit reforms (Johnson and Webb, 1992).

  Decentralisation in the civil service (Elliott and Bender, 1997).

Distribution of income

- Tax and transfer reforms contributed to rising income inequality (Blundell and Preston, 1995; Goodman and Webb, 1994; Giles and Johnson, 1994).
- 30 per cent of the income growth in the 1980s went to the richest 5 per cent of the population (Jenkins and Cowell, 1994).
- The extreme form of the poverty trap, where marginal tax rates exceed 100 per cent was eliminated, but high marginal tax rates, those of over 80 per cent, affect a larger group (Dilnot and Webb, 1988).
- The number of families with incomes below the supplementary benefit line increased by 18 per cent between 1979 and 1987 (Johnson and Webb, 1990).

Industrial relations

- The proportion of work places with recognised unions fell from 64 per cent in 1980 to 53 per cent by 1990 (Milward *et al.*, 1992).
- Unionisation fell from 39 per cent of all employees in 1989 to 32 per cent in 1995 (HMSO, 1996).
- In the first half of the 1990s, labour disputes in the UK private sector fell below the OECD average (HMSO, 1996).

The internal environment

The environment within which organisations will structure their reward strategies at the end of the 1990s is far less circumscribed by legal regulation, and by statutory and collective bargaining provisions than at any time in the last two decades. But the changes in patterns of work that this greater flexibility has produced and the greater diversity of rewards that are evident in the market place present new challenges to management. Reward strategies must be attuned to a more rapidly changing and more diverse environment than has existed in the past fifty years. This changing environment and the opportunities and threats it presents are reported below.

Work organisation

- Managements are now able to achieve greater flexibility in employment and working practices, and to redesign bargaining and consultation machineries to suit their business needs throughout large areas of the public and private sectors, yet the re-organisation of work practices has proceeded at a variable pace in the public sector. Doctors, nurses and school-teachers have all proved effective in moderating the pace of change, but in other areas, such as the civil service, it has continued apace. Further, the complexity of government reforms and the pace at which they have been introduced have placed new demands on public-sector managers. The limited resources available to public-services managers have meant they cannot always implement this radical agenda of change.

- Enhanced labour market flexibility has resulted in greater diversity in working patterns and in the number of part-time jobs and female job holders. This in turn has resulted in a fracturing of traditional patterns of work and labour supply.
- The patterns and distributions of working time have changed, reflecting the greater spread of part-time, short-term and self-employment, but again, affording employers the opportunity to propose new patterns of work and employment.

Pay policy

- The greater diversity in market rates of pay may exert pressure on pay differentials and could disrupt the internal pay structure of established organisations.
- Increasing returns to education and skill reveal a substantial shift in the pattern of the demand for labour. In the face of intensified competition for skills in short supply, organisations must devise reward strategies which enable them to retain their most valued employees.
- The virtual demise of industry-wide bargaining in the private sector means that firms of all sizes must now develop their own coherent and appropriate reward structure.
- In the absence of a structure of collectively bargained minimum rates of pay, there is no simple external guide as to the rates small firms should pay.
- Reward systems focused on attracting women to and retaining women in employment need to be sufficiently sensitive to the changing household context in which such decisions are taken.

Employee relations

- Expectations of job loss may reduce employee commitment and morale and these concerns may be greatest in the public sector (Rubery, 1995).
- The dilution of union influence on bargaining procedures and creeping de-recognition necessitates the construction of alternative mechanisms to enable employees to voice their concerns over pay and conditions.

In summary, the reforms have had far-reaching effects on both the external and internal environments in which firms operate. In areas such as employment, pay and work practices, firms more than ever before have to construct their own systems and strategies.[6] But these new employment policies must avoid creating a climate of fear and insecurity, or the resulting demoralisation of the workforce will in the end prejudice the very productivity gains they seek.

CONCLUSION

So far, it seems clear that the new Labour government is, like its predecessors, concerned to promote labour market flexibility. Indeed, in one important respect, labour market flexibility seems likely to increase as the supply of labour to relatively low paid jobs increases as a result of welfare benefit reform. Moreover, the impact of any change in the level and availability of benefit will be reinforced by the introduction of a minimum wage. Thus, firms are likely to be confronted by an increased supply of labour at the new minimum wage. However, such a change occurs at a time when the pattern of demand continues to swing toward more highly skilled labour. It is by no means clear that the supply of skilled labour will improve dramatically in the short run. Thus, firms need to have a clear strategy for developing and retaining the skills they require. The construction of reward strategies which encourage skill development and worker attachment to the firms will be essential to the success of firms over the next few years.

NOTES

1 For a discussion of the debate surrounding the effectiveness of incomes policies, see Fallick and Elliott (1981).
2 See Fallick and Elliott (1981) for a chronological summary of the principal regulations and exceptions.
3 These reforms rationalised the relationship between the three most important income related benefits. The twin goals of these reforms were poverty prevention/alleviation and improved incentives to work. Under the reforms, entitlements to income support (which replaced supplementary benefit), family credit (which replaced family income support) and housing benefit were put on the same basis. The needs allowances for families of different sizes were brought into line between the various benefits, and the income definitions and the rules relating capital were unified. The idea was to concentrate benefit expenditure on low-income families with children and to this end, resources were shifted away from housing benefit and towards family credit and income support.
4 For a concise summary of the public sector pay reforms, see Elliott (1997) and Elliott and Murlis (1997). For a comparative assessment of the reforms, see Elliott and Bender (1997).
5 See Crouch (1995) for a review of the changes to the management structure in the different areas of the public sector.
6 The reforms already meet many of the OECD Jobs Study (1994) recommendations regarding promotion of labour market flexibility.

LEARNING ACTIVITIES

1 Review the changes that have taken place in your organisational structure and employment patterns within your organisation over the last ten years and identify the extent to which these can be attributed to economic policies pursued by the government.

2 This chapter highlights two of the aims of successive governments over the last 20 years: one is increasing labour flexibility the second is to reduce trade union influence. To what extent have these aims been reflected within your organisation?

3 After many years of de-regulation of the labour market two significant moves towards re-regulation will affect employment in the next decade. These are the introduction of a minimum wage and the working time directive. How do you anticipate these affecting organisations?

4 How has government economic policy of the last 20 years contributed to the development of new and diverse approaches to reward systems?

REFERENCES

Blundell, R. (1992) 'Labour Supply and Taxation: A survey', *Fiscal Studies*, 3: 15–40.

Blundell, R. and Preston, I. (1995) 'Income, Expenditure and the Living Standards of UK Households', *Fiscal Studies*, 16: 40–54.

Colling, T. and Ferner, A. (1995) 'Privatisation and Marketisation', in P. Edwards (ed.), *Industrial Relations, Theory and Practice*. Oxford: Blackwell Publishers.

Crouch, C. (1995) 'The State: Economic Management and Incomes Policy', in P. Edwards (ed.), *Industrial Relations, Theory and Practice*. Oxford: Blackwell Publishers.

Dilnot, A. and Kell, M. (1988) 'Top-Rate Tax Cuts and Incentives: Some empirical evidence', *Fiscal Studies*, 9: 70–92.

Dilnot, A. and Webb, S. (1988) 'The 1988 Social Security Reforms', *Fiscal Studies*, 9: 26–53.

Elliott, R.F. (1997) 'Controlling Personnel Costs in Central Government in the United Kingdom', Budgeting and Monitoring Personnel Costs, Sigma Paper 11: 46–56, Paris: OECD.

Elliott, R.F. and Bender, K.A. (1997) 'Decentralisation and Pay Reform in Central Government: A study of three countries', *British Journal of Industrial Relations*, 35: 447–75.

Elliott, R.F. and Murlis, H. (1997) 'The State of the Art in the Public Sector', in H. Murlis (ed.), *Pay at the Crossroads*. London: Institute of Personnel and Development.

Fallick, J.L. and Elliott, R.F. (1981) *Incomes Policies, Inflation and Relative Pay*. London: George Allen & Unwin.

Giles, C. and Johnson, P. (1994) 'Tax Reform in the UK and Changes in the Progressivity of the Tax System, 1985–95', *Fiscal Studies*, 15: 64–86.

Goodman, A. and Webb, S. (1994) 'For Richer, For Poorer: The changing distribution of income in the UK, 1961–91', *Fiscal Studies*, 15: 29–62.

HMSO (1985) *Reform of Social Security: Programme for action*. London: HMSO.

HMSO (1996) *Labour Market Trends*. London: HMSO.

Ibbs, Sir Robin (1988) *Improving Management in Government: The next steps*. London: HMSO.

Jenkins, S.P. and Cowell, F.A. (1994) 'Dwarfs and Giants in the 1980s: Trends in the UK income distribution', *Fiscal Studies*, 15: 99–118.

Johnson, P. and Webb, S. (1990) 'Low Income Families, 1979–87', *Fiscal Studies*, 11: 44–62.

Johnson, P. and Webb, S. (1992) 'Recent Trends in UK Income Inequality: Causes and policy responses', paper presented at the Royal Economic Society Conference, March.

Leslie, D. and Pu, Y. (1996) 'What Caused Rising Wage Inequality in Britain? Evidence from time series 1970–93', *British Journal of Industrial Relations*, 34: 111–30.

Local Government Management Board (1992) 'Survey of the Employment Effects of Central Government Initiatives', London: Local Government Management Board.

Local Government Management Board (1993) 'CCT Information Service', Survey Report No. 8, London: Local Government Management Board.

Machin, S. (1997) 'The Decline of Labour Market Institutions and the Rise in Wage Inequality in Britain', *European Economic Review*, 41: 647–57.

Machin, S. and Manning, A. (1994) 'The Effects of Minimum Wages on Wage Dispersion and Employment: Evidence from UK wage councils', *Industrial and Labour Relations Review*, 37: 319–29.

Milward, N., Stevens, M., Smart, D. and Hawes, W.R. (1992) *Workplace Industrial Relations in Transition*. Aldershot: Dartmouth Publishing.

OECD (1993) *Employment Outlook*. Paris: OECD.

OECD (1994) *The OECD Jobs Study: Evidence and explanations*. Paris: OECD.

OECD (1996) *OECD Economic Surveys: United Kingdom*. Paris: OECD.

Rubery, J. (1995) 'The Low-Paid and the Unorganised', in P. Edwards (ed.), *Industrial Relations, Theory and Practice*. Oxford: Blackwell Publishers.

FURTHER READING

Blaug, M. (1997) *Economic Theory in Retrospect*. Fifth edition, Cambridge: Cambridge University Press.

Edwards, P. (1995) *Industrial Relations, Theory and Practice*. Oxford: Blackwell.

Murlis, H. (ed.) (1997) *Pay at the Crossroads*. London: IPD.

5 Motivation and reward

Angela Bowey and Richard Thorpe

INTRODUCTION

To be effective, remuneration systems need to be based on a sound understanding of how people at work are motivated. HRM practitioners will, however, be under no illusion that this is an extremely complex topic and as, Pfeffer (1996) points out, reward systems used by employers have often been based on simplistic motivation theories, and have often failed. This chapter offers an overview of the most significant contributions to the theory of motivation. We then attempt to draw links between the assumptions made about reward motivation theory and reward strategy, and to explore the strategy for integrating reward systems into strategies for changing other human resource management systems.

Payment-by-results systems of various kinds are still extensively used in Britain, with around 30 per cent of the male workforce covered by such schemes and some 20 per cent of the female workforce (New Earnings Survey, 1997). In the United States, the figure is somewhat also significant, illustrating the reliance placed on pay as a means of motivating high performance.

Theories of motivation to work have passed through many stages, and, over the last decade, have influenced and been influenced by the prevailing management ideologies and philosophies of each era. Although we can trace the sequence of this development, it does not mean that the old theories have died and gone away. On the contrary, what we have learnt is that managers are extremely confident in their beliefs about what motivates, whether these beliefs are based on research evidence, or just personal experience or folk lore (Pfeffer, 1998). This lower level of understanding of how reward systems work to affect behaviour can be blamed partly on the confusion generated by so many opposing theories of motivation, partly on real life offering conflicting examples, and partly on research evidence not being disseminated properly over the years.

PAYMENT SYSTEM DEVELOPMENTS – THE HISTORICAL CONTEXT

Scientific Management and Rational Economic Man

If we go back to the management practices and theories that existed before 1940, we would find that the predominant theory about employee motivation was the classical 'scientific' management approach. This view held that, since employees came to work to earn money, they would work better if they were given more money for increased performance. Incentive payment schemes were therefore devised to reward extra work with extra pay, and a great deal of interest was aroused and effort expended in determining the best way to relate the two. The most basic form was piecework whilst other schemes paid a basic hourly rate for performance up to some standard level, with additional premium or bonus payments for higher rates of working. Gearing of various kinds was also a feature. This adjusted the relationship between the work rate and bonus earned, in that the relationship between pay and effort was not from a straight proportional one. 'More than proportional' schemes yielded more income for a given amount of effort than 'directly proportional' ones. This theory, that money provided the motivation to work, was rooted in the belief that employees made rational choices. As a consequence, employers did not doubt that their employees were doing their best to work as hard as they could. But differences in productivity were still observed between different factories. The conclusion drawn, which was consistent with the 'theory' of the day, was that some workers must be being impeded in their efforts to work hard by factors beyond their control of which fatigue was considered to be the most likely.

As a consequence, and again in keeping with the 'scientific' research approaches of the time, interest focused on ways to improve productivity by reducing the causes of worker fatigue. These studies were conducted on both sides of the Atlantic – here by the Industrial Fatigue Research Board. By far the more influential – mainly because of the weight of their academic press – was, however, research conducted in the United States, at Harvard Business School.

Studies conducted in organisations in the 1920s examined the effects of giving workers more frequent rest pauses, varying the temperature or humidity, adjusting the intensity of the lighting, providing free meals and so on. This early research appeared to confirm that differing performance levels were due to physical or psychological factors. Elton Mayo and his colleagues from Harvard studied a Philadelphia textile mill where the company introduced more frequent rest periods, gave free meals and shortened the working day. The predominantly female workers responded by improving their rates of working. When the company took away the new benefits, they fell back to working at their former rate.

Mayo and his colleagues then set up a major series of studies at the Hawthorne works of the Western Electric Company to more scientifically study the effect of fatigue-inducing factors on productivity, and to study worker behaviour in detail. These studies went on for almost ten years, and subsequently became so famous as to become part of the folklore of management, adding terms such as 'the Hawthorne effect' to managers' everyday language (Landsberger, 1958). As the studies developed and new insights were gained, so the methods of research changed to take account of and better reflect the phenomena they were studying. For example, as the researchers' focus of attention moved from the physical and psychological to the social and anthropological aspects of individuals, the research methods became more qualitative and less experimental. Natural settings were used and control groups abandoned. The main finding was that relationships between people at work had a far greater effect on job performance than did any of the fatigue-inducing factors tested or the financial incentives built into the company's payment system. Pfeffer (1998) reiterates these points in a recent *Harvard Business Review* article. In some of the experiments, the working environment was changed drastically to assess how it would influence productivity. For example, the lighting was changed in small stages, first increasing it to a high intensity and then gradually reducing it to little more than moonlight. Through all the changes, the productivity of the employees rose steadily, due mainly to the effect on morale of the new relationships established both within the groups and between the researchers and the group (the Hawthorne effect).

These results together with other evidence about how employees behave under incentive conditions (Roy, 1952) led managers to reject the prescribed 'wisdom' which held that incentives improved productivity, and to turn instead to 'human relations' as the answer to the question, 'How do I motivate my employees to produce superior performance?'

Human relations

Following the results outlined above, thousands of managers and supervisors were sent on training courses to learn how to improve their relationships with other staff. Others, meanwhile, preferred to stick doggedly to the view that money was the best way to motivate people. During this period (the 1940s and 1950s), then, managers believed that there could only be one answer to the problem of motivation, and they sought simple panaceas to guide their actions. Even now, the great majority of managers in Britain, the United States and, quite worryingly, Central and Eastern Europe (as well as other developing countries) believe that there is one best way to motivate employees to work well, whether through financial reward, job design, conducive working environments, good human relations, enriched jobs, participation, or any of several other factors.

An example is perhaps useful here to show how panaceas are not always appropriate. The human relations management movement believed that conflict in the work place was a bad thing and could be the cause of poor work performance. As a consequence a manager wishing to improve productivity should concentrate on resolving conflict at work, and establishing sound and friendly relationships with and between their staff. In some situations this works well but not in all. One example might be a manager voicing concern for an individual whose colleague has just been made redundant! In a famous example of Angela Bowey's, a manager of a small UK garment factory built a wall between two departments in order to reduce what he perceived to be arguments between employees, only to find that productivity dropped rather than improved. This was because the conflict had in fact been about the slow pace of work in one of the departments, the conflict had been the only thing to maintain pressure on this department to produce, and thus to allow the other neighbouring department to make a reasonable bonus.

The motivation theories that underpinned or built upon the 'human relations' findings belonged to the behavioural school and had as their new focus the search for the satisfaction of human needs. This approach swept through management thinking in the 1950s and 1960s. The field, as usual, was dominated by the North Americans and in many ways reflected, as it still does today, their own cultural context. Although the findings of their research are often viewed as universal truths, they have been criticised on cultural as well as methodological grounds (Hofstede, 1980, 1991).

Maslow (1954), for example, offered his '*needs hierarchy*' which claims that human beings have their needs arranged in a hierarchy such that they are motivated to seek satisfaction of the lower levels first. Once that level of need is satisfied it is no longer a motivator, and the person is motivated by the next level in the hierarchy. Basic needs such as shelter, food and warmth are in the bottom level, followed by physical well-being, social acceptance and self-esteem with '*self-actualisation*' (realising one's own potential at the top).

Herzberg, Mausner and Snyderman (1959), another American writer/researcher from this period, theorised that human beings needed to satisfy '*hygiene factors*' before they would begin to work at superior levels of performance. He argued that individuals would only work at what he called a '*performance-motivated performance*' by the fulfilment of so-called '*motivator factors*', achieved primarily through enriched jobs.

McGregor (1957) warned us against Theory X (the view that people are lazy and reluctant to work unless threatened, cajoled or offered incentives) and offered us Theory Y, with its emphasis on people's need for achievement and satisfaction from a job done well. McClelland (1967), following the work of Murray in the 1930s, emphasised the importance of needs for achievement, power and affiliation.

All these writers were the glamorous management gurus of the 1960s. Their theories were simple, their remedies straightforward. If you followed Maslow then you accepted his assurance that most Western working people already had most of their basic needs satisfied, so could not be motivated by money (which can buy basic necessities but not relationships, affection, self esteem, etc.). Managers following this theory turned their attention to providing more satisfactory relationships, more interesting work and more opportunities for self-fulfilment. Employers who followed Herzberg also rejected money as a motivator, and focused their efforts on providing more enriched jobs and greater satisfaction from work. McGregor led managers to provide opportunities for reward and satisfaction from a job well done. McClelland focused attention on giving people the opportunity to satisfy their needs for achievement, power and affiliation.

Like many management ideas, theories and tools, much of the literature is written from an 'upstream' position simply focusing on what the idea or concept will do; there are few 'downstream' evaluations of what has actually happened to organisations following the implementation of a particular idea or theory.

It was not until the 1970s that case studies of organisations which had followed these exhortations began to be published. Unlike the first rash of converts, whose massive efforts and successful results had contributed to the popularity of the 'needs' approach in the 1960s, these second-generation studies showed very mixed results. There were job-enrichment programmes which resulted in most of the staff leaving; human relations programmes which reduced conflict but caused output to fall; and companies which, having removed incentive payment systems, found they could not manage the resulting need for more directive supervision. At the same time, there were other companies achieving the good results promised of the programmes they introduced.

Contingency theory

By the 1960s, there was considerable confusion and debate about the relative value of incentive bonus schemes and human relations management, and a number of studies conducted indicated that the same management practice could be a resounding success in one organisation and a miserable failure in another. For some time, as is common when paradigms change, the proponents of each technique blamed the failure on ineptness of application. Again, this is a standpoint still held by many managers. But, in the light of evidence that improvements in productivity can be obtained with one technique in one situation and a different technique in another, it gradually became clear that there could be no single panacea for low motivation among employees. Contingency theory was therefore developed as a response.

Joan Woodward (1958) was one of the first researchers to produce the kind of evidence that showed how contingency theory operated. In her example she examined organisation structure and technology. Classifying organisations into technological types (from batch through to mass production and continuous process) she found that the most successful firms in each category conformed closely to the typical structure for that technology (in terms of features like levels in the hierarchy, spans of control, the ratio of industrial workers to staff and so on). Her work suggested that a company that wished to be successful ought to match its structure to its technology.

At about the same time, Burns and Stalker (1961) made similar discoveries in their studies of textile mills and electronics factories. They found that firms in the electronics industry operating with '*organic*' management systems (characterised by loosely defined responsibilities and relationships, free communications, and co-operation across hierarchical and divisional boundaries) were more successful than those using the alternative '*mechanistic*' management systems (typified by clearly defined duties, responsibilities and authority; specific chains of command; and structured channels of communication). Yet in the textile industry, the reverse was true; the 'mechanistic' firms were more successful than the 'organic' ones. The major differences between textiles and electronics, which Burns and Stalker put forward as the reason for these results, were rate of change and degree of uncertainty. These were held to be greater in the electronics industry and its market than in textiles. Rapid change and uncertainty were handled better by an organisation with a flexible structure, one capable of learning from and adapting in response to information and knowledge that arose from anyone at any organisational level. In textiles, however, where everything was much more certain 'organic' systems resulted only in time being wasted on unnecessary communications and conflict resolution (at least at that time).

Just as the work of Woodward and Burns and Stalker, showed that the principles of designing organisations for high effectiveness varied with the nature of the industry, and its technology and environment, so those searching for the key to high productivity reached the conclusion that factors which produced this in one situation could be different from those which did so in another.

One of the clearest examples of this and one which also demonstrates the importance of social context, was in a television components factory in the North West of

England, where Milward and Legge were asked to help the management to understand why some of the young women they employed seemed to be highly motivated by the incentive bonus scheme, whilst others working alongside them showed no interest in it at all. They found that when a young woman first left school and started work, she took her unopened pay packets to her mother, who gave her daughter a fixed sum as her pocket money. The younger workers consequently had little interest in the bonus system because they did not benefit from it; their mothers keeping the variable part of their pay. At the age of about 18, young women were allowed to open their own pay packets and give their mothers a fixed sum for board and lodgings. At this point, they became more concerned about higher earnings (Milward, 1968).

This and other research which also showed different factors affecting motivation and productivity in different people and organisations, led to the development of a 'contingency' approach to payment system design. This would produce the desired result in any particular set of circumstances.

Other researchers have also reported variations in motivators. In his sample of several thousand managers, Michael White (1973) found that he could show six distinctive patterns of motivation. Material rewards, status and prestige, social issues, job interest, variety and challenge and leadership. Blackburn and Mann (1979) too found in a sample of 1,000 low-skilled workers a wide range of 'orientations', or motivations to work. These included such things as pay, hours of work, promotion opportunities, autonomy, work location (indoors or out), intrinsic features of the work, how worthwhile the work was perceived to be, relationships with colleagues and working conditions. Nichols (1981) also showed the range of *satisfactions* miners gained from work, many of which had little bearing on the incentive bonus scheme in place.

All these studies support the 'contingency theory' approach, which suggests that management strategies (including payment systems) should be designed specifically to suit the particular characteristics of the organisation, and its employees and managers.

However, the picture is even more complicated by the fact that there is also a body of research which indicates that needs are neither instinctive nor fixed for individuals. They vary with changes in personal circumstance and with development, and can be modified by making desired rewards more or less available. White's study showed that the managers who were most likely to be motivated by security and social needs were those who had reached a peak in their careers and for whom some of the other motivators were no longer available. Job interest was a motivator for people who had interesting jobs, variety and challenge were motivators for people with challenging jobs and so on. In many cases, it is impossible to ascertain which came first, that motivation or the choice of career. Schein (1980) would suggest that motivation stems from an enduring *'career anchor'*. But, if this were true, people might, equally, adapt their needs to match the rewards available. It would explain why Goldthorpe *et al.* (1968) had found so many Luton car assembly workers motivated by the high wages they could earn in their boring, repetitive jobs rather than choosing more interesting work for lower pay. Their motivational needs were largely being met outside the factory.

The Wage Payment Systems Research Team led by Tom Lupton at Manchester Business School, conducted a series of studies of payment systems in order to learn about the factors which could influence the way a pay system operated. This work led to proposed guidelines for the design of wage systems, which took account of some 29 organisational and environmental factors known to have an influence on wage system effectiveness

(Lupton and Bowey, 1974). For each kind of payment system, the Manchester Business School team set out to produce information for determining when a situation was suited to the introduction of a particular kind of scheme. This 'contingency approach' was entirely consistent with the work being done in other fields of management at the time – for example, by Fiedler on managerial style (Fiedler and Chemers, 1974); by Morris and Burgoyne on management development (Morris and Burgoyne, 1973); by Lawrence and Lorsch on organisation design (Lawrence and Lorsch, 1967); and by Vroom and Yetton on leadership (Vroom and Yetton, 1973). Each of these studies was examining the links between alternative management practices (in each specialist field), relevant organisational and environmental characteristics (measurement of which is not as simple as it at first sight appears), and the effects on the organisation's performance. Their findings were always intended to be of practical relevance to managers wishing to choose or design the most suitable and effective management techniques for the particular contingent characteristics of their own organisation and its situation. So what can we conclude from all this? The first conclusion is that we cannot accept uncritically any simple model which seeks to explain human motivation as deriving from generally applicable needs, such as for money, achievement, interesting work, or relationships at work. People both between and within organisations have differing needs. A final conclusion to this could of course be that we need a 'contingency' approach that produces reward systems tailored to each individual's needs – like cable television! But, unlike television producers, HR managers would find this a nightmare, and it has never been seriously advocated except for fringe benefits ('The Cafeteria Plan', see Thierry, 1978).

The second conclusion is that it may be possible to encourage people to seek the rewards employers are able or willing to offer. Employees do not expect individually tailored rewards and there is ample evidence that some organisations have motivated their employees with money, some have motivated them with enriched jobs, some with growth opportunities, some with improved relationships and so on.

A constructivist perspective – the importance of process

Our own contribution to the evidence took place in the late 1970s, at a time when many new payment systems were being designed because of the governments prices and incomes policy. We set out to design a research project based on the contingency model of payment systems. At the time we hoped it would produce evidence of the links between pay systems appropriate to the situation, resulting in improvement in performance. As we expected, the findings gave very little support to the view that the type of payment system has a major effect on the results achieved. All kinds of payment systems we studied both succeeded and failed in different organisations. Many produced benefits, but often not those the scheme was designed to deliver, and there were some objectives towards which certain types of scheme tended to contribute better than others. One of the major findings of the study was that payment systems do not fall neatly into categories, but, in fact, vary in a multitude of respects – time, size, basis of payment, measures used and so on. This makes designing a suitable payment system much more complicated.

Surprisingly, the study produced little evidence to support a contingency model of payment system results. Neither did the effects of a given payment scheme become significantly more similar when our sample was re-analysed, holding various aspects of organisation and environment constant. This suggests that, at least for our sample during the period 1977–80, it was not true that the most effective systems were those best suited to the traditional contingencies of the organisation and its environment (size, technology, market, industry, rate of change, etc.). If we draw on the prevailing theories of management, this finding could perhaps be explained by Child's assertion that strategic decision makers often intervene between the management practice and organisational context, inhibiting or preventing any natural gravitation of organisations towards the most appropriate practice for their situation. But, from our findings, we can perhaps explain more than Child's view of 'strategic contingencies' (Child, 1972).

Our findings suggest that a major factor in the degree of success of schemes was the amount of time and effort expended by management on the scheme, in the planning and design and in consultation. Consultation produced a better understanding of individuals and the organisation and, as a direct consequence, allowed the views and issues put forward by managers, supervisors, employees and their representatives to be taken into account. This helped communication – both downwards, of the organisation's priorities for success, and upwards, of just what would be the most appropriate measures on which to base payment systems so as to ensure that they met the strategic priorities of the organisation.

Through our case studies, we recognise that the means by which these benefits can be realised require considerable time and effort together with a research approach that can map and make sense of the perspectives of a wide range of individuals within an organisation. The implicit motivation theory in use here is a behavioural or phenomenological one. It suggests that improved motivation is achieved by managers and staff developing increased critical awareness through more information and better understanding. Change is no longer something that is imposed on them from outside. The process is one that reduces the reactance of individuals to change.

Table 5.1 illustrates eight theories of motivation and their implications for pay systems. The first two relate to the economic theories based on the psychological rationality of individuals. These theories assume that simple logic will predict and dictate individuals' behaviour in similar situations when faced with incentives. Exhibit 5.1 illustrates the model. Flat weekly wages will ensure attendance, payment by results will ensure output, merit rating will secure appropriate bands of commitment, and profit sharing will ensure that employees put the organisation first.

The Human Relations school suggests that different rewards might motivate people to achieve higher performance. In a review paper, Guest (1984) identified a number of categories under which the various theories of motivation can be grouped. Goodridge (1986) has taken the assumptions behind these different motivation theories and considered how they might relate to different pay systems. Theories relating to needs, goals and orientations encompass the ideas of Maslow (1954), Herzberg (1966), Alderfer (1959), and McClelland (1962). In these hierarchical theories of motivation, 'lower-order' needs, such as existence and security signal, are thought to be met by the use of rewards such as basic salary and job security, whereas promotion through salary scales, and fringe benefits, are thought to 'satisfy higher-order' needs.

The second category of Guest's is expectancy theory. This group of theories (Vroom, 1964 and Porter and Lawler, 1968) attempts to show the complexity of the motivational process and the design choices made by employees. In pay terms, these

Table 5.1 Pay linked to specific theories of motivation based on economic, human relations and contingency theory

Motivation theory	Reward system implication
Economic Man	Payments directly linked to measured increments of work, as in payment by results.
Economic Man with periodic fatigue	As above, but with regular rest and meal breaks and possibly subsidised canteens.
Needs, goals and orientations ● Human relations ● Maslow ● Herzberg ● McClelland ● McGregor	Hours or weekly wage/salary with no incentive elements. Emphasis on motivating through human relations skills, job enrichment or opportunities to satisfy higher-order needs, such as achievement.
Expectancy theory	Payments directly linked to effort, care taken to ensure employees believe they can achieve the goals through their efforts, that the rewards are desirable, and that performance will improve, and produce the expected reward if they put in the effort.
Reactance theory	Employees free to choose any kind of reward system, provided there is extensive consultation and involvement of all staff prior to its implementation. People need to feel they have some control over the rewards.
Goal theory ● goals ● targets ● behaviour modification theory	Payments related to achieving goals of modified ways of working, which have been identified as desirable, accepted by the employee, such as pay for performance.
Contingency theory	Rewards systems tailored to an individual's needs. Cafeteria Plans, Different kinds of motivation, offering growth, enriched jobs, salary plans.

Exhibit 5.1

> ## Payment based on motivational assumptions
>
> Flat weekly wage ────────▶ Payment for being present
>
> Payment by results ────────▶ Payment for producing results
>
> Merit rating ────────▶ Payment for 'appropriate' attitude or commitment
>
> Profit sharing────────▶ Payment for putting the organisation first

theories have been used by managers in an attempt to diagnose the perceived link between effort, performance and those rewards considered attractive to individuals. It has been thought that diagnosing such relationships will help to ensure that the rewards offered are sufficiently visible and deliverable. Moreover, there will not only be a perceived link between effort and reward, but also the opportunity for managers to better ensure the likelihood of any particular effort producing a reward. Research has shown that employees may still be motivated by an incentive provided that: employers have ensured that workers understand what rewards will result from higher effort; employers know what the effort required is; employers have provided the facilities to do the job; and employees possess the necessary competence. Where any of these constituents are missing, the attempt to motivate will fail. This does appear to support expectancy theory.

Research by Wannus, Keon and Latack (1983) produced evidence to suggest that employees do not, as the model suggests, rationally weigh up probabilities in the calculation of expectancy but rather base their decisions and actions on things like habit, their own past experience, and the advice and experience of colleagues. There can be little doubt that an employer who spends time ensuring that all the requirements of expectancy theory are met will have undertaken considerable consultation with managers and employees. The good results from this approach are thus quite consistent with the findings of our Strathclyde study which found the successful remuneration schemes to be those where the most time and effort had been spent in consultation and involvement with workers and managers.

The third category Guest cites is Locke's goal theory, 1975. This theory proposed that motivation and the ensuing performance will be higher if feedback is given on performance. It was probably the application of this theory to payment systems that spawned the growth of merit pay linked to appraisals, and there are clear overlaps with aspects of expectancy theory. Latham and Locke (1979) motivated workers with the prospect of achieving relatively difficult goals. This put the source of motivation not on the fulfilment of a 'need' but on the achievement of a goal which they had been involved in setting. Management by objectives was first proposed by Drucker (1964) but became overly bureaucratic and produced poor results. A study of the coal industry (Bowey and Thorpe, 1986) shows the power of incentives based on goals as a motivator. Similar to goal theory are those theories of behaviour modification, such as guidance prompting, feedback and reinforcement.

Reactance theory is Guest's final category. This approach offers a bridge to the notion of authority and control in relation to pay. It suggests that individuals, managers and employees do not passively receive and respond to information as might be thought, but try to make sense of their environment and to reduce uncertainty in order to influence the rewards they gain.

In contingency theory, the rewards are tailored either to an individual's needs, through cafeteria plans to a group's needs, or through a deep understanding of the other ways in which reward might motivate workers, whether in the form of progression, security or pay.

Although these five stages of development in the thinking about payment systems were all based on underlying theories of the motivation to work, they have not always been made explicit. Also, methods of motivating high performance have been developed, based on different theories of motivation. When considering the design of a payment system, it is important to be aware of the limitations of pay and to consider the alternatives which have been developed, such as job enrichment and participation. As enthusiasm for incentive payment systems waxes and wanes, so these alternative approaches become more prominent.

ALTERNATIVE MOTIVATION PRACTICES

As we have discussed, a major problem of using pay to motivate high performance is that money fulfils several different purposes in an organisation. By focusing on designing incentive schemes, it is only too easy to upset the balance of other systems, such as the skill and responsibility hierarchy; recruitment and retention situation; willingness to work overtime; measurements of work or price charged for products or services; recognition of powerful bargaining groups; desirability of promotion; traditional differentials; reward for age or length of service; compensation for working conditions; recognition of merit; and attempts to control inflation.

Money, is of course, used as an indicator as well as an influencing factor for all of these systems and should not be thought of simply as a motivator. Some types of incentive schemes upset these other systems more than others, and the question must be asked whether it is possible to separate out these different purposes, decide on the most important, and try to avoid using money for those where it is unnecessary. As there are many other ways of offering employees rewards, money-based incentive schemes might well fall into this category.

Over the last half of this decade, a great deal of attention has been given to what these other, non-money-based rewards might be. Job enrichment and participation are considered the two major alternatives to incentive payment as ways of motivating employees to improve their performance.

Herzberg, as we have seen, has suggested that money is never in fact a motivator, but only a '*hygiene factor*' which can just as easily demotivate people if it is thought to be inadequate. It is the enriching of their jobs that Pfeffer (1998) believes is the way to motivate. The main shortcoming of this suggestion, as we have already stated, is that it proposes another panacea. It is simply not true that the same solution will work in all situations where human motivation is concerned. People are different in the same way that situations are different, as the studies of White and Goldthorpe showed.

The transfer of responsibility to employees through, for example, delayering or through the use of autonomous working groups has had consequences for the design of jobs – particularly in terms of job enrichment. Two forms of job enrichment are job flexibility, which offers employees the opportunity to undertake different tasks throughout the day, and job enlargement, which increases the range of skills an employee has and as a consequence the range of work an individual can undertake.

In what used to be referred to as job enlargement but is now more usually referred to as multi-skilling, the number of tasks undertaken by the employee is increased to include many more activities. Although one of the reasons why this is done is clearly so the organisation is able to respond more quickly to change, another can be to improve the satisfaction of employees by enlarging the tasks on a job and thereby reducing boredom and gaining benefits through such things as reduced absence or reduced labour turnover. In the early 1970s, young women assembling radios at the Philips Eindhoven factory had their jobs enlarged from repetitively fitting the same parts on each radio to putting together a complete radio. The view was that the quality of working life would be improved, as well as product quality and performance – especially if the work required some discretion or creativity. But the Philips' women were not happy with their newly enriched jobs, and many left. These individuals disliked the additional concentration required by the new jobs, and were apparently happier performing repetitive tasks which left them free to think and talk. This again highlights the danger of making assumptions about what will enrich someone else's job! There is a very real irony in managers designing enrichment into a job and, by so doing, denuding that job of autonomy. Given the correct opportunities, most people can probably think of ways to improve their own jobs, and they do not necessarily appreciate someone else's ideas of an improvement. To give this kind autonomy can reduce the likelihood of 'reactance'.

When multi-skilling involves some degree of self-direction, it is usually referred to as being 'vertical'. Here, responsibilities that were formerly the duties or prerogatives of managers and supervisors, are incorporated into the employee's job (for instance, quality inspection, work allocation within a group and work scheduling). This kind of enrichment can be popular with the recipients. Its most common problem is not the failure of the employees to respond, but the resentment generated among first line managers/supervisors, whose jobs have been denuded through the enrichment. For this reason, it is recommended that any programme of vertical job enrichment should start with re-designing management jobs.

On the theme of re-designing jobs, at whatever organisational level, a word of warning is called for. Reward systems are very often tied to existing work arrangements. If jobs are to be changed, it is desirable to assess how the new jobs will affect the incentive schemes, overtime arrangements, job evaluation systems, promotion procedures and merit and appraisal procedures. Where necessary, systems should be re-designed to fit the new situation. Some of the most successful changes in payment system have been those which were part of a programme of complementary changes introduced by the management – working as a 'systems component' of wider change.

Vertical job enrichment has features in common with some kinds of participation, the other major alternative to incentive payment as a way of motivating higher performance. Both involve employees in decision making which was formerly a management activity. But, whereas job enrichment is usually introduced as a means of improving either efficiency or industrial relations, increased participation is advocated for a wide range of reasons, such as that it is believed it will:

(a) satisfy employee needs or demands and enable management to implement its policies more smoothly and with less resistance, leading to improved efficiency;

(b) enable the organisation to make fuller use of the expertise and knowledge which each employee can contribute, making the system more effective in adapting and improving;

(c) allow differing points of view to be expressed, and decisions made which achieve a compromise between the interests of different groups, avoiding conflict at later stages, when it would be more disruptive;

(d) allow employees more influence over their own working situation and improve both the quality of their working lives and their job satisfaction which, whether or not it leads to improvements in performance, is an important objective in its own right;

(e) allow employees their rightful share of influence and control in the organisation.

As the close of the century approaches many managers believe that participation through job design, participation and other commitment strategies (Walton, 1986) will bring increased efficiency and productivity. In many ways, the popularity of added-value or gain-sharing schemes of various types is associated with the idea of offering employees

Table 5.2 Strategies for competitive advantage from control to commitment in the workplace

	Control	Commitment
Job design	Single job skills Single task Fixed job definition	Multi-job skills Whole task Teams and flexible roles
Performance expectations	Measured standards of output	Measured standards of input
Organisation structure	'Tall and thin' 'Top–down'	'Short and fat' 'Bottom-up'
Management	Positional authority	Problem solving relevant 'expert knowledge' Harmonisation
Compensation policies	Variable pay related to individual effort Pay geared to evaluation	Gain sharing linked to organisation 'goals' Pay geared to skill and mastery
Employee assurances	Employees seen as a variable cost	Employees seen as major assets
Employee participation	On a narrow agenda	Participation encouraged
Labour relations	Adversarial or conflict of interests	Mutuality – joint planning and problem solving

Source: Walton, 1986

opportunities for greater involvement in the success of the whole organisation.

One popular way of improving performance is through empowering employees. The evidence for the success of this method lies in studies of self-directed work groups, for example Hill (1971) and research by Marchington (1977) and Hill (1991) in a factory which introduced participative decision-making linked to a company-wide bonus scheme based on added value. In both cases, participation was introduced as part of a wider package of changes all designed to increase commitment to the organisation and to improve efficiency and productivity. Table 5.2 shows the kind of changes that might need to be made over a number of dimensions. These are not 'pick and mix' alternatives but have an important synergy and coherency which would be undermined by failure to address all dimensions.

Table 5.3 shows the two key dimensions of participation, namely its intensity (ranging from merely informing to handing over complete control to a co-operative) and its content (ranging from aspects of the working environment up to policy decisions). This demonstrates the very wide variety in types of participation, about the values and results of which we still have a great deal to learn.

Participation can have real advantages. The research evidence presented in this chapter shows that the involvement of employees in the design, operation and monitoring of the pay system (whatever its type) considerably improves its chances of success. As a management practice, however, participation suffers from unfortunate ideological connotations, being viewed by some as a threat to managerial prerogatives and the natural order of control.

Table 5.3 Dimensions of participation

A	B	C	D	E
1 *Intensity of Participation*				
informing	consulting	partially sharing decisions	co-determination	worker determination (i.e. co-operative)
2 *Content of participation*				
working environment (e.g. health and safety)	working practices (e.g. work place layout)	management systems and procedures (e.g. job evaluation system)	policy decisions affecting employees directly (e.g. redundancy)	all policy decisions (e.g. investment)

Exhibit 5.2

The importance of pay in management

Purposes of pay:
- recognising what the job deserved (status, skill, responsibility)
- retaining good employees
- motivating high performance
- encouraging interest in promotion
- encouraging loyalty to the company
- rewarding merit generally
- compensation for adverse conditions

At the same time, pay is a key component in:
- controlling costs
- complying with government policy aims
- maintaining a company image

As alternatives to payment, job enrichment and participation have offered alternative methods of motivation and reward and are now a permanent feature of many management strategies.

THE CONTINUED IMPORTANCE OF PAY IN MANAGEMENT

As mentioned in chapter 2, it is important to take a broad view of the role played by pay within management. Pay is one means by which employers seek to control or influence the workforce, managers often relying on it, as we have seen for all kinds of aims within organisations. It is a major component of the employment contract, both formal and informal. Employees work for money and also for other rewards, but, on the whole, they will not work without money. Employers have tended to see money as a tool for achieving numerous and wide-ranging management responsibilities (see exhibit 5.2).

We believe that using money for all these different purposes is often self-defeating. Achieving any one of the objectives depends on paying those employees to whom it applies more money than other employees. But, by paying more money to groups of employees to whom each objective applies, the employer often ends up cancelling out the impact of one differential by superimposing on it another, which may encourage different behaviour. Nevertheless, vast sums of money are spent by British managers on designing, implementing and modifying payment systems.

The attraction of focusing on payment system design, which places a large share of the responsibility for organisational success or failure on the workforce, may be based on the belief that the organisation will succeed if only the employees can be motivated to perform their jobs better. A theme that is developed in other chapters of this book, however, is that quite often payment systems have very little bearing on the real problems in an organisation. Indeed, the pay system may be changed in an attempt to solve a problem which is in fact unrelated. Meanwhile, the solution of problems that the payment system can address frequently does very little to resolve the organisation's real difficulties. The major organisational effort required to change a payment system creates, however, a situation conducive to bringing about other changes. It is the inter-relationship between changes to payment systems and changes to other systems and procedures that produces benefits in those organisations which 'succeed' with a new system of remuneration.

The underlying reason why integrated packages of change incorporating a payment system are associated with greater success is that a payment system designed to motivate employee performance can only form part of the effort–reward bargain. Reward is much broader than pay, and effort involves far more than measured results. Figure 2.2 in chapter 2 showed some of the rewards that employees may seek or may receive from their work experience and, on the right-hand side, the various dimensions of effort which the organisation may need. One of the problems with much past work on payment systems is that focusing narrowly on pay, risks missing the opportunity to contribute to employee motivation through some of the other reward systems – which may even cause frustration. And a narrow focus on those aspects of effort which can be measured sometimes makes employees turn all their attention to those efforts, and neglect or refuse to make effort in other possibly more important areas.

For payment systems to succeed, three key measures must be followed. First, there is a need to recognise that you cannot measure everything, and that what you do measure will become important if payment is attached. There is therefore a need to prioritise. Second, these priorities should ideally be related to the priorities of the business; they may be genuinely different between departments (for example, between research and development, and production) and between processes. Third, there is a need to view the organisation's products or services as a process not a series of fragmented activities. Customers buy whole products, the decision to purchase being based not only on the efficiency of accounts in sending out invoices, but also on how they are treated by the salesperson, and the quality of the product.

Much progress has been made in the area of performance measurement in recent years to recognise these issues, the balanced score card (Kaplan and Norton, 1996) 360° assessment and the value chain (Porter, 1985), all recognising the importance of process and the need for qualitative as well as quantitative measures.

CONCLUSION

This chapter has considered different ways in which employers have sought to bring about improvements in productivity, looking first at philosophies and ideologies, and later at the implications for pay design of the main theories of motivation. The contingency approach to pay design, to which we subscribe, suggests that there can be no one answer to the question, 'How do I motivate my employees to work well?' Indeed, the particular characteristics of the employees concerned, the work that they are doing, and the context in which they work will affect both the extent to which they would expect and respond to different kinds of rewards from work, and the extent to which different dimensions of effort are important to their job performance.

The manager who wishes to bring about improvements should therefore take a careful look at their employees, their organisation, and the environment in which they are operating.

However, the results of our own research suggest that even this is not enough. A key factor in the successful design, implementation and operation of a new scheme for motivating employees lies in the process adopted by management. These processes should involve wide discussion of the proposed changes at all levels and with all functions of the organisation, and an integrated programme of complementary changes designed to ensure effective operation of the new scheme.

Although no one approach has been shown to be entirely satisfactory, theories on exactly what motivates people and how they can be most appropriately rewarded do have elements that support one another and that are consistent with empirical research findings. If we take an eclectic approach, we can define the six key principles which might be worthy of incorporation into reward systems strategies. These are illustrated in exhibit 5.3.

Lessons for managers

The views about payment system design that we summarise here are not the dominant ones to be found in British management today. Theories about pay and motivation have been through many phases in the second half of the decade, and there is a wide spectrum of views among managers concerning the role which payment systems can play in relation to employee job performance and concerning the design of payment systems.

Managers may, at some stage in their careers, have experienced a particular type of payment system which they considered successful, perhaps because of a particular 'industry recipe' (Spender, 1982). They then transfer this particular payment system design to another situation, believing unquestionably that it is the best, and ignoring both culture and circumstances. This also applies to managers who have been convinced by the exposition of a particular system either in texts or at seminars. Wise managers meanwhile recognise that the best design for a payment system will greatly depend on the circumstances in which it is to be applied, and do not try to impose favour or fashion without careful analysis.

A final point for managers to bear in mind is that pay design requires as much if not more effort from supervisors and managers as from the workers they are managing. Too often in the past, poor performance has been blamed entirely on employees,

Exhibit 5.3

Key principles for possible incorporation into reward systems strategies

1 Involvement
Employees should be involved in the development of any new remuneration system and consulted about problems they may foresee. They should be encouraged to develop a commitment to the success of the system, and a sense of ownership which will carry it through its teething difficulties (from reactance theory, goal theory and expectancy theory).

2 Demotivators
All the difficulties which prevent workers from achieving high levels of performance should be removed. It is no use trying to motivate high performance if employees' efforts to perform well are frustrated by not having the right amount and quality of equipment, space, materials, spare parts, instructions, support systems, co-operation from others or other required resources (from expectancy theory, behaviour modification theory and reactance theory).

3 Equity
Any performance standards which are to be applied to goals, targets or behaviour changes for the remuneration calculations should be fair, i.e. comparable for all employees doing the same job in the same organisation (from equity theory, referred to in chapter 1).

4 Reinforcement
Procedures should be put in place with care to give employees reinforcement, encouragement, guidance and feedback, so that they are aware of their employers' interest in their performance and they can quickly learn how to earn the desired reward (from expectancy theory, also behaviour modification theory and reactance theory).

5 Relevance of reward
Time should be spent making sure employees are interested in earning the proposed rewards (from expectancy theory and contingency theory).

6 Goals
Employees should be consulted about the goals, targets or behaviour changes which will earn the reward, and these should be made as specific and clear as possible (from goal theory, expectancy theory and reactance theory).

and only recently have writers recognised that poor employee performance is often related to poor management. Seeking to motivate employees is a red herring that is sometimes used to turn attention on others, rather than managers facing up to their own responsibilities in this area.

LEARNING ACTIVITIES

1 Using table 5.1, analyse your organisation's human resource strategies in terms of control and/or commitment.

2 Using the profile gained from exercise make a contrast between this and objectives of your organisations reward strategy. Assess the degree of 'fit'.

3 Using the information gained in question 1, analyse the assumptions that underlie your firm's approach to the psychology of the individuals who work there that underpin your organisation's reward strategies.

4 Using the six principles in exhibit 5.3, discuss how an effective practical process for determining reward strategy might be constructed.

REFERENCES

Alderfer, C.P. (1959) 'Job Enlargement and the Organisational Context', *Personnel Psychology*, March.

Blackburn, R.M. and Mann, M. (1979) *The Working Class in the Labour Market*. London: Macmillan.

Bowey, A.M., Thorpe, R. with Hellier, P. (1986) *Payment in Systems and Productivity*. London: Macmillan.

Brown, W. (1982) *Piecework Abandoned*. Heinemann.

Brun, W.J. ed. (1992) 'Performance Measurement, Evaluation and Incentives', Harvard Business School, Cambridge, HA.

Burns, T. and Stalker, G. (1961) *The Management of Innovation*. London: Tavistock.

Child, J. (1972) 'Organisation Structure, Environment and Performance: The role of strategic choice', *Sociology*, 6(1): 1–22.

Davis, T.R. (1996) 'Developing an Employee Balances Scorecard: Linking front line performance to corporate objectives', *Management Decision*. MCB University Press.

Drucker, P. (1964) *Management for Results: Economic tasks and risk-taking decision*. New York: Harper & Row.

Fiedler, F.E. and Chemers, M. (1974) *Leadership and Effective Management*. Illinois: Scott, Foresman, Glenview.

Goldthorpe, J. *et al.* (1968) *The Affluent Worker*. Cambridge: Cambridge University Press.

Gomez-Meija, L.R. and Balkin, D.B. (1992) *Compensation, Organisational Strategy and Firm Performance*. South Western Publishing.

Goodridge, M. (1986) 'Practical Payment Systems: Training for the future', Industrial Relations Services and Employment Relations Workshop, Oxford.

Guest, D. (1984) 'What's New in Motivation?', *Personnel Management*, May.

Harvard Business Review, (1991) 'Managing Change: A collection of articles', Harvard Business Publishing.

Herzberg, F. (1966) *Work and the Nature of Man*. Ohio: World Publishing.

Herzberg, F. (1966) 'One more time: How do you motivate employees?', *Harvard Business Review*, January 1968 (reprinted in same journal in September 1987).

Herszberg, F., Mausner, B. and Snydermann, B.B. (1959) *The Motivation to Work*. Second edition, New York: Wiley.

Hill, P. (1971) *Towards a New Philosophy of Management*. Epping: Gower Press.

Hill, S. (1991) 'How Do You Manage a Flexible Firm: The total quality model', *Work, Employment and Society*, 5(3): 397–415.

Hofstede, G. (1980) *Culture's Consequences: International differences in world-related values*. London: Sage.

Hofstede, G. (1991) *Cultures and Organisations: Software of the Mind*. London: McGraw Hill.

IRR (1984) 'Productivity Circles at John G Kincaid', *Industrial Relations Review and Report*, no 325, August.

Kaplan, R.S. and Norton, D.P. (1996) 'Using the Balanced Scorecard as a Strategic Management System', *Harvard Business Review*, Jan.–Feb.

Kessler, I. (1994) 'Performance Related Pay: Contrasting approaches', *Industrial Relations Journal*, 25: 2.

Kessler, I. and Purcell, J. (1994) 'Performance Related Pay: Objectives and application', *Human Resource Management Journal*, 2: 3.

Landsberger, H.A. (1958) *Hawthorne Revisited*. Ithaca.

Latham, G.P. and Locke, E.A. (1979) 'Goal Setting – A Motivational Technique that Works', *Organisational Dynamics*, 8.

Lawler, E.E. III (1971) *Pay and Organisational Effectiveness: Psychological view*. New York: McGraw Hill.

Lawler, E.E. III (1988) 'Pay for Performance: Making it work', *Personnel*, October.

Lawrence, P.W. and Lorshe, J.W. (1967) *Organisation and Environment: Managing differentation and integration*. Homewood, Illinois: Irwin.

Locke, E.A. (1976) 'The Nature and Causes of Job Satisfaction', in Marvin D. Dunnette (ed.), *Handbook of Industrial and Organisational Psychology*. Chicago: Rand McNally, pp. 1300–7.

Lupton, T. (1963) *On the Shop Floor*. Pergamon.

Lupton, T. (1968) *Payment Systems*. Harmondsworth: Penguin.

Lupton, T. (1974) *Management and the Social Sciences*. Harmondsworth: Penguin.

Lupton, T. and Bowey, A. (1974) *Wages and Salaries*. Harmondsworth: Penguin (second edition by Gower Press in 1983).

Marchington, M. (1977) 'Worker participation and plan-wide incentive schemes', *Personnel Review*, 6, Summer: 3.

Maslow, A.H. (1954) *Motivation and Personality*. New York: Harper & Row.

Mayo, Elton, (1949) *Hawthorne and the Western Electric Company, The Social Problems of an Industrial Civilisation*. London: Routledge.

McClelland, D.C. (1962) 'Business Drive and National Achievement', *Harvard Business Review*, 40, July–August.

McClelland, D.C. (1967) *The Achieving Society*. New York: Free Press.

McClelland, D.C. (1975) *Power: The inner experience*. New York: Irvington.

McGregor, D.M. (1957) 'An Uneasy Look at Performance Appraisal', *Harvard Business Review*, 35: 3.

Milkovich, G. and Newman, J. (1996) *Compensation*. Fifth edition, New York: McGraw Hill.

Milward, N. (1968) 'Family Status and Behaviour at Work', *Sociological Review*, 16: 2.

Morris, J. and Burgoyne, J. (1973) *Developing Resourceful Managers*. London: Institute of Personnel Management.

New Earnings Survey (1997) Part D. 'Analysis by Occupation', Office for National Statistics.

Nichols, G. (1981) *A Study of the National Coal Board's Productivity Bonus Scheme*, M.S.c. thesis, Strathclyde University – Business School.

Peters, T.J. and Waterman, R.H. (1982) *In Search of Excellence: Lessons from America's best-run companies*. New York: Harper & Row.

Pfeffer, J. (1998) 'Six Dangerous Myths about Pay', *Harvard Business Review*, May–June.

Porter, L.W. and Lawler, E.E. (1968) *Managerial Attitudes and Performance*. Homewood: Irwin.

Porter, M.E. (1985) *Competitive Advantage: Creating and sustaining superior performance*. New York: Free Press.

Roethlisberger, F.J. and Dixon, W.J. (1939) *Management and the Worker*. Cambridge, MA: Harvard University Press.

Roy, D. (1952) 'Quota restriction and gold-bricking in a machine shop', *American Journal of Sociology*, 57: 427–42.

Roy, D. (1953) 'Work Satisfactions and Social Reward in Quota Achievement: An analysis of piecework incentives', *American Sociological Review*, 18: 4.

Roy, D. (1954) 'Efficiency and the "Fix"', *American Journal of Sociology*, 64: 255–66.

Schein, E. (1980) *Organisational Psychology*, Englewood Cliffs, New Jersey: Prentice-Hall.

Spender, J.C. (1982) *Industry Recipes: the Nature and Sources of Managerial Judgement*. Oxford: Blackwell.

Taylor, F.W. (1947) *Scientific Management*. New York: Harper & Row.

Thierry, H. (1978) 'The Cafeteria Plan', in Bowey (ed.), *Work and Pay*, Management Decision monograph.

Tjosvold, D. and Tjosvold, M.M. (1995) *Psychology for Leaders: Using Motivation, conflict and power to manage more effectively*. New York: Wiley.

Vroom, V. (1964) *Work and Motivation*. New York: Wiley.

Vroom, V. and Yetton, P. (1973) *Leadership and Decision Making*. University of Pittsburg Press.

Wannus, J.P., Keon, T.L. and Latack, J.C. (1983) 'Expectancy Theory and Occupational/ Organisational Choices and Review and Test', *Organisational Behaviour and Human Performance*, 32.

Walton, R.E. (1986) 'From Control to Commitment in the Workplace', *Harvard Business Review*.

White, M. (1973) *Motivating Managers Financially*. London: IPM.

Whyte, W.F. (1955) *Money and Motivation*. New York: Harper & Row.

Woodward, J. (1958) *Management and Technology*. London: HMSO.

FURTHER READING

Kaplan, R.S. and Norton, D.P. (1996) 'Using the balanced scorecard as a strategic management system', *Harvard Business Review,* Jan.–Feb.

McCoy, T. (1992) *Compensation and Motivation: Maximising employee performance with behaviour*. New York: Amacom.

Pfeffer, J. (1998) *The Human Equation: Building profits by putting people first*. Boston MA: Harvard Business School.

Pitts, C. (1995) 'Motivating your organisation: achieving business success through reward and recognition'. Maidenhead: McGraw Hill.

Robbins, S.P. (1998) *Fundamentals of Management: Essential concepts and applications*. London: Prentice Hall.

6 Authority and control – the carrot or the stick?

Emma Bell

INTRODUCTION

This chapter centres upon the aspect of organisations referred to as 'culture'. It considers the way in which a set of values and beliefs, which constitute a 'programmed way of seeing' (Hofstede, 1980), is affected by and affects payment systems. The payment system is therefore an important component in the management of change. Every culture has its own particular values, and these provide an iterative cycle around which the meaning of payment systems in organisations is defined, and continually redefined, to employees. A culture is, thus, a 'way of seeing' that is common to many people; the job of managers involves attempts to manipulate or affect an organisation's culture (Pheysey, 1993) by changing the basis upon which people are rewarded. Furthermore, cultures are subject to change. Research suggests (Hendry and Pettigrew, 1992) that structural transformation of administrative processes which govern the payment of employees often forms a necessary precursor to more fundamental organisational value shifts.

In this chapter we focus specifically on *cultural ideologies*, as expressions of the 'beliefs, moral principles and values which undergird organisation decision making' (Ulrich, 1984), the shared adherence to which has been argued to be a contributor to organisational success (Peters and Waterman, 1982; Schein, 1992). An ideology can be seen as a way of promoting a set of assumptions about the basis for organisational rewards, through the talk and action of managers whose job it is to communicate the rules of payment to employees and their representatives. According to Barley and Kunda (1992), this kind of managerial ideology is, in some part, based on managerial theory.

By looking at payment systems for blue-collar or shop floor workers, it is argued that there has been a shift, within the espoused management theory, from values which emphasise *compensation* for work tasks, to *rewards* for employees who demonstrate teamwork, loyalty and motivation. This may be intended to extend the timespan over which action and consequence (or effort and reward) are negotiated, and increase the 'line of sight' for these workers. Findings of mine from a qualitative, ethnographic study indicate the commonsensical way in which British chemical industry workers and managers make sense of pay as a 'carrot' which is offered to the workforce. The removal of 'old' payment systems, based on an ideology of compensation, does not seem to be matched by a recognition of the ideology of reward by the shopfloor workers. It is also clear that the workers quoted in this chapter do not recognise the polarised distinctions between compensation and reward that are proffered within the management literature.

Chapter 7 will deal with the role of trade unions in responding to the means and methods of pay administration which management proposes; this discussion considers management's interests in mediating the interests of the various stakeholders in pay determination, and how they communicate the 'management reward strategy' in a way which generates, at least, compliance or, at best, commitment from employees.

PHASES IN PAYMENT THEORY

Against measurement

Payment theory has passed through several significant eras. Melville Dalton (1948), Donald Roy (1958) and Tom Lupton (1963) charted the preoccupation with rational provision of economic incentives and, in particular, piecework payment systems. They showed how the behaviour of the individual actually relates to the social group of which they form a part, rather than being determined by a logical concentration on the piece rate bonus. Most significant was the finding that 'the adoption of financial incentives relies on an atmosphere of worker–management co-operation and trust' (Whyte, 1952), in reaching an agreement that the rates were 'fair'. Concluding that these systems of financial incentives probably access only a small fraction of the energy and intelligence that workers have to give to jobs, these writers endorsed a return to theoretical preoccupation with worker thoughts and emotions, rather than prioritising worker's self-interested behaviour. The tenor of the ideology of these theorists was oriented towards control over shared values, through moral participation, which would unite unions and management in pursuit of the goal of improved organisational productivity. The Scanlon Plan for gainsharing (see also chapter 19) provides an alternative, and suggests that collectively shared values would enable management and labour to work as a team.

Contingency theory

The second phase was a movement towards systems theory in managerial thought, which led to an interest in contingent approaches to the design of payment systems. One such was the Lupton–Gowler '7-box model' for contingent pay system design (Lupton and Gowler, 1969). They identified 'several different kinds of effort–reward relationships that the rules and procedures comprising the payment systems embody' (Legge, 1978), and illustrated these relationships as a logical grid. In each case, the firm should consider which payment system is best suited to its circumstances, based on an understanding of the impact of technology, labour markets, dispute procedures and the structural characteristics of the organisation. The authors outline 23 dimensions on which to profile a firm, chosen on the basis of their relevance to the payment system (Lupton and Gowler, 1969). They warn against poor payment system 'fit'. This is seen when the behaviour of individuals or groups is not reinforced by appropriate payment systems, leading to tensions which may erupt into overt conflict. The Lupton–Gowler 7-box model for selecting a wage payment system 'embodies a belief that take-up may be assured by the inherent rationality of the product' (Hendry, 1980).

Part of the appeal of contingency approaches to pay system design has been their explicit solution-seeking focus. This focus means that 'views are ultimately directed toward suggesting organisational designs and managerial actions most appropriate for specific situations' (Kast and Rosensweig, 1970). In seeking to make a practical contribution to managing change in organisations, contingency theorists are located in a 'middle ground', rejecting universal principles and seeking to achieve congruence between organisations of particular types and their environments. The popularity of this approach led managers to believe that they could consciously design more effective payment systems by manipulating organisational structures and decision processes. The theoretical ideology of this phase in payment system thinking was based on 'systems rationalism' (Barley and Kunda, 1992), seeking to develop universal principles to enable managers to plan, forecast and act more effectively.

Contingent approaches to payment system design have, however, been increasingly criticised for not adequately concerning themselves with key processes which make an organisation a *living system* (Hendry, 1980). Most notably, the eighth box of the Lupton–Gowler '7-box model', representing 'conflict resolution mechanisms', has not received the same critical or theoretical attention as the others. This has led to a more recent, and more ambitious, preoccupation with an incorporation of the effects of culture into the contingency model, which attempts to overcome the rational emphasis upon structural factors such as technological development and product market.

Strategic pay

Hendry and Pettigrew argue that structural change is a necessary part of first shifting the power base in order to make effective strategy; human resource management change may be an important part of this change process. Thus, the introduction of a new payment system might be a necessary precursor to strategic organisational development (Hendry and Pettigrew, 1992). Bowey and Thorpe present an argument which runs along similar lines; they suggest that present payment systems act as potential agents for initiating wider organisational change (Bowey and Thorpe, 1986). Potential exists, on the basis of these authors' case study illustrations, to implement further structural changes, such as the introduction of new technology or operating systems, or to develop a cultural shift in relation to management style and procedures, on the back of pay system changes. Pay can be seen as key to managing change.

More recently, the pay strategy literature has sought to re-apply contingency principles, on the premise that 'compensation strategies and organisation strategies should "fit" each other; the better the fit, the better the organisation's performance' (Milkovich, 1988). This normative view of contingency is based upon the assumption that degree of fit between compensation strategy and organisation strategy contributes to organisation performance by signalling and rewarding the behaviours that are consistent with the organisation's objectives.

The 'strategy paradigm' (Gomez-Mejia and Balkin, 1992) of pay system design requires strategic firm alignment. This stretches from business strategy, through to human resource management policies which, in turn, shape and influence corporate pay policy. The greater this alignment, so it is argued, the more effective payment systems will be. This raises the profile of pay systems, and advocates its incorporation at high-level organisational decision making. This requires the design of payment systems having a major role in strategy formulation, whilst continuing to reflect the wishes of the major constituencies or stakeholders (Gomez-Mejia and Balkin, 1992). Payment systems need to support business strategy in terms of:

1 maintaining the consistency of internal wage differentials;
2 ensuring the competitiveness of wage rates in relation to local labour markets;
3 reflecting relative employee contributions;
4 representing a centralised, or decentralised, administrative style, as appropriate to the organisation (Milkovich and Newman, 1996).

Balanced against these technical requirements to reinforce and define the *structure* of the organisation (Lawler, 1984), however, is the need for payment systems to reflect corporate philosophy, or the organisation's culture and values.

Gomez-Mejia and Balkin (1992) classify organisational culture according to whether it promotes a 'moral commitment'. This involves identification with organisational goals, or 'calculative commitment'. This means an instrumental, utilitarian attachment to the company; they then seek to explore the consequences of these alternative organisational orientations for pay strategy. This promotes a value-free taxonomy of cultural values which relate to pay, independent of any statement of managerial best practice surrounding the 'new pay' (Lawler, 1995), or 'high commitment' models (Walton, 1985) which have typically been associated with human resource management (HRM) of the 1980s and 1990s.

HRM and payment systems

A HRM-inspired view of the design and management of payment systems seeks to engage the commitment of employees. This is ideally based on a superior relationship between employees and their organisation, and 'to make human resource management an integral part of the strategic arena in organisations' (Tichy, Fombrun and Devanna, 1982). According to HRM principles, in the well-designed payment system employees are not driven to 'compensate for their dissatisfaction with intrinsic rewards by demanding improvements in extrinsic rewards, particularly pay' (Beer *et al.*, 1984). This symbolic view of pay emphasises the common identity or *Gemeinschaft* of the organisation, and suggests that 'communication, participation and trust can have an important effect on people's perceptions of pay, the meaning they attach to a new pay system and their response to that system. In short, *the process may be as important as the system*' (original emphasis) (ibid.). The payment system, thus, constitutes part of the new-value system whereby culture is reformed, by way of 'reward systems which praise those who serve the new values' (Ulrich, 1984).

The HRM/best-practice approach to strategic pay can be regarded, even more than best-fit standpoints (Milkovich and Newman, 1996), as advocating a normative ideology. This kind of ideology is broadly complementary to the surge in popularity of 'organisational culture' literature during the 1980s and 1990s (see Barley and Kunda, 1992, for a comprehensive summary of this body of work). This ideology endorses 'self conscious attempts to formulate corporate cultures' as a normal 'part of organisational life', through the management of pay systems. A central tenet of this approach is that 'economic performance in turbulent environments requires the commitment of employees who make no distinction between their own welfare and the welfare of the firm' (ibid.). It represents a resurgent interest in the thoughts and feelings of the workforce as a unified whole, over and above the employee characterised as being driven by narrow, economic self-interest.

'COMPENSATION' AND 'REWARD': A CULTURAL DUALISM

This historical overview of phases in pay theory illustrates one of the ways in which management ideology has progressed in a succession of phases which alternate 'repeatedly between ideologies of normative and rational control' (Barley and Kunda, 1992). In anthropology, it has long been maintained that traditional cultures revolve around core ideas that are oppositional or dualistic in nature (Maybury-Lewis and Almagor, 1989), such as 'good' versus 'evil', 'life' versus 'death'. These dualisms are seen as playing a crucial role in determining cultural values, language and symbols. In modern organisations, cultural dualisms remain; for example, the contrast between individualism and collectivism (Kessler and Purcell, 1995), which is strongly associated with the underlying management style and with the design of payment systems. In this chapter, it is proposed that there is a second competing dualism at work in relation to pay. This is the distinction between the 'carrot' of reward versus the 'stick' of compensation.

Unfortunately, the terms 'compensation' and 'reward' tend to be used interchangeably within payment systems literature in a way which fails to engage with their cultural significance. This is more than just a semantic debate. Language frames the way we see the world, which, in turn, shapes our organisational reality. Eccles and Nohria (1992), for example, look at managerial use of language 'both in the sense of how language is used *in* organisations and in the sense of how it is used in ways – such as business books and journalism – that *span* organisations' (original emphasis). The particular words chosen to express the basis of organisational exchange with employees, therefore, influence the way in which payment is perceived. Language is not neutral – it expresses a view of the world. This discussion attempts to foreground some of the contested meaning surrounding pay terminology. It is suggested that only by recognising the contradictory nature of the counterpunctual themes of compensation and reward are we able to analyse their significance within organisational culture.

Lawler (1990) refers to 'payment' and 'reward' systems interchangeably. 'Compensation' is often integral to 'strategy'; it is the preferred term of the new pay writers in the USA, as can be seen from the title of one of the most prestigious journals of the field, *Compensation and Benefits Review*. On this side of the Atlantic, the term 'payment systems', prevalent in the 1970s and 1980s (Lupton, 1972; Bowey and Thorpe, 1986), appears to have fallen out of favour. It has been replaced by the pay specialists' use of the broader term, 'reward' (Armstrong and Murlis, 1994), in pursuit of a 'more strategic approach' to the management of remuneration (Smith, 1993). Moreover, 'pay conflict', formerly a key identifier in industrial relations and organisational behaviour (White, 1981), appears to have been backgrounded. So what are the classical connotations of the competing payment scheme terminologies?

A compensation ideology

The ideology associated with the term 'compensation', if interpreted literally, emphasises a 'fair day's work for a fair day's pay', as a 'purely extrinsic *quid pro quo* contract' (Tichy, Fombrun and Devanna, 1982). Furthermore, it is suggested that this extrinsic motivation is 'provided *to* the individual by someone else' (original emphasis) (Steers and Porter, 1987). Forms of compensation include:

- overtime payments
- piecework
- measured daywork
- traditional merit pay awards or bonuses (based on measurable performance indicators, such as attendance or productivity)
- shift supplements
- 'danger money' or 'dirt money'.

The ideology of compensation can, thus, be located within a historical overview of industrial sociology, by the need to financially recompense employees for disruption to their non-work life. Many blue-collar jobs fit this description, and workers have been shown to exhibit a primarily instrumental orientation to work, in that they see work as a means to an end, and that they seek to maximise economic returns for this disruption (Blackburn and Mann, 1979; Goldthorpe *et al.*, 1968). Pay satisfaction is expressed in terms of the ability to attain a 'good life', measurable in terms of a house, car and holidays. In studies of this era, manual workers are shown to define employment as a means of acquiring a certain standard and style of living outside of work, through their calculative involvement with the firm. As a result, there have been criticisms of payment schemes which 'take a man's earnings away from his shovel' (Edwards and Heery, 1989), by moving away from payment-by-results. Workers are rarely portrayed as having a moral (Goldthorpe *et al.*, 1968) or ideological commitment to the corporate culture, brought about by managers through a successful 'battle for the minds and wills of the men' (Nichols and Beynon, 1977). Compensation systems tend to be *retrospective*, or immediate in focus, in line with reinforcement theory. This suggests that, the closer the outcome is to the actual behaviour which precipitated it, the greater its motivational impact. The specific task environment where an employee performs his or her duties is emphasised, and employee satisfaction is perceived as transitory, rather than stable over time, based on immediate reactions to pay as a tangible aspect of the psychological contract (Mowday, Porter and Steers, 1982). Employees and managers are seen to act as if there were an implicit 'effort-bargain' which permits a clear and concrete 'tradeoff between pay and effort' (Brown and Walsh, 1994).

A reward ideology

The ideology of reward, on the other hand, is located within the field of human resource management (Beer *et al.*, 1984), as part of a broader overall strategy of enhancing loyalty, motivation and satisfaction. Rewards are defined as encompassing career opportunities, job security and learning opportunities (Tichy, Fombrun and Devanna, 1982). For the purposes of this discussion, we take the term in a more limited sense to refer to pay, in its various forms, including salary, bonuses, stock options and benefits. In this context, the exchange with employees stresses the provision of challenging, meaningful work, in return for loyal, committed, and self-motivated employees. Rewards are seen to be partly intrinsic, provided by the individual himself, or herself, as a result of performing some task (Steers and Porter, 1987). Similar to the human relations movement, the ideology of reward emphasises psychological growth and satisfaction of emotional and social needs and the opportunity for achievement, responsibility, recognition and learning *as an integral part of the job* (Herzberg, 1968).

Reward systems tend to be more *prospective* in focus, in that they tend to operate a longer time horizon in the measurement of performance and the distribution of rewards. They emphasise a general affective response to the organisation as a whole, rather than transitory, day-to-day events in the workplace (Mowday, Porter and Steers, 1982). This encourages a longer-term view towards the provision of monetary rewards proportionate to inputs. In other words, it serves to extend the 'line of sight' between effort and payment (Lawler, 1995; Bell, 1999).

One way in which this can be achieved is through the appraisal system, objective setting, and review process, which provide the means whereby individual performance is reviewed over time, and reward allocation is anticipated on the basis of achievements. In the UK, 'a range of surveys have highlighted the spread of schemes which relate pay directly to an assessment of individual performance' (Kessler, 1994); these changes affect a growing number of non-executive employees in British organisations (Heery, 1996). Although there have been studies looking at the effects of tying managerial compensation to organisational performance using merit pay (Morris and Fenton-O'Creevy, 1996), relatively little attention has been paid to the application of shop-floor incentive schemes over a similar time period (Smith, 1989). The ideology of reward moves towards paying the person. The new 'bottom line', suggests Kanter (1987), is what you contribute. However, the 'decision to reward individual contributors makes otherwise latent concerns about equity much more visible'.

Another aspect of reward ideology involves emphasis on career development. In the words of a General Motors manager, 'we don't have jobs at GM, we have careers' (in Tichy, 1982). In a manufacturing context, the removal of the 'command and control structure' and 'levels of plant hierarchy', coupled with the integration of quality and production activities and amalgamation of production and maintenance operations, has opened up new 'career possibilities' for workers (Walton, 1985). Furthermore, in delayered organisations, careers are more likely to develop 'within broadly homogeneous areas of responsibility rather than progressing up a number of steps in a clearly defined hierarchy' (Armstrong and Murlis, 1994). Lawler suggests (1994), therefore, that there is growing evidence to suggest that it may be appropriate for many organisations to move away from a focus on jobs and towards a focus on individuals and their competencies.

By loosening the relationship between job assignment and pay level, organisations are moving away from a situation of 'paying for the job', using traditional job evaluation, towards an emphasis on the individual as a unit of value over and above the job. Cross-functional teams and an emphasis on a broadly skilled workforce has led some UK and US organisations to replace point-factor job evaluation and payment systems with simplified structures, such as broad banding or salary banding (Townley, 1994). This is complementary to a high commitment strategy, and implies that 'each team member has the training to perform many or all of the tasks for which the team is accountable, and pay reflects the level of mastery of required skills' (Walton, 1985).

A third aspect of reward ideology is built upon the value of collectivity, sharing in the commercial and financial success of the organisation. It is suggested, therefore, that payment systems such as profit sharing or stock options 'should increase the felt responsibility of employees and thus their commitment to the organisation' (Mowday, Porter and Steers, 1982). Attempts are made 'not only to persuade employees to identify themselves as producers, but to constitute themselves as productive subjects', and to become 'concerned with the performance of the company as a whole' (Townley, 1991). However, as Townley notes, 'the difficulties of such schemes for "creating the productive subject" involve, amongst other things, the *time lag* between effort and reward' (emphasis added).

THE 'CARROT' AND THE 'STICK' AS FORMS OF CONTROL WITHIN THE BRITISH CHEMICAL INDUSTRY

Management terminology of compensation and reward rarely surfaces in the everyday lives of workers and managers in the British chemical industry.[1] In relation to pay, the distinction mentioned most often in the organisations studied was between the 'carrot' and the 'stick'.

Etzioni (1961) outlines a fairly straightforward typology showing managerial techniques as strategies for control. These he identifies as:

1 coercive,
2 remunerative,
3 normative.

Coercive control derives from employer use of the 'stick', to control the labour force. In modern Britain, coercive sanctions take the form of disciplinary rules and procedures, breach of which leads to discipline such as suspension without pay or dismissal. The 'stick' then, is a form of punishment threatened, or actually meted out, to non-compliant workers. Its existence demonstrates the ultimate authority of managerial control, although it often underlies or complements other, more subtle, forms of incentivisation at work:

They came round with this bloody big stick, the 'Scheme Z' [review of terms and conditions]. [It] was handled in an atrocious manner.

The threat of [plant] closure . . . was a big stick initially.

We have some carrots and some sticks, for those that need it.

Yet coercive control is regarded as relatively outdated and, as a consequence, needs to be understated. It was seen, by this management consultant, to signify a failure of management to achieve and maintain control by other means:

I would say, if management feel they have got to get the big stick out all the time to everybody, then they clearly don't understand what they are trying to achieve.

The alternative, that of remunerative control, involves employers in the utilisation of financial rewards as a basic means of motivation and control, based on calculative involvement. 'In Britain, employers traditionally placed very great reliance on incentives such as payment-by-results and today there is still considerable emphasis on performance pay as a way of motivating workers' (Gospel and Palmer, 1993: 42). Workers and managers expressed the view that many of the traditional 'carrots', such as overtime payments and grade progression, had been removed from their discretion. These forms of pay, as *compensation*, which constituted the traditional–historical means of controlling blue-collar workers, were seen to still have functional relevance in the work place. The removal of 'carrots', such as overtime, left management impotent in this particular use of remunerative control. In the words of one manager, without overtime payments:

> I don't have the carrots to induce people to come in and work on a Saturday night.

> You no longer have the carrot available, to say, well we need extra production out this week, there might be a few overtime shifts going.

Nor was there sufficient remunerative incentive towards grade progression, without which, the notion of skill and career failed to have relevance:

> To get to the top half, and then to go on to the next grade, there's no money – like dangling the carrot, you know, there's nothing there.

Reliance on the 'cash nexus' as a form of control is argued to invite instrumental attachment from employees but, without it, there was little motive to progress. Being 'in it for the money' was a sentiment broadly expressed and generally adhered to, and it was considered (unsurprisingly perhaps in a capitalist-consumer society) to be an inevitable part of the way of life for everyone from board directors to shop floor workers:

> We pay the main board extremely good salaries, they get extremely good bonuses, they get share options. If you thought there was job satisfaction, it should be at that level. The carrot we give them isn't job satisfaction, the carrot we give them is money. So why should we be any different? Why should we think that the carrot at the shop floor should be any different from the carrot in every boardroom across the UK?

Normative control, as the last possible option for control, seeks to give employees a sense of belonging, a voice in the organisation, and more satisfying work by attempting to build mutual reciprocity and trust. Such a moral involvement is argued to be more likely in situations where the worker thoroughly identifies with the organisation. Such references are beyond the scope of this paper, but they tend to manifest themselves in terms of an understanding about 'culture' and are, as has already been suggested, complementary to the ideology of *reward*.

Based on research by Skinner and Winckler (1980) and Hofstede (1980), Pheysey (1993) suggests that it is possible to classify organisational goals in relation to the appropriate type of power. Different types of power encourage certain types of behaviour. The cultural values of 'competition' and 'independence' are, thus, attainable via 'remunerative' power, i.e. the ability to reward people. As a consequence, the organisation will elicit 'indifferent' behaviour. By this, Skinner and Winckler imply that people are primarily self-interested, will seek personal benefits, but neither support nor oppose the sources of those benefits (in Pheysey, 1993). Hofstede's (1980) cultural values of

Table 6.1

Form of control	Commonsensical term	Theoretical term
Coercive –encourages order and obedience through use of discipline and threat	'stick'	
Remunerative –encourages competition and independence through use of rational measures	'carrot'	'compensation'
Normative –encourages sharing, friendship and involvement through diffuse, abstract indicators		'reward'

'sharing', 'involvement' and 'friendship' are argued to be best reached through utilisation of normative power, in order to obtain the commitment (as a form of behavioural involvement) of employees.

These value associations map closely on to the preceding distinction between compensation and reward, in that the cultural values of 'competition' and 'independence' are endorsed and encouraged through an ideology of compensation and the values of 'sharing' and 'involvement' relate closely to the ideology of reward. We can start to see a pattern which relates these commonsensical terms of 'carrot' and 'stick', to the theoretical terms of 'compensation' and 'reward', as they are used within the literature. Table 6.1 locates them within the overall framework of Etzioni's distinctions between different forms of control.

It is evident that there is a high degree of dissonance or incongruency between the theory and the practice, the rhetoric and the reality (Legge, 1995), or 'the talk and the action', of payment system operation within these case study organisations. What we have is two *independent* dualistic relationships; the 'compensation' versus 'reward' dichotomy within the literature, and the 'carrot' or 'stick' debate within the case studies themselves. The crucial point of overlap, in terms of understanding pay systems, is in the 'carrot' as a form of 'compensation' for work activity, which is used to achieve remunerative control within these organisations. It is this nexus which gives us insight into understanding the role of pay in the management of meaning.

CONCLUSIONS

Is the 'new pay' really changing the 'line of sight' for blue-collar workers?

Remunerative power, exercised through the manipulation of the 'fetishised brown wage packet' (Willis, 1979), has historically constituted the predominant source of control in blue-collar industries, where manual workers represent the bulk of an organisation's participants. By contrast, reward ideology has spawned a variety of 'new pay' approaches which challenge the received orthodoxy of compensation.

The new pay model, summarised by Heery (1996), comprises a number of themes which broadly correspond to a reward ideology. These comprise:

1 a strategic orientation
2 market flexibility
3 performance-related or 'at risk' variability
4 unitarism, or the pursuit of 'mutual gains'.

On a broad scale, there is evidence to suggest that there has been some movement towards the new pay model in Britain (CBI, 1995). What is not clear, however, is the impact and extent of an associated shift in values and ideology, initiated by these pay system reforms. Indeed, it may be the case that these progressive systems of remuneration generate the same kinds of 'perverse effects' as the more traditional forms of compensation, such as employee dissatisfaction and resistance (Scott, 1994); without further qualitative research it is almost impossible to tell.

The reward ideology represents an attempt to change the basis of exchange relationships with shopfloor workers, with direct consequences for methods of payment. This is based on the premise that employee commitment can be 'equally strong up and down the organisational hierarchy' and, contrary to popular myth, blue-collar workers are no less committed than top executives (Mowday, Porter and Steers, 1982). This involves extending the 'line of sight' (Gomez-Mejia and Balkin, 1992) between employee behaviours and organisational rewards, so that, instead of being based simply on immediate reinforcement of physical, observable inputs of effort, time and skill, rewards are being placed increasingly 'at risk' (Heery, 1996), and are dependent on expectations of a diffuse, and at times vague, emphasis on the 'total behaviour of the individual', rather than on their 'productive behaviour' alone (Townley, 1991).

The new pay is said to match a less-certain organisational environment which demands a more fluid organisational form (Heery, 1996). This, however, obscures the fact that both traditional and so-called 'new' forms of remuneration are *both* attempts at managerial control. What has changed, through the ideological movement away from compensation and towards reward, is a shift from rational to normative rhetorics. The prescriptive writing of the new pay specialists supports a move away from rational, hierarchical, bureaucratic measures, towards more diffuse cultural indicators of individual or collective value or worth.

So why the shift? According to Barley and Kunda (1992), 'rational rhetorics prospered when the economy expanded; normative rhetorics surged when the economy contracted'. In a similar vein, Fox (1985: 14) suggests that when 'labour scarcity tips the balance of power at the workplace towards the employees and management feels its disciplinary powers slipping', there is likely to be an increase in managerial interest in eliciting the 'moral involvement' of employees, as 'methods of control which do not require the exercise of overt discipline or coercion'. Ramsay (1977: 496) has, in earlier work, suggested that waves of enthusiasm for participation schemes seem to have arisen out of a managerial response to threats to management authority, in order to 'nullify pressures to change the status quo', rather than to 'stimulate its reform'. 'The tenor of our theorising' in pay system research may, thus, 'amount to little more than the turning of a small cog within a larger socioeconomic clock over which one has no control' (Barley and Kunda, 1992).

Building and sustaining an ideology, however, is always a social process. This case study research would suggest that reward ideology is, at best, partial and incomplete. Though the words have changed, to reflect progressive, non-bureaucratic organisations, in the 'merry-go-round which is the search for the newest management ideas' (Eccles and Nohria, 1992), their efficacy must be judged by how well they are used to generate widespread meaning, as well as action. The illustrator of the book jacket of Vroom and Deci's (1970) Penguin edition of 'Management and Motivation' depicts a luscious carrot. As Sievers (1994) remarks, 'this does not seem . . . to be a joke, but an accurate expression of the hidden truth behind the predominant thoughts about management and its functions *vis-à-vis* the worker'.

NOTE

1 This chapter contains data from ethnographic case study research within three chemical industry organisations in the North West of England, which was carried out during 1997 and 1998, over a period of one year. More than one hundred interviews were carried out as part of the research and these have been analysed with the assistance of the software analysis tool, NUD.IST.

LEARNING ACTIVITIES

1 Assess the language that is used in your organisation to discuss pay generally and reward systems in particular using table 6.1 as an assessment tool.

2 Using the data from question 1, critically assess whether languages used differ for different pay constituencies (i.e. at different levels and for different groups).

3 To what extent can reward systems both *reflect* organisational culture and be used to *change* organisational culture?

4 Select three different types of payment system and discuss the form of managerial control that each represents and how it is achieved.

REFERENCES

Armstrong, M. and Murlis, H. (1994) *Reward Management: A handbook of remuneration strategy and practice*. Third edition, London: Kogan Page.

Argyris, C. and Schön, D.A. (1978) *Organisational Learning: A theory of action perspective*. Reading, MA: Addison-Wesley.

Barley, S.R. and Kunda, G. (1992) 'Design and Devotion: Surges of rational and normative ideologies of control in management discourse', *Administrative Science Quarterly*, 37: 363–99.

Beer, M., Spector, B., Lawrence, P.R., Quinn Mills, D. and Walton, R.E. (1984) *Managing Human Assets*. New York: Free Press.

Bell, E. (1999) 'Changing the Line of Sight on Payment Systems: A Study of Shop Floor Workers in and Managers within the British Chemical Industry', *International Journal of Human Resource Management*, 10(5): 924–940.

Blackburn, R.M. and Mann, M. (1979) *The Working Class in the Labour Market*. London: Macmillan.

Bowey, A.M. and Thorpe, R., with Hellier, P. (1986) *Payment Systems and Productivity*. Basingstoke: Macmillan.

Brown, W. and Walsh, J. (1994) 'Managing Pay in Britain', in K. Sisson (ed.), *Personnel Management*. Second edition, Oxford: Blackwell.

CBI (1995) *Trends in Pay and Benefits Systems: 1995 CBI/Hay survey results*. London: Confederation of British Industry.

Dalton, M. (1948) 'The Industrial "Rate Buster": A characterisation', in T. Lupton (ed.), *Payment Systems*. Harmondsworth: Penguin.

Eccles, R.G. and Nohria, N. (1992) *Beyond the Hype*. Boston: Harvard Business School Press.

Edwards, C. and Heery, E. (1989) *Management Control and Union Power*. Oxford: Clarendon Press.

Etzioni, A. (1961) *A Comparative Analysis of Complex Organizations*. New York: Free Press.

Fox, A. (1985) *Man Mismanagement*. Second edition, London: Hutchinson.

Goldthorpe, J.H., Lockwood, D., Bechhofer, F. and Platt, J. (1968) *The Affluent Worker: Industrial attitudes and behaviour*. Cambridge: Cambridge University Press.

Gomez-Mejia, L.R. and Balkin, D.B. (1992) *Compensation, Organisational Strategy and Firm Performance*. Cincinnati, Ohio: South Western Publishing.

Gospel, H.F. and Palmer, G. (1993) *British Industrial Relations*. Second edition, London: Routledge.

Heery, E. (1996) 'Risk, Representation and the New Pay', *Personnel Review*, 25(6): 54–65.

Herzberg, F. (1968) *Work and the Nature of Man*. Crosby Lockwood Staples.

Hendry, C. (1980) 'Contingency Theory in Practice, II', *Personnel Review*, 9(1): 5–11.

Hendry, C. and Pettigrew, A. (1992) 'Patterns of Strategic Change in the Development of Human Resource Management', *British Journal of Management*, 3: 137–56.

Hofstede, G. (1980) *Culture's Consequences: International differences in work-related values*. London: Sage.

Kanter, R.M. (1987) 'The Attack on Pay', *Harvard Business Review*, 65: 60–7.

Kast, F.E. and Rosensweig, J.E. (1970) *Organisation and Management: A systems and contingency approach*. New York: McGraw Hill.

Kessler, I. (1994) 'Performance Pay', in R. Sissons (ed.), *Personnel Management*. Second edition, Oxford: Blackwell.

Kessler, I. and Purcell, J. (1995) 'Individualism and Collectivism in Theory and Practice', in P. Edwards (ed.), *Industrial Relations Theory and Practice in Britain*. Oxford: Blackwell.

Lawler, E.E. (1984) 'The Strategic Design of Reward Systems', in C.J. Frombrun, N. Tichy and M. Devanna (eds), *Strategic Human Resource Management*. New York: Wiley.

Lawler, E.E. (1990) *Strategic Pay*. San Francisco: Jossey Bass.

Lawler, E.E. (1994) 'From Job-Based to Competency-Based Organisations', *Journal of Organisational Behaviour*, 15: 3–15.

Lawler, E.E. (1995) 'The New Pay: A strategic approach', *Compensation and Benefits Review*, July–August: 14–22.

Legge, K. (1978) *Power, Innovation and Problem-Solving in Personnel Management*. Maidenhead: McGraw Hill.

Legge, K. (1995) *Human Resource Management: Rhetorics and realities*. Basingstoke: Macmillan.

Lupton, T. (1963) *On the Shop Floor*. Oxford: Pergamon Press.

Lupton, T. (ed.) (1972) *Payment Systems*. Harmondsworth: Penguin.

Lupton, T. and Gowler, D. (1969) *Selecting a Wage Payment System*. London: Engineering Employers' Federation.

Maybury-Lewis, D. and Almagor, U. (eds) (1989) *The Attraction of Opposites*. Michigan: University of Michigan Press.

Milkovich, G.T. (1988) 'A Strategic Perspective on Compensation Management', *Research in Personnel and Human Resources Management*, 6: 263–88.

Milkovich, G.T. and Newman, J.M. (1996) *Compensation*. Fifth edition, Chicago: Irwin.

Morris, T.J. and Fenton-O'Creevy, M. (1996) 'Opening up the Black Box: A UK case study of top managers' attitudes to their performance related pay', *International Journal of Human Resource Management*, 7(3): 708–20.

Mowday, R.T., Porter, L.W. and Steers, R.M. (1982) *Employee-Organisation Linkages: The psychology of commitment, absenteeism and turnover*. New York: Academic Press.

Nichols, T. and Beynon, H. (1977) *Living with Capitalism: Class relations and the modern factory*. London: Routledge & Kegan Paul.

Peters, T. and Waterman, R.H. (1982) *In Search of Excellence: Lessons from America's best run companies*. London: HarperCollins.

Pheysey, D.C. (1993) *Organisational Cultures*. London: Routledge.

Ramsay, H. (1977) 'Cycles of Control: Worker participation in sociological and historical perspective', *Sociology*, 11(3): 481–506.

Roy, D. (1958) 'Quota Restriction and Goldbricking in a Machine Shop', *American Journal of Sociology*, 57: 427–42.

Schein, E.H. (1992) *Organisational Culture and Leadership*. Second edition, San Francisco: Jossey Bass.

Scott, A. (1994) *Willing Slaves? British workers under human resource management*. Cambridge: Cambridge University Press.

Sievers, B. (1994) *Work, Death and Life Itself*. Berlin: Walter de Gruyter.

Skinner, G.W. and Winckler, E.A. (1980) 'Compliance Succession in Rural Communist China', in A. Etzioni and E.W. Lehman (eds), *A Sociological Reader on Complex Organizations*. Third edition, New York: Holt, Rinehart & Winston.

Smith, I. (1993) 'Reward Management: A retrospective assessment', *Employee Relations*, 15(3): 45–59.

Smith, I.G. (1989) *Incentive Schemes: People and profits*. Surrey: Croner.

Steers, R.T. and Porter, L.W. (1987) *Motivation and Work Behaviour*. Fourth edition, New York: McGraw Hill.

Tichy, N.M., Fombrun, C.J. and Devanna, M.A. (1982) 'Strategic Human Resource Management', *Sloan Management Review*, 23(2): 47–61.

Townley, B. (1994) *Reframing Human Resource Management*. London: Sage.

Townley, B. (1991) 'Selection and Appraisal: Reconstituting "Social Relations"', in J. Storey (ed.), *New Perspectives on Human Resource Management*. London: Routledge.

Ulrich, W.L. (1984) 'HRM and Culture: History, ritual and myth', *Human Resource Management*, 23(2): 117–28.

Vroom V.H. and Deci, E.L. (eds) (1970) *Management and Motivation*. Harmondsworth: Penguin.

Walton, R.E. (1985) 'From Control to Commitment in the Workplace', *Harvard Business Review*, 63: 76–84.

White, M. (1981) *The Hidden Meaning of Pay Conflict*. London: Macmillan.

Whyte, W.F. (1952) 'Economic Incentives and Human Relations', in T. Lupton (ed.), *Payment Systems*. Harmondsworth: Penguin.

Willis, P. (1979) 'Shop Floor Culture, Masculinity and the Wage Form', in J. Clarke, C. Critcher and R. Johnson (eds), *Working Class Culture: Studies in history and theory*. London: Hutchinson.

7 Design and implementation of remuneration systems

Richard Thorpe

INTRODUCTION

This chapter examines a number of the process issues that should be considered when managers consider making major changes to reward and remuneration systems. Rather than dealing solely with the technical and operational aspects of particular types of payment system, it concentrates instead on those aspects of process that are likely to promote a link between an organisation's priorities for success and the reward policy, systems and structures.

A number of writers (Bowey and Thorpe, 1986; Lawler, 1990; Mahoney, 1992 and Crowe, 1992) have all indicated the importance of linking the strategic aspects of pay with the operational. Pay cannot only attract, reward and retain the right kind of people, and signal to them what the organisational priorities are but act as a catalyst for wider organisational change. Payment systems offer a good two-way communication tool for linking business strategy with company culture, and a change in the reward system can enable the accommodation of a wide range of changes that fit a particular philosophy or approach. It can, so to speak, send messages about what is important and what is valued. Some might go even further and suggest that, unless changes are made in key areas of the organisation, a change in the payment system alone will not deliver its potential and probably fail completely.

Seen in this way, the payment system is important not simply as a means of rewarding individuals for their contributions at work, but also as a policy instrument that carries messages which encourage appropriate behaviour. The payment system thus becomes an important systems component and should not be viewed in isolation from the full range of business objectives and performance measures.

This chapter begins by examining a number of ways of thinking about how change might be brought about before going on to suggest how research has suggested that a process that includes a wider group of stakeholders in the design process can offer more successful outcomes. The chapter concludes with a blueprint for practitioners.

TYPES OF PAY SYSTEM PROCESS

A great many ways have been advocated as to how payment systems should be designed and implemented. In the field of pay there has always been interest taken in any new system or approach which quickly develops into a fashion. Yet another is the analytical approach that encourages the examination of certain key organisational variables and a third is to seek wide involvement from a wide group of organisational stakeholders.

The history of payment scheme design, as we have seen in previous chapters, is a catalogue of various fads or fashions, many developed for a particular purpose but then used in situations without discrimination. Harvey Ramsay referred to the circular fashion of ideas in a paper entitled 'Cycles of Control'. (He argued that in one era the measurement of work systems directly might be important to control labour costs.) When they decayed through wage drift, they may be replaced by a form of measured day work – to peg output but to avoid the disadvantages of piecework. Later, participation might be seen as important, but then a time may come when direct measurement is once more seen to be important and the whole cycle would begin again. Over the last half-century, academics and pay practitioners have seen these cycles come as the balance of power has moved in the labour market. This is one reason why it is perhaps important for a pay practitioner to have a perspective on history. In other words, what's been around, comes around.

The second group of pay change practices have focused on 'best-fit' approaches. This approach is consistent with the contingency view of pay. Here the focus is on certain key variables relating to organisational characteristics and context. An analysis of these will suggest that particular types of payment systems are likely to be more successful than others in improving performance.

Yet a third approach recognises that whilst a diagnosis of variables is important, there are certain process issues involved which, unless they are understood, could result in poor performance. It is this third approach that is the main focus of this chapter.

MANAGING CHANGE – SCHOOLS OF THOUGHT

As Mabey and Maynard-White (1997) point out, the competitiveness of an organisation owes much to the way change is managed, particularly the extent to which attention is paid to the environment. The same is true for payment system changes, especially if the system is to remain healthy and serve to buttress the objectives and priorities of the organisation. There can never be a recipe for how to manage change in an organisation. There are, according to Whittington (1993), two main schools of thought when it comes to change – planned and emergent.

Those advocating planned approaches to organisational change see it as a process of moving from one fixed state to another. Different writers advocate different ways as to how this can be achieved, and disciplines, such as organisational development, offer very many behaviourally based approaches to how interventions can be made. But the approach can be criticised for the emphasis that is placed on incremental change, and, often, its lack of recognition of the very real issues of power and politics that exist within organisations.

The alternative method of managing change is the emergent approach. Emergent strategies focus not on planning but on the unpredictable nature of change and the importance of making sense of the contested issues; for example, differences in views and perspective between members of the same board, or from individuals performing different functions that inevitably arise in organisations. As Burnes (1996) indicates this approach views change as a process that emerges through the interplay of a range of variables in an organisation. Context and political processes are seen to be very important.

These are aspects that Eden, Sim and Jones (1983) have focused on when they argue that organisations are social entities where problems are not so much related to corporate objectives and to 'objective' criteria, as to the subjectivity in a situation. The personal perspectives of individuals and political issues arising from the idiosyncratic values held are therefore relevant. Required in such a context are ways of helping people bring their concerns to the surface and make sense of them with one another.

APPLICATIONS OF THE EMERGENT CHANGE MANAGEMENT APPROACH TO PAY SYSTEM DESIGN

Learning and change

Concepts such as learning and change are becoming increasingly central to current debates about life of organisations. The question of how payment systems should best be designed so that they fit and support the business is a case in point. It is somewhat of a truism that all organisations need to be 'learning organisations', whether they are labelled in this way or not. However, not all individuals and organisations learn as well as they might, and the question then becomes one of how learning in the design of payment systems can be supported. The ability to manage and facilitate learning, development and change is now being recognised by many as a crucial organisational competency (Pedler, Burgoyne and Baydell, 1997). A task for contemporary management, therefore, is to make the processes of organisational learning more explicit, systematic and intentional, and to capture the learning that takes place so that it can be more manifest in new pay practices.

Pay change processes that involve consultation, negotiation, and debate

As we have reported in various other chapters, research conducted in the 1980s (Bowey and Thorpe, 1986) demonstrates the importance of an inclusive process of consultation and participation when organisations change and design payment systems.

Figure 7.1 illustrates this process simply. The process begins with recognising that it might be a mistake to believe that senior managers know and can clearly articulate

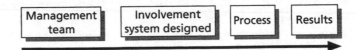

Fig. 7.1 An inclusive pay change process

just what the priorities of the business are, and, even if they do and can, that they all understand these in exactly the same way. In a recent piece of consultancy conducted in the food industry, the eight senior managers held eight different views of what the priorities of the business should be. Each of these views would require a different emphasis for the payment system. So what is required is a system whereby senior managers are able to articulate without fear, their views on the priorities for the success of their organisation. As I have indicated, this is not always as easy as it sounds and, in most organisations, when attempting to do this, I have had to adopt a tactic that will engender a debate and allow the differences in beliefs and perspectives to surface (however subtle). Using a cognitive mapping process such as that provided by Eden and Ackermann (1998) is one way to do this. (see Easterby-Smith, Thorpe and Holman, 1996). Based on personal construct theory, cognitive maps offer ways of representing ideas and individuals' perceptions of issues and problems, and of making links between these that allow key relationships to be analysed. However, what is important in cognitive mapping is not so much the technology but the process whereby people come together to discuss, argue and debate more or less-contested issues, and the actions that result from these discussions. A balance between content and process is therefore essential. Through such a process, not only is a complex organisational issue captured as each individual member of the group perceives it, but these views and perspectives are also challenged. It is the ensuing discussion which often proves the most useful (Ackermann and Belton, 1994).

Cognitive mapping however, is, just one of many ways to facilitate pay system change. There are other nominal group techniques. Lupton and Tanner (1986), for example, have produced an approach that recognises that any change needs to combine the rational objectivities of a situation with the social. In a similar way to Eden they advocate the use of a coalition of organisational members. This group first brainstorms the organisational variables that will affect performance, then measures where the organisation is now in terms of each variable. It is then considered in which direction and by how much the organisation might reasonably be changed. The approach then, through a matrix that is sound, establishes which factors are easier to change than others and which will have the greatest impact on performance. Through this process, priorities are set and measures established for these.

So, it is the discussion of the ambiguities and quandaries that arise, together with the resulting shared understandings (often new) of the participants that take part, that is important.

Once completed, this process can be repeated involving as wide a coalition of managers and staff as is needed to reflect the character of the organisation. There may, for example, be a need to conduct such an exercise in a range of different departments, particularly where the activities required to meet the overall organisational objective processes and behaviours would be quite different. Once identified, measuring these activities, processes and behaviours would be established with managers and staff. For example, research and development would contribute in very different ways than sales and marketing. When measurement had taken place, the objectives for the reward system, and the most appropriate reward strategies, could be determined.

Exhibit 7.1 shows a whole range of processes and factors that can influence the outcome of a payment system. Each will affect the organisation's eventual performance in its own way, and each can in turn be affected by the payment system. An incentive

Exhibit 7.1

Processes and factors influencing the outcome of a new incentive scheme

Cell 1: Environmental conditions

- product market
- labour and other factor markets
- technology and production methods
- level of investment
- structure of industry
- government policy

Cell 2: Company profile and structure

- ownership
- size
- organization structure
- management, style, philosophy, policy and objectives
- centre of decision-making power
- degree of consultation and active participation
- past economic performance
- characteristics of the labour-force
- physical working conditions

Cell 3: Incentive scheme design and implementation

- type of scheme
  - initiation of scheme
  - management's aims
  - suitability of scheme
  - responsibility for scheme design
- management effort
  - depth and breadth of consultation with employees
  - degree of help provided by managers and supervisors about introduction and operation of scheme
  - amount of time, effort and resources committed to the scheme.

Cell 4: Features of work

- nature of work: complicated– simple, varied – repetitive, worker paced – machine paced, individual-group, closely supervised – independent
- manual, machine or automated
- product quality
- material usage, waste, scrap
- maintenance hours
- order lead time

Cell 5: The behavioural system

- work performance
  - number of employees, skill distribution
  - absenteeism, labour turnover, overtime, mobility
  - disputes, time lost, frequency, industrial relations climate
  - union membership, level of bargaining, bargaining issues
- individual and group attitudes and motivators
  - what rewards sought
  - attractions of this work
  - attitude to incentive scheme
  - attitude to work, the organisation management, other workers

Cell 6: Operating systems

- work schedule and flow
- job differentials, transfers and recruitment
- stock levels, work in progress and work allocation procedures

Cell 7: Changes in productivity

- output – input relationships
- increases in jobs or work
- effects on the nature of work, behavioural systems, structure or environment
- unexpected changes
- other changes that have occurred to affect productivity

Cell 8: Changes in production costs

- direct unit costs: material, labour, maintenance
- indirect costs: stock, work in progress, maintenance, tools spares, advertising.
- work study and costing methods.

Cell 9: Other changes introduced in operating and control systems by management, e.g.

- job evaluation
- centralised maintenance
- group technology
- quality circles, etc, etc.

Source: Bowey et al., (1982)

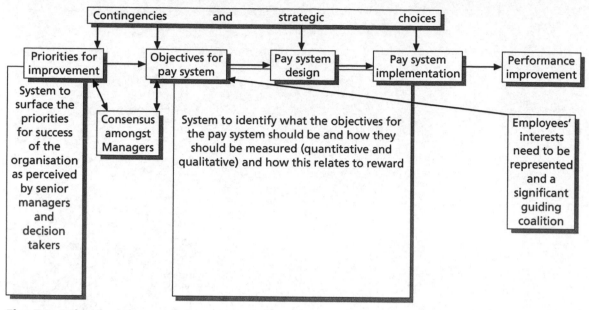

Fig. 7.2 Enlarging the model

bonus scheme could, for example, increase the turnover rate of staff and lead to a drop in quality, possibly costing the organisation far more in the long run than the higher output achieved through the scheme. The exhibit also illustrates a point made by Pfeffer (1998) – that it is not labour rates that are important in an organisation, but labour costs, and high labour costs can just as easily be brought about by low wage payments and unskilled staff. This refutes the commonly held view that it is high wages that are the root of all evil.

Figure 7.2 enlarges on the process outlined above showing how contextual factors and strategic choices pervade each stage of the pay system design and implementation process, from the establishment of priorities for success, to the linking of these to pay system objectives, to the developing of a consensus among all those in the organisation about what these objectives are. Of course, the consultation process also helps managers learn about the perspectives of those who will have to work with the scheme. The discussion, argument and debate generated have the effect of eliciting better-quality information from those who know more not only about the detail of how performance can best be improved, but also how it might be measured. This kind of intelligence is often all the more important because it is the sort of information about which management is, in many cases, misinformed. As has already been argued, this occurs even at the highest levels in organisations. Indeed it may well be at these levels that misinformation about objectives is most significant. Galbraith (1967) claims that the technostructure (the controlling executives) of an organisation usually has primary goals that are not identical with those of the employing organisation. For example, growth is more important to the technostructure than is return on investment, since growth protects the executive's position. How much more likely it must be that at lower levels in the organisation there will be a disparate array of objectives.

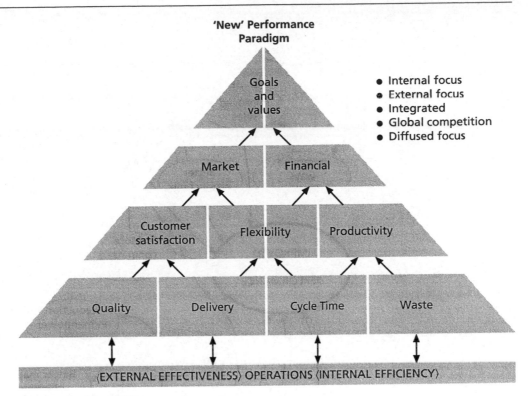

'New' Performance Paradigm

Goals and values

- Internal focus
- External focus
- Integrated
- Global competition
- Diffused focus

Market — Financial

Customer satisfaction — Flexibility — Productivity

Quality — Delivery — Cycle Time — Waste

(EXTERNAL EFFECTIVENESS) OPERATIONS (INTERNAL EFFICIENCY)

Source: Lynch and Cross (1991)

Fig. 7.3 The importance of multiple measures

Individuals' positions in the organisational hierarchy will also affect the measures they use to assess their performance and the time horizons these span (Thorpe and Horsburgh, 1991). This is because as one descends the organisational hierarchy, the measures used to some extent are reflective of the means by which the objectives of the level above were achieved, and thus become increasingly easier to define and measure, and are more short term. As a consequence, the higher up in an organisation a person is, the broader will be the measures, and the longer the time horizons. At the lower organisational levels, partial measures of productivity replace the more global ones. At shopfloor level, measures used tend to be single indices of output.

Problems, of course, arise when the performance measures used cease to relate to the company's longer-term needs and objectives, as perceived by those responsible for its direction. As noted earlier, a consultation process facilitates the development of a more satisfactory top management view of organisational priorities. In addition performance measures should address processes, not just fragmented activities, and to do this they can look both inside the organisation and outside (e.g. at customer satisfaction), and be qualitative as well as quantitative. Figure 7.3 shows diagrammatically the kind of measures that offer an external as opposed to an internal focus. Many of these have qualitative aspects. Of course, there is a range of analytical tools which can be used to focus on key aspects of strategic performance or their measures, for example, Porter's value chain (Porter, 1981), getting the measure of your business (Neeley *et al.* (1998) and Kaplan and Norton's (1996) balanced score card approach.

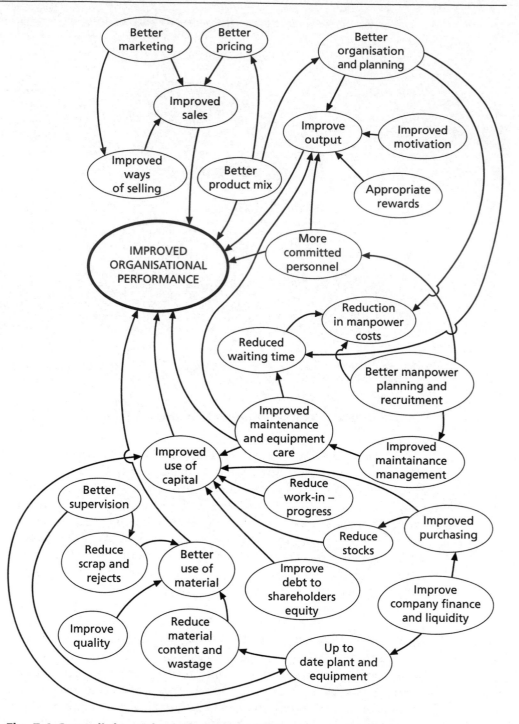

Fig. 7.4 Some links and relationships within an organisation

Taking a systems perspective on performance can be affected by a great many things, all of which are interrelated. What activities and measures are important in one part of an organisation can be quite inappropriate in another. Figure 7.4 illustrates some of these links and relationships.

A process of consultation can also help here by avoiding the problems of over-emphasis on means at the expense of goals. For example, over-reliance on labour performance indices, collected at individual or department level, may fail to take account of where current and future sales are coming from, resulting in a less than optimal product mix, or too much time being devoted to work which is not of the highest priority. Without a mechanism of communicating the organisation's priorities downwards, misunderstandings can arise. Consider the following quotation gained from research conducted in an engineering organisation.

> A lot of frustrations are creeping into manual and staff employees alike because the management does not do enough to explain why they do things. They think we should automatically understand the company's problems irrespective of what they are. Twelve months ago, the company could have concluded an agreement by co-operation and a ballot of the members taken. Now when it was offered again it was forced on the workforce and proved to be far more costly to the company than the first deal would have been.

Organisations can become locked into once important working practices that no longer relate to the corporate objectives. A consultation process closes the gap of understanding, making the organisation's priorities better understood and translating these into appropriate performance measures, objectives for a payment system and, from there, the design of a practical system. This approach is not new to American pay researchers as the following contribution illustrates. Lawler and Bullock (1978) two well-known American researchers into pay and reward comment:

> Most approaches to changed pay systems are top down; they assume that people above those on the pay scheme should make the decisions. What about letting the people who will be affected by the plan be a fundamental part of the decision?

Vroom and Yetton (1973) also suggested that some degree of participation and co-operation in the design and implementation of payment systems leads to a greater understanding of their workings and of the need for their introduction. Morse and Reimer (1956) commented that a company encouraging more participation in decisions regarding pay is a major part of any longitudinal participation exercise.

Three distinct benefits of adopting a strategy of consultation can therefore be identified:

1 Management will learn about the contingent and contextual variables that are associated with performance improvement. These can be translated into measurable objectives for all levels in an organisation. As Lawler and Bullock indicate when people are involved in design, they can provide information that would not have been considered had they not been involved. In addition, a great deal of useful information is learned about the organisation which can be the basis for identifying more appropriate priorities and payment system objectives.

2 Management will also learn about the contingent social and behavioural variables which need to be taken into account if the design and implementation of a new system is to 'fit' the people who are to work with it. Quite often, management and

employee perceptions differ widely and what management may think motivates and rewards may be quite different from the reality, and vice versa.

3 The third benefit is that the very process of consultation and participation will lead to understanding and commitment. Lawler and Bullock also found this to be the most important benefit of a participative system because it substantially increased the chances of the successful implementation of a new approach. If staff and managers at middle and lower levels contribute significantly to the design, they become more conscious of the organisation's priorities and how these can best be met. They might also become more committed to making the outcome a success, the new scheme becoming something in which they have a vested interest and in which they are more likely to place their trust.

Undertaking a process of systematic analysis of an organisation in this way will highlight where development and change are needed to meet a company's objectives, and change is of course far better attempted when a climate of uncertainty is dispelled. As White (1978) remarks:

> When environmental uncertainty is high, it is only by different groups or individuals pooling their own bits of information to piece together the environmental 'jigsaw' that the pattern becomes clear to any of them; that is, the reduction of uncertainty is dependent on communication.

An example: sources of work satisfaction for coal miners

In research in which I was involved, Geoff Nichols (1980) conducted a diary study in the coal mines of North West England.[1] He uncovered some interesting and hitherto little understood 'satisfaction' for the miners in their work. One of these, for all the men, was money. But we found it to be of varying importance to different people. Face teams which were predominantly composed of men highly motivated by money, responded best to monetary reward. B88 face was very often the one which performed best during the week. The colliery manager attributed its high performance level to the fact that the workers were 'a very young team and they like the money'. Others saw them as 'just plain greedy'.

Money was clearly important to men like Peter, who had made a decision to enter mining from another industry. He would usually work an hour's overtime between 6.00 a.m. and 7.00 a.m. to obtain extra pay. He had two children to support. On 25 February, he wrote, 'I hope I can make it for 6.00 a.m. all week, as the overtime will help towards my holidays, but I have a habit of oversleeping.' However, the money did not appear to be sufficient to induce many men to work weekends, as evidenced by another entry in Peter's dairy: 'Barry came around again and was asking the men who wanted to work at the weekend, and it was the same old faces that told him they wanted to work, and the rest of the men are always joking about them and saying that they must have a lot of things on H.P. and cannot afford to have a weekend off and in some cases I think it is true.'

A second source of satisfaction was the attainment of set targets. Most men were aware of the 'norm', the number of cuts needed to achieve the standard level of take per shift, on their face. Satisfaction was always gained from achieving this number of cuts for its own sake regardless of how it translated into money. For example, on one day that the shift had done two and a half cuts, one miner commented, 'That is the first time this week we even reached our norm but I checked our face advance rate for this week so far . . . our weekly norm cannot be reached this week.' And again the following week, he wrote, 'No doubts about reaching our norm. By 12.30 a.m. the cutter starts on the third strip.' Jim too, an overman, noted, 'This made just over two full cuts for 18 men and myself, which is a very good day.' The incentive scheme offered the miners a target level of performance that they had never had before.

Yet a third motivator we detected was the respect derived from achievement. This was related to targets, as particular respect was gained by being a member of, or particularly the overman of, the face team which had made the highest contribution to the pooled incentive each week. Although the incentive payments were pooled between the faces, the performance of each individual face, and hence its contribution to the pool, was recorded on the 'bonus board'. This board was displayed near the lamp room, which every incentive worker had to pass through during the day. The satisfaction of knowing that their face team had made the biggest contribution to the pool was very important to the miners. The importance of achievement as a motivator is reflected in an entry in Jim's diary: 'On Friday some men went home early. Even so, the face had an average advance of 12.75 metres, which was over two metres more than any other face in the pit, and this gave me the Yellow Jersey.' The Yellow Jersey was a fictitious item that the overmen at the pit strove to get. It was a term borrowed from the Milk Race and meant your face had the best advance of the week. As Jim added, 'It's all about honour you know.'

The 'bonus board' also created a sense of rivalry and competition, as shown again in Jim's diary: 'S8 had been doing OK, but not as good as they (F3) did. F3 did the best advance it's ever done, 12 metres, and it was great to go around S8's and rib them and tell them to get their fingers out.' The men on different shifts were motivated as much by personal pride and the professionalism with which they approached the job, as they were by the cash incentive. The achievement of high output in the eyes of their colleagues also served to maintain production at a high level.

A fourth source of satisfaction, of particular importance to overmen and deputies, was simply the knowledge that they had done their job well. The norm might not have been reached and the incentive pay might not have been high, but the men walked away from their job at the end of the day pleased that it had been done well. This concern with doing a job well was closely related to the particular dangers encountered in mining. It was especially important that the overmen were more concerned with safety than with monetary reward bonus, as this helped to ensure that the former was not disregarded for the sake of the latter. As Jim wrote, 'Yesterday I came out of my district (F3) with some degree of satisfaction. It had been a particularly good day for a number of reasons. First we had done two full cuts for the first time for several weeks. Although this is one third of a cut down on the norm set by the Manager it is still good performance on what I consider a very difficult face to work.' Indeed, safety was a major priority of all the men. As Andy wrote, 'While tackling a difficult job, I was seriously injured a few years ago and this was at the back of my mind all the time. I was off work on crutches for eight months and all the bonus in the world is not worth being injured again.'

A fifth source of satisfaction, and one that was mainly of importance to managers, was the regard in which they were held by their superiors in the Coal Board. The National

Coal Board used management by objectives, and the area officials at Head Office gave the managers at Hillend certain targets to reach. While the managers were keen to reach the targets for their own personal satisfaction, they were particularly concerned to satisfy their area officials.

A sixth source of satisfaction of great importance to the miners in general was leaving work. On Friday afternoons, the men would often leave early, even though their pay was reduced by this. It would happen to a greater extent on the day preceding a holiday. The men were supposed to leave the pit at 7.30 p.m. on Friday. The early leaving was described by Jim on F3: 'When the cutter gets to the end of the face on Friday afternoon the men won't start cutting again for love nor money. . . . When they stop at 6.00 it grieves me but unless you go around bawling at everybody there is little else I can do.' As Andy put it, 'Friday today, thank God. It seems that the life of a coal miner is all darkness and dust. All week long I have been looking forward to Friday. It's a pity that it's not Friday more often.' These examples of source of satisfaction gained in miners were gained from close contact and study, and serve to reveal something of social and behavioural variables (and the different motivations) that were present in the mine.

Diagnosis of factors

Diagnosis of variables such as those described above can be conducted in a number of different ways. All, though, involve a commitment to listening.

The Manchester Business School researchers advocated the use of a range of detailed measurements which profiled features of the organisation. In practice, many of these were difficult to measure quantitatively, for example the percentage loss in output due to work-flow problems, but nevertheless some attempt at measurement was thought to be beneficial.

Others have advocated the use of surveys, which have the advantage of recording the views of a great many people in a short period of time. Although thorough, they are impersonal, and only allow individuals to answer the questions asked (which may not give them the opportunity to provide the information they wished). This approach and the use of groups can be useful as an 'unfreezing' mechanism (Lewin, 1947), to help 'soften' the prevailing norms of a group prior to introducing change. Through debate, group norms can be brought out and considered afresh.

Lawler and Bullock (1978) and Bowey and Thorpe (1986) also advocate the use of groups. They believed that small task forces of between five to nine people should undertake diagnosis of the current situation, which would form the basis for future decisions (as with quality circles, action learning, or the productivity action teams in Total Quality Management programmes), sometimes in conjunction with a detailed survey undertaken by management.

Although the factors important to the design of a payment system are not the same for every organisation, Table 7.1 shows those which might be considered (cf. Thorpe, 1980).

Application of these techniques can be illustrated by one case study where we found that the system dictated that, regardless of ability or aptitude, operators could not progress up the hierarchical structure unless they had seniority over their colleagues. They were also restricted from taking over the jobs of more senior colleagues except through absence.

Table 7.1 Possible factors in pay system design

Technical and organisational
- Current customer requirements or dissatisfactions
- Technology used now and likely developments
- Nature of the work and likely changes
- Prospective changes in product market segment
- Aims of management in introducing the scheme
- Type and level of communication and consultation
- Size of the work unit and organisation
- Design of jobs
- Organisational structure
- Interdependence of jobs
- Machine breakdown and maintenance system
- Availability of substitute machines and/or workers
- Physical characteristics of the workplace
- Manufacturing or servicing costs *vis-à-vis* competitors (market tolerance)
- Delivery performance
- Pricing policy
- Working conditions
- Interdependence of work between sections

Social and behavioural
- History of individual and collective industrial relations
- Current industrial relations climate
- Management style
- Orientations of the workforce and management, including aims and interests
- Relevant dimensions of the dominant value system in the organisation
- Fatigue
- Human relations inside work
- Participation
- Autonomous work groups
- Level of belief in the need for incentives among managers

Environmental
- Competitiveness of product market
- Product market buoyancy
- Market share
- Economic and political climate
- History of incentives locally and in the industry
- Local culture and the traditions of the industry

The introduction of the incentive scheme had an impact on the everyday running of the plant for both operatives and management. The workers interviewed openly admitted to jumping in on others' jobs to preserve their level of bonus. Most suggested that this was one of the better unseen benefits of the scheme. There was a much greater feeling of teamwork than ever before, and most workers felt that their jobs had become more interesting as a result. Reward had shifted from pay for seniority to more interesting work and greater job satisfaction.

CONCLUSION

It is possible to begin to draw some conclusions about how change might be effectively brought about, and about how payment systems might be designed and implemented – particularly how they might be linked to the strategic priorities of an organisation (Kotter, 1996 and Pettigrew and Whipp, 1993).

Lessons for managers

From the experience of the increasing number of 'action research' interventions in organisations focused on changing their systems of pay there appear to be a number of lessons that practitioners might learn about the processes.

Expand the information base

What managers might begin to consider is how they can develop a process that un-covers the understandings, expectations and motivations of organisational members and matches these to a thorough environmental assessment of the priorities the organ-isation will need to focus on if it is to be successful. This process might well need to be undertaken at two levels – at a senior level to clarify the organisation's priorities and at a more operational level to communicate these to the workforce to learn how best they might be achieved.

Such a process appears to be more important than matching the type of payment system to non-social characteristics of the organisation and its environment (such as new technology, location and size), even though some of these characteristics do, as research has shown, have an effect on results. The process by which a payment system is designed and implemented is crucial to its success, and success is associated with the extent to which managers really understand their organisation. It must be recognised that the problems of collecting information, consulting and revising ideas prior to imple-menting a change is likely to demand considerable time and effort and there are few short cuts.

Ensure the involvement and commitment of managers

It must be remembered that David beat Goliath, in other words, ensure that the scheme is not modified or subverted in its implementation. This to a large extent requires appropriate leadership by management. Much research evidence on change (Kotter, 1996 and Pettigrew and Whipp, 1993) clearly shows that senior managers need to be involved from the beginning and to have the commitment and competence to carry through the programme if it is not to be modified or subverted by others in the organ-isation pursuing different goals and objectives. This will also serve to ensure that there is a close link established and maintained between the strategic and the opera-tional, and that coherence in the payment system is maintained. If the reader refers to table 5.2 in chapter 5 it will be seen, for example, that rewarding individuals might well undermine the working provision of team working and co-operation.

Middle managers should have a clear role in the process so that they do not feel threatened and disenfranchised. Prior training and briefing is often necessary before people are comfortable conducting their roles.

The commitment of employees at a junior level can be greatly influenced by how they perceive and experience the commitment of those at more senior levels. Powerful messages can come from relatively small symbolic acts, serving to undermine change.

Encourage the participation of staff

Encourage participation by establishing a large enough coalition of staff to drive through the change. The experience of organisations making change has shown that providing opportunities for participation, both formal and informal dramatically improves company performance. The key does appear to be good human resource man-agement practice (Pettigrew and Whipp, 1993), in particular are the involvement of organisational members at any level (preferably those who can see a wider context than simply their own current role) with a contribution to make. Useful techniques here include involving trade union officials, and establishing a joint steering group representing the main staff groups to be affected by the change. This latter technique has the added advantage of ensuring a close link between the strategic and the operational (Pettigrew and Whipp, 1993).

Be process-led

The importance of process is vastly underrated, and it is important to recognise the important social, idiosyncratic and subjective aspects of individuals and change, as well as the rational ones (Lupton and Tanner, 1986). It is the process that will deliver the content and context of the change, and it needs to be made explicit.

There are usually debates about whether outsiders should be involved in facilitating the process. There may well be advantages in engaging a facilitator or external agent to act as a 'felt fair' broker to assist the change process. This person can help both by bringing new knowledge or information into the organisation, and by ensuring that existing knowledge can be fed into the areas where it can be heard and acted upon.

The strategic nature of such an approach to changing pay systems cannot be understated. As this type of change permeates a large area of the organisation and requires the re-organisation and revision of procedures, it provides an opportunity for improving performance in a variety of ways – what Pettigrew and Whipp (1993) refer to *as coherence*. These improvements might be in the area of communication control procedures, technology or training. Lawler and Bullock (1978) also saw this possibility, writing:

> The compensation system is important to every employee and it impacts on each organisation member. Many time change programmes are limited to a sub-section of the organisation, such as a department or functional area, or to an issue that is not important to everyone. As a result change is slow and often is not very significant. Compensation provides a broad base upon which to begin organisational change. Beginning with compensation can provide a model for how other problems can be dealt with. Usually organisations have no historical reference for the process of solving system-wide problems that affect the quality of working life and organisational effectiveness. These mechanisms and processes can be developed and made explicit by changing the compensation system.

Research studies have shown that when payment systems are used as interventions and catalysts for broader organisational changes they have led to improved motivation and attitudes towards pay. As Lawler and Bullock observe, 'A physicist once remarked that every time we try to separate something to study it, we find it hitched to everything else in the universe.' Payment systems affect almost all other sub-systems of an organisation, not only performance, but also appraisal procedures, information systems, measurement systems, job design, management style and organisational culture.

Practical steps for a process-led approach

A programme of intervention using a process-led approach to change could follow a schedule similar to that given below.[2]

Establishment of business priorities through discussions with senior managers

An initial discussion amongst senior managers in the organisation about the programme, with the purpose of identifying the main priorities for the business. Sometimes it is not easy to get this started. Beginning a process of effective participation might, for example, require a change in management style and the establishment of some new structures.

Various strategic decision support methods (such as cognitive mapping) might be helpful here. Alternatively, confidential interviews could be conducted with all senior managers, and their different views and perspective played back for analysis, discussion and debate. An outside facilitator may be useful, or a mature team might feel able to conduct this process itself. Yet another way would be for managers to send round a questionnaire to all workers, both to diagnose the problems the organisation faces on a number of dimensions and to alert all staff members that change is under way and that they have a contribution to make.

Since an aim of payment systems is to improve performance, perhaps a key focus in the participative process should be the identification of ways of improving performance. Payment systems could then be designed which would reinforce appropriate behaviours. It must be remembered, however, that the payment system alone can not lead to improved performance, but can only influence behaviour in one part of a whole system.

Encouragement of participation of all organisational members

Managers need to communicate to workers the purpose, implications of change for individuals' work and what contribution they can make. One way of enabling this part of the process is to establish small groups of six to ten people from different departments and organisational levels (such as shopfloor workers, supervisors, managers, research and development people and so on). The work of group members needs to be interdependent (i.e. they should be from the same section, department or function of the company). Groups need to meet fairly regularly to discuss ways of tackling particular problems related to performance improvement. These problems could be of two kinds – those which the group itself puts forward which, if solved, would improve performance, and those which management feeds into the groups as priorities. It is important for both types of problem to be debated and discussed, decisions reached and action implemented.

Decisions in these groups should be reached by discussion and based on full information. A process of organisation and debate should result in consensus. By such a process, employees will be able to influence the decisions, the strategic and operational will be linked and commitment will be gained. It is considered (Bowey *et al.*, 1982) that issues about which management and the workforce are likely to disagree fundamentally, are better left for the normal channels of negotiation. Care should therefore be taken to recognise any such issues and to remove them to another forum as soon as possible so as to avoid bringing them into team discussions.

The focus of discussion can be all those aspects of the business which involve the organisation working more effectively, such as methods of working and ways of organising the work systems for increasing efficiency (i.e. managing technology). There is little satisfaction for any member of an organisation in seeing activities being administered inefficiently, and teams working participatively can engender enthusiasm in everyone to perform better at work.

As we have indicated, this kind of participative approach does require a change in management style. Instead of managers taking decisions about pay independently, based solely on their own judgement and experience, they will need to involve in the decision-making process those individuals whose work will be affected. Some managers for whom this may be a major departure from their established management style, will need support and encouragement until they can practise the new style independently.

A participative team may sometimes draw its individuals from different sections of the company. This may be a sensible approach where the traditional departmental boundaries are expected to have to shift to meet some change in customer needs as a result of new technology, or where a project affects several different sections of the company. Such teams or 'sets' (in action-learning terms) might be either temporary (if the project is one which does not require a permanent realignment of responsibilities and change of organisation structure) or permanent (especially if the process measures to be used are likely to change rapidly). It is advisable to change the membership of these terms periodically to gain the perspectives of others in the organisation. One might, for example, replace two members annually. It is also desirable to try to retain a manager in each team, so that changes in the environment can be quickly passed into the organisation for discussion.

Programmes of work for the management team

The first stage should involve managers in discussions on how to manage the process, and the difference it will make to their own decision-making responsibilities. For example, managers should consider the need to open up decisions for discussion with the workers affected, how this approach differs from what is currently done, and the effects it will have on their authority.

Discussions should focus on how to cope with the proposals which will inevitably arise from employees within groups, particularly the need to respond positively and to demonstrate that action is being taken, to be flexible and to continue to encourage teams and their members to research their proposals adequately and to review how much change has been made in response to team proposals.

Managers should at this stage decide which discrete part of the company each team will represent, based on a clear rationale. Teams that can relate to particular processes are increasingly seen as important in helping to establish the most appropriate performance measures for that aspect of work. Finally, managers must identify the priorities and future plans which they will communicate to teams.

Discussions with workers for whom participative teams are intended

The first step here is to make a convincing case as to why workers should take part in the exercise, explaining that it will offer them the opportunity to influence decisions that affect their work. To be able to win the support of the workers, it is important to ensure that there is nothing in the approach which could run counter to the aims of trade union or other representatives, whose support for the exercise will greatly assist its acceptance by members. It is wise to ensure at this stage that such representatives know what the project is about, how it has worked elsewhere, and that they can play a vital role in its operation.

The next step is to invite the workers or staff to nominate or volunteer to make up a team (of, say, six people) for their area. There are pros and cons as to whether management should identify individuals or employees should choose their representation. Either way it is a good idea to ask the group to select one member as a joint chair. The management team should nominate the formal line manager as a joint chair, checking first that this person is willing to perform the role.

131

The last stage is to train all the joint chairs in matters relating to operation of teams. This will include procedures, remit and how to chair meetings, how to write reports and so on, as well as skills such as team membership roles and additional information on to what the team should focus. In addition, issues which the management team feels is relevant to the functioning of the team should be addressed.

Recruitment of a full-time coordinator

It would be hoped, that if communication has taken place correctly, all those in the organisation will know how the change will take place and their role in it, as well as how much commitment the company is giving to the process. At this time, it is probably appropriate to appoint a full-time co-ordinator. This person's role would be to ensure that the teams operate smoothly and are adequately serviced, and that their ideas are co-ordinated.

Pilot teams followed by extension to other areas

In line with other changes, it is often a good idea to try out the process in one part of the organisation before extending it to the whole company. It is also important to remember that the process will, as likely as not, work differently in different parts of the organisation, given different personalities and issues. The structure of the process and content should not therefore be seen as a panacea but instead should remain flexible. Kotter, (1996) suggests that successful change programmes feature short-term wins, where performance is improved incrementally.

Six-monthly review

As with all change, it is important to review achievements and progress on a regular basis, in order to resolve difficulties and adapt the process, as well as to provide greater impetus where necessary.

Co-ordination

In order to ensure coherence and co-ordination between each group's different measures and suggestions, it is important that the co-ordinator formally reviews what has been achieved with a view to ensuring 'fit'.

It will be recognised that this blueprint of how to set about developing a process to design and implement an incentive scheme is rather different from what often seems practical. Case studies of how they can work in practice however illustrate for themselves, the effectiveness of the approach.

NOTES

1 The examples of sources of satisfactions from Coal Miners was undertaken as part of an M.Sc. thesis. This study is reported in chapter 6 of *Payment Systems and Productivity* (Bowey and Thorpe, 1986).

2 The process outlined is based on applied research conducted at John G. Kincaid Ltd and written up by John Taylor (Production Director) and Angela Bowey. Suggestions for practical steps for a process led approach are contained in the conclusion to chapter 8 of *Payment Systems and Productivity* (Bowey and Thorpe, 1986).

LEARNING ACTIVITIES

1 Identify the organisational variables that will affect performance in your organisation and their relative importance in terms of impact.

2 Assess the extent to which the variables identified in question 1 vary in impact in different areas of the organisation.

3 Now, identify which of these factors you would consider require change and how that change might be facilitated by the re-design of the reward system.

4 This chapter advocates a processual approach to designing and implementing a remuneration scheme. Discuss the extent to which this approach might vary, and why, within non-unionised and unionised organisations.

REFERENCES

Ackermann, F. and Belton, V. (1994) 'Managing Corporate Knowledge Experience with SODA and VISA', *British Journal of Management*, 5: 163–76.

Bowey, A.M. and Thorpe, R. with Hellier (1986) *Payment Systems and Productivity*. London: Macmillan.

Bowey, A.M. Thorpe, R., Nichols, G. Mitchell *et al.* (1982) 'Effects of Incentive Payment Systems: United Kingdom 1977–1980', Research paper no. 36, Department of Employment, September.

Burnes, B. (1996) *Managing Change: A strategic approach to organisational dynamics*. London: Pitman.

Crowe, D. (1992) 'A New Approach to Reward Management', in M. Armstrong (ed.), *Strategies for Human Resource Management*. London: Kogan Page.

Easterby-Smith, M.P.V., Thorpe, R. and Holman, D. (1996) 'Using Repertory Grids in Management', *Journal of European Industrial Training*, 20: 4.

Eden, C. and Ackermann, F. (1998) *Making Strategy: The journey of Strategic Management*. London: Sage.

Eden, C. Sims, D. and Jones, S. (1983) *Messing about in Problems*. Oxford: Pergamon Press.

Galbraith, J. (1967) *Organisational Design*. Reading, MA: Addison-Wesley.

Jessop, G. (1997) 'The Case for Shop Floor Participation', *Department of Employment, Gazette*, June.

Kaplan, R.S. and Norton, D.P. (1996) *The Balanced Scorecard*. Boston: Harvard University Press.

Kotter, (1995) 'Leading Change: Why transformation efforts fail', *Harvard Business Review*, March–April.

Lawler, E.E. and Bullock, R.J. (1978) 'Pay and Organisational Change', *The Personnel Administrator*.

Lawler, E.E. (1990) *Strategic Pay: Aligning organisational strategies and pay systems*. San Francisco: Jossey-Bass.

Lewin, K. (1947) 'Frontiers in Group Dynamics', *Human Relations*, 1: 16–40.

Lupton, T. and Tanner, I. (1986) *Achieving Change*. Aldershot: Gower.

Lynch, P.L. and Cross, K.F. (1995) *Measure up: How to measure Corporate Performance*. Oxford: Blackwell.

Mabey, C. and Maynard-White, B. (eds) (1997) *Managing Change*. London: Routledge.

Mahoney, T. (1992) 'Multiple Pay Contingencies: Strategic design of compensation', in M. Salman (ed.). *Human Resource Management*.

Marchington, M. (1992) *Managing the Team*. Oxford: Blackwell.

Morse, N.C. and Reinier, E. (1956) 'The Experimental Change of a Major Organisational Variable', *Journal of Abnormal and Social Psychology*, 52: 120–9.

Neeley, A. *et al.* (1981) 'Getting the measure of your Business', *Work Management*, University of Cambridge.

Nichols, G. (1980) 'A Study of the National Coal Board's Productivity Bonus Scheme', M.Sc. Thesis, Strathclyde University Business School.

Pedler, M., Burgoyne, J. and Boydell, T. (1979) *The Learning Company: A Strategy for Sustainable Development.* Second edition, London: McGraw-Hill.

Pettigrew, A. and Whipp, R. (1993) 'Understand the Environment', in C. Mabey and B. Mayon-White (eds), *Managing Change.* Second edition, London: The Open University/Paul Chapman Publishing.

Pfeffer, J. (1998) 'Six Dangerous Myths about Pay', *Harvard Business Review*, May–June: 109–19.

Porter, M. (1980) *Competitive-Strategy.* New York: Free Press.

Thorpe, R. (1980) 'The Relationship Between Payment Systems, Productivity and the Organisation of Work', M.Sc. Thesis, Strathclyde University Business School.

Thorpe, R. and Horsburgh, S. (1991) 'Productivity', *The Management Services Handbook.* London: Holt Rineholt Winston, Chapter 15.

White, M. (1978) 'Pay Methods: Attitude survey, diagnostic and change', *Personnel Review*, 7: 4.

Vroom, V.H. and Yetton, P.W. (1973) *Leadership and Decision Making.* University of Pittsburgh Press.

Whittington, R. (1993) *What is Strategy and Does it Matter?* London: Routledge.

FURTHER READING

Burns, B. (1996) *Managing Change: A strategic approach to organisational dynamics.* London: Pitman.

Crow, D. (1992) 'A New Approach to Reward Management', in M. Armstrong (ed.), *Strategies for Human Resource Management.* London: Kogan Page.

Lawler, E.E. (1990) *Strategic Pay: Aligning organisational strategies and pay.* San Francisco: Jossey Bass.

Neeley, A. *et al.* (1998) 'Getting the Measure of Your Business', *Work Management*, University of Cambridge.

PART II

Reward as a systems component

8 Strategic reward systems – pay systems and structures

Colin Massey

INTRODUCTION

At some stage every organisation has to consider changing their reward system. As features of the organisation change, the way in which the reward system supports them will also require change. This chapter discusses the ways in which this can be achieved.

The process of developing a pay structure seems mechanistic, yet at the same time it draws from concepts of motivation and communication and the softer elements of business management. It seems complex and full of mystery, with just a hint of the black art, yet virtually all managers, trade union representatives, and not a few employees would claim to be experts in the subject. People have been paid for what they do for time immemorial and usually there has been some kind of structure around both the content of the payment, the process by which the level of payment is determined, and the physical payment made. Nevertheless, theory on the role of pay and, importantly, how rewards, recognition and benefits should be configured in a way that aligns the thoughts and actions of employees with business strategy was a comparatively barren area until quite recently. Thinking and practice in the management of people is developing rapidly and nowhere more so than in the field of pay and how a payment system should be structured to stimulate improved individual and organisational performance. Good scheme design must also balance the potentially conflicting aspirations of shareholders, customers and employees.

PAY DESIGN AND RE-DESIGN

The payment systems paradigm is changing, as it always has done, in line with the prevalent management philosophy of the time. Thus the approach in the 1960s and 1970s was characterised by scientific management (for example, detailed job descriptions, job evaluation and work-measurement-based payment-by-results); an inclination towards the theory X view of what inducements needed to be offered to get a fair days work (for example, a strong perception that blue-collar workers needed piecework to ensure reasonable effort); and collective bargaining to set pay levels, which were then often applied uniformly across a bargaining group.

An increasing use of performance-related pay in the late 1980s and early 1990s saw the beginnings of a shift from pay for the job towards the individualisation of pay and pay for the person. Now there is a growing recognition that an effective pay system can be central to business success.

There have been several attempts to devise methods of systematically selecting a payment system. In 1969 Lupton and Gowler described 'an effort bargain' referred to in chapter 1 in which the employee and the manager implicitly or explicitly concluded to regulate the relationship between contribution and reward. In this effort/reward relationship 'effort' had a wide interpretation and covered, for example, physical effort, mental effort, contribution, performance and attendance.

Four kinds of influence affected the operation of a payment scheme – technology, labour markets, disputes and disputes procedures, and structural characteristics. These could be further sub-divided into 21 factors. A second dimension identified the type of effort (time, energy or competence) and the unit of accountability (individual, group or plant). These in turn each had three sub-divisions (reciprocal-immediate, reciprocal-deferred, and non-reciprocal). Thus Lupton and Gower proposed that a 23 by nine factor profile of a company could be produced and that this could be used as part of the process of selecting a payment system. Organisations would make a profile of themselves against these criteria and a 'best-fit' payment system would suggest itself. The first part of this template is shown below with the beginning of a profile marked on (see figure 8.1).

1 (g)	Type of effort	Time			Energy			Competence		
2 (g)	Unit of accountability	Individual			Group			Plant		
		1	2	3	4	5	6	7	8	9
1	Length of job cycle									
2	Number of job modifications									
3	Degree of automation									
4	Number of product changes									
5	Etc.									

Fig. 8.1 A profile of a company

Lupton and Gower's approach also endeavoured to encourage managers to find the answers to four critical questions:

1 What should the objectives of a firm be when installing or modifying a payment scheme?
2 What payments systems are available to choose from?
3 How should a firm go about deciding which of the available schemes is best suited to its circumstances?
4 Which of the available schemes satisfies its objectives?

This four-stage approach still remains valid today despite the shift away from the formulaic approach contained in Lupton and Gower's seminal work.

Thomas Wilson (1994) proposes the development of a reward strategy that is 'a plan of action for the way an organisation can direct its resources to reinforce desired behaviours'. The economics of an organisation ('the way it uses resources to serve customers and achieve competitive advantage') and the values of the organisation (a reflection of 'an organisation's determination of which behaviours get reinforced and which get punished') are what the payment system must focus on to support the organisations business strategy.

Flannery, Hofrichter and Platten (1996) argue that there are four major cultural models: functional, process, time-based and network. Organisations are unlikely to fit a model precisely however and there are hybrids, for example, a process/time-based culture. There may also be more than one culture within an organisation. Some types of payment system are more appropriate to some of these work cultures than others. Thus the type of grading structure, application of incentives, access to benefits, and so on, that suit best the culture of the organisation can be identified. It should not be overlooked that pay can also be used as one of the ways in which the culture can be changed by identifying the desired cultural model and putting in place the appropriate payment system to encourage employees to behave in the desired way.

Some organisations have adapted mission statements with the objective of producing a vision for their payment system, a statement of the values that underpin it, set goals and objectives, developed action plans for implementation and measures against which to evaluate their achievements.

All these methods which identify 'the best-payment system' call for a logical step-by-step analysis of the requirements of the business and in the selection of the most appropriate scheme to satisfy those requirements. What they reject is the selection of what may be called the airport panacea – the choice of a solution because it is in vogue at the time and appearing on the shelves of the airport departure lounge stationers. The best fit for one organisation is unlikely to be so for another. They may seem to be the same type of organisation facing the same type of problems, employing the same type of people but investigation will reveal differences that will require a different solution, even if that difference is relatively subtle.

Defining the requirements

In designing or re-designing a scheme multiple factors need to be analysed both for the current state and future, the framework shown in exhibit 8.1 offers the reader a checklist to establish the organisation's current position and what will be required to meet its strategic objectives. The gap between the two represent features the payment system will need to reinforce or assist in developing if the organisation is to achieve its priorities for success.

Taking each in turn, managers should consider the following before any payment system is completed.

Business objectives and strategy: the objectives of the business three to five years hence; the strategy, and action plans required to achieve those objectives.

Exhibit 8.1

Business objectives and strategy		
Human resource objectives and strategy		
Critical success factors for the business		
Strengths and weakness of the payment system	Current	Future
Organisation culture	Current	Required
Organisation structure and processes	Current	Required
Product type and range	Current	Future
Processes technology	Current	Future
Type and degree of flexibility	Current	Required
Decision-making process	Current	Required
Focus of contribution	Current	Required
Performance levels	Current	Required
Performance management	Current	Required
Employee attitudes and aspirations	Current	Required
Employee skills and knowledge	Current	Required
Industrial relations and pay determination	Current	Required
Labour market competitiveness	Current	Required
Management skills	Current	Required

Human resource objectives and strategy: the consequential human resource objectives, strategy and action plans; behaviours required to achieve those objectives.

Critical success factors for the business: a specification of what the organisation must do well if it is to be successful and also identifying what it must not do; the behaviours essential for success and those that will be detrimental.

Strengths and weakness of the payment system: a SWOT analysis of the current pay and reward systems from the perspective of the customer, the shareholder and the employee; relevance of the grading structure and job evaluation scheme.

Organisation culture: the beliefs, attitudes and values Williams (1996) of the organisation and, if necessary, elements within it; how these impinge upon behaviours; use of pay and recognition to communicate vision and values.

Organisation structure and processes: consideration of the number of layers in the structure; the extent to which the organisation is structured around functions (sales, finance, etc.) or processes (customer, quality, etc.); the extent of functional or multifunctional project working; whether the organisation has a conventional or team-based structure; the extent of formal or informal networking required.

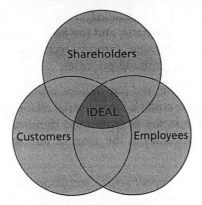

Fig. 8.2 Swot analysis of pay and rewards system
Note: The same process should be repeated when the new scheme is designed by way of a check that it will deliver.

Product type and range: type of products and services; demand forecasts for products and services; product and service changes and the influence of these on the skills and knowledge of employees.

Processes technology: types of process machinery, equipment and systems in use; changes in technology and the influence of these on the skills and knowledge of employees.

Type and degree of flexibility: the ability to change headcount through sub-contract, part-time employees, temporary, casual, short-term contracts, or fixed-term contracts; the ability to move employees between activities and tasks; the inherent ability of employees to adapt to change.

Decision-making process: the extent to which decision making and accountability is centralised, devolved or team based; where authority sits; the amount of discretion given to employees at different levels and in varying circumstances.

Focus of contribution: the relative importance of the individual contribution of employees or collaborative team working.

Performance levels: operational performance measures and achievements; performance relative to external measures; performance relative to competitors; opportunities for performance improvement; the relationship between pay and performance; what behaviours need to be reinforced to improve performance.

Performance management: ability of management to conceptualise what constitutes good performance; balance of target setting versus development; performance reviews, feedback, assessment of potential, succession planning and career management; extent to which individual employees are made aware of their contribution and competence relative to company, departmental, team or personal objectives; the extent to which opportunities for and constraints on performance improvement are identified and acted upon.

Employee attitudes and aspirations: attitudes to change; attitudes towards and understanding of customers, competition and key issues for the business; employee priorities in the areas of pay and reward.

Employee skills and knowledge: competence in relation to the business objectives, strategy and action plans, and the factors critical to success; competence in relation to product type and range, process technology, flexibility and performance; employee development and training priorities.

Industrial relations and pay determination: labour turnover, absence, age, gender and length-of-service profiles; the industrial relations and pay-bargaining context; trade unions and their role in the organisation; significant agreements on pay and performance; trade union priorities in the areas of pay and reward, policies, procedures and work organisation.

Labour market competitiveness: recruitment or retention difficulties; the actual and desired position in the salary and benefits league in the relevant labour market.

Management skills: ability to manage performance; ability to manage the payment system; competence in relation to the business objectives, strategy and action plans, and factors critical to success; competence in relation to product type and range, process technology, flexibility and performance; the extent to which managers should have delegated authority or flexibility for elements of the pay bill; management development and training priorities.

BRIDGING THE GAP

The whole point of the above exercise is for the organisation to obtain clarity about the current circumstances, the future state, and the behaviours that need to be reinforced. A payment system can be the most powerful communications mechanism in the business. It will indicate to employees what is important and what is not. Often though they receive the wrong message through managerial behaviour or develop a wrong impression based on the behaviours that they perceive the payment system to reward. Two examples emphasise how contradictory and confusing messages can be:

1 A team-based organisation had a performance appraisal process, the outcome of which affected the annual performance-based salary increase. Management communications, through various media, stressed the importance of collaboration and team working. However, the word 'team' did not appear in the vocabulary of performance assessment and the performance appraisal documentation emphasised individual contribution and the achievement of personal objectives. Additionally, a significant minority of managers wrongly emphasised the need for individuals to achieve their targets 'no matter what'. Such slips serve quickly to undermine important priorities, as one message the employees receive is cancelled out by another.

2 A firm had multiple and equally balanced performance measures of: contribution to sales generation, personal and business development and income earning. Very few employees believed that the first two sets of objectives were worth chasing because they had the perception that those employees who excelled in the third set of objectives got the biggest rewards.

Setting the scheme objectives

Once the task of obtaining clarity about the organisations circumstances has been undertaken the organisation should specify what it wants the payment system to do. It should identify what objectives the payment system should have and the behaviours it needs to reward. It is a fallacy to believe that a payment system can address all issues, and some of the problems identified will be better dealt with by some other action. Importantly, at this stage financial and non-financial rewards need to be separated out. Table 8.1 gives examples of some of the financial and non-financial rewards that can be built into a reward system – the non-financial aspects of reward are rarely given the same prominence and emphasis in the design of payment systems.

Table 8.1

Financial rewards	Non-financial rewards
Basic pay	Recognition
Individual, team, and corporate bonuses	Career opportunities
Performance related pay	Status
Skill and competency based pay	Responsibility
Pension and other benefits	Achievement

Pay needs to be aligned to business objectives and strategy, and the desired culture of the organisation, so that the behaviours that are important for the success of the enterprise are reinforced. In this context a critical review is required. Associated with this should be the development of non-financial forms of reward and recognition.

Purpose of pay structures

The purposes of payment structures are numerous and so too are the possible objectives an organisation may want to achieve when designing a system. Some of the typical possibilities are shown in the list below, which is by no means exhaustive.

- Accommodate market rates
- Attract employees
- Balance interests of all stakeholders
- Conform to equal value legislation
- Create a career structure
- Ensure consistency of reward
- Control costs
- Encourage individual growth
- Ensure no unjustified differential or benefits
- Provide career opportunities for specialists
- Foster a common purpose
- Improve customer service
- Improve quality

- Increase output
- Increase participation
- Internal equity
- Reflect levels of authority
- Reduce throughput time
- Reflect organisational needs
- Reinforce vision and values
- Reinforce organisation structure
- Retaining employees
- Reward performance, skill and competence.
- Support lateral movement
- Support occupational flexibility
- Support teamworking

DESIGN CHOICES

There are essentially three key decisions that need to be made in relation to the choice of design. How many structures? What type of structures? How many grades?

How many structures?

The first question is whether there should be one single integrated structure or should there be different structures, for example, for (a) blue-collar, white-collar and managerial jobs or (b) technical, administrative, and managerial jobs or (c) different labour market groups or (d) different bargaining groups? Of course all of the above have advantages and disadvantages and these are set out below. A 1997 Industrial Society survey revealed that nearly two thirds (64 per cent) of organisations have separate pay structures for different types of employees with differentiation between manual workers and others and between managers and staff. Organisations might want to consider different grade groupings for the following occupational groups:

- Executive management
- Management
- Professional
- Technical
- Administrative
- Skilled manual
- Manual

Employers however should be conscious that one of the major trends of the past two decades has been towards the harmonisation of terms and conditions of employment for different types of employees and the removal of distinctions such as 'staff' and 'manual' workers.

Single plant-wide grading structures

It is difficult to have harmonised conditions and 'single status' organisations yet separate payment schemes. Separate structures raise the prospect of the continuation of separate bargaining, differences in status and unnecessary distinctions between jobs. A single integrated grading structure is a prerequisite to flexibility, team working and single status employment. The administrative advantages of a single structure and a single method of job evaluation can be significant. A single integrated grading structure may well be introduced because it is attractive to remove complex multi-grade arrangements, perhaps based on separate bargaining units. But this is missing the point and losing the potential added value. Single integrated grading structures are a vehicle to promote harmony amongst the workforce, encourage the acquisition of skills and promote job growth.

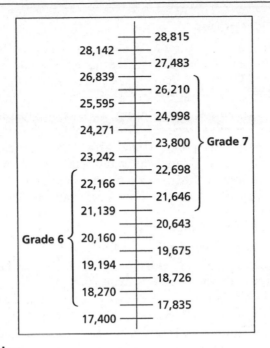

Fig. 8.3 A pay spine

Types of grading structures

Job or 'spot' rates

A single rate of pay for each grade with no differentiation, in terms of basic pay, between employees in the grade on the basis of performance, skill or contribution. There may, however, be non-consolidated performance bonuses paid in addition to the grade rate. This type of arrangement is typical of conventional manual worker payment schemes.

Pay spine

Figure 8.3 shows a hierarchy of rates of pay on a single spine. When such a system exists, when pay levels are reviewed either the spinal rates or the location of the grades on the spine can be changed. This type of arrangement is typical of traditional public-sector pay scales. The diagram shows the number of rates of pay encompassed by grades 6 and 7. Note in this spine there is an overlap between the grades.

Individual job range

Each job has its own rate of pay, often based on relative job evaluation results. This method can be used where there is a need to pitch rates of pay close to the labour market rates.

Grades

Jobs are grouped together; often according to some measure of job size, which may be determined by job evaluation. Jobholders may progress within their grade on the basis of performance, skill, length of service, etc.

Job family grades

Separate grade structures for different job families. Used where there is a need to treat occupations or professions differently; perhaps for career development purposes or to respond to labour market pressures. Basically job families group together a number of jobs which have some dimension of commonality defined by the organisation, this is usually a particular area of work, such as accountancy or information systems. The grade structure for each family would normally cover all associated jobs from entry levels through to the most senior, providing a vertical structure. The diversity of jobs within the organisation will normally determine the number of job families developed.

Job families can offer technical career structures and allow for increased responsiveness to labour market demands. They are sometimes called labour market structures.

Broad-band structures

Many organisations are finding that broad-banded payment systems, in which there are a small number of grades, work much better where there are flatter organisation structures and where there is team working. Where broad-banded systems are developed they tend to cover a greater proportion of the workforce, sometimes even used as a mechanism to harmonise disparate blue-collar, white-collar and managerial pay structures. Indeed, some broad-band systems are constructed by 'collapsing' existing multiple narrow bands into broad bands. Their use facilitates flexible or constantly changing job descriptions. They also enable lateral career paths and broadly defined areas of responsibility, both important features of delayered organisations.

Certainly, broad bands offer more freedom of movement and flexibility than narrow-banded systems but the advantages these offer in making decisions about pay, that will reflect the current and future needs of the organisation, also bring with them a loss of control. Loss of control within the system can result from an increased line management input into the decision-making process, without the restraint imposed by the multiple layers of narrow bands, and an increased tendency for pay to drift upward. The end result can be a system which, unless carefully monitored, can increase wage costs and lose that transparency that contributes to 'felt fairness'. The development of broad-banded systems and their control mechanisms are discussed more fully in chapter 9.

Grading choices

The four variables are number of grades, width, overlap and differentials. They are interdependent because, within the limits of the minimum salary of the bottom grade and the maximum salary of the top grade, a decision about any one of the variables will influence the other three. For example, on the one hand, if large differentials are required there will be fewer grades but if, on the other hand, the organisation wants to have a large number of grades it must accept smaller differentials. Whilst a spreadsheet can be a useful tool to inform the decision-making process, these choices are necessarily judgemental to meet the organisation's objectives and pay policies.

Number of grades

There is not an 'ideal' number but typically there will be five to ten but sometimes more. In broad-band structures there may be six or less. There are both internal and external factors of influence on the number chosen. These are shown below.

- Organisational structure
  - Number of levels
  - Reporting relationships
- The degree of flexibility required
  - High flexibility requirements leads to fewer and wider grades
  - Many narrow grades can reinforce job boundaries and demarcation
- Collective bargaining arrangements
  - Separate bargaining
  - Single table bargaining or single union agreement
- Job evaluation
  - Clusters of similarly sized jobs

- Pay policy
  - Size of differentials
  - Extent of grade overlap
  - Grade width
- Career paths
  - Within the grades
  - Through the grades
- Personal growth
  - Lateral movement or job enlargement easier with fewer broad grades
- Labour market issues
  - Labour market may make significant differentiation between some jobs

Differentials between grades

There are different approaches to measuring differentials; sometimes the relationship between the bottom of one grade to the bottom of the next grade below is used. More commonly it is the difference between the mid points of the grades. Thus if the mid point of the first grade is £18,000 and the mid point of the second grade is £21,240 then the differential is 18 per cent. Differentials in conventional structures will be between 15 per cent and 25 per cent but greater in broad-band structures and less in some manual or clerical grades. A constant percentage differential will result in the grades progressively increasing, in money terms, towards the higher grades. Often the percentage differential is increased so that, for example, differentials at the lower grades are approximately 15 per cent but in senior management grades 25 per cent. In structures where the lower grades are paid for overtime but the higher grades are paid a 'professional' salary, and expected to work whatever reasonable hours are necessary to do the job, an increased differential may be introduced where overtime pay ceases (see figure 8.4).

Overlap

The desirability of overlap of grades is one of the important matters of pay policy. Key questions are:

1 whether the organisation wishes to recognise exceptional contributions from employees who have progressed towards the top of their grade by rewarding them similarly to, or greater than, low contributors in the grade above;
2 whether trainees and new entrants in a grade are adding less value than experienced employees in the grade below.

Grade overlaps can also help to reinforce the idea that it is not necessary to obtain a promotion to be recognised and rewarded. Where there is overlap it is typically 25 per cent to 50 per cent. Overlaps of more than 50 per cent might be de-motivating to those

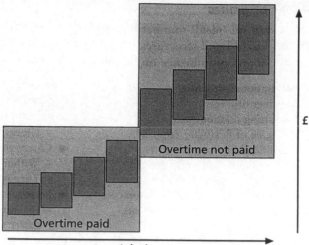

Fig. 8.4 Differentials between grades

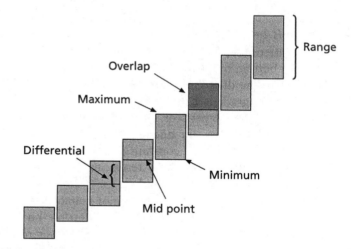

Fig. 8.5 Width of grades

at the lower end of the grade payments, particularly if the individual is managing the work of employees who are to the top end of the scale below.

Width of grades

Typically 20 per cent to 60 per cent if the width is measured as a percentage of the bottom of the grade. Also sometimes measured around the mid point (see figure 8.5).

PURPOSE OF JOB EVALUATION

In any grouping of jobs into a grade structure there are two sets of comparisons that need to be made. First, there is the need to produce a 'felt fair' rank order of jobs or grading, and, second, there is the need to compare these jobs with jobs in the labour market that are the same or substantially similar. The first is concerned with internal relativity, the second with external comparability. There can be a tension between these two because it is not unusual for the internal relativity to say that Job X is bigger than Job Y but for the labour market to say Job Y is paid more than Job X because of skill shortages.

Job evaluation is the means by which many organisations establish the internally acceptable rank order. It is a process by which judgements about the relative merits of one job versus another can be made in a logical manner against predetermined criteria. It is in effect controlled judgement. The various methods of job evaluation are covered in chapter 12. Job evaluation is concerned with:

- determining the relative value of jobs to the organisation
- the systematic comparison of jobs either against each other or against a set of factors

In applying job evaluation organisations often gain a number of additional benefits. These are often:

- clarifying organisation structure and relationships
- clarifying the duties and responsibilities of job holders
- identifying opportunities for the rationalisation of jobs and job re-design.

Job evaluation is a means to an end – the creation of a rank order of jobs. It is not however an essential prerequisite to grading but it can provide a logical basis for a grade structure and a system that is 'felt fair' that employees will accept. The benefits of job evaluation are being questioned in the context of reducing the administrative burden and the production of simplified broad-band grading structures.

CONVERTING JOB EVALUATION RESULTS TO GRADES

One way of converting job evaluation results into grades is to prepare a scattergram in which job size, perhaps in terms of the points scored through a points factor job evaluation system, is compared with the current internal salaries. A visual representation is shown in figure 8.6. Once obtained a trend line can then be plotted. This can either be done by judgement, but it is preferably calculated using a spreadsheet or database. A note of caution here is that many text books seem to assume that the line of best fit will be a straight line, as shown in the schematic diagram above. This however is rarely the case and the best fit is often a curve or sometimes a dogleg with the line accelerating as job sizes increase. This does not represent a particular problem but will give some challenges to the practitioners if they wish to design more than proportional schemes or schemes that are progressive or regressive through the grades.

Market rates

The process should be repeated but this time to create a comparison of job size with salaries paid for the same or similar jobs in the appropriate labour market. It is unlikely that data can be found for all the jobs and so a representative sample of jobs should be chosen. Data are usually obtainable as upper quartile, median and lower quartile

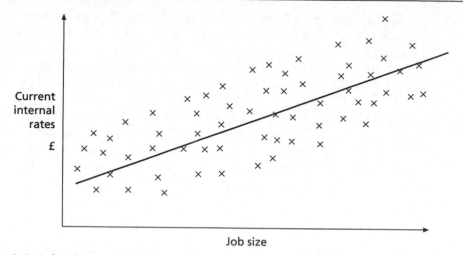

Fig. 8.6 Selecting a grade

salaries. Occasionally upper and lower deciles are available. Figure 8.7 shows what the market rate analysis might look like.

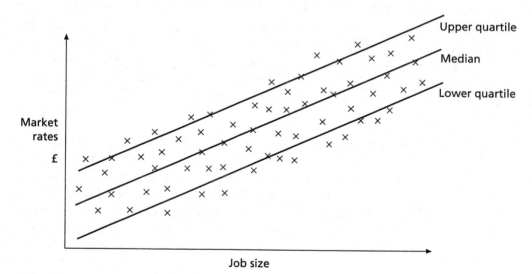

Fig. 8.7 Company grades within a market

Policy line

Some organisations prefer to take all this information (internal and external) into account to make a judgement and produce a line that represents the pay policy around which grades and payments will revolve.

Converting job size to grades

There are four approaches to deciding how the rank order of jobs determined by job evaluation can be sub-divided into grades.

1 An arithmetic progression of the job sizes.
2 Curvilinear progression of the job sizes.
3 Around clusters of similarly scored jobs.
4 To minimise the cost of implementation.

These are represented below as separate methods but often a pragmatic approach is required which may draw elements from each.

1 Arithmetic progression

This method divides up the grades equally, in the example below 100 points per grade.

99 points and less	Grade 1
100–199 points	Grade 2
200–299 points	Grade 3
300–399 points	Grade 4
400–499 points	Grade 5
500–599 points	Grade 6
600 points and over	Grade 7

2 Curvilinear progression

In this approach the grade size increased in size through the grades. The example below shows grades increasing from 99 points to 149, 299, 499 and so on.

99 points and less	Grade A
100–249 points	Grade B
250–549 points	Grade C
550–849 points	Grade D
850 points and over	Grade E

3 Clusters of similarly scored jobs

This is a process whereby the practitioner attempts to identify gaps in the progression of job sizes. Often this reveals a significant change in job size. Figure 8.8 shows how the second and third grade is significantly smaller than grades 1, 3, 4 and 5.

4 Minimum cost

Too rigid an application of the arithmetic progression of job sizes to arrive at a structure can produce a high-cost solution if this results in substantial uplifts in salary for individuals or even small increases if they affect a large number of employees. The same problem can arise if there is an inflexible application of grade differentials. In the example below the current situation is that the job of Grunger (see table 8.2) with 202 points fits into grade X. If the job is at the bottom of the new grade Y, where it more properly fits, the upshot will be that each Grunger will receive a £441 increase to bring them on to the bottom of the new grade because of the number of employees, (73) the total cost to the organisation would be £32,193 per annum. If a minimum cost answer is required then the possible solutions would be:

1 change the boundaries of grade X to 100–209 and change the boundaries of grade Y accordingly thereby bringing the job of Grunger into grade X;

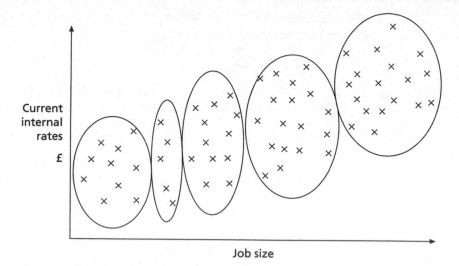

Fig. 8.8 Company grades within a company

Table 8.2

Points range	Grade	Min–max. salary (£)	Jobs	Score	Salary (£)	Employees	Total increase
100–199	X	14,500–15,950	Widget Banger	115	14,500	1	0
			Sump Filler	130	14,700	3	0
			Smudger	145	14,890	10	0
			Fence Mender	162	15,570	3	0
			Tide Turner	175	15,235	7	0
			Bridge Builder	191	15,796	4	0
200–299	Y	15,951–17,545	Grunger	202	15,510	73	32,193
			Line Marker	210	15,980	10	0
			Grass Cutter	235	16,700	5	0
			Dimpler	260	16,509	15	0

2 alter the differentials so that grade X ends at 15,800 and grade Y starts at £15,801 and the total cost is reduced to £21,243 or;

3 introduce a grade overlap so that grade Y starts at £15,500.

Grade structure

Bringing all these elements together to produce a final structure as shown in table 8.3.

Table 8.3

Points Range	Grade	Differential (%)	Range (%)	Overlap (%)	Minimum (£)	Maximum (£)
99 and less	1	–	30	–	15,000	19,500
100–199	2	15	40	33	17,250	24,150
200–299	3	20	40	42	20,700	28,980
300–399	4	20	40	42	24,840	34,776
400–499	5	20	40	42	29,808	41,731
500–599	6	20	40	42	35,770	50,077
600 and over	7	25	50	24	44,712	67,068

Organisation structure and payment grades

A not unreasonable question is 'why not have one grade for each level in the organisation?' Thus in a typical medium-sized organisation there might be separate grades for:

1 Directors
2 Senior managers
3 Middle managers
4 Junior managers
5 Staff

A difficulty presented by this approach is to decide where to place any professional staff who say, for example, report to middle managers or technical staff that report to junior managers. For this reason an organisation might decide that a more appropriate structure might be:

1 Directors
2 Senior managers
3 Middle managers
4 Professional staff
5 Junior managers
6 Technical staff
7 Staff

A team-based organisation might want to have a grading structure that reflects the different roles.

1 Direction leaders (directors)
2 Leader of teams (line managers)
3 Team leader (project leaders, work group leaders)
4 Team member (professional)
5 Team member (operations)

Market supplements

A further consideration is whether there should be any market supplements. Supplements tend to affect individual jobs rather than an entire grade. If the basic salary range for a grade should prove to be uncompetitive for a particular job, the job should not be regraded to a higher salary grade. Instead a market supplement should be paid. The advantages of supplements are:

- Cost control because the supplement can be varied, frozen or terminated to match changing circumstances.
- If an individual employee does not demonstrate performance at the market rate level, the supplement can be frozen to reflect the actual performance.
- There is a stronger potential defence against equal value claims as the supplement may be seen to be a genuine material difference unrelated to gender.

Pay modelling

Before finalising any pay structure it is always a good idea to attempt a number of simulations in order to determine how it will respond to different scenarios. The implication on the salary bill can be produced using available computer models. These use databases or spreadsheets to:

- forecast the effect of different grading options on the total pay bill
- forecast the effect of different grading options on individual earnings
- enable 'what if?' exercises to be performed

The advantage of pay modelling is in harnessing information so that informed pay decisions can be made in line with business objectives; conducting 'what if?' analyses to determine the cost impact of varying the elements of the pay package and the cost/benefit of defraying changes over several years. The extent of modelling can be kept to the minimum level practicable because most costs are influenced by comparatively few elements of pay.

Other methods of producing grades

No exposition on designing structures would be complete without some discussion of the alternative methods of producing grades. Job evaluation is not the only method that can be used to create a grade structure. One alternative method of producing a grade is to have specifications of the type of job that would fit into a grade and to then compare each job with this specification (see exhibit 8.2).

PROGRESSION CHOICES

In any scheme, other than for spot rates, there is the need to decide how movement up each of the grades will be managed. Here again there are a number of decisions that need to be made.

Exhibit 8.2

Characteristics of jobs

Grade 6
Jobholders: implement policy and strategy to achieve corporate goals and objectives established by directors; set objectives for operating units and departments; determine resources required; allocate new and existing resources; submit proposals on medium and long term strategy; monitor and review performance of the departments, units, programmes or projects under their control; determine corrective action to ensure objectives are met; manage multi-disciplinary programmes and projects. This grade may also include specialists with a strong professional role who provide strategic advice on scientific and technical matters to directors, throughout the organisation and to customers.

Grade 5
Jobholders: interpret and implement strategies and programmes formulated by higher grade staff; determine how allocated resources will be used; develop departmental and project goals, objectives and plans to support business and functional strategies; monitor and review performance of departments and projects; take action to ensure time, cost and quality and customer requirements are met; provide information and advice on technical, financial, operational and commercial matters to jobholders in higher grades; investigate and recommend new techniques, processes and business opportunities.

Fixed increments

Service related

Service related increments are where employees are guaranteed to move increment-ally up the scale according to seniority in the grade. This may be conditional on them performing satisfactorily. In some organisations employees obtain an incremental increase, typically in the range of 1.5 per cent to 2.5 per cent, in addition to whatever general increase is agreed. Increasingly this approach is being questioned and its use is in decline because increases bear no relationship to the performance of the individual or the organisation's ability to pay.

Qualifications

Incremental progression, based on qualifications are where movement is dependent up on the employee obtaining a professional qualification. This approach is to be found in research and development and knowledge-based organisations.

Skill modules

Here incremental increases are awarded when the employee is assessed and can apply an additional skill module.

Semi-fixed increments

Semi-fixed increments are often service related with additional increments being awarded if the employee's performance is exceptional. Conversely increments may be withheld or even withdrawn if the employee's performance is unsatisfactory.

Variable

There are four main types of variable progression in common use and movement can be by any one or a combination of these.

Individual performance progression

Here progression is through the achievement of objectives that contribute to business objectives or to the development of the individual. A performance increase might, for example, be applied by producing a score for each employee, then aggregating the score for all employees in the same grade and awarding individuals a salary increase equal to their proportion of the budget available to all employees in that grade. An example of such a calculation is given below:

Another method is to use a salary increase matrix. In the example shown in table 8.4 individuals would be able to progress depending both on their performance and their position in the grade. If the individual was in the fourth quartile of the salary grade and their performance was assessed as good they would receive a 2% increase in salary. If the individual was in the first quartile, however, and their performance was again assessed as good they would receive a 5% increase.

Table 8.4

| Performance | Position in grade | | | |
	First quartile	Second quartile	Third quartile	Fourth quartile
Exceptional	6%	5%	4%	3%
Good	5%	4%	3%	2%
Satisfactory	4%	3%	2%	1%
Less than satisfactory	3%	2%	1%	0%
Poor	2%	1%	0%	0%

Skill progression

Skill progression can be a highly effective approach in circumstances where there is a need to raise general skill levels, replace old skills with new ones or generate flexibility. Through broad-banding there can be training and development of employees at lower organisational levels so that they obtain additional skills.

Organisations need to decide if each skill module will be of equal weight in terms of the training and development requirements and of responsibility. Where they can be constructed to be equal, a module or group of modules can equal a pay increment. Where they are not a method can be devised, such as points for each module, so that a given number of accumulated points equal an increment. Table 8.5 has a 20 point break between increments within the grade. The salary each yields is also shown.

Competency progression

In competence progression the competencies of the individual are matched against the competencies required in the role. Table 8.6 shows competency statements and the points that relate to each competency statement.

Table 8.5

Points	Increment	Pay (£)
100	Top of the grade	16,500
80	Four	16,100
60	Three	15,750
40	Two	15,450
20	One	15,200
0	Starting salary	15,000

Total points awarded to all employees = 714
Points awarded to employee X = 6
Employee X's proportion 6/714

Table 8.6

Competency levels	Points
Well above required competency	10–12
Above required competency	7–9
Meets competency requirements	4–6
Developing competency	1–3
Below required competency and not developing	0

Managers may be given discretion to award points within a range, as above, to take into account other factors, such as the contribution of the employee.

Team performance objectives

Team performance objectives are those that contribute to the performance of the team as a whole. The salary increase that is appropriate to any increase in performance can be determined using the kind of matrix shown in table 8.7.

Salary bars

Some grades may have a bar, perhaps half to three quarters up the grade range. Progression to the bar will be on one set of criteria and above the bar will be on a different

Table 8.7

Contribution to team performance	Performance of the team				
	Exceptional	Good	Satisfactory	Less than satisfactory	Poor
Exemplary	7%	6%	5%	4%	3%
Significant contribution	6%	5%	4%	3%	2%
Satisfactory contribution	5%	4%	3%	2%	1%
Some positive contribution	4%	3%	2%	1%	0%
None or negative influence	0%	0%	0%	0%	0%

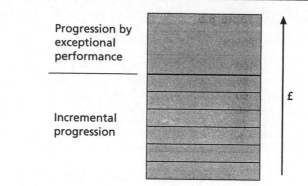

Fig. 8.9 An incremental scale with a bar

set. Alternatively, there may be a critical assessment when the employee reaches the bar and further progression will depend on that assessment confirming that the individual is considered to have the right potential. Figure 8.9 is an example of an incremental scale leading to a bar with performance-related progression above the bar.

No maximum

Some grades have minimum rates of pay but have no maximum. The inference of there being no maximum is that the employer will pay whatever is necessary to attract and retain good employees. This approach gives managers complete flexibility but this can be abused to contain most salaries within a tight grouping close to the minimum.

SUMMARY

This chapter has reviewed the various ways in which organisations can produce logical payment systems that are aligned to their business needs. The link between business objectives, performance and behaviours has been explored. Some of the more recent developments in pay have been touched upon but emphasis has intentionally been placed on the more conventional approaches.

The migration from traditional structures through which managers controlled employment costs and rewarded conformity in behaviour to alternative and more flexible arrangements seems to be gaining momentum. The alternative strategies have been developing for over a decade. Wallace and Fay (1988) identified eight features in this trend:

- performance-based pay
- merit awards or incentives not tied to base pay
- lump-sum bonuses
- gain-sharing plans
- skill-based pay
- all salaried workforce
- profit-sharing plans
- cafeteria plans

As more organisations embark on a methodical analysis of business requirements and an exploration of the relationship between pay and performance they are likely to conclude that new and more dynamic approaches are needed to contribute to competitiveness. Managers, employees and trade union representatives will need to think in a different way about the nature of individual and team contributions, the development of competence, and how pay can both motivate and reward. In most respects new pay is more challenging for scheme designers and more demanding for operational managers for it places pay firmly at the centre of performance management.

LEARNING ACTIVITIES

1 Within your organisations, audit the current numbers of payment systems for different groups of employees and the numbers of levels.

2 Identify the factors in your organisation that should influence the structure of the reward systems.

3 Discuss the merits of job families and job evaluation schemes.

4 Why do organisations need to structure their reward systems. In what circumstance might these structures inhibit organisational effectiveness.

REFERENCES

Flannery, Hofrichter and Platten (1996) *People, Performance and Pay*. The Free Press.
Industrial Society (1997) 'Pay Structures', 39, Managing Best Practice.
Lupton, T. and Gowler, D. (1969) *Selecting a Wage Payment System*. London: Engineering Employers' Federation.
Wallace, M.J. Jnr. and Fay, C.H. (1988) *Compensation Theory and Practice*, Boston: PWS-Kent Publishing.
Williams, A. Dobson, P. and Walters, M. (1989) *Changing Culture*. Institute of Personnel and Development.
Wilson, T.B. (1994) *Innovative Reward Systems for the Changing Workplace*. New York: McGraw Hill.

FURTHER READING

Armstrong, M. (1996) *The IPD Guide on Broad-banding*, London: IPD.
Armstrong, M. (1996) *Employee Reward*, London: IPD.
Bergman, T. *et al.* (1998) *Compensation Decision Making*. Third edition, Fort Worth: Dryden Press.
Industrial Society (1997) 'Pay Structures', 39, Managing Best Practice.
McAdams, J. (1996) *Aligning Business Objectives and Reward Systems*. London: Jossey Bass.
Milkovitch, G. and Newman, J. (1996) *Compensation*. Fifth edition, Chicago, Irwin.

9 Strategic rewards systems – flexible pay

Colin Massey

INTRODUCTION

Trends in flexible pay involve the elimination of rigid job boundaries and detailed job descriptions, linking the competence and contribution of employees to business objectives, encouraging flexibility and the acquisition of skills and knowledge, and rewarding excellence. Flexible and responsive organisations need flexibility in the way in which they reward employees so that they may respond to labour market pressures, stimulate improved organisational and individual performance and encourage employees to increase their job size and flexibility. This chapter explores the options available.

A 1997 Industrial Society survey found a positive trend towards more flexible pay structures with 59 per cent of respondents reporting that their structures had become more flexible in the previous five years. But there is no universally recognised definition of flexible pay (which US journals sometimes call 'nimble' pay or 'new' pay). Recent Department of Trade and Industry information suggests that flexible pay covered three main areas:

- changes in the way pay is determined; for example, opting out of national agreements, or moving to 'single-table' bargaining;
- linking reward to performance, skills or profit; these include merit pay, team performance incentives or profit-related pay;
- restructuring arrangements, such as more flexible grading, or working time patterns, which break down former rigidities in pay structures.

That publication also recognised that the 'introduction of flexible payment systems is often an integral part of wider corporate initiatives, such as total quality management, quality circles and teamworking, or other cultural change'.

Flexible pay should be considered:

1 against the historical backdrop of legal, quasi-legal and collectively bargained inflexibilities in the labour market that have now, for the most part, diminished;
2 in the context of the search for competitive advantage necessitated by increasingly global competition;

3 and in relation to the various forms of organisational and occupational flexibility that have emerged and which flexible pay often reinforces.

It should be recognised that flexible pay also provides employers with the means of ensuring value for money and better control of payroll costs. For example, with broad-banded payment systems, it is possible to respond to labour market pressures without increasing total employment costs, as a high market rate for a particular job can be absorbed without necessarily inflating the rates for the remainder of the grade. In addition annual increases can be applied in such a way that more is given to some and less to others enabling the organisation to remain within its planned limits for the overall increase in the pay bill.

HISTORICAL CONSTRAINTS

The extent to which flexibility now exists within organisational, occupational and pay structures, and the challenge of introducing it where it does not, is best understood by examining some of the major changes that have occurred over the past two decades or more. Various restrictions will be described, which limited the freedom of managers to manoeuvre resources and to introduce innovative practices to deal with competitive pressures.

Restrictive practices

Industry, commerce and the public sector in the UK have long been dogged with arguments about who does what. Although these problems have diminished they still do exist in places. Restrictive practices and demarcation take many forms. There may be boundaries around jobs, which restrict the ability of a manager to get jobholder A to do any of the work of jobholder B. There may be trade boundaries which mean that trade A won't do work that is considered that of trade B. There may be restrictions created by the perceived spheres of influence of trade unions whereby work normally performed by members of one trade union cannot be performed by members of other trade unions.

Sometimes restrictive practices manifest themselves as constraints on mobility. Characteristic of these circumstances is where an employee will not move from work-place A to work-place B without some form of extra pay.

In some organisations there are restrictive output norms whereby it is 'understood' by groups of employees that no more than a certain amount of work will be done within a specific period. Output restrictions of this type are found in various forms in all kinds of industries.

Statutory inflexibilities

Perhaps motivated by attempting to find ways round the government incomes constraints that existed in the late 1970s early 1980s, trade unions submitted numerous claims under Schedule 11 of the Employment Protection Act or the Fair Wages Resolution. First passed by Parliament in 1891, the Fair Wages Resolution was renewed several times through to 1946. In its final form the Resolution meant that a government department was able to write clauses into any contracts they awarded that required the contractor not only to pay 'fair' wages but also to agree to permit workers to join a trade union. The contractor also had to guarantee that these obligations were passed on to any sub-contractors. Disputes over the observance of the clauses were resolved by arbitration. The Central Arbitration Committee (CAC) also heard claims that employers were not awarding employees recognised terms and conditions or that they were not equivalent to the general level of terms and conditions observed by comparable employers. Schedule 11 of the Employment Protection Act, was repealed in 1980 and the Fair Wages Resolution was rescinded in 1983 by the Conservative government who considered both to be artificial constraints on market forces and vehicles for organised labour to improve the position of the already comparatively well paid.

National minimum wage

There is an argument that a national minimum wage (NMW) reduces mobility in the labour market, and that an artificially created baseline for pay such as this is a restraint on labour flexibility and pay. The question is not whether a NMW restrains the natural market forces – because it does and deliberately so – by requiring employers to have a minimum pay level that is higher than they might otherwise pay but rather whether this in turn reduces flexibility. The logic runs that since pay is not truly flexible one of the options that employers might use to respond to commercial pressures has been removed. Some employers argue that this is particularly onerous if the competition is from a country that does not have minimum wage legislation. Although linked, this is a different argument than saying that a NMW discourages employers from employing (say) part-time or young workers.

A contradictory proposition is that a NMW encourages firms to seek to gain maximum added value from employees because they are less able to compete on the basis of low wages. Thus a NMW can be a spur to managers to search for improved productivity through, for example, additional flexibility in working practices.

We should be mindful of the historical origins of minimum wage legislation and the wages council system, following the growing concern about the use of 'sweated labour' at the end of the nineteenth century. The development of Trade Boards and Wages Councils, emerged though legislation such as the 1909 Trade Boards Act and later the 1945 Wages Council Act. At its peak in 1962 Wages Council coverage was 3.5 million workers.

The debate about the economic benefits and disadvantages of a legally enforced minimum wage will be one that will continue. Assessing the overall impact of minimum wage controls on employment, unemployment, poverty and economic effectiveness – both on individual businesses and the UK in general – is a complex and contentious problem.

DECLINE IN NATIONAL AND CENTRALISED BARGAINING

Flexible working practices and flexible pay have in most cases been bargained for. But the structure and processes of collective bargaining in the United Kingdom have

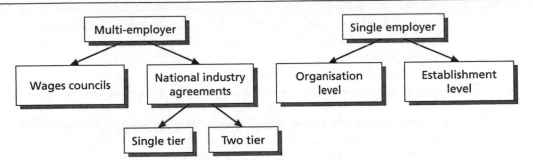

Fig. 9.1 The complex structure of collective bargaining in the UK – circa 1980

needed reform for this to happen. In parallel with the introduction of organisational and occupational flexibility, and flexible pay, the locus of collective bargaining has shifted from multi-employer and centralised agreements to company and establishment agreements that are better able to reflect local business needs.

Structure of pay determination

The pay of most of the UK workforce is still determined through collective bargaining. Until quite recently the actual pay received by an employee might have been the result of negotiations conducted at several different levels. Whilst a few industry-wide agreements were used to set actual rates, the vast majority set minimum rates. Some reserved specific items such as hours, pensions and holidays for negotiation at national level. Despite this there was often a divergence between basic rates of pay in national agreements and actual rates at company and establishment level.

Multi-employer bargaining had its origin in the late nineteenth century. By 1945 national agreements covered approximately three quarters of all employees in the UK. As a consequence of the arrangements that developed the structure of collective bargaining in the UK was diverse and complex.

From the 1950s the coverage and influence of multi-employer agreements steadily declined, although there was a resurgence in the late 1970s because of the industrial relations difficulties of that period combined with the influence of employment legislation, particularly Section 11 of the Employment Protection Act, which has since been repealed. Figure 9.1 shows the complexity of the structure of collective bargaining in the early 1980s.

At company and establishment level it was often the multiplicity of bargaining arrangements that presented the greatest impediments to change in human resource practices; including flexible working and flexible pay. The UK's complex mix of payment systems, trade unions and bargaining units often resulted in different bargaining groups in a company competing with each other. This has been one important reason for the emergence of single-union agreements and single-table bargaining.

The breakdown of national and centralised bargaining

Multi-employer collective bargaining and wages councils were regarded by the 1979–97 Conservative government to create institutionalised rigidities which prevented wages from fully responding to the circumstances of the relevant labour market, the profitability of companies and the differences in individual performance and skills. The government advocated the break up of national wage bargaining on the grounds that it was inflationary and created unemployment by providing pay increases unrelated to company performance or local circumstances.

But it was the achievement of business objectives that was the motivation for most organisations to want to bargain locally. Organisations in both the public and private sectors increasingly wished to take a business centred approach to pay, which was difficult to do within the constraints of national agreements. Decentralisation of bargaining allowed for the complex relationship between pay and performance within an organisation to be examined and acted upon, whereas these local initiatives to achieve a high pay/high performance relationship could be constrained by centralised bargaining. The ability to develop effective policies to deal with recruitment and retention problems was also an important consideration for many. Moves to remove unjustified differentials between blue- and white-collar workers by the creation of single-status harmonised payment systems was also a motivation for some. Many national agreements covered only blue-collar employees or, as in the public sector, there were separate arrangements covering different groups of employees.

As companies devolved decision making to put a greater focus on business units they have introduced flatter, less-functional organisational structures. For such arrangements to work effectively managers have needed to be able to control all elements of the business for which they are accountable, including pay. Simultaneously they have needed to obtain improvements in performance and productivity by introducing flexible working practices, which were constrained by some multi-employer agreements.

Wage bargaining in the public sector

Public-sector pay determination for long remained a seemingly intractable problem in the UK. From the early 1990s public-sector pay determination underwent a procession of change aimed at facilitating organisational change and increasing levels of efficiency. Addressing a conference on delegated bargaining in 1995 a senior Treasury official identified the benefits of devolved bargaining in the public sector to be:

1 better pay-bill control;
2 more focused reward;
3 a closer match between the pay and grading arrangements and the culture and purpose of the organisation with its performance management system;
4 where appropriate, re-balancing between the centre and local offices; and
5 a capacity to target particular kinds of recruitment or local markets.

Collective bargaining and flexible pay

The decline in national and centralised bargaining has removed a strait-jacket from company and local negotiators and has facilitated the development of flexible pay. At the same time, however, flexible pay is also a threat to the traditional forms of collective bargaining at company and establishment level. The individualisation of pay which results from flexible pay, emphasises the relationship between the employee and employer at the expense of the third party. It is not surprising therefore that trade unions have sought to secure agreements on the content and process of flexible working and flexible pay. The employers' case is that flexibility leads to greater efficiency, increased competitiveness and better customer service, and that this in turn results in security of employment. Another argument is that a multi-skilled flexible worker will be more employable should his or her current employment cease. Trade unions have nevertheless often sought to trade off flexibility for job security. One example of the type of agreement that has emerged is the 'partnership' agreement.

THE SEARCH FOR THE FLEXIBLE ORGANISATION

Conventional pay systems tend to be conservative and to discourage change, initiative and personal growth. Many of the current pay practices have their origins in scientific management, e.g. merit pay and job evaluation. They were developed when one of the priorities for managers was to ensure uniformity and conformity. Now the challenge is to manage diversity. Alvin Toffler (1981) described the need neatly when contrasting employees within the 'traditional' organisation with that of the more flexible responsive organisation of the future. He saw the increasing need for employees to accept responsibility, understand how their work dovetailed with that of others, to be able to handle larger tasks and to adapt swiftly to changing circumstances. 'The difference is like that between classical musicians who play each note according to a predetermined, pre-set pattern, and jazz improvisers who, once having decided what song to play, sensitively pick up cues from each other and, on the basis of that, decide what notes to play next.'

Indeed there have emerged an abundance of organisational forms – semi-autonomous business units, decentralisation of decision making, cross-functional teams, networking, project-based working, teamworking.

What is flexibility?

In their search for competitive advantage organisations have needed to embrace many forms of organisational flexibility. 'Whether one is referring to products, production volumes, or manufacturing processes, flexibility is about increasing range, increasing mobility, or achieving uniform performance across a specified range' (Upton, 1994).

Increasing customer expectations required organisations to be more flexible. So that organisations could increase the range of products or services, increase mobility, increase the speed of response to changing customer demands, or achieve a better balance of workload and capacity, different forms of organisational flexibility have emerged. Employers have needed to obtain the flexible use of labour as part of a business or human resource strategy to achieve the best utilisation of resources, whilst meeting customer needs.

- *Numerical or contract flexibility*. The ability to quickly increase and reduce head-count through sub-contract, part-time employees, agency workers, temporary or casual employees, home workers and consultants; the use of short-term contracts, fixed-term contracts and job sharing; also more flexible working hours for full-time staff, including annual hours contracts.

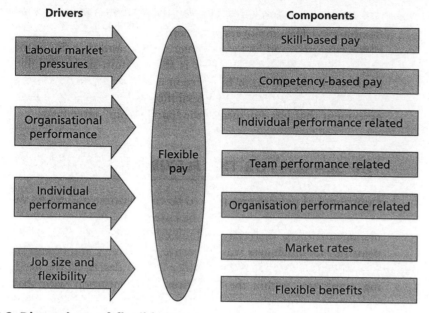

Fig. 9.2 Dimensions of flexible pay

- *Functional or occupational flexibility.* The creation of a flexible and adaptable workforce, through training and retraining, so as to be able to move employees between activities and tasks.
- *Pay or financial flexibility.* The application of variable pay, flexible pay, flexible benefits, market rates, skill- and competency-based pay.
- *Dimensions of Flexible Pay.* Figure 9.2 illustrates how the need to improve efficiency, at both organisation and national levels, has resulted in a new configuration of payments.

THE ROLE OF JOB EVALUATION

Whilst job evaluation remains in extensive use throughout all sectors of the economy, in the context of flexible pay the use and usefulness of 'traditional' job evaluation is being questioned. In a few cases employers have abandoned job evaluation entirely. (For example one manufacturing company now has six broad-band grades below managing director, only 15 job titles and no job descriptions.) The question raised by managers is 'why define jobs in detail and then, through job evaluation, identify fine distinctions between them when we are trying to encourage flexibility and job growth such that the job performed changes from that which was evaluated?'

Inflexible and excessively bureaucratic approaches to job evaluation and grading are increasingly recognised as inappropriate in a flexible working environment. These traditional job evaluation systems were often designed to support a hierarchical structure with vertical lines of communication with authority vested at the top. The job evaluation scheme then reinforces the notion that power, authority and status are associated with the hierarchy. In flexible organisations this is undesirable. Many schemes are based on outdated ideas of clearly defined duties and responsibilities and work on the premise that the more resources managed or used (money, people, equipment) the more responsible a job must therefore be. As a consequence they do not easily measure the relative worth of specialist, advisory or knowledge based jobs. One employer describes his organisation's job evaluation system as a 'management imposed restrictive practice'.

Job evaluation is a resource rich process. Complex multi-factor schemes are unwieldy and administratively expensive. Over time the factors, and the weighting of those factors, lose their relevance. Because of the need to arrive at fine distinctions between jobs, evaluators must rely on experience and guesswork to arrive at points totals and grades. A substantial industry has grown to support these systems, which in its self creates inertia against change.

Jobs are often influenced by the competence of the jobholder, who may develop the job in a particular way, or enlarge it to the advantage of the employer. In these circumstances job evaluation needs to consider both a combination of tasks to be performed and competence (i.e. both what the jobholder brings to the job and how he or she develops it). Jim Hillage (1994) describes how in these circumstances 'the role of job evaluation has changed to become the job of role evaluation.'

JOB DESCRIPTIONS

Flexible working, flexible pay, wide payment bands and a small number of generic job descriptions fit well together. With general or non-specific job descriptions the emphasis is on describing the functions of the job, what is done not how its done or what it's done to. Thus, for example, in any given organisation the functions of administrators are usually substantially the same irrespective of the department or office in which the administration is done. So separate job descriptions are not needed for finance clerk, personnel clerk, purchasing clerk, sales clerk and so on, because close scrutiny will show that what they do is much the same: what is different is what they do it to and where they do it. Often in job evaluation it is found that in reality some of the differences between jobs are small. For example:

- The same job description apart from changes of words such as 'simple' to 'complex' and 'several' to 'numerous'.
- Duties, responsibilities and skills are substantially similar but it is the point of application that is different.
- Differences in job titles may also reflect differences in the competence, contribution, or experience of the job holder rather than in the job content itself. Examples of this might be the use of words such as senior, principal or chief before a job title.

A large number of job titles is not conducive to job flexibility or simplified job evaluation and grading. Often opportunities exist to merge individual job descriptions into more generic roles. There may also be opportunities to produce generic job descriptions for jobs at the same level but being performed in different departments. The maintenance of large numbers of job descriptions has several disadvantages:

1 it is administratively burdensome;
2 it encourages employees to emphasise differences in their jobs that in reality are small and have no impact on grading; and
3 the introduction of broad salary grades, which facilitate flexibility, makes the emphasis on small differences between jobs unnecessary.

Why have job descriptions at all? A potential employee relations difficulty resulting from job descriptions is that if the task is not on the document the employee may be reluctant to do what is being asked, even if it is well within his or her capability; or they might ask for extra money. Certainly there has been a move, albeit only slight, to dispense with job descriptions, particularly in the context of a small number of wide payment bands.

A difference of opinion that exists in management texts is whether the content of job descriptions should describe what actually happens or what should happen? Many say that it should be the former. This surely is nonsense since it has the effect of confirming the status quo: be that good, bad or indifferent. If for example an organisation has performance-related pay, what is the employee in a singleton post to be judged against if a job description has been written to describe the job as it is currently being performed? In these cases the description must be written to capture what should happen.

A solution in some circumstances is to have role descriptions, which, in effect, describe both the job and the people. Role descriptions cover the 'hows' of a job as well as the 'whats' by incorporating the technical expertise required, behaviours that must be displayed, tasks that must be undertaken and the essential outcomes of the role. One way of visualising the difference in approach is to consider a part in a play, as it is described by the playwright in the written text, as the equivalent of a job description. How different directors and actors might bring to the play their own individual expertise and interpretation of the text, whilst still delivering what the playwright wanted is the equivalent of a role description.

FLEXIBLE PATTERNS OF WORK AND FLEXIBLE PAY

Some organisations have sought to achieve the maximum utilisation of resources whilst at the same time providing high levels of customer response. Some of these approaches are excellent examples of forms of flexible pay.

Annualised hours

Annual Hours is a system designed to allow predictable seasonal variations in workload to be covered through a work rota which fixes the total hours worked over a year but varies the weekly hours according to predicted demand, thereby reducing or eliminating overtime. A variation of annual hours, committed hours, is a system which fixes the majority of working hours but allows for the often unpredictable variations in demands by having a bank of additional hours from which management may draw to cover increased needs or absenteeism, or to use for training. Annualised hours are discussed in more detail in the chapter on time-based pay.

Time off in lieu

Time off in lieu is a means of reducing or removing overtime payments by allowing employees who work additional hours the same amount of time off at a future time by agreement between the individual and management.

Flexitime

Although not strictly flexible pay, flexitime nevertheless fits into the pattern of arrangements that have emerged in the pursuit of flexibility. The system is commonplace, particularly in the public sector. Employees are permitted to work a minimum and a maximum number of hours within a daily or weekly envelope. Any additional hours worked in the envelope are 'banked' and may be taken off within a specified time frame. There is much disenchantment with flexitime since in practice many organisations have found that it gives considerable flexibility to employees and little to managers.

SKILL AND KNOWLEDGE-BASED PAY

Payment systems based on the acquisition of skills and knowledge first gained prominence in the United Kingdom in the second half of the 1980s when they were applied in the manufacturing sector – which is still the major user – to operator and technical jobs. The approach is people rather than job oriented and focuses on what the individual is capable of doing, if required.

Skill- and knowledge-based pay is particularly appropriate where:

- the level and range of skills required is high but the current skill base is low;
- there is continuing change in technology, or products and skills must be constantly updated;
- flexible working is needed;
- teamworking is needed;
- the organisation is capital-equipment intensive rather than labour intensive and there is the need to ensure the maximum utilisation of assets.

Skill- and knowledge-based pay can be expensive to install and maintain for it requires the identification of skill modules and extensive training and development. Progression is usually incremental and can become the norm, and there may be pressure to lift the top of the scale once the majority of employees have developed the full range of skills. What has to be managed is the expectation that all staff can reach the maximum of the band as this can be inflationary and in any case it may not be necessary for everyone to have the full range of skills. Skill-based progression may therefore be more appropriate for grades towards the bottom of a structure, or for narrower grades, because costs can escalate unless there are effective methods of testing and assessment. In a dynamic business, skill requirements continue to change and the skill payments should change. An alternative to incremental progression therefore is to pay skill bonuses, which allow for payments to continue to reinforce skill acquisition as each new cluster of skills is acquired.

Schemes need not be entirely skill based. They can be very effective if incorporated into a performance-related pay system.

Two things are important for successful implantation and control. First, the actual flexibility required in practice must be identified and it should not be assumed that, for example, it is necessary for all operators in a manufacturing cell to have all the skills. Failure to understand the cost/benefit relationship at an early stage has caused some organisations to find it difficult to quantify the advantages. Secondly, there needs to be a rigorous assessment of the skills gained and, importantly, whether the individual can apply them to satisfactory standards of output, quality and safety. Experience in skill-based pay schemes, that do not have a robust method for judging proficiency, is that they inevitably result in an upward drift in earnings without a commensurate upward movement in performance. Despite these reservations, as Michael Cross (1992) suggested, successful implementation can 'increase productivity by 20 to 30 per cent, reduce labour turnover, improve quality and safety, and increase flexibility and efficiency'.

COMPETENCY-BASED PAY

Organisations are increasingly recognising that their image in both product markets and labour markets is influenced significantly by how they go about their business. The beliefs, attitudes and values of the organisation, as perceived by 'customers', impact upon their competitiveness. This means that how employees do things can be as important as what they do. In a competency-based approach, pay and recognition is used to communicate vision and values to employees and to reinforce desired behaviours and performance.

Objectives, strategy and the desired culture of the organisation are examined to identify the competencies required for business success. Roles are defined and the competencies required in each role are described using behavioural definitions. This enables the competencies of the individual to be matched against the competencies required in the role (see table 9.1).

Table 9.1 Competency levels

Well above required competency
Above required competency
Meets competency requirements
Developing competency
Below required competency and not developing

The outcome is (a) an assessment of performance in terms both of 'what' the employee achieved and 'how' it was achieved and (b) an identification of development opportunities.

VARIABLE PAY

A feature of flexible pay is the increase in the amount of pay 'at risk' and dependent on the individual, team, or organisation doing well.

Individual performance-related pay

For performance-based progression effective performance measures need to be defined that are appropriate to the job. This means that they probably should be different for each grade and maybe for different jobs within a grade. It is better to have progression criteria that are best suited to the particular roles within the grades and reflect the different impacts of jobs (see figure 9.3).

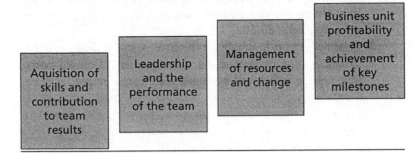

Fig. 9.3 Performance measures defined

Ad hoc awards and bonuses

A manager can be given a small budget to use for discretionary awards, for those who excel in some way. This is an approach to incentives similar to that practised in sales teams for many years. The award need not be great and may cost only a few pounds. In team-based organisations it can be left to the team to decide which of their number should receive a reward.

Team performance-related pay

It is difficult to visualise circumstances in which team working and continuous performance improvement can be successfully introduced without some form of assessment of the competence and contribution of the individual and the team as a whole. The object is to reward the behaviours that lead to effective team working. There are several approaches (see table 9.2).

Providing the assessment is suitably team focused, it is also possible to use individual performance-related pay.

Table 9.2

Input based	Output based
Skill related pay	Achievement of team targets
Competence related pay	Gainsharing

Pay related to corporate performance

Schemes through which the financial gain made from a productivity improvement is shared between organisation and employees according to a predetermined ratio are a valuable component of flexible pay. Of these gainsharing plans are particularly appropriate. There are many types of gainsharing plans but they fall into four broad categories:

1 *Scanlon* which are based on the principle that in many companies there is a consistent relationship between the sales value of output (less customer returns) and total employment costs. This relationship is defined in terms of a reference period, typically a year, to produce a base ratio. Any positive change from the base ratio is then shared between the employees and the company according to a predetermined split, typically 50/50.

2 *Cost reduction* in which a reference period is chosen and the ratio of defined costs to sales value of production is determined. Defined costs might include any costs that can be influenced by employees, for example:
    – salaries
    – sickness absence payments
    – scrap and rework
    – consumable materials
    – maintenance and repair of plant and equipment
    – heating and lighting
    – expense claims

Again any positive change from the base ratio is then shared between employees and company according to a predetermined split. Providing the data are available this type of scheme can be related to a department or team.

3 *Added value* is the sales value of production, minus materials and supplies consumed in producing the output. The proportion of the added value that is spent on employment costs provides a ratio for sharing out any improvements made. Any positive change from the historical measure of employment costs as a proportion of added value provides a gain to be shared with employees.

4 *Share of improvement*: these schemes are simple in concept in that a base ratio is determined by measuring the relationship between the total hours of output in a reference period with the total attendance hours used. This then provides a ratio for calculating any gains made, which are shared 50/50 between employees and company. In reality there are subtleties which can make the approach very powerful.

BROAD-BAND PAY

Flexible organisations that have de-layered, or are team-, process- or project-based may well seek ways of valuing jobs that are more compatible with the needs of the organisation. Broad-banded payment systems, within which there is more scope to reward people for their capacity to adapt to change and develop their skills and knowledge can provide a solution.

Grades can represent symbols of authority and status. A grading structure can encourage people in higher grades to believe that their jobs are more important than those in lower grades. Broad-band schemes typically have only four, five or six, wide and overlapping salary bands. The salary range for each band is likely to be at least 75 per cent. It is preferable to designate the bands with a generic description of the

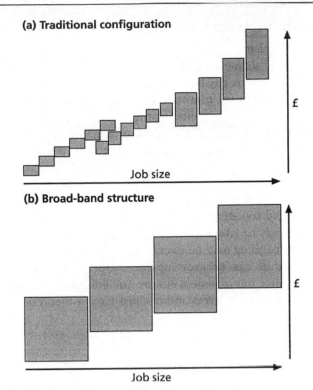

(a) Traditional configuration

Job size

£

(b) Broad-band structure

Job size

£

Fig. 9.4 Bands of pay, traditional and broad band

jobs within it (professional, technical, team leaders, etc.) rather than to label them with a hierarchical reference (1, 2, 3, etc.). Progression up the bands can be by performance, skill, competence or a mixture of these. Figure 9.4 is an example typical of traditional arrangements with multiple grades and three separate structures (say blue-collar, staff and managerial). This is contrasted with a broad-banded structure for the same hypothetical organisation. How these fit within considerations about pay structures has been discussed in the previous chapter.

The Institute of Personnel and Development (1997) define broad banding as 'the compression of a hierarchy of pay grades or salary ranges into a small number of wide bands, typically four or five. Each of the bands therefore spans the pay opportunities previously covered by several separate pay ranges. The focus is on lateral career movement within the bands and on competence growth and continuous development.'

Some broad-band structures are a collapse of old multi-tied grade structures into a smaller number of grades, which also retain many of the features and administrative arrangements of conventional structures. True broad banding is not a device for reducing the number of pay grades. A thorough understanding of business objectives and strategy and of the desired culture is needed for a well-designed scheme to be introduced.

Gilbert and Abosch (1996) introduce the idea of career-band structures, which are a more significant move away from conventional structures, with a small number of bands and an emphasis on flexibility and growth in competence and job size through individual career development.

Managing progression and careers

Since one of the motives of broad-band pay is to promote job growth, it is important to precisely define what constitutes additional responsibilities, worthy of progression and an increase in pay but within the same band, and what constitutes additional responsibilities, warranting promotion to a higher salary band.

Because the opportunities for a series of promotions, each with an increase in pay are gone, an impression of broad banding is that the reduction in the number of grades increases the problem of providing the right calibre employees with career development opportunities and rewards. Closer consideration reveals that employees who excel need not necessarily be promoted to be rewarded. Duties and responsibilities can be enlarged and there can be salary movement without promotion. Employees can be encouraged to extend their jobs to the advantage of themselves and the organisation. The barriers to lateral movement are also reduced.

Broad banding may be essential with flat structures that restrict promotion prospects so that staff can progress up the band. It must however be an integral part of a performance improvement culture and employees in a band must be able to obtain the wherewithal to progress and not just have a theoretical opportunity.

The use of zones

Sometimes bands include zones, perhaps to reflect market rates or competency levels. It can be conceptually difficult to accept that zones within a band are anything other than bands-within-bands. This is sometimes the case but there are mechanisms that can make such an approach attractive.

The shift in emphasis from jobs to people creates the opportunity for the individualisation of pay and flexibility in employee remuneration. Greater importance should be given to performance and market rates than to general increases. Good quality labour market data to provide benchmarks and information on changing competitive conditions are needed.

One approach is to constrain progression within the market value for the job with progression being linked to personal growth and performance. The salary zone is aligned with benchmark market rates. Jobholders can increase the market value of their job by demonstrating an increase in responsibilities, skills or competence (i.e. making the job bigger). Progression within the zone is dependent upon the jobholders demonstrating that they have increased their contribution (i.e. by doing the job better). By this means the two dimensions of performance – the skills or competencies of the jobholder and the extent to which the jobholder applies them – can be accommodated. Again, a more detailed discussion of how these fit within the general structure of a payment system has been discussed in the previous chapter.

Figure 9.5 demonstrates the use of zones to align jobs to the market whilst rewarding individual performance. Zones may also be based on competence or job families (see figure 9.6).

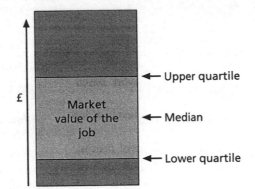

Fig. 9.5 Market rate zone

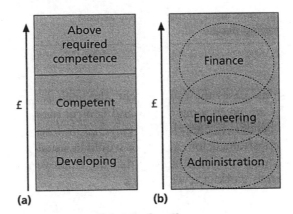

Fig. 9.6 (a) Competency zone, (b) Job family zone

FLEXIBLE BENEFITS

So far flexible pay has been discussed in the context of the search for competitive advantage, the need for organisations to be responsive to changing market and customer demands, and the utilisation of resources. Flexible benefits have a different focus in that they contribute to the recruitment, retention and motivation of staff. A second purpose is to give both the employer and the employee better value for money. Flexible benefits fit well with flexible working, and devolved responsibility and benefits can be used to reinforce the direction, values and culture of the organisation.

The range of benefits that might be included:

- childcare payments
- company cars
- dental care
- disability insurance
- extra holidays
- eye care
- healthcare
- life assurance
- medical insurance
- nursery places
- personal pensions
- sports facilities

Table 9.3

Favourable circumstance	Unfavourable circumstance
Flat structures	Bureaucratic centralised, organisations
Team, process, project or network based organisations	Low trust organisations
Need multi-skilling and high levels of job flexibility	Points means pounds job evaluation and grading
Good performance management process	Trade union opposition
Many advisory roles and knowledge workers	Low investment in training and development
Empowered devolved decision making	Poor performance management process
Encourage and reward personal growth	Technical excellence preferred to excellence in managing people
Line managers want to manage pay as part of managing people	

In some cases the range might also include individual financial counselling. Employees are given some choice and control over their own rewards so that they may match benefits to lifestyles and personal preference. But flexibility and choice are normally constrained, for example it would be usual for the employer to prescribe the minimum number of days holiday that the employee must take.

Schemes work in several ways:

1 Each of the benefits has a cost and the employee is able to choose more of some and less of another, usually in the form of a monthly allowance.
2 Each of the benefits has a cost and the employee is able to acquire the benefits instead of pay. If the employee decides to take pay they may not get as much (say 90 per cent). This approach is more widely available to executives and senior managers.
3 A core package plus options with a sum of money either to increase some of the core package or add some of the options.

Schemes may be based on age, length of service or salary or a combination of these things.

WHERE WILL FLEXIBLE PAY WORK?

Flexible pay is only appropriate for flexible organisations. This means that the organisation implementing it either has to be flexible or want to be. Flexible pay is not compatible with bureaucratic, hierarchical organisations.

SUMMARY

A simple but sometimes salutary process is to test the relevance of current pay and benefits against the emerging needs of the business. What attitudes and values should be reinforced? What is it important for employees to be good at? What kind of performance should be rewarded? By identifying the key requirements and then rating the current arrangements against them using a simple scoring system, a profile of the added value of the scheme is produced. Figure 9.7 below shows one way in which this might be done.

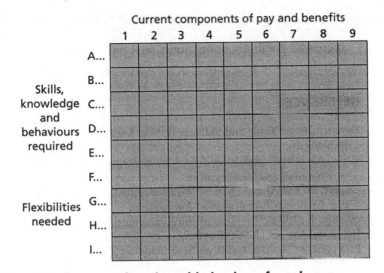

Fig. 9.7 A profile for assessing the added value of a scheme

Flexible and responsive organisations need new approaches to rewarding employees. Flexible pay systems can provide the link between the contribution and competence of employees and business plans. But flexible pay must not be viewed as just a payment system. Business strategy, organisational and individual competence, performance management, flexible working and flexible pay are all intertwined. Flexible pay will not of itself produce benefits but used as an integral part of a bigger package of performance improvement measures it can help create the high performing organisation.

Line managers are in the best position to know what flexibility and performance they need and how individual employees are contributing. Inevitably more pay-related decisions will be made by them. This calls for good performance management systems and assessment procedures. As a result the role of the personnel specialist becomes more advisory than administrative. They must provide advice, coaching and training for line managers on payment systems and performance management.

The development of flexibility will continue. As yet occupational flexibility has hardly touched managerial and professional jobs. We should expect the conventional wisdom that it is difficult for management and professional jobs to be enlarged, merged or treated as generic job descriptions to be challenged.

LEARNING ACTIVITIES

1 Using the three dimensions of flexibility outlined in the chapter assess and prioritise your organisations need for flexibility.

2 Using the data gained from the activity in question 1 analyse the extent to which your organisation's current reward systems support and facilitate the required flexibility.

3 Different organisations require different forms and levels of flexibility in their reward systems. Discuss the reasons for this and how it might impact on their payment systems.

4 To what extent does government economic and social policy affect the options for increased flexibility in organisational payment systems.

REFERENCES

Department of Trade and Industry (1996) *The Rewards for Success*. Department of Trade and Industry.

Cross, M. (1992) *Skill-based Pay: A guide for practitioners*, edited by Michael Cannel, Institute of Personnel and Development.

Gilbert, D. and Abosch, K.S. (1996) *Improving Organisational Effectiveness through Broadbanding*. American Compensation Association.

Hillage, J. (1994) 'The Role of Job Evaluation', Institute of Manpower Studies, Report 269.

Industrial Society (1998) 'Pay Structures', No. 39, *Managing Best Practice*.

IPD (1997) 'The IPD Guide on Broadbanding', Institute of Personnel and Development.

Toffler, A. (1981) *The Third Wave*. Pan Books.

Upton, D.M. (1994) 'What Really Makes Factories Flexible?', *Harvard Business Review*, July–August.

FURTHER READING

Chatterton, A. and Leonard, R. (1979) *How to Avoid the British Disease*. Northgate Publishing.

Cross, M. (1992) *Skill Based Pay: A guide for practitioners*, London, IPD.

Edwardes, M. (1983) *Back from the Brink*. Collins.

Gilbert, D. and Abosch, K.S. (1996) *Improving Organisational Effectiveness through Broadbanding*. American Compensation Association.

Hillage, J. (1994) 'The Role of Job Evaluation', Report No. 269, Brighton Institute of Manpower Studies.

Industrial Society (1998) Pay Structures, No. 39, *Managing Best Practice*.

10 Trade unions and reward

Hamish Mathieson

INTRODUCTION

The purpose of this chapter is to discuss the role of trade unions in relation to pay. The chapter opens with a consideration of the vital importance of pay for unions and also its significance for those with whom unions interact. The changing contexts within which unions influence pay determination are then reviewed. Particular attention is paid to the responses of unions to management initiatives on pay arising from the decentralisation of industrial relations to enterprise and unit levels. The final section focuses on emergent union strategies on pay and considers the factors which will influence their effectiveness.

THE IMPORTANCE OF PAY FOR TRADE UNIONS

> The employment relationship is formed around the payment of labour, payment is the most conspicuous focus of collective concern for labour. (Brown, Marginson and Walsh, 1995: 123)

Pay and its determination is a central concern of British trade unions for the principal reason that the creation and permanence of, and methods adopted by, trade unions may be attributed in large part to an endeavour to overcome the disparity in economic power between individual employees and employers in labour markets. While there is, of course, diversity in the particular market situations of different groups of employees in terms of actual income levels and so on, there is also an underlying commonality in the position of all wage earners. In explaining the tendency for employees to form unions one commentator succinctly sums up the market position of the employee thus:

> In the first place an employee on his own is at a marked disadvantage in labour market trans-
> actions. In all labour markets there are many employees and few employers so that employers
> are in a position where they can select employees according to their own criteria, dispense
> with them if need be, discriminate between one employee and another, displace employees by
> machines, contract out labour market transitions altogether. The employee cannot avoid the
> market superiority of the employer for he is forced on to the labour market because only by
> selling his labour can he subsist. He is in an inherently unstable position which is reflected in

the determination of his wages, conditions of work and hours of work. In other words because of the operation of the market situation it is the employer who argues, negotiates, acts, from a basis of power. (Allen, 1966: 12)

This analysis of the labour market situation not only points to the inequality of the terms of economic exchange but suggests that the employment relationship must also be seen as a relationship of control in which 'the concentrated economic power of capital confronts the far more vulnerable sellers of labour power' (Hyman, 1980: 308). Transactions in the labour market, therefore, have a significance beyond the mere fixing of pay or salaries since employers, motivated by a belief that the purchase of labour power assigns them 'rights' of control over labour, will typically seek to exert their 'prerogatives' over individuals in the performance of work.

Given this context the rationale for collective organisation in trade unions is that, by combining, employees can reduce the disadvantages they are prone to experience as individuals subject, on the one hand, to the unfettered exercise of management authority over the labour process and, on the other hand, to the inequality of bargaining power in pay determination. Writing over a century ago the Webbs identified a main function of trade unionism as the establishment of the 'common rule'. The defining principles underlying the 'common rule' were laid out as follows:

> Instead of the employer making a series of separate contracts with isolated individuals, he meets with a collective will, and settles, in a single agreement, the principles upon which, for the time being, all workmen of a particular group, or class, or grade, will be engaged. (Webb and Webb, 1913 edn: 173)

So far as pay determination is concerned the 'common rule' implies 'payment according to some definite standard, uniform in its application' (1913: 279). The adoption by unions of the 'common rule' and insistence on a 'standard rate' aims to enhance employees' bargaining strength by seeking to eliminate competition between members through the substitution of a single collective agreement 'thereby both raising the supply price at which labour is sold and making the rate of wages uniform over a whole trade' (Dobb, 1955: 160). As Burkitt remarks: 'the common rule introduces equivalent conditions for equivalent work' (Burkitt, 1975: 13).

However it is important to note that in pursuing the objective of the 'common rule' different organised groups of employees tend to utilise different beliefs and norms – or 'doctrines' as the Webbs termed them – to guide their methods. An illustration of this is provided by Seifert (1992) in his discussion of employee organisations in the National Health Service (NHS). While the 'closed' professional organisations have historically relied on the 'doctrine of vested interests', entailing among other things the defence of customary pay and conditions from encroachment, the 'open' general unions have been wedded to the doctrines of 'supply and demand' and the living wage' to be realised through the medium of collective bargaining. 'Supply and demand removes trade union demands beyond that of custom to what the market will bear. So in good times efforts are made to force wages up' (Seifert, 1992: 114). But the 'doctrine of the living wage' also has salience in informing the bargaining objectives of those unions whose members experience low pay and downward pressure on pay resulting from, for example, contracting out. Finally, the position is not static: as professional associations in the NHS, such as the British Medical Association (BMA), are increasingly subject to market forces and the force of custom diminishes such organisations are turning more to collective bargaining to look after their members' interests. An additional reason why pay is a major concern of trade unions derives from the priority it has for their members and for the other industrial relations parties with which unions interact – management and the state.

Trade unions

Turning to union members first: there is recent evidence of the importance attached by members to the union role in determining pay. In a large survey of new members Waddington and Whitston (1997) found that 'improved pay and conditions' scored second only to 'support if I had a problem at work' when respondents were questioned about their reasons for joining the union. Further, evidence shows that the most common manifest cause of discontent in industry is discontent with pay. For example, approximately two-thirds of the working days lost due to strikes in the 1986–96 period were accounted for by disputes centring on pay grievances (*Employment Gazette*, 1987–95; *Labour Market Trends*, 1996–7). This is, according to Hyman (1980), to be expected:

> We live in a society in which the importance of money is pervasively emphasized: in which vast resources are devoted to encouraging new and more sophisticated material aspirations among consumers; but in which workers receive far lower income to satisfy these aspirations than the more privileged social strata. Moreover, the **legitimacy** of wage bargaining as a focus for trade union activity is widely accepted, whereas the propriety of demands which challenge managerial authority is more commonly disputed. (Hyman, 1980: 309)

Employees' discontent with pay and related union demands can be linked to several factors. First, employees may protest about the terms of the wage–effort bargain; that the level of effort expended and discomfort experienced in work is not adequately compensated by the wage paid. Second, claims for higher pay may be based on the inadequacy of existing pay in relation to rises in the cost of living, i.e. inflation. Third, employees may complain that current pay levels do not provide for what is perceived as an acceptable standard of living. Fourth, employees may feel justified in seeking higher pay on the grounds that they have increased efficiency and profitability.

Fifth, discontent may stem from dissatisfaction with the perceived 'unfairness' of the prevailing wage structure in the enterprise, that is, the rates paid to different grades of employees. As Brown (1995) remarks:

> Employees' sensitivity to relative pay is all the more acute because they are in daily contact with the people in their comparative reference groups. The closer the point of comparison, the closer it is watched. Unless they accept that some rationale of 'fairness' underlies the disturbance of established internal pay differentials, employees are liable to become distressed, demotivated and thereby less productive. (Brown, 1995: 133)

To underline this point, evidence, such as that commissioned by the TUC, shows that pay differentials within companies increased sharply in the decade from the mid 1980s with the average ratio between the highest paid director salary and average employee salary growing from 7.8 to 12.94. In arguing that pay differentials seen in many companies 'do not sufficiently value and reward the work of those at the bottom of the company in relation to those at the top', the TUC concludes that actions which suggest 'that there is one rule for the directors and another for the majority of the employees will not develop constructive staff relations' (TUC, 1996: 45). Concern about the lack of 'felt fairness' in pay differentials is not confined to the private sector: commenting on pay awards made to NHS Trust Chief Executives at twice the percentage rate of increases to other staff, Unison's assistant general secretary said that they revealed 'the glaring gap that persists between those at the top and staff on the wards' and that 'we have a long way to go before equality becomes a reality in the health service' (*Financial Times*, 16 April 1998).

The importance of comparability in influencing employee pay demands may extend further than intra-firm relativities to take in comparators in other industries, organisations and occupations. Yet whatever the precise 'orbits of comparison' adopted in a particular situation the perceived frustration or denial of 'fair pay' may result in discontent or even industrial action, a point underlined by recent experience in the public services where, as Elliot and Duffus (1996) report, the relative pay of most groups of non-manual workers declined during the 1980s. In the 1990s pay pressures in the public sector began to build up against the background of government pay freezes, pay awards below the cost of living and a growing gulf with earnings trends in the private sector.

Sixth, discontent may arise in relation to the method of payment, that is the wage payment system. Historically a considerable cause of disputes, particularly in engineering, surrounded the introduction and operation of individual payment by results systems. Employees' objections to such schemes focused on the question of control over work and the stability of earnings. As Goodrich noted in his classic 1920 study: 'The motives of the workers who oppose the system are various – a distaste for being speeded up and the past experience and fear of rate-cutting are the chief' (Goodrich, 1975: 163). In his study of piece work bargaining half a century later, Brown found shop steward dissatisfaction with the system on the grounds that it 'led to inequalities' which 'splits up the men' and was a 'dog eat dog rat race' (Brown, 1973: 124). However, at the same time, the existence of the perceived threat to a uniform wage–effort bargain often had the effect of strengthening worker solidarity and the bargaining power of stewards. Discontent with the payment system is also a feature of the contemporary scene: for example, the attempt by Barclays Bank to introduce a performance pay scheme led to a series of one day strikes in 1997. In explaining the industrial action, the assistant general secretary of the bank workers' union, BIFU, said: 'Our members in Barclays want a pay system that is fair and rewards them for record profits. A pay freeze is a kick in the teeth for staff from one of the richest companies in UK' (*Financial Times*, 5 August 1997: 7).

Although the preceding discussion focuses on the economic concerns of trade unions, it would be wrong to conclude that this exclusively defines the role of unions. Unions are also social and political entities pursuing more than one set of objectives, so that in any given situation non-economic factors may be a decisive determinant of their behaviour. 'Moreover, trade union influence gradually extends beyond wage negotiations to the regulation of managerial control over labour after hire, so that due account must be taken of this aspect of their policy when assessing their overall impact' (Burkitt, 1975: 46). Unions thus have political objectives relating to the structure of power and authority in the enterprise, and in society in general (Martin, 1992). The non-economic roots of some wage demands have also been documented (see Hyman, 1984: 127–9).

Nevertheless British unions have been strongly concerned to defend the economic interests of their members through collective bargaining, thus emphasising the salience of pay as a measure of their effectiveness. The unions' economic objectives lead them to focus on the two sides of the reward–effort bargain: on the one hand, on issues such as pay, pensions and holidays and, on the other hand, on hours of work, staffing levels and labour intensification issues. With regard to union justifications for higher pay, Kessler notes that 'cost of living and comparability have perhaps been the most important of these arguments' (Kessler, 1983: 86).

Management

Pay is also of considerable importance to the achievement of employers' objectives. At root labour is a commodity. Consequently 'the wages and conditions which the worker naturally seeks as a means to a decent life are a cost to the employer, cutting into his profits, and he will equally naturally resist pressure for improvements' (Hyman, 1975: 19). Moreover, pay can represent a very significant proportion of total costs, as is the case, for example, in the public services. But, as Brewster and Connock (1985) note, the significance of pay to management stretches beyond the fact that it represents a controllable cost. Pay is also perceived as a means to the achievement of fundamental organisational objectives, such as the maximisation of labour productivity and flexibility and the improvement of product or service quality. Finally, the 'spectacular increase in the sophistication and prominence of accounting control in British companies' (Armstrong, 1995: 144) implies that policies on pay are increasingly subject to the setting of corporate financial targets and associated budgetary controls. Evidence collected by Marginson et al. (1993) reinforces this observation: in a survey of large multi-site companies it is reported that in 80 per cent of the firms the finance function played an active part in calculating the cost of the pay offer or ensured that offers remained within budget (see Marginson et al., 1993, chapter 4).

The state

In its roles as economic manager, legislator and employer the state seeks to exert varying degrees of direct and indirect influence on pay. Economic policy is fundamentally concerned with employment, unemployment and inflation. Though the relative emphasis placed by different governments on these issues varies Robinson and Mayhew (1983) observe that 'political necessity leads each government to implement policies designed to influence the rate of inflation and this inevitably leads it to seek to alter in one way or another movements in pay' (Robinson and Mayhew, 1983: 3). Government has thus sought to intervene in pay bargaining activity in a range of ways: through the imposition of incomes policies, by changing the legal framework of bargaining in such a way as to shift power between the parties, by its use of arbitration and in its stance in relation to public-sector pay claims. Unions' pay objectives, therefore, inevitably intersect with the prevailing 'political contingency' as expressed in terms of overall economic management and in the mode of management encouraged among public-sector employers.

Having pointed to the centrality of pay negotiation as a trade union function we now turn to the factors which affect the union role in pay determination. Following a discussion of the wider economic and political environment and the coverage of collective bargaining, consideration will be given to the impact of management initiatives, particularly the growth of enterprise-centred employment policies since the 1980s, on union behaviour in relation to pay issues.

THE ECONOMIC, POLITICAL AND LEGAL CONTEXT

The economic, political and legal context within which trade unions operate has been significantly revised since 1979. For most of the period between 1945 and 1979, as Wrigley (1996) notes, economic and political conditions favoured the expansion of trade unionism and collective bargaining. A combination of a boom in international trade, low unemployment, rising inflation, an expanding welfare state and government legitimisation in various ways lay behind the growth of unions to their greatest size by 1979. Figures compiled by Bain and Price (1980) show that union density rose from 38 per cent to 55 per cent between 1945 and 1980. In sectional terms growth in density was particularly marked in manufacturing, where it rose from 51 per cent in 1948 to 70 per cent in 1979, and in the public sector (up from 71 per cent to 82 per cent over the same period) (Bain and Price, 1983).

Kessler and Bayliss (1995) summarise the principal changes in the economic environment since 1979 as comprising four key developments: the decline in manufacturing industry, the sharp growth in unemployment, the restructuring of the economy with a redistribution of employment towards private-sector services and a sharpening of international competition. In place of what was perceived as the 'failed' post-war consensus the government set about shaping policies which emphasised the primacy of 'free' deregulated markets, competition, individualism and a 'smaller state'. In the terminology of Smith and Morton (1993) these strategic policies provided the foundations for a programme of 'union exclusion' comprising 'reduction in the power of unions and workers in relation to employers, creation of new rights against unions for members and non-members alike, reduction in the institutionalisation and scope of collective bargaining, de-legitimisation of unions within the political process, and the rejection of all proposals for co-determination' (Smith and Morton, 1993: 98). The aim of such measures was to remove many of the institutional arrangements which had supported union influence in the earlier period and to make the labour market more exposed to 'market forces' (Purcell, 1993).

In *broad* terms the effects of such changes have reduced union bargaining power (see Martin, 1992). Changes in employment structure have posed greater recruitment and organising problems; the existence of a 'reserve army' of the unemployed might be expected to have reduced the willingness of union members to press their demands with as much force as they might under 'full employment' conditions, and legislative changes have eroded solidarity. Trade union density has markedly declined: from the high water mark of 55 per cent in 1979 to 31 per cent reported in the *Labour Force Survey* in 1996 (Cully and Woodland, 1997). Declines have occurred across all sectors but the rate of decline has been uneven: while density in manufacturing is equal to that in the economy in general, public-sector levels are still significantly higher than the average (at around 60 per cent).

The coverage of collective bargaining

The principal collective mechanism for setting pay and conditions in the twentieth century has been collective bargaining. Data presented by Milner (1995) shows a growth in the proportion of the workforce covered by collective bargaining from an estimated 20 per cent in 1906 to a high point of 73 per cent in 1973. Since then all estimates point to declining coverage. The third *Workplace Industrial Relations Survey* (WIRS) records that aggregate collective bargaining coverage fell from 71 per cent to 54 per cent between 1984 and 1990 for work places of 25 or more (Milward *et al.*, 1992), or 47 per cent if the calculation takes in work places of under 25 employees (Brown, 1993). Data from the Labour Force Survey indicates that just 37 per cent of employees were covered by collective bargaining in 1996 (Cully and Woodland, 1997). In sectional terms WIRS 3 shows that in manufacturing coverage declined from 64 per cent to 51 per cent between 1980 and 1990; the corresponding figures for private services were from 41 per cent to 33 per cent and for the public sector from 95 per cent to 78 per cent. The *Labour Force Survey* of 1996 also points to considerable variation in collective bargaining coverage by industry, ranging from relatively high levels in public administration (78 per cent) to 34 per cent in manufacturing and 8 per cent in hotels and restaurants (Cully and Woodland, 1997). In aggregate terms the period since 1980 has been one in which union influence over pay through collective pay arrangements has severely contracted. As Milner (1995) remarks:

> The recent decline in collective bargaining coverage is the most prolonged ever recorded and has been noticeably steeper than the fall in union density, such that the proportion of British workers covered is lower now than in the 1940s. With the abolition of wages councils in 1993, collective pay-setting machinery now affects the pay and conditions of fewer workers than it did in the 1930s. (Milner, 1995: 69)

Some qualifications to the foregoing picture may be mentioned. The union/non-union wage differential, or 'union mark-up', remains a feature of industrial relations. Though the number of workers enjoying this premium has fallen, due to factors such as declining union membership and recognition, the mark-up itself has in general stayed intact, and in the case of male production workers has increased (Hildreth, 1997). Second, in his analysis of the impact of unions on performance Metcalf (1993) points to the unions' role as a 'sword of justice' and 'force for equality'. While the 1980s saw 'a huge growth in the inequality of pay' (see also Kessler and Bayliss, 1995: chapter 10), the unions' longer-term effect has been to 'narrow the overall dispersion of pay and . . . compress the wage structure between blacks and whites, women and men, the disabled and able-bodied and the unskilled and skilled' (Metcalf, 1993: 263).

MANAGEMENT STRATEGIES, PAY AND TRADE UNIONS

We now turn to consider the role of trade unions in relation to the contemporary management of pay. Few would dispute that the shift in power relations since the 1980s has resulted in employers in the private and public sectors being accorded greater scope and a more pro-active role in structuring employment relations and pay. While the underlying drivers of change may be 'a crisis of international competitiveness in the private sector, and of finance in the public', the implication for trade unions is that 'more than at any time this century their role depends upon the use that employers choose to make of them in the management of labour' (Brown, 1986: 164).

By far the most dominant trend in large private-sector enterprises (and increasingly also emulated in the public sector) has been 'the development of the firm-specific labour market and organisation-based employment systems in contrast to the traditional reliance on the external labour market for labour supply, and on industry-wide wage-fixing institutions for the determination of basic terms and conditions of employment' (Purcell, 1991: 33). Several initiatives illustrate the trend.

The decentralisation of bargaining

A major change in the conduct of collective bargaining, particularly in the private sector, has been the decline of multi-employer industry- (or sectoral-) level pay bargaining machinery and a shift of focus to negotiation at company level, sometimes further decentralised to lower-level units (Brown, 1993; Gregg and Yates, 1991; Milward et al., 1992). What explanations have been put forward to account for employers moving away from national bargaining? First, pressure from government to deregulate the labour market entailed exhortations to employers to break with traditional methods of pay determination based on comparability and the cost of living and instead relate pay more to individual and company performance, local labour markets and the company's 'ability to pay' (Jackson, Leopold and Tuck, 1993). Second, decentralised pay bargaining can enhance management control over pay and tailor it to business needs and structures. As Purcell puts it:

> The development of single employer bargaining, often at a level consistent with profit centres or business units, enables the firm to bring in new payment systems and grade structures (as in banking) and link the management of labour more to the product market than the external labour market. (Purcell, 1993: 11)

Third, decentralisation can be an opportunity for recasting union recognition and representation arrangements. For example there has been growth in the incidence of 'single-table' bargaining where, by bringing together unions which had previously bargained separately, employers hope to emulate the benefits accruing from single union deals on greenfield sites; to avoid the complexity and possible conflict potential of fragmented arrangements; to introduce harmonised pay and conditions; and to facilitate wide-ranging changes in working practices (Gall, 1994).

From another angle decentralisation may entail the marginalisation of union influence or even the exclusion of unions altogether from pay determination. In the former scenario, local bargaining takes place against a background of other employment policies focused on the individual, while, in the latter, a move away from industry bargaining provides an opportunity not to recognise unions at the local plant/site level (Purcell, 1991). Kinnie (1987) also highlights the potential of decentralisation to permit the deliberate isolation of the level at which bargaining is conducted, and union influence exerted, from that at which strategic decisions are taken. Such 'institutional separation' is thus an important element in the parochialisation of union influence and a basis for 'enterprise unionism'. At the same time the degree of local influence over pay is qualified by the extent of central control exercised by head office over the parameters of ostensibly local bargaining.

Empirical studies provide evidence for the varying rationales for decentralisation. In her study of large multi-divisional/multi-site companies Walsh (1993) found that the main reasons for decentralisation of bargaining were a desire to 'bring pay determination under the firms' direct control and to rationalize bargaining levels' together with a need to match pay determination structures to geographical and product market diversification (Walsh, 1993: 412–13). In a survey of 57 private-sector employers the most common reasons given for decentralisation of pay were to take account of local labour market conditions and individual performance and a desire to get control over business strategy at unit/site/profit centre level (Industrial Relations Services, 1996). Marchington et al. (1994) and Purcell (1994) point to the growth of non-recognition in the context of the decentralisation of industrial relations. Marchington and Parker (1990) see the relevance of 'institutional separation' in analysing two of their case study plants, although they take issue with the assumption that this necessarily occurs out of a purposive desire to marginalise trade union influence at strategic level.

Although a trend pioneered in large private-sector companies in manufacturing and services, decentralised pay bargaining has also spread to the public sector, most notably in the Civil Service where from April 1996 the four central civil service agreements on pay were abolished and replaced by bargaining at departmental or executive agency level (Incomes Data Services, 1997). Motivated by 'hostility to the system of centralized collective bargaining involving strong trade unions committed to the principle of comparability and standardised conditions of employment' (Winchester and Bach, 1995: 316) government aims for decentralisation were similar to those espoused by private employers – pay related to productivity, individual performance and labour market conditions (White, 1996).

However progress toward decentralised pay in the public sector has been patchy outside of the privatised industries, with the majority continuing to have their pay determined nationally either through collective bargaining or independent pay review bodies (Bailey, 1996). For example, only around 10 per cent of NHS staff are covered by local arrangements with the rest on either nationally determined pay or Trust contracts which closely mirror national agreements (Corby and Mathieson, 1997). Also, in the case of civil service agencies central Treasury (and Departmental) oversight is a feature of pay delegation, exercising a role analogous to Head Office in the private-sector multi-divisional company. Additionally, the role of comparability has been maintained via pay indexation arrangements for the police and fire-fighters and through the pay review body system.

Trade union responses

How have trade unions been reacting to pay decentralisation trends? In general terms unions have tended to oppose moves by employers to abandon national bargaining. Union concerns centre on the threat posed by decentralised pay bargaining to the principles of the 'common rule' and 'the rate for the job' which protect those members in weaker bargaining positions. Moreover unions may fear that decentralised bargaining is only the 'thin end of the wedge', presaging de-recognition and the eventual abandonment of collective bargaining itself. Once workers are paid different rates according to market and performance criteria the 'incentive to combine' (Martin, 1992) is eroded and the union is undermined. Among public service unions high priority has been given to the retention of national salary and grading structures. 'In their view they not only define terms and conditions of employment but also shape career expectations, influence mobility patterns and safeguard professional standards of service' (Bach and Winchester, 1994: 275).

Opposition to proposals for decentralisation has been expressed in a spate of localised industrial disputes, many of them in the public sector – involving further education lecturers, health staff, librarians and residential care workers (Labour Research, 1996b). But typically unions have responded more pragmatically: in their case studies Jackson, Leopold and Tuck (1993) found unions seeking by various means to ensure a common bargaining approach across decentralised units to ensure that advances in one area were spread to others. Further, Corby (1998) remarks that delegated bargaining in civil service agencies had given unions at local level a *raison d'etre* and 'something to hang on to'.

At TUC level the view taken is that unions 'attempting to oppose all moves to decentralisation and flexibility – some of which have clear immediate financial benefits to members – would be in danger of finding themselves by-passed' (TUC, 1991: 4). In recognition of the shift of focus 'emphasis will tend increasingly to be given to the enterprise – taking into account that "national agreements" in the public sector correspond more closely to enterprise level bargaining in the private sector'. The preferred TUC model is for bargaining to take place on a single-table basis where central enterprise agreements taking into account the entire pay structure can 'establish a clear positive framework within which local elements could be negotiated' (TUC, 1991: 14). Union support for single-table arrangements reflects perceived benefits, such as increased inter-union unity and the preservation of collective bargaining where national agreements have been terminated. Another advantage is that it can promote co-ordination between unions to ensure greater equity in enterprise pay structures. 'Single-table bargaining with a single salary structure, or salary structures where processes for comparison are in-built, should encourage pay parity' (Gilbert and Secker, 1995: 205).

But it also signals union willingness to respond to the employers' agenda in providing a forum to deal with the host of issues involved in restructuring, such as the alignment of pay review dates, regrading and job evaluation and changing working practices. In its evidence to a parliamentary Select Committee the TUC emphasised the role of unions as a steadying influence in the potentially 'confusing' world of enterprise pay setting. 'The presence of a union allows the problem to be internalised and solved in a stable way' (House of Commons Select Committee, 1994). However, there seems to be doubt as to whether STB arrangements result in enhanced union bargaining power translating into higher pay: according to Gall (1994) the experience is of 'no great change compared with pre-STB negotiations, while more have witnessed pay freezes and lower settlements rather than greater pay rises because of the alleged inability of companies to fund "large" rises' (Gall, 1994: 70). Further, the proportion of enterprises with single-table arrangements remains limited (Industrial Relations Services, 1995).

Single-table bargaining arrangements may be seen as only one aspect of a broader trend by unions to develop a new 'partnership' orientation and to adapt to enterprise-focused industrial relations. The shift from a traditional 'highly adversarial class conscious attitude towards employers' (Freeman, 1995) among union leaders is reflected in the introduction to the TUC's *Partners in Progress: Next Steps for the New Unionism* policy document of 1997:

At the workplace social partnership means employers and trade unions working together to achieve common goals such as fairness and competitiveness; it is recognition that, although they have different constituencies, and at times different interests, they can serve these best by making common cause wherever possible. (TUC, 1997a: 1)

Evidence of the growth of 'partnership agreements' is apparent (Industrial Relations Services, 1997c). So far as pay is concerned the agreements often involve unions in moving away from traditional annual bargaining rounds providing across the board increases taking place in an 'adversarial' union-based JNC context towards longer-term agreements, sometimes negotiated in directly elected 'consultative' forums and incorporating elements contingent on factors such as individual performance and company profitability. Further, such agreements reflect a broader formulation of the effort–reward bargain. Pay is seen as one (important) element of reward but the provision of training opportunities and employment security accompanies agreement to work 'beyond contract' and to cooperate in flexibility schemes.

However, much depends on the terms of partnership, i.e. on the degree of equality in the relationship. In some cases employment security guarantees have been accompanied by union concessions on traditional pay practices. For example, in the 1998 agreement between Vauxhall and its unions there is provision for the company to take on new employees at lower pay rates for their first three years and to link pay to the strength of the pound (*Guardian*, 22 April 1998).

Unions have also responded to decentralised bargaining by reviewing their organisational structures. First, union activity is re-focusing on the workplace with changes in the roles of lay reps and full-time officers. As the role of the workplace rep has broadened from tasks such as information giving to include pay negotiation, unions have been directing resources to support these activities (Industrial Relations Services, 1992). Apart from training in negotiating skills unions have increased the flow of information to local reps: for example UNISON has developed a software package, 'Local Negotiator', which by drawing on electronic data bases allows negotiators to calculate the effect of a pay claim on members' earnings and the employers' paybill (Labour Research, 1996a). Local pay bargaining may also strengthen the link between members and the union and promote greater interest or 'union renewal' from the grass-roots as Fairbrother (1996) has dubbed it. Second, the advent of enterprise bargaining has been a factor promoting union merger activity. The merger of three public service unions creating UNISON in 1993 was partly driven by a concern to enhance the eligibility of the new union representing all sections of the workforce in terms of employer recognition for local bargaining (Waddington and Whitston, 1995). The merger has indeed ensured that UNISON has achieved a pre-eminent role in employee representation in NHS Trust bargaining forums (Bryson, Jackson and Leopold, 1995). A similar strategy may be seen in the amalgamation which produced the Amalgamated Engineering and Electrical Union in 1992: the AEEU has sought to position itself as the premier manufacturing industry union, as a 'partner in profits', in return for sole recognition rights on new sites (AEEU, 1997).

Performance-related pay

A significant development since the 1980s has been the growth of a 'pay for performance' culture in organisations and 'a shift to relating pay more directly to individual characteristics and away from a reliance on pay for grade or job' (Kessler and Purcell, 1995: 350). For example, survey results produced by Waddington and Whitston (1996) record a marked growth in the incidence of pay, linked to appraisal, of 21 percentage points over a three year period, indicating, they argue, 'a closer monitoring of individual effort, and, by extension, individual job content' (Waddington and Whitston, 1996: 157). Moreover, research conducted by Heery and Warhurst (1994) shows that the majority of the 61 unions surveyed reported that they had at least a proportion of their members covered by individual performance pay with the greatest coverage among non-manual unions and in sectors such as financial services. But performance pay is less in evidence in the public sector (Milward *et al.*, 1992).

From a trade union viewpoint individual performance pay tends to be regarded warily. Heery and Warhurst (1994) outline the potential 'disorganising' threats posed by it: first, it may 'reduce the perceived need for union protection among employees and replace identification with the union with identification with the employing organisation'. Second it 'may fragment workers' interests, by placing a new emphasis on the relationship between the individual employee and the employer at the expense of the collective relationship between management and union' (Heery and Warhurst, 1994: 6). As Kessler and Purcell note: 'Placing important pay-related decisions in the hands of line management, opening up a direct dialogue between managers and workers on how the company and the individual performs, can be seen to challenge collective bargaining as the main means of pay determination' (Kessler and Purcell, 1995: 355). Further union concerns turn on the damage which can be done to fairness, motivation, co-operation between employees and equal opportunities at the workplace. Speaking of the public sector, Bailey (1996) notes that 'the shift from the rate for the job to individual contribution redefines notions of equality in a manner quite alien to most public sector workers' (Bailey, 1996: 147).

While most unions are opposed in principle to individual performance pay their behaviour in practice has tended to be conditioned by the approach adopted by employers to it, i.e. whether it is part of a strategy to exclude unions from pay determination altogether or not. Only limited evidence exists of the former approach (Claydon, 1996). A more common strategy is a 'dualist' one in which performance pay is introduced alongside collective bargaining arrangements. In such circumstances Heery and Warhurst (1994) note that unions are likely to strike a position of 'principled opposition' initially but modify their approach to one of seeking to shape and regulate the scheme through collective agreements once members are transferred on to it. This approach is echoed in a guide prepared by MSF for its representatives.

There is evidence that union influence over performance pay schemes has not been negligible. Kessler and Purcell (1995) report instances in which unions have been engaged in detailed negotiation of the design of schemes. Moreover, a survey of 128 mainly private-sector employers shows negotiation taking place on a range of substantive issues, such as salary scale minima and maxima – the pay 'range for the job', minimum annual awards for staff, budgets available for awards, the award for satisfactory performers and the distribution of awards (Industrial Relations Services, 1997b). In another study the Inland Revenue Staff Federation, responding to its members complaints about the operation of a scheme, commissioned independent research which was subsequently used in negotiations resulting in a modified scheme (TUC, 1994). Further, Heery and Warhurst (1994) note that most unions in their survey had claimed to have negotiated procedural rules (e.g. on appeals) surrounding the operation of schemes. Finally, even in cases where collective bargaining has been ousted in favour of personal contracts, for example among senior managers, unions have responded by developing individual services to members, such as legal advice on contractual matters (Kessler and Purcell, 1995; Pickard, 1990).

In sum, unions have responded collectively and with some effect to moves to individualise pay. However, the precise combination of collectively bargained and individually determined pay varies considerably between organisations. As IRS says, 'The breadth and depth of union involvement depends in part on what employers consider appropriate' (IRS, 1997b: 16).

Financial participation

Recent years have seen a significant growth in the presence of financial participation schemes in British companies. According to Pendleton (1997) such schemes can be divided into two categories: 'cash-based profit sharing, where rewards are paid from profits more or less immediately, and share-based schemes, where the rewards are primarily gained from a long term increase in share value' (Pendleton, 1997: 104).

Turning to profit sharing first: following the provision of tax relief in 1988 for companies adopting such schemes a period of rapid growth occurred with 2.5 million employees covered by profit-related pay (PRP) by the mid 1990s. Trade union reaction to profit-sharing schemes has been broadly negative. The principal objections levelled against PRP by the TUC are that it fails to 'give workers a real stake in the company', that 'profit levels are only distantly related to the real efforts of workers', and that fluctuations in profits intensifies the financial insecurity of workers, particularly the lower paid (TUC, 1996: 47). Further there is concern that many schemes are introduced unilaterally by management and that they represent a means to get workers to accept a lower basic pay award. Indeed, reporting on case studies carried out in the 1980s (Baddon *et al.*, 1989) found that 'in no case was the introduction of the scheme the subject of bargaining . . . The unions remained aloof from the process' (Baddon *et al.*, 1989: 249).

But despite the rather cool reception to PRP in principle, and often the lack of a central policy at individual union level, negotiators 'on the ground' are now seeking to place PRP within a negotiated framework. For example, in the bus industry the Transport and General Workers Union is insisting on a fall-back rate to protect gross earnings if the scheme comes to end. In the clothing and footwear industry union negotiators require that PRP must be 'underwritten' in that, if it fails to match the nationally negotiated settlement over the year, members' pay rises by that settlement (Labour Research Department, 1995).

Growth has also occurred in employee share-ownership schemes (see chapter 20) although at a lesser rate than PRP. Debate has continued over the years about whether trade unionism and collective bargaining is weakened by employee share ownership. The case for the non-involvement of unions rests on the argument that institutions of employee ownership can supplant traditional union forms of representation or alternatively that the union role in pursuing the distinctive economic interests of its members through bargaining with the employer becomes blunted by having to also express ownership concerns such as profitability. However, research findings in the UK repudiate the view that employee ownership necessarily weakens traditional union representation and functions. In the conclusions to their studies on the bus industry Pendleton, Robinson and Wilson (1995) remark that in 'most cases union membership remains unaffected, and collective bargaining continues to be the main forum of establishing rates of pay and other conditions of employment. Most employees continue to perceive an important role for union representation' (Pendleton, Robinson and Wilson, 1995: 579). Such findings echo those of an earlier study (Wright *et al.*, 1990). Such findings have no doubt helped to commend employee ownership to the TUC: in its policy document *Your Stake At Work* (1996) this form of financial participation is endorsed not only as carrying less risk for workers but also because it provides a mechanism for workers to take part in decision making as 'stakeholders'.

UNION INITIATIVES IN THE 1990S

Addressing the TUC in 1990 John Edmonds, General Secretary of the GMB, declared that 'the requirement for unions and their members to move beyond the role of simply responding to either government or employer initiatives is imperative if we are to set our own agenda on issues important to men and women at work' (TUC, 1990: 402). In the policy document *Collective Bargaining Strategy for the 1990s* published in 1991 a key bargaining priority was identified as 'fair pay', in particular improving the status and pay of low-paid workers within the framework of a statutory minimum wage and 'appropriately valuing, revaluing and upvaluing women's jobs' (TUC, 1991: 12). In regard to the public sector 'fair pay' is seen to be dependent on 'comparability arrangements backed by independent evidence' (TUC, 1991: 13).

Equality of pay and status

Issues of equal pay have moved up the union bargaining agenda. The backcloth to change is the traditional 'conservatism and parochialism' of collective bargaining as revealed in a study by Colling and Dickens (1989). They found that bargaining agendas tended to 'narrowness and stability' and that the focus of negotiation was often increases in pay within existing structures with little concern about the structure itself. But the 1990s have seen some developments in 'equality bargaining'. First, a study by the Labour Research Department shows that the combination of local bargaining and concern by employers about the cost of defending equal pay claims in court is increasing the amount of workplace negotiation over the issue (Labour Research Department, 1998). Second, the ground-breaking national agreement between local authority employers and unions in 1997 is based on principles of equality and equal pay. It provides for single status between manual and non-manual staffs and for a jointly developed job evaluation scheme based on the equal pay for work of equal value principle which is to be used to produce a non-discriminatory grading structure (Industrial Relations Services, 1997a).

Low pay

While the goal of a statutory national minimum wage lies at the heart of TUC policy on low pay 'it is important to emphasise that the NMW is not seen by the trade union movement as a substitute for collective bargaining but as a floor on which agreements can build' (TUC, 1997b: 15). However there is evidence prior to the establishment of the NMW of union influence on low pay via collective bargaining. Unions have been using the imminent prospect of legislation as a negotiating tactic to raise employers' pay offers to low-paid staff. Results of a survey of 800 collective agreements in 1996–7 show that above-average increases have been won by the lowest paid (Labour Research Department, 1997).

The recommendations of the Low Pay Commission in May 1998 that the National Minimum Wage be set at £3.60 for those over 21 years of age were met with mixed reactions within the trade union movement. While there was widespread support for the establishment of a nationally applicable minimum, Rodney Bickerstaffe, Unison's General Secretary, also spoke of the need 'to press for the implementation, effective enforcement and uprating of the minimum wage to something nearer the half male median earnings figure' (*Guardian*, 28 May 1998). Union disappointment deepened when, in June, the government decided to lower the floor of the minimum wage for young persons to £3.00 initially and to extend the lower rate to 21 year olds.

CONCLUSION

Given the underlying inequality in bargaining power between employers and individual employees, influence over pay determination is a central issue for unions in terms of improving members' living standards and promoting fairness at work. Union influence over pay is, of course, variable between and within industries and is affected by a range of economic, political and technical factors. In broad terms, however, union influence increased in the 1945–80 period and declined thereafter. In the former period, relative security of employment, the growth of a bureaucratised welfare state, 'Taylorised' work organisation and state support for collective bargaining underpinned a strong role for unions in an effort–reward bargain focused narrowly on pay based on the rate for the job and seniority. The post-1980 period saw union influence challenged by rising unemployment, deregulation of labour markets, privatisation and a hostile legislative climate. Pay became more unequal, more contingent and more likely to be determined at the local level than through standardised national agreements.

Unions have sought to secure influence over pay in part by reacting to the employers' agenda but latterly also by developing a more strategic approach of their own. At enterprise level unions have been seeking to co-ordinate local bargaining and also to place the operation of performance-related and profit-related pay schemes within a negotiated framework. But the TUC has set its own agenda for increasing union influence over pay. One prong in the strategy is 'fair financial rewards' which encompasses a statutory minimum wage, action to make pay structures more equitable, for example via the adoption of the equal pay for equal value principle, employee share ownership, and a return to national standards in the public services. A second prong is the related emphasis on 'partnership': here the approach is on placing unions at the centre of company competitiveness. This also implies a broadening in the terms of the effort–reward bargain: in return for employee flexibility there are pay benefits but also guarantees of job security, development opportunities and fulfilling work.

The effectiveness of the unions' strategies depends on three things. One is the reciprocation of employers in the 'partnership' project. Second, the effectiveness of a partnership approach is dependent on the degree of commitment to a cooperative as opposed to an adversarial conception of work place relations by full-time and lay union officials (Claydon, 1998). Third, there is the impact of the change of government in 1997. The collective bargaining environment under Labour is a friendlier one from the union viewpoint: there has been legislation on union recognition and the minimum wage, and in addition there will be legislation flowing from the EU Social Chapter. Unions will also hope that public-sector collective bargaining will be strengthened by the abolition of compulsory competitive tendering while action is taken to tackle the relative decline in public-sector pay and to restore national pay standards.

Finally, trade union support for European monetary union may increase the likelihood of pay agreements with European characteristics. The advent of monetary union is a force for convergence in labour markets: while Europe-wide collective bargaining is some way off there are signs, such as the 1998 agreement at Vauxhall, that British unions are prepared to conclude pay agreements linked to the exchange rate. Moreover there is evidence of the emergence of an informal 'European pay area' characterised by convergence in national collective agreements on pay, hours and other conditions (Taylor, 1998). A possible further extension of this trend is the formulation of formal pay bargaining strategies based on the single currency and the euro. Time will tell.

LEARNING ACTIVITIES

1 Catalogue the mechanisms for determining pay in your organisation. To what extent do arrangements vary between different groups, extend up the hierarchy, are collective or individually based and involve trade unions?

2 What are the major influencing factors in the annual pay round in your organisation?

3 Discuss the advantages and disadvantages of union involvement in pay system design.

4 What factors might influence the successful development of a partnership agreement with a trade union?

REFERENCES

Allen, V. (1996) *Militant Trade Unionism*. London: Merlin Press.

Amalgamated Engineering and Electrical Union (1997) *Partners in Success*. Bromley: AEEU.

Armstrong, P. (1995) 'Accountancy and HRM', in J. Storey (ed.), *Human Resource Management: A critical text*. London: Routledge.

Bach, S. and Winchester, D. (1994) 'Opting out of Pay Devolution? The prospects for local pay bargaining in the UK public services', *British Journal of Industrial Relations*, 32(2, June): 263–82.

Baddon, L., Hunter, L., Hyman, J., Leopold, J. and Ramsay, H. (1989) *Capitalism? An analysis of profit-sharing and employee share ownership.* London: Routledge.

Bailey, R. (1996) 'Public sector industrial relations', in I. Beardwell (ed.), *Contemporary Industrial Relation: A critical analysis.* Oxford: Oxford University Press.

Bain, G. and Price, R. (1980) *Profiles of Union Growth.* Oxford: Blackwell.

Bain, G. and Price, R. (1983) 'Union Growth in Britain: Retrospect and prospect', *British Journal of Industrial Relations*, 21(March): 46–68.

Brewster, C. and Connock, S. (1985) *Industrial Relations: Cost-effective strategies.* London: Hutchinson.

Brown, W. (1973) *Piecework Bargaining.* London: Heinemann Educational Books.

Brown, W. (1986) 'The Changing Role of Trade Unions in the Management of Labour', *British Journal of Industrial Relations,* 24(2, July): 161–8.

Brown, W. (1993) 'The Contraction of Collective Bargaining in Britain', *British Journal of Industrial Relations*, 31(2, July): 189–200.

Brown, W. (1995)

Brown, W., Marginson, P. and Walsh, J. (1995) 'Management: Pay determination and collective bargaining', in P. Edwards (ed.), *Industrial Relations: Theory and practice in Britain.* Oxford: Blackwell.

Bryson, C., Jackson, M. and Leopold, J. (1995) 'The Impact of Self-governing Trusts on Trade Unions and Staff Associations in the NHS', *Industrial Relations Journal,* 26(2): 120–33.

Burkitt, B. (1975) *Trade Unions and Wages: Implications for economic theory.* London: Bradford University Press.

Claydon, T. (1996) 'Union Derecognition: A re-examination', in I. Beardwell (ed.), *Contemporary Industrial Relations: A critical analysis.* Oxford: Oxford University Press.

Claydon, T. (1998) 'Problematising Partnership: The prospects for a cooperative bargaining agenda', in P. Sparrow and M. Marchington (eds), *Human Resource Management: The new agenda.* London: Financial Times Pitman Publishing.

Colling, T. and Dickens, L. (1989) 'Equality Bargaining – Why Not?', *Equal Opportunities Research Series.* London: HMSO.

Corby, S. (1998) 'Industrial Relations in Civil Service Agencies: Transition or transformation?', *Industrial Relations Journal,* 29(3, September).

Corby, S. and Mathieson, H. (1997) 'The National Health Service and the Limits to Flexibility', *Public Policy and Administration,* 12(4, Winter): 60–72.

Cully, M. and Woodland, S. (1997) 'Trade Union Membership and Recognition: An analysis of data from the 1996 Labour Force Survey', *Labour Market Trends,* June: 231–9.

Dobb, M. (1955) *Wages.* Fourth edition, Cambridge: Cambridge University Press.

Elliot, R. and Duffus, K. (1996) 'What has been Happening to Pay in the Public-service Sector of the British Economy? Developments over the period 1970–2', *British Journal of Industrial Relations,* 34(1, March): 51–86.

Fairbrother, P. (1996) 'Workplace Trade Unionism in the State Sector', in P. Ackers, C. Smith and P. Smith (eds), *The New Workplace and Trade Unionism.* London: Routledge.

Freeman, R. (1995) 'The Future for Unions in a Decentralised Collective Bargaining System: US and UK unionism in an era of crisis', *British Journal of Industrial Relations,* 33(4, December): 519–36.

Gall, G. (1994) 'The Rise of Single Table Bargaining in Britain', *Employee Relations,* 16(4): 62–71.

Gilbert, K. and Secker, J. (1995) 'Generating Equality? Equal pay, decentralisation and the electricity industry', *British Journal of Industrial Relations,* 33(2, June): 191–208.

Goodrich, C. (1975) *The Frontier of Control.* London: Pluto Press.

Gregg, P. and Yates, A. (1991) 'Changes in Wage-Setting Arrangements and Trade Union Presence in the 1980s', *British Journal of Industrial Relatoins,* 29(3, September): 361–76.

Heery, E. and Warhurst, J. (1994) 'Performance Related Pay and Trade Unions, Impact and Response', Kingston University Business School, Occasional Papers, 30, August.

Hildreth, A. (1997) 'What has happened to the Union Wage Differential in Britain in the 1990s?' Essex University: Institute of Labour Research.

House of Commons Select Committee on Employment (1994) *The Future of Trade Unions*. London: HMSO.

Hyman, R. (1975) *Industrial Relations: A Marxist introduction*. London: Macmillan.

Hyman, R. (1980) 'Trade Unions, Control and Resistance', in G. Esland and G. Salaman (eds), *The Politics of Work and Occupations*. Milton Keynes: Open University Press.

Hyman, R. (1984) *Strikes*. Third edition, London: Fontana.

Incomes Data Services, (1997) 'Delegated Pay Bargaining in Departments and Agencies', IDS Report 729, January: 25–30.

Industrial Relations Services (1992) 'The Changing Role of Trade Union Officers: The devolution of pay bargaining', *Employment Trends*, 526, December: 5–12.

Industrial Relations Services (1995) 'Single-table Bargaining: An idea whose time has yet to come?', *Employment Trends*, 577, February: 10–16.

Industrial Relations Services (1996) 'Collective Bargaining and Pay Determination Levels: A survey, *Employment Trends*, 601, February: 4–9.

Industrial Relations Services (1997a) 'Historic Single-status Deal in Local Government', *Employment Trends*, 639, September: 5–10.

Industrial Relations Service (1997b) 'New Pay Drives Hard Bargaining', *Employment Trends*, 640, September: 7–16.

Industrial Relations Services (1997c) 'Partnership at Work: A survey', *Employment Trends*, 645, December: 3–24.

Jackson, M., Leopold, J. and Tuck, K. (1993) *Decentralisation of Collective Bargaining*. Basingstoke: Macmillan.

Kessler, I. and Purcell, J. (1995) 'Individualism and Collectivism in Theory and Practice: Management style and the design of pay systems', in P. Edwards (eds), *Industrial Relations: Theory and practice in Britain*. Oxford: Blackwell.

Kessler, S. (1983) 'Comparability', in D. Robinson and K. Mayhew (eds), *Pay Policies for the Future*. Oxford: Oxford University Press.

Kessler, S. and Bayliss, F. (1995) *Contemporary British Industrial Relations*. Second edition, Basingstoke: Macmillan.

Kinnie, N. (1987) 'Bargaining within the Enterprise: Centralised or decentralised?', *Journal of Managment Studies*, 24(5, September): 465–77.

Labour Research Department (1995) 'Who Profits from PRP?', *Labour Research*, 84(7, July): 17–18.

Labour Research Department (1966a) 'High-tech Bargaining for UNISON Branches', *Labour Research*, 85(2, February): 5.

Labour Research Department (1996b) 'Local Bargaining may Spell Disputes', *Labour Research*, 85(7, July): 17–18.

Labour Research Department (1997) 'Unions Deliver on Low Pay', *Labour Research*, 86(10): 16–17.

Labour Research Department (1998) 'Equal Pay Cases – A Reps' Job', *Labour Research*, 87(2, February): 21–2.

Manufacturing Science Finance (no date) *New Management: An MSF guide*. London: MSF.

Marchington, M. and Parker, P. (1990) *Changing Patterns of Employee Relations*. Hemel Hempstead: Harvester Wheatsheaf.

Marginson, P., Armstrong, P., Edwards, P., Purcell, J. and Hubbard, N. (1993) 'The Control of Industrial Relations in Large Companies: An analysis of the second Company Level Industrial Relations Survey', *Warwick Papers in Industrial Relations,* 45(December).

Martin, R. (1992) *Bargaining Power*. Oxford: Clarendon Press.

Metcalf, D. (1993) 'Industrial relations and economics performance', *British Journal of Industrial Relations*, 31(2, June): 225–84.

Milner, S. (1995) 'The Coverage of Collective Pay-setting Institutions in Britain, 1896–1990', *British Journal of Industrial Relations*, 33(1, March): 69–92.

Milward, N., Stevens, M., Smart, D. and Hawes, W. (1992) *Workplace Industrial Relations in Transition*. Aldershot: Dartmouth Publishing.

Pendleton, A. (1997) 'Charcteristics of Workplaces with Financial Participation: Evidence from the WIRS', *Industrial Relations Journal*, 28(2, June): 103–19.

Pendleton, A., Robinson, A. and Wilson, N. (1995) 'Does Employee Ownership Weaken Trade Unions?: Recent evidence from the UK bus industry', *Economic and Industrial Democracy*, 16: 577–605.

Pickard, J. (1990) 'When Pay gets Personal', *Personnel Management*, July: 41–45.

Purcell, J. (1991) 'The Rediscovery of the Management Prerogative: The mamagement of labour relations in the 1990s', *Oxford Review of Economic Policy*, 7(1): 33–43.

Purcell, J. (1993) 'The End of Institutional Industrial Relations', *Political Quaterly*, 64(1): 6–23.

Purcell, J. (1994)

Robinson, D. and Mayhew, K. (eds) (1983) *Pay Policies For The Future*. Oxford: Oxford University Press.

Seifert, R. (1992) *Industrial Relations in the NHS*. London: Chapman & Hall.

Smith, P. and Morton, G. (1993) 'Union Exclusion and the Decollectivisation of Industrial Relations in Contemporary Britain', *British Journal of Industrial Relations*, 31(1, March): 97–114.

Taylor, R. (1998) 'New Strategies Called For', *Financial Times Survey*, 30 April: 2.

Trades Union Congress (1990) *Annual Report*. London: TUC.

Trades Union Congress (1991) *Collective Bargaining Strategy for the 1990s*. London: TUC.

Trades Union Congress (1994) *Human Resource Management: A trade union response*. London: TUC.

Trades Union Congress (1996) *Your Stake At Work*. London: TUC.

Trades Union Congress (1997a) *Partners in Progress: Next steps for the new unionism*. London: TUC.

Trades Union Congress (1997b) *Low Pay Commision: TUC evidence*. London: TUC.

Waddington, J. and Whitston, C. (1995) 'Trade Unions: Growth, structure and policy', in P. Edwards (ed.), *Industrial Relations: Theory and practice in Britain*. Oxford: Blackwell.

Waddington, J. and Whitston, C. (1996) 'Empowerment versus Intensification: Union perspectives of change at the workplace', in P. Ackers, C. Smith and P. Smith (eds), *The New Workplace and Trade Unionism*. London: Routledge.

Waddington, J. and Whitston, C. (1997) 'Why do People Join Unions in a Period of Membership Decline?', *British Journal of Industrial Relations*, 35(4, December): 515–46.

Walsh, J. (1993) 'Internalisation v. Decentralisation: An analysis of recent developments in pay bargaining', *British Journal of Industrial Relations*, 31(3, September): 409–32.

Webb, S. and Webb, B. (1913) *Industrial Democracy*. London: Longmans, Green.

Winchester, D. and Bach, S. (1995) 'The State: The public sector', in P. Edwards (ed.), *Industrial Relations: Theory and practice in Britain*. Oxford: Blackwell.

White, G. (1996) 'Public Sector Pay Bargaining: Comparability, decentralization and control', *Public Administration*, 74(Spring): 89–111.

Wright, M., Chiplin, B., Thompson, S. and Robbie, K. (1990) 'Management Buy-outs, Trade Unions and Employee Share Ownership', *Industrial Relations Journal*, 21(2, Summer): 137–46.

Wrigley, C. (1996) *A History of British Industrial Relations 1939–79*. Cheltenham: Edward Elgar Publishing.

FURTHER READING

Ackers, P. *et al.* (eds) (1996) *The New Workplace and Trade Unionism*. London: Routledge.

Edwards, P. (eds) (1995) *Industrial Relations: Theory and practice in Britain*. Oxford: Blackwell.

Heery, E. (1996) 'Risk, Representation and the New Pay', *Personnel Review*, 25(6): 54–65.

Heery, E. (1997) 'Performance Related Pay and Trade Union Membership', *Employee Relations*, 19: 5.

Storey, J. (1995) *Human Resource Management: A critical text*. London: Routledge.

Trade Union Congress (1977) *Partners at Work: Next steps for the new unionism*. London: TUC.

Also Industrial Relations Services Employment trends publications.

11 Women, pay and equal opportunities

Sue Shaw and Mary Clark

INTRODUCTION

The issue of a gender pay differential has been central to the whole debate of equal opportunity. Pay inequality between the sexes has always existed and continues to exist. Although the gap is narrowing there are still substantial differences in earnings. Results from the 1997 New Earnings Survey show for example that full-time women earn on average £110 less per week than their male counterparts.

Whilst the existence of a gender pay gap is not in dispute, the reasons for its existence are less clear cut. To what extent can it be explained by women's lower labour market participation, their industry and occupational distribution or by institutional factors such as organisational pay structures; or are women discriminated against in a way that is illegal? The significance lies not so much in the explanations themselves but in the policy solutions that flow from them.

Equal opportunities legislation was introduced in the 1970s to help improve women's pay position and has undoubtedly done so in the time that it has been in existence. However, the gap exists despite the law. Institutional and structural factors such as payment systems and job evaluation schemes together with perceptions and stereotypes which have led to the under-valuation of women's work and women's skills are powerful constraining forces.

Gender and pay inequality and low pay are inextricably linked. Much of the wages gap can be explained by the fact that large numbers of women have low pay. It is therefore interesting to speculate whether proposed minimum wage legislation will improve women's pay position where equal pay legislation has failed.

Women make up half the workforce and their pay position is therefore a barometer of the level of equality and fairness in the labour market at large and in organisations in particular. That pay position also impacts more widely on society because it has implications for women's economic independence, for their incentive to work and for their retirement income.

This chapter examines the nature of gender inequality and reward, the reasons why it has come about and persists, and the legal framework that is in place to eradicate it. It goes on to consider what can be done to improve women's pay position and concludes with a consideration of issues for the future.

THE NATURE OF REWARD INEQUALITY

The gender pay gap is one of the central features of inequality between the sexes. Women generally earn less than men throughout their working lives.

Size of the gender pay gap

Results from the 1997 *New Earnings Survey* showed that women's average gross hourly earnings excluding overtime were 80.24 per cent of men's (table 11.1). The aggregated figures for average gross hourly earnings mask variations between manual and non-manual occupations with the gender pay gap wider at the higher grades (72.16 per cent as compared with 69.01 per cent).

It is important to distinguish between hourly and weekly average earnings as the gender gap is greater for weekly earnings. The increased pay gap for the latter arises because it includes additions to basic pay such as overtime, shift premiums and incentive pay which are earned by a smaller proportion of women than men. In 1997, women's earnings averaged 72.72 per cent of men's, again with the aggregated figure masking variations between manual and non-manual occupations (table 11.2).

In the same year, on average men worked 41.8 hours including 3.2 hours overtime compared with women's 37.6 hours and just 0.9 hours overtime. Table 11.3 examines

Table 11.1 Average gross hourly earnings (excluding overtime) full-time employees, Great Britain – 1997

	Manual	Non-manual	All
Full-time men	£6.79	£12.39	£9.82
Full-time women	£4.90	£8.55	£7.88
Differential: male/female	£1.89	£3.84	£1.94
Women's earnings as % of men's	72.16%	69.01%	80.24%

Source: New Earnings Survey, Part A 1997.

Table 11.2 Average gross weekly earnings full-time employees, Great Britain – 1997

	Manual	Non-manual	All
Full-time men	£314.30	£483.50	£408.70
Full-time women	£201.10	£317.80	£297.20
Differential: male/female	£113.20	£165.70	£111.50
Women's earnings as % of men's	63.98%	65.73%	72.72%

Source: New Earnings Survey, Part A 1997.

Table 11.3 Make-up of average weekly pay, Great Britain – 1997

	Men		All	Women		All
	Manual	Non-manual		Manual	Non-manual	
Average weekly earnings	£314.30	£483.50	£408.70	£201.10	£317.80	£297.20
Comprising:						
overtime payments	£45.30	£13.60	£27.60	£13.40	£6.10	£7.40
profit-related payments	£4.50	£6.20	£5.40	£2.40	£3.90	£3.60
other incentive payments, etc.	£12.30	£15.60	£14.10	£7.40	£5.50	£5.80
shift, etc. premium payments	£11.10	£3.60	£6.90	£5.90	£2.80	£3.40
All additions	£73.20	£39.00	£54.00	£29.10	£18.30	£20.20
Basic	£241.10	£444.50	£354.70	£172.00	£299.50	£277.00

Source: New Earnings Survey, 1997.

Table 11.4 Trends in the pay gap, Great Britain – 1987 to 1997 (all women's as % of all men's)

Year	Average gross hourly earnings	Average gross weekly earnings
1987	73.62	66.12
1988	75.09	66.80
1989	76.43	67.64
1990	77.03	68.17
1991	78.29	69.74
1992	79.31	70.89
1993	79.38	71.46
1994	80.02	72.22
1995	80.25	72.02
1996	80.49	72.32
1997	84.46	72.72

Source: New Earnings Survey, Part A 1997.

the makeup of average weekly pay and indicates that all additions accounted for 13 per cent (£54) of male average gross earnings but just 7 per cent (£20.20) of those of females.

Trends in the gender pay gap

An examination of the figures over the past decade shows that there has been a gradual narrowing of the gap (table 11.4).

Distribution of the gender pay gap

One of the main reasons for the pay gap is that men and women are generally employed in different industries and in different occupations. Women tend to be concentrated in low-ranked industries such as hotel, catering, retailing, clothing manufacture and health

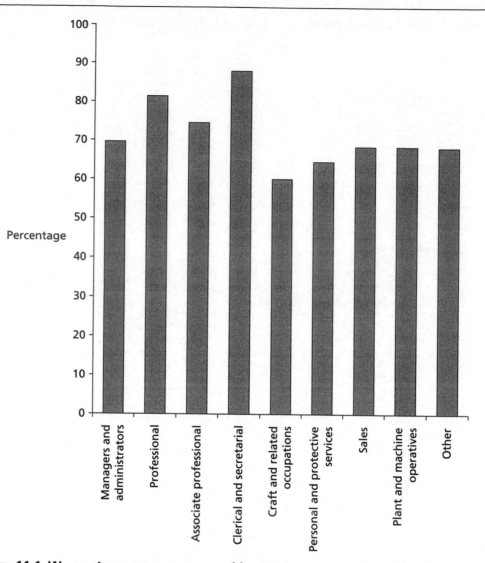

Percentage

Fig. 11.1 Women's average gross weekly earning as a percentage of men's by occupational group, Great Britain, 1997

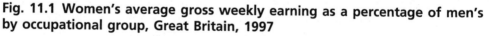

Source: New Earnings Survey, part A, 1997.

care and in low-ranked occupations such as childcare and related occupations, retail checkout, hairdressing and machining. Moreover, even when men and women are employed in the same occupational group, men's average earnings are usually higher, although the extent of the gap varies considerably. Figure 11.1 shows the pay gap by occupation.

Women and low pay

Women (and ethnic minorities) are particularly vulnerable to low pay. Indeed, women are almost twice as likely as men, to be low paid. For example, 30 per cent of women

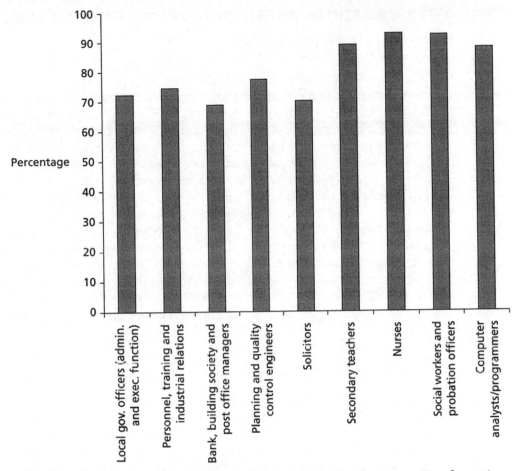

Fig. 11.2 Women's average gross weekly earning as a percentage of men's by managerial and professional groups, Great Britain, 1997

Source: New Earnings Survey, part A, 1997.

compared to 14 per cent of men earn less than £4.00 per hour, whilst at less than £3.00 per hour the respective percentages are almost 10 per cent for women and just over 5 per cent for men (EOR, 1997).

One of the main reasons for this, is the fact that part-time jobs are largely undertaken by women (eight out of ten) and part-time workers are disproportionately represented among the low paid. In addition to being employed in part-time work, there are a number of other features which characterise women in low-paid work (Labour Research, 1998). They are most likely to be working in manual jobs and employed in one of three sectors (wholesale/retail/motor industry, hotels/restaurants or health/social work). What is more, they are typically found in smaller, non-unionised work places and ones which often just employ women.

EXPLANATIONS OF THE DIFFERENCES BETWEEN MALE AND FEMALE EARNINGS

The question of male/female wage differentials has pre-occupied economists, sociologists and feminists for some time. Their differing disciplinary perspectives give rise to numerous and at first glance conflicting explanations for the gender pay gap. However, closer examination of the different studies suggests the explanations are neither mutually exclusive nor necessarily competing. What they do show is that there are numerous factors which impact on women's relative pay position and contribute to what is undoubtedly a complex interaction. The significance lies not just in the explanations themselves but in so far as the different interpretations affect how policy solutions are perceived and implemented. A central consideration is the extent to which the explanations can be attributed to discrimination. This is exemplified by the orthodox economists who attribute a significant proportion of the pay gap to the legitimate operation of the labour market and human choices and preferences rather than inherent discrimination.

Explanations have tended to be classified according to whether they are either supply or demand driven, although Dex *et al.* (1994) extend the classification further to include institutional–structural elements and policy influences. The key explanations are reviewed below.

Differences between men and women

A number of the explanations focus on differences between the sexes. One of the most significant contributions to the supply-side explanation has been that of the orthodox or neoclassical economists. They attribute a significant part of the pay gap to differences in productivity-enhancing characteristics amongst men and women, which in turn are due partly to taste or preference and partly to pre-market behaviour. Consequently, it is argued that women and men make different but legitimate choices about the occupations they go into, their labour-market activity and also about education and training as well.

Human capital theory, is a way of calculating the extent to which an individual consciously decides and is able to invest in him or herself through the acquisition of additional qualifications, skills and knowledge. The theory was developed to explain the differences in individuals' productive capacity. In applying the theory to women's earnings it was argued, first in the United States (Mincer and Polachek, 1974) and subsequently in Great Britain (see, for example, Wright and Ermisch, 1991) that women made different investments and accumulated less human capital than men because they had differing expectations about labour-force participation. Whilst these and numerous other studies show that productivity differences between men and women do impact on the wage gap, the critical issue is just how much of the gap can be attributed to differences in human capital. As Humphries (1995) has argued this in part depends on how broad the concept of human capital is and some classical economists have endeavoured to provide a very extensive definition. Consequently, estimates vary between 44 per cent and 75 per cent of the total gap (see Dex *et al.*, 1994). Differences in human capital certainly do not explain all the gap and the various studies have led, according to Humphries (1995), to a standard procedure for decomposing an overall male–female wage gap into a component attributable to differences in the endowments of human capital (explained) plus a residual (unexplained) which is identified with discrimination. This is important, as the underlying implication from this is that there are two separate problems and two different solutions. So, whereas supporters of equal opportunities would argue for intervention, economists are much more likely to go for wage flexibility.

To what extent can the pay gap be accounted for by women attaching less importance to pay relative to other factors and consequently being inclined to accept low-paid work? Dex, Lissenburgh and Taylor's (1994) review of a range of studies suggests that male and female attitudes towards the relative importance of pay in a job and the relative satisfaction with pay when differences are controlled for are in fact more similar than dissimilar. However, they go on to argue that further research into employee satisfaction is necessary before we can say that women are satisfied with low pay.

The apparently continuing preference of a large number of women to pursue part-time jobs (Martin and Roberts, 1984; Shaw and Taylor, 1997) goes some way to explaining the situation. Such work provides a way for women to combine childcare or other caring responsibilities with paid employment and balance home and work. The issue of course is that of choice and women's decisions have to be seen in the context of constraints, such as the availability of jobs, lack of affordable childcare, economic necessity and the remuneration levels in part-time work.

Whilst a full critique of human capital theory and the differences between male and female attitudes to paid employment is outside the scope of this chapter it is important to consider some of the challenges to the arguments presented above. Feminists have not only questioned whether differences between the sexes are sufficient to account for the current earnings gap but have also argued that choice/taste differences rather than being exercised freely are in fact the product of discrimination and gender stereotyping. So they would refute the orthodox economists claims that women's interrupted market activity and the household division of labour are a freely exercised choice and one which maximises the contributions of both wives and husbands based on specific preferences. Labour market structure and segregation have therefore been used alongside human capital differences and a difference in tastes and preferences to explain earnings differentials between men and women and it is to this that we now turn.

Labour market structure and gender segregation

To what extent are women's earnings a product of the industry they work in and the occupations they undertake? Differences in male and female earnings have been attributed to structural factors within the labour market and the fact that women are disproportionately represented in certain less well-paid jobs. 'The essential feature of segregation is that males and females do not compete in the same labour market; their wages, as a result, are subject to different forces of supply and demand and different institutional forces' (Milward and Woodland, 1995: 223). It is widely acknowledged that women are concentrated in industries and jobs which are amongst the most poorly paid. This is borne out by the extent to which they exist in industries which were formerly represented by Wages Councils and their disproportionate representation in the service sector at large; a sector which, despite being the major growth area of the economy during the past three decades, continues to have lower pay rates than other sectors.

Labour Market Segmentation Theory, which came to prominence in the 1960s and 1970s, has been used to explain low pay. The early formulations of this theory depicted a dual labour market comprising a high-paying, high-skilled primary sector and a poor-paying, low-skilled secondary sector. Its relevance for women's relative pay position was first made by Barron and Norris in 1976 (cited in Dex, Lissenburgh and Taylor, 1994) through their location of women in the poorer secondary sector. Later models of labour market segmentation have recognised the inappropriateness of treating women workers as a homogeneous group located in a single (secondary) sector. Consequently they present a much more complex picture which takes account of women's position in professions such as teaching and clerical jobs and the more general division of full- and part-time work (Hakim, 1996).

Hakim (1996) has examined the trends in occupational segregation of men and women over the last century and particularly since the introduction of equality legislation in the 1970s. A number of developments have significance for earnings differentials: first, the extent to which women's employment is polarising not only between managerial/professional/technical and lower-level service and clerical occupations but also between full- and part-time occupations; second, the extent to which vertical segregation and women's apparent failure to advance up an occupational ladder to higher-paid posts depresses their pay.

Whilst gender segregation is usually defined at the occupational level, Milward and Woodland (1995) examine its incidence between and within work places and consider its impact on pay levels for similar occupational groups across establishments, using the 1990 WIRS data. They conclude that female concentration has a depressing effect on women's wages at the work-place level and that there are grounds for suggesting the existence of a substantial establishment-level male premium.

The apparently depressing effect on wages of female concentration is part of the wider issue of employers under-valuation of women's services compared with those of men. In her exploration of the concept of skill and how it is defined, Dex (1988) examines how these different valuations manifest themselves. She reports a number of studies where jobs are 'labelled' differently according to whether they are undertaken by men or women and assigned a higher skill level when undertaken by men. She also reflects on the fact that employers and society fail to value caring roles and part-time work, seeing them both as unskilled. This under-valuation comes about and persists not only because of society's view of paid versus unpaid work, specifically in the home, and women's and men's acceptance of the gender divide, but also through the trade unions and the way in which they have been created and maintained along gender lines. The role of the trade unions in the creation of the gender pay gap is covered in the following section.

Trade unions

The role of trade unions in influencing pay levels cannot be ignored, both in terms of supply- and demand-side explanations. Dex, Lissenburgh and Taylor (1994) suggest that women's lower levels of trade union membership and therefore exclusion from collectively bargained agreements is significant for two reasons. First, it prevents them from benefiting from the general union mark up on wages over and above industry variations (Dex, Lissenburgh and Taylor, 1994, report studies which suggest this might be as high as 14 per cent on men's pay and 15.35 per cent on women's pay).

Second, it might exclude them from shift and overtime premiums. However, how significant this is or continues to be has to be seen within the context of the more general decline in membership for both sexes.

Dex, Lissenburgh and Taylor (1994) suggest that there is a demand-side consideration as well in that employers who are anti-union may prefer to employ women since they think women will be less likely to agitate for union status or better terms and conditions, a point made by Humphries and Rubery (1984).

Other studies, notably Armstrong (1982) have charted the institutional mechanisms of pay negotiations and their complexity, and the way formal pay negotiating mechanisms, informal arrangements and social conventions all play a part in keeping women and low-paid workers in a weak bargaining position. The concept of skill has already been referred to and trade union attitude to skill has been the subject of bargaining procedures. The situation has been exacerbated by male-dominated trade unions who have arguably created the situation in the first place.

Organisational payment structures

Whilst early explanations of the gender pay gap have focused on human capital explanations and labour market structure, more recent research has looked within organisations for explanations for women's relative pay position. Whilst there are relatively few studies which have looked at the link between payment structure and practice and gender pay inequality, those that have been undertaken reveal not only considerable differences in organisational practice in setting pay for men and women but also the extent to which different structures and systems impact on the gender pay gap.

Rubery *et al.* (1997) suggest that there are three dimensions to payment structures that are likely to have an influence. These are: the form of payment system, the size of pay differentials (by industry, occupation and type of organisation) and the job grading system.

Payment systems

Payment systems for men and women are often different. The extent to which women work in organisations where pay is often determined by employers at a local level and outside of any collective negotiating process has already been referred to. Studies undertaken in the early 1990s (IRS, 1991; IRS, 1992; Bevan and Thompson, 1992) showed considerable differences in organisational practice in such aspects as pay enhancements, shift premiums and pay scales when setting pay for men and women. Women's jobs were less likely to attract merit payments, individual-performance-related pay, shift premiums or have regular overtime or bonuses and were more likely to have pay supplements removed during a recession. Furthermore, women's pay scales were shorter, possessed fewer points and did not rise to the same levels as men's. In their comparative study of the UK, Germany and Italy, Rubery *et al.* (1997) have looked at the ways in which different forms of payment systems result in different levels and forms of gender pay inequality and generate different obstacles. In their evaluation they stress the importance of the national context for determining the overall balance of advantage or disadvantage.

Two recent developments in pay, and their potential to discriminate, are worthy of fuller consideration. These are performance-related pay and competency- and skills-based pay. It could be argued that both these systems have the potential to improve women's position. The former because it depends more on superiority in the job than position in the hierarchy and the latter because it is based on performance as measured by the individual's level of skills or competencies. However, studies (Rubery, 1995, Strebler, Thompson and Heron, 1997) show that both developments introduce a number of potentially discriminatory elements which may even widen rather than reduce the gap. In her examination of performance-related pay, Rubery (1995) identifies three problems: its inherent subjectivity; the fact that it might be applied in a way that introduces market-based rather than job-content factors as a way of overcoming recruitment and retention problems; and the extent to which it is used to widen differentials between grades, with higher grades having greater opportunities for higher bonuses. Whilst recognising the need for further research, Strebler, Thompson and Heron (1997) point to potential difficulties with skill- and competency-based schemes, not in the way that pay decisions are taken, but rather in unequal access to training and skill acquisition. What is more they suggest that employers' use of occupational standards and achieved level of National Vocational Qualifications (NVQ) in pay and promotion decisions may be detrimental to women if, as appears to be the case, young women achieve lower levels of NVQ than young men.

Pay differentials

The size and ranking of pay differentials is significant too. Rubery *et al.* (1997) argue that when differentials between sectors and organisations are changing, it is important for female-dominated sectors to maintain their relative position in the hierarchy. The last two decades have seen considerable structural changes in wage determination in the UK, including the decline of public-sector pay. The fact that this has not been uniform has according to Rubery *et al.*: 'seen many female-dominated groups slip down the pay hierarchy while others such as nurses have improved their relative pay' (Rubery *et al.*, 1997: 138).

Job grading

The division of jobs into separate families or groups, the way groups are linked together and individual gradings also have an impact on gender pay equality. In the United Kingdom female and male dominated jobs may be graded and paid on completely separate systems. So an organisation might have a managerial pay structure (male dominated) and a clerical pay structure (female dominated). A situation could arise where a skilled clerical worker could have a lower salary than a semi-skilled production worker in the same factory. The implications for the gender pay gap and for equal pay for work of equal value are obvious.

   The significance of the country context is exemplified here and Rubery *et al.* (1997) show that this situation could not arise in Italy, for example, because of the existence of four legally recognised categories of workers and a national unified grading system which applies to the first three categories in most industries.

THE LEGAL FRAMEWORK OF EQUAL PAY

The Equal Pay Act 1970 ('EPA') was implemented in order to give accessible legal redress for pay inequality based on sex. There was a five year gap between the royal assent to the EPA in 1970 and its enforcement – so that employers should have an opportunity to sort out the problem of pay inequality before it became a legal obligation. Despite the gap and the lapse of time since, the EPA has not achieved the hoped for bridging of the differences between men's and women's pay. The EPA did initially lead to a closing of the gap but then this stabilised.

Complexity of the legislation

A feature of equal pay legislation is its great complexity which is comparable with the complexity of maternity legislation. Tribunals were designed to provide a venue for dispensing speedy 'industrial justice', but in the specific areas of gender equality, for example relating to pay rights and maternity, they have proved to be the antithesis of 'user friendly'. Also, while the jurisprudence is very complex and the amounts at stake high (because unlike unfair dismissal awards are not capped at the current limit of approximately £18,000 and the pending European case of *Levez* [see below] may well have profound effects), legal aid is not available to assist claimants. Without trade union support, or the financial support of the Equal Opportunities Commission (EOC), which is increasingly hard to obtain, the vast majority of potential claimants would be deterred from claiming equal pay because of the arcane methods of bringing and pursuing claims. Bringing a claim, also requires stamina and fortitude because claims are rarely heard within months and are more likely to take years to come to a conclusion. This acts as a deterrent to potential claimants who are often involved in employment which is insecure, low paid and possibly part time. If cases take years to come to a conclusion, there may be a difficulty in sustaining the interest and support of claimants in continuing with their claims.

Establishing a claim for equal pay

For those who obtain support in bringing a claim or who are prepared to conduct it for themselves, reliance must be placed on the EPA. Claims may also be brought under the provisions of Article 119 Treaty of Rome but only where the EPA does not provide redress. The EPA has been substantially amended since it was first introduced and there are now three ways in which a claim for equal pay may be established.

The basis of the legislation is often misunderstood. It is aimed at eradicating discrimination on the grounds of sex and not at introducing fair wages. This means that a woman cannot claim pay parity with a man unless the differential in pay is caused by conscious or unconscious sex discrimination. Thus the employer may successfully defend the claim if he can show that the difference in pay between the woman and her comparator is attributable to genuine factors other than sex. In *Wallace and others* v *Strathclyde Regional Council 1998 IRLR 146 HL*, nine women who performed the duties of principal teacher brought equal pay claims with men employed as principal teachers by the local authority. The House of Lords held that section 1(3) EPA would provide a defence if the employer Council could show that the variation between the men's and the women's contracts was genuinely due to a factor which was (a) material and (b) not the difference of sex. The reason must not be a 'sham or a pretence' and causally related to the difference in pay. The employer only has a burden to justify the factors giving rise to the difference in pay where the employer relies on a factor

209

which is gender discriminatory. This case will have potentially far-reaching effects on equal pay claims and represents a shift in the way in which the law is applied. Prior to *Wallace*, once a potential claim was established, the burden effectively passed to the employer to rebut the claim for equal pay. Following *Wallace*, it seems that employers will be able to defend claims on the basis of agreeing that women are paid less but arguing that the causative factor is unrelated to sex. It is difficult to predict the full ramifications of the decision in practice which remains to be seen in subsequent cases.

The starting point of the EPA is that it implies an equality clause into all terms of contracts of employment, i.e. not simply those concerned with pay. The clause therefore covers, e.g. holiday pay, pensions, car allowance, contractual share schemes, etc. The equality clause modifies the woman's contract to bring it up to the same standard as the man's.

In order to establish an entitlement to equal pay, a woman 'in the same employment as a man' (the comparator) may establish that she is engaged on

- like work with a male comparator under section 1(4) EPA or
- work which is rated as equivalent under a job evaluation study under section 1(5) or
- work which is of equal value

One of these three steps is the starting point for any claim and if a woman cannot establish one of them, then there is no case for the employer to answer. The pay differential must also be directly or indirectly discriminatory for there to be a claim. 'Like work' has to be established for there to be a claim under this heading, but tribunals are instructed not to be over-technical in their approach to the definition. Importantly, it is the actual work which the woman and the comparator do which is analysed – not the work which they are contracted to do. The distinction is for obvious reasons: if the tribunal only had to analyse the terms of the contract, employers could always avoid successful claims by drafting contracts showing extreme differences in the work which could be required in principle between men and women, even if never demanded in practice.

Once the work has been analysed, and found to be like work, it is then possible to move to the second stage which is to decide if there is a material difference between the two cases so that the employer can justify the differential in pay. For example, women on a day shift may be paid less than men working on a night shift. The difference in pay is not based on sex, but on the time when the work is done and therefore there is an objective justification for the pay difference which is regardless of sex.

The second method of establishing an entitlement to equal pay is that the work done has been rated as of equal value under the terms of a job evaluation study ('JES'). Provided the JES is objective and not itself gender biased, then it will provide a defence to any equal pay claim. Any employer is well advised to conduct such a scheme in order to make pay differentials between men and women defensible. Once such a scheme has been conducted objectively, it is not open to a tribunal to find that there is pay inequality to found a claim.

However, it is open to the tribunal or court to challenge the basis of the JES, a fact which was demonstrated in *Bromley v H&J Quick 1988 IRLR 249*. In that case an evaluation exercise had been conducted and formed the basis of the employer's defence to an equal pay claim. It was argued on behalf of the women applicants for equal pay that section 1(5) EPA required that their work should be evaluated as part of the job evaluation exercise. The section requires that the jobs are compared for equal value purposes under various headings, for instance effort, skill and decision making. It was not sufficient that sample jobs had been evaluated and benchmarked. To rely on the JES, the employer had to show that the job of the complainant and her comparator had been evaluated and this could not be done simply on the basis of samples.

The third way in which a claim for equal pay may be established is by showing that the work done is of equal value with that of the comparator in the same employment under s 1(2) c. The 'equal value' provision was introduced into the EPA in 1984. While it is potentially the most powerful weapon in establishing equal pay, it has been described in the case of *Leverton* v *Clwyd County Council 1989 IRLR 28* as 'lengthy, elaborate and expensive' – an overriding criticism of the legislation as a whole. Equal value claims can only be brought if the work is not like work or work which is rated as equivalent under a JES.

A woman must compare herself with males employed in the same establishment or by any associated employer. In *British Coal Corporation* v *Smith and Others 1996 IRLR 404* women canteen workers compared themselves with surface coal workers – (predominantly men) at 14 different establishments. BCC took a preliminary point that the men and women were not employed on the same terms and therefore not in the same employment. Obviously any restrictive interpretation of 'same employment' reduces the opportunity for a successful equal pay claim. The House of Lords agreed with the interpretation of the tribunal – that there should be a common-sense approach to what 'same employment' means.

Article 119 may also assist: in *Scullard* v *Southern Regional Council for Education and Training 1996 IRLR 344* the applicant compared herself with managers who worked for 11 other regional councils. They were not associated employers for the purposes of the EPA. She successfully relied on Article 119 which states that a woman is entitled to equal pay where the comparators are employed in the same establishment or service.

Who constitutes a valid comparator is a crucial issue in determining equal pay: a claimant must compare herself with a real person – not a hypothetical man and she is entitled to choose as her comparator someone who is employed at the same time as her or her predecessor or successor in post.

Even if the work is found to be of equal value, the employer can still show that the difference in pay is unrelated to gender – i.e. there is a material factor defence unrelated to sex and that the pay difference is not based on sex. Therefore the fact that the woman establishes that she is employed on like work, work rated as equivalent or work of equal value means that the implied equality clause in the contract of employment comes into operation unless the employer can show that the variation is genuinely due to a material factor other than sex.

The employer's defence

The material factor defence has taken a number of forms in reported cases. These can be:

- personal factors – skill, seniority or experience
- red circling
- differences due to a genuine non-sex-biased grading scheme

- collective bargaining where the collective bargaining itself is not tainted by sex discrimination
- market forces

and since *Wallace* employers can argue that the *difference is unrelated to sex.*

IMPROVING WOMEN'S PAY POSITION

Women's pay position relative to men's has to be improved not just because that position may be based on discrimination, but also for wider social and moral reasons as well. The fact that many women are locked into low-paid jobs not only impacts on morale and productivity, but has wider implications for women's economic independence and retirement income. Solutions have not only been advanced in terms of reforming the legislation, but also through policy changes as well.

Improving the legislation

It is rare for employers consciously to pay women less *because of their sex*. Differences may result from the time when the work is done, or the place where it is performed. Some cases suggest that market forces will lead to pay differentials because of the desirability of certain skills or qualifications over others. There are problems in that many pay differentials arose from the fact that people might be paid more 'in times of plenty' and that especially in the public sector, when less cash was available, people would be paid less. This is clearly a defence to a claim.

The greatest problems in equal pay claims arise from the 'equal value' provisions. They are the most difficult to prove and there is the greatest scope for argument about what constitutes value.

The EOC has strongly criticised the legislation, especially the equal value aspects since its capacity to eliminate discrimination against women who are lower paid than men has been most disappointing. The EOC has argued that the UK has failed to implement Article 2 Equal Pay Directive which requires member states to introduce measures which are necessary 'to enable employees who consider themselves wronged by failure to apply the principle of equal pay to pursue their claims by judicial process after possible recourse to other competent authorities.'

Statistics suggest that claims are inordinately protracted and that very few reach a speedy and satisfactory conclusion, getting lost in procedures or the appointment of experts, or simply bogged down by appeals to higher courts including to Europe. Some cases have taken over seven years to be adjudicated. Even then, the award of equal pay may lead to confusion and the need to revert to the tribunal to deal with problems which arise after the award.

Some potential improvements to the legislation may be proposed. The position of employers would be significantly improved if what constitutes an acceptable JES were to be set out – perhaps by Code of Practice. Employers could achieve compliance with legal requirements simply by applying the correct scheme. If agreed guidelines could not be implemented then the scheme operating in Ireland could be adopted where state appointed inspectors investigate and reach decisions on pay inequalities.

This scheme would be cheaper and more user friendly than the current system of litigation.

The recent elimination of the need for an independent expert always to be appointed in any claim should assist in cutting down the delay in achieving a hearing date since tribunals can now decide for themselves if work is of equal value. This development is the effect of the EOC reforms to procedure in the 1997 Code of Practice. As an alternative the use of one expert only with agreement to accept his/her recommendations as binding might also assist the speedier disposal of proceedings. Under present rules, both parties are entitled to challenge any independent expert appointed by the tribunal which can simply elongate the proceedings and the scheme also favours the employer since it is the employer who can afford to appoint an independent expert to challenge another expert's evidence. Employers know that it is likely to be worthwhile to appoint their own expert – if only to delay the ultimate decision.

Increased intervention of tribunals in the conduct of proceedings would also assist. The evidence is anecdotal – but tribunals have been criticised for being too prepared to delay proceedings, in contrast to the 'hands on' approach of tribunals to other claims, especially unfair dismissal, where delays and postponements are not tolerated and the tribunal is entirely master of the timetable of its own procedures. Independent experts have also been subject to much criticism for contributing to the delay in proceedings.

As the law stands, a claim for equal pay is limited to arrears or the difference in pay for two years preceding the submission of the application to the tribunal. This limitation on damages has been challenged on the basis that it failed to provide a proper remedy under the provisions of European law. In contract, claims are limited to six years of losses and there is no logical reason for the limitation of damages in equal pay to two years since this is a contract claim also. The case of *Levez* was referred to the European Court on the point, and the Advocate General has produced a favourable opinion, agreeing that the claim is a contract claim and therefore should be limited only in the same way as are contract claims. It remains to be seen if the ECJ will follow the Opinion.

It is arguable that the amount of any possible remedy affects the speed with which employers are prepared to deal with claims or compromise them. *Levez* may therefore have a profound effect on equal pay claims and settlements.

Differentials in pay often arise because of the gender segregation of jobs – it is frequently the case that on apparently arbitrary grounds work will be defined either as men's or women's work. Given that such segregation is one of the major causes of pay disparity, the greater equalisation of pay is not assisted by the need to prove that the difference in pay is the result of direct or indirect discrimination.

If the issue of pay equality were to become one of fairness rather than discrimination, so it were unnecessary to prove discrimination to achieve pay parity, this could have a much greater effect on the elimination of gender segregated jobs giving differentials in pay, although it is difficult to envisage the precise method for achieving this.

Re-visiting employer's equal opportunities policies and practices

Employers not only need to ensure that women are treated equally in terms of training, appraisal and promotion, they also need to examine their payment structures, grading systems and job evaluation criteria to ensure that these do not discriminate unfairly against women.

Moreover, if the issue of women's low pay is to be tackled they need to go further than this by ensuring that women have opportunities to break out of the low-skill, low-pay spiral. The attachment of low-paid women to the labour market can be facilitated in a number of ways. First, through the introduction of family friendly policies, such as extended maternity rights and childcare facilities. Second, by placing low-paid jobs and part-time jobs within a proper career structure which provides opportunities for promotion or career development and finally by the re-evaluation of the skills content of these low-paid jobs.

The role of trade unions

The role of trade unions goes beyond the backing of equal value cases and using the legislative principles as a basis for collective negotiation. Unions need to tackle issues such as the representation and involvement of women and the extension of collective bargaining into the low-wage sector. This means putting women's issues higher on their agenda and increasing the numbers of women in positions of power.

Removal of patriarchal controls in the workplace

Writers have argued that the solutions outlined above are not sufficient in themselves and that what is needed is the removal of patriarchal controls in the work place – the controls that exclude women from certain occupations or levels of occupation within them and that lead to the under-valuing of women's work. This requires commitment not only from the trade unions but also changes in attitudes by men and women.

The future

Despite the steady convergence of men's and women's pay since the introduction of the equal pay legislation in the 1970s, pay inequality still exists. Arguably, the solutions outlined above, will not be sufficient in themselves. What is needed is a more fundamental change.

The significance of a statutory minimum wage is that it has the potential to raise the pay of women relative to that of men by disproportionately benefiting women, because of their predominance in the low-pay sector. However, the critical issue is the level at which any minimum wage will be set and the extent to which employers might try to recover any additional costs by reducing working time. At the time of writing, it is only possible to speculate.

Moreover, as has been suggested earlier, the issue is wider than the question of low pay and encompasses questions of exclusion and value as well. If true equality of reward is to be achieved then substantial shifts in attitudes are necessary, by organisations, institutions and the men and women who constitute them. This perhaps presents the biggest challenge of all.

LEARNING ACTIVITIES

1 Assess the capability of the payroll systems in your organisation to provide information on gender based pay differentials.

2 To what extent are other, wider, issues such as access to training or family friendly policies monitored for their impact on gender equality and pay?

3 What advice would you offer an organisation introducing a competency- or skills-based pay system to ensure that their scheme was defensible in terms of an equal value claim?

4 Outline why, nearly 30 years after the introduction of the Equal Pay Act of 1970, there are still substantial differences between men's and women's pay.

REFERENCES

Armstrong, P. (1982) 'If It's Only Women It Doesn't Matter So Much', in J. West (ed.), *Work, Women and the Labour Market*. London: Routledge & Kegan Paul.

Bevan, S. and Thompson M. (1992) 'Merit Pay, Performance Appraisal and Attitudes to Women's Work', IMS Report No 234, Brighton: Institute of Manpower Studies.

Dex, S. (1988) 'Gender and the Labour Market', in D. Gallie (ed.), *Employment in Britain*. Oxford: Blackwell.

Dex, S., Lissenburgh, S. and Taylor, M. (1994) 'Women and Low Pay: Identifying the issues', Manchester, Equal Opportunities Commission, EOC Research Discussion 9.

EOR (1997) 'Minimum Wage Benefits Women and Ethnic Minorities', *Equal Opportunities Review*, 73, May/June.

Hakim, C. (1996) *Key Issues in Women's Work. Female heterogeneity and the polarisation of women's employment*. London: Athlone.

Humphries, J. and Rubery, J. (1984) 'The Reconstitution of the Supply Side of the Labour Market: the relative autonomy of social reproduction', *Cambridge Journal of Economics*, 8(4).

Humphries, J. (1995) 'Economics, Gender and Equal Opportunities', in J. Humphries and J. Rubery (ed.), *The Economics of Equal Opportunities*. Manchester: Equal Opportunities Commission.

IRS (1991) 'Pay and Gender in Britain', A Research Report for the EOC, IRS/EOC.

IRS (1992) 'Pay and Gender in Britain', A Second Research Report for the EOC, IRS/EOC.

Labour Research Department (1998) 'A Minimum Boost to Equality', *Labour Research*, March.

Martin, J. and Roberts, C. (1984) *Women and Employment: A lifetime perspective*. London: HMSO.

Milward, N. and Woodland, S. (1995) 'Gender Segregation and Male/Female Wage Differences', in J. Humphries and J. Rubery (eds), *The Economics of Equal Opportunities*. Manchester: Equal Opportunities Commission.

Mincer, J. and Polachek, S. (1974) 'Family Investment in Human Capital: Earnings of women', *Journal of Political Economy*, 82: 2.

New Earnings Survey (1997) Part A. Office for National Statistics.

Rubery, J. (1992) 'Pay, Gender and the Social Dimension to Europe', *British Journal of Industrial Relations*, 30: 4.

Rubery, J. (1995) 'Performance-Related Pay and the Prospect for Gender Pay Equity', *Journal of Management Studies*, 32: 5.

Rubery, J., Bettio, F., Fagan, C., Maier, F., Quack, S. and Villa, P. (1997) 'Payment Structures and Gender Pay Differentials: Some societal effects', *International Journal of Human Resource Management*, 8: 3.

Shaw, S.R. and Taylor, M.E. (1997) 'Warning Handle With Care – Careers in Transit', Paper presented to the Strategic HRM Conference, Nottingham Business School, December.

Strebler, M., Thompson, M. and Heron, P. (1997) *Skills, Competencies and Gender: Issues for pay*, Brighton: Insitute for Employment Studies.

Wright, R.E. and Ermisch, J.F. (1991) 'Gender Discrimination in the British Labour Market: A Reassessment', *Economic Journal*, 101, May.

FURTHER READING

Clarke, L. (1995) *Discrimination*. London: IPD.

Dijkstra, A.G. and Plantenga, J. (1997) *Gender and Economics – A European perspective*. London: Routledge.

EOC (1997) *Code of Practice on Equal Pay*. London: Equal Opportunities Commission.

Hakim, C. (1996) *Key Issues in Women's Work – Female heterogeneity and the polarisation of women's employment*. London: Athlone.

Humphries, J. and Rubery, J. (ed.) (1995) *The Economics of Equal Opportunities*. Manchester: Equal Opportunities Commission.

Lewis, D. (1997) *Essentials of Employment Law*. Fifth edition, London: IPD.

Pitt, G. (1997) *Employment Law*. Third edition, London: Sweet and Maxwell.

12 Job evaluation

Peter Smith and Geoff Nethersell

INTRODUCTION

This chapter begins by describing the purpose of job evaluation and the various types of schemes in common use. It goes on to identify the various processes essential to the effective management of a job evaluation system before exploring some recent trends in the development of methods and how these have arisen. The public sector is given separate treatment to the private sector and, although the chapter focuses on job evaluation as a support to pay in the way it establishes relativities and provides a basis for grouping jobs for the purpose of pay and as a support to benchmarking, it concludes by highlighting how job evaluation systems can also help to develop jobs and align these to the organisation's priorities for success.

JOB EVALUATION DEFINED

Job evaluation is the term which describes a systematic process used to assess the relative size of jobs within and sometimes between organisations. Despite the fact that the output from a process of this kind is frequently represented as a 'score' it is important to recognise that job evaluation is essentially comparative and judgemental. Job evaluation judgements are never capable of scientific proof.

PURPOSE

Traditionally, job evaluation has been associated with order and control; the emphasis has been on producing a broadly accepted and defensible pattern of internal relativities which have primarily been used for grouping jobs together in grades. Grades in turn have provided a convenient vehicle for salary administration and supporting pay has historically been the main focus of job evaluation. But grades have also afforded overt recognition of status. Sometimes this has been associated with differential benefits, but even without this a difference in grade label is often highly prized as a status symbol.

The expression of evaluation relativities in these terms is, in many organisations, a powerful shorthand – a common language that speaks volumes about the perceived relative worth of an individual in a job: 'He/she is only a grade x' immediately communicates how much weight should be given to an individual's statements. In this sense, job evaluation can be seen to be part of a culture which emphasises hierarchy and status and it has been argued to conflict with new organisational values which are explored later in this chapter.

In fact, despite dramatic/transformational organisational change in many companies, there has been continued growth in the use of formal job evaluation. This reflects its continued importance in the determination of pay and also its several wider purposes of measuring job size in:

- underpinning sound decisions on career development. It is important, particularly in newer, leaner organisations to have some means of assessing the weight and nature of a position which may be used to offer career development opportunities.
- helping in the design of efficiently structured lean organisations which have appropriate distance between jobs.
- *accurate* market comparisons. Again, as organisations have sought to achieve competitive advantage through the redesign of work and the creation of different flexible roles, market comparisons based on job title or capsule job description have become even more unreliable as an accurate measure of market worth. Comparison across organisations based on job size has therefore remained important.
- establishing a 'fully satisfactory' reference point for performance-related-pay progression arrangements.

In addition, job evaluation has continued to play an important role in underpinning internally equitable pay arrangements. This, despite much of the rhetoric of some modern management gurus, has continued to be important to many organisations both because of inherent organisational values and, as we will demonstrate below, because of an increased emphasis on equal value.

JOB EVALUATION METHODOLOGY

By way of introduction to a review of job evaluation methodologies it is important to differentiate between method and process:

- the term 'method' refers to the measuring instrument used to assess job size
- 'process' refers to how decisions are made: what information is presented, who is involved in making judgements, etc.

Looking first at method, it is possible to distinguish four principal methodologies which can be sub-divided into two non-analytical methods and two analytical methods. Non-analytical methods make whole job comparisons whilst analytical methods assess job size by reference to specific pre-determined criteria. Further differentiation between methods reflects the nature of the comparisons made; job with job or job with scale. The four main methodologies are distinguished in this way in table 12.1 and further explained below.

Table 12.1

	Method of analysis	
Basis of comparison	Job elements	Whole job
Job with job	Factor comparison	Ranking
Job with scale	Points rating	Classification

Ranking

Ranking involves comparing whole jobs and arranging them in a rank order which reflects their perceived relative size. Under this arrangement relative worth is all in the eye(s) of the beholder(s). Ranking is often an implicit rather than explicit methodology. Any small entrepreneur deciding to pay his/her bookkeeper more or less than his/her secretary is making a ranking judgement.

Ranking is, in historical terms, the oldest and simplest form of job evaluation but is most suited to circumstances in which the individual(s) making judgements are in a position to view and understand all the jobs in an organisational unit. In larger and more sophisticated organisations it is difficult to achieve the degree of understanding which enables consistent judgements to be made. In these circumstances there is normally a search for a more formal process which will limit subjectivity.

Classification

Job classification was pioneered in the United States in the Federal Classification Act of 1923. Classification requires the advance definition of the number and characteristics of grade levels in an organisation. Each of the levels is described in terms which will enable the levels to be clearly differentiated from each other. Job evaluation involves matching actual jobs to the level definitions to determine the appropriate grade.

Whilst classification schemes were initially developed for large organisations – the United States Federal Government being the first example – the major problems with approaches of this kind are associated with the difficulty of constructing level definitions to accommodate diverse and changing jobs in large and complex organisations. Classification works best in cohesive, stable, hierarchical organisations and organisations of this kind may be seen to be the exception rather than the rule in the new millennium. However the advantages of defining, in broad terms, levels of work have been acknowledged in 'new' organisations in the form of *job family modelling* where levels of work are defined in relation to related groups of roles. Unlike traditional classification schemes a job family model has a restricted focus and does not try to embrace all positions in an organisation. Rather a series of models are developed for different job families, with formal analytical job evaluation underpinning the development of the models with provision made to enable individuals to make comparison between models.

Non-analytical schemes, involving consideration of the whole job, share the difficulty of evaluating very different jobs. Individual relative judgements may be very different because those making the judgements implicitly value different aspects of jobs differently. Consensus may therefore be difficult to achieve and differences in judgement difficult to reconcile. This led to the development of analytical methods which require the advance definition of the criteria on which relative judgements will be based. Analytical schemes take two main forms: points rating and factor comparison.

Points rating

The development of a job evaluation method of this kind demands:

- the determination of the 'factors' which are to be used to identify the differences between jobs;
- the identification of the levels or degrees at which each of the factors can be present in jobs in the population to be evaluated;
- the determination of a maximum score associated with each of the factors – factor weighting;
- the determination of scores for each factor level – identified by dividing the maximum available score by the number of levels or degrees.

Clearly the selection of factors is critical to the success of a method of this kind. The factors themselves and the language used to describe them are an important opportunity to reinforce the values of the organisation, they also need to be selected to ensure that they are not discriminatory (see paragraphs on equal value below). Points-rating methods will usually contain between three and 12 factors and, whilst a superficial review of the wide range of methodologies around suggests a large number of different factors are in use, in practice these can be considered under three broad headings:

- *Input*: under this heading factors seek to define what jobholders must bring to the job in terms of their skills and knowledge. This will encompass education and training and formal qualifications as well as skills gained through experience and softer interpersonal skills.
- *Process*: these factors are concerned with capturing the demands associated with translating inputs to outputs. Typical factors will focus on complexity, scope for innovation and need for initiative and judgement.
- *Output*: authority, responsibility for resources – finance, people, assets – are examples of factors which focus on the contribution of a job to the end results of the organisation.

Points-rating methods reduce the degree of subjectivity in job evaluation and provide the basis for explaining differences between jobs. They force evaluators to consider the range of factors which can impact on relative job size and therefore reduce the likelihood of bias and over-simplified judgements. They can – subject to a wide variety of other criteria – be acceptable in equal-value cases. On the down side they are complex to develop and are only as good as the assumptions on which they are based – in particular the assumptions around the factor weights.

Factor comparison

Like points rating, factor comparison begins with the identification of factors which are to be used to determine the differences between jobs but uses agreed current pay rates to produce weightings. Job evaluation using factor comparison involves four steps:

- The selection of benchmark jobs is made. Elsewhere we refer to a benchmark as a representative sample of job in the population to be evaluated. In factor comparison the term 'benchmark' has a further and particular meaning since benchmark jobs are those where there is advance agreement that the current rates of pay are, in some way, 'right'. In principle these would be market rates with the objective of job evaluation being to identify appropriate rates for those positions which could not be priced by reference to the market.
- Benchmark jobs are then ranked against each of the identified factors and 'profiled' by determining the relative importance of each factor in the total (100 per cent) score for each of the jobs.
- Current pay levels are taken to specify the overall rank order and the pattern of relativities, and provide the basis for allocating money values to the factors, effectively specifying the relative contribution of each factor to the 'price' of the job.
- The values establish factor scales and non-benchmark jobs are then compared factor by factor with the benchmark scales to produce ranking/pricing for each of the positions.

Conceptually, factor comparison has a number of advantages enabling direct job to job comparisons rather than comparisons with a sometimes artificial or abstract scale. It produces directly a price for a job. However, it does require advance agreement on the correct rate for benchmark jobs and is seen as too complex and difficult to communicate. As a result, it is rarely if ever used directly today, but factor comparison was the basis of the development of the Hay Guide Chart Profile method of job evaluation, the most widely used methodology around the world. Readers requiring a more substantial analysis of the pros and cons of each method are recommended to read Armstrong and Baron (1995).

JOB EVALUATION PROCESS

The process of job evaluation is concerned with the application of the agreed methodology. The methodology is designed to enable consistent and defensible judgements about relative job size, and the wider process is also underpinned by 'rules' which seek to limit the degree of subjectivity in the job size judgements. Irrespective of the method being used the operating rules tend to be common. Job evaluation:

- focuses on the job and not the person
- assumes fully acceptable performance
- considers the job at a particular point in time
- ignores current pay and status

In designing the overall process the two most critical issues concern the way in which job information is gathered and who (or what in the case of computer-assisted job evaluation) makes the judgements required by the chosen method. There is also an important question of whether and how to review judgements once made.

Job analysis

Job evaluation needs to be based on a full and up-to-date understanding of the jobs which are being evaluated. Job analysis refers to the process of gathering, analysing and presenting information about jobs, usually in the form of a job description, for evaluation. It is necessary to determine the nature of the information that should be contained in the job description and the way in which it is to be presented in the light of the requirements of the job evaluation methodology. Job analysis then seeks to obtain the appropriate information about jobs, either through interviews conducted by trained job analysts or through questionnaires. Traditionally it has been assumed that the people who are best placed to provide information about a job are jobholders and/or the person to whom they report. Job analysts would therefore conduct face-to-face interviews with jobholders to obtain job information, draft this in the required format and have the draft reviewed and approved by the boss. Where information was gathered through questionnaires, jobholders would complete these after a briefing and again submit them to their superior for review and sign off.

As organisations have sought to cope with constant change and achieve competitive advantage through the redesign of work processes and the creation of new roles they have increasingly seen the need to reorientate the job analysis process from one which captures information about the roles which exist to one which proactively designs jobs/roles to align with business strategy. Job-family modelling is frequently deployed in this way.

Evaluation judgement

As was indicated at the start of this chapter, job evaluation is essentially a subjective, judgemental activity. Even with a well-developed and refined analytical method the judgement about the score to be given under a certain factor heading is never absolute. This means that job evaluation has usually been seen to benefit from a collective approach – evaluation panels 'representative' of the population being evaluated are assembled to read reviews and discuss job descriptions and to reach consensus about the evaluation in terms of the chosen methodology.

The size and nature of panels varies depending on the scale and diversity of the population being evaluated but conventional wisdom argues that a panel of less than six may risk being unrepresentative and over-dominated by individual strong personalities whilst a panel of more than ten may be too large to enable the efficient conduct of focused discussions on relative job size. The process of reviewing the content of a wide range of positions in an organisation has often been a powerful learning and development opportunity for those involved, but it also has a high opportunity cost. Again conventional wisdom regarding the strike rate – the number of unique positions evaluated by a panel in a day – suggests that this is typically around eight. Assembling a panel of eight or so individuals for this purpose is clearly expensive.

The search for greater efficiency has been traditionally reflected in the distinction between benchmark and non-benchmark positions. A programme of job evaluation commences with the identification of a (benchmark) sample of positions which are seen to be appropriately representative of the total population. These have been subject to rigorous job analysis and full and thorough scrutiny by the job evaluation panel. Once the benchmark framework is in place non-benchmark positions can be evaluated more rapidly through a process of 'slotting'. The precise form of slotting varies but in all cases the objective is to significantly increase the daily strike rate.

More recently the search for efficiency and productivity has been reflected in the use of computers to assist the job-evaluation process. Approaches of this kind will typically require the manual evaluation of a benchmark sample of jobs in the way outlined above but this is followed by the development of a questionnaire and algorithm to reproduce the benchmark evaluations. The questionnaire and predictive model are then used to evaluate non-benchmark positions. Whilst computer-assisted approaches of this kind can play an important part in job evaluation (and job analysis) processes it is important to maintain a sense of perspective about the nature of the 'judgements' which can be made in a black box. Computer-based job analysis and job evaluation still requires rigorous quality assurance on the nature of the questionnaire responses and input – rubbish in, rubbish out is a truism which needs to be borne in mind in developing approaches of this kind.

Appeals/maintenance

The final stage of the job evaluation process usually provides for jobholders to appeal against the outcome of a job evaluation exercise. This is further recognition of the imprecise nature of job evaluation and enables individuals who feel unable to accept the relative positioning of 'their' job to seek a further review. Appeals arrangements vary widely but normally attempt to inject some measure of independence and 'felt fair' consideration into the review rather than simply asking the evaluation panel 'to think again'.

Job evaluation is frequently described in project terms – a programme to be implemented – but continuing change in organisation and jobs means that job evaluation is for most organisations an ongoing activity with new and changed positions needing to be evaluated all the time. Job evaluation can therefore become something of an industry with large quantities of paper and administration adding to the opportunity cost issue referred to above. These and wider changes described later in this chapter have led to significant changes to job evaluation as it is positioned as a business process to meet the needs of current organisations. Before looking at this in detail we will however consider the implications of equal value for job evaluation.

EQUAL VALUE

The detail of equal value requirements is covered elsewhere (chapter 9), but a brief reference here is inevitable given the link between evaluation and equal value assessment.

The current requirements derive from the Equal Pay Act of 1970 and the 1984 amendment, which provides that women and men are entitled to equal pay where the work is of equal value in terms of the demands of the job – 'for instance effort, skill and decision'.

If an equal pay claim is brought, the employer may argue that they have a method of job evaluation which shows the jobs to be unequal. At this point, the employers' scheme may be examined to test its validity. If the claim proceeds to a full hearing on the substantive issue, expert assessment of job relativities is likely to be required. This often involves a tailored method, designed to compare specifically the jobs of applicant and comparator.

These requirements and the way they have been applied in thousands of cases carry two main implications for employers. First, they do need to have a valid job evaluation approach. Both the method and the process by which it is applied have to be free of sex bias. The method has to be analytical, i.e. to break down consideration of job demands under a number of factor headings and definitions (*Bromley and others v H & J Quick, Court of Appeal 1988*). The process must involve the right people, use trained evaluators and exercise care in 'slotting' or matching jobs against a benchmark sample.

Second, there is some uncertainty about exactly what constitutes an acceptable method. This is partly due to a tension between the realities of job evaluation in organisations (where a wide range of job types and levels will be examined using the same generic framework of factors) and the expert process in Tribunal (where tailored factors are used to conduct paired comparisons). It is also partly because there have not been enough appeal cases focusing specifically on questions of methodology for the guidelines to be completely clear. Organisations have to make their own choice about how to proceed, based on their own needs and circumstances, and on general advice.

In practice, as we outline below, this has led to a wide variety of approaches to job evaluation. The relationship of many modern grading and pay systems to equal value law is far from clear, and some would argue that the law itself needs modernising if it is to be effective and relevant.

DEVELOPMENTS IN RECENT DECADES

General trends in the private sector

Exhibit 12.1

> **Yorkford Building Society, 1978**
>
> Job evaluation introduced to cover all jobs at all levels in headquarters, regions and branches. The aims were to support the introduction of a clear reward system, with effective disciplines and cost control, and to enable external pay comparisons.
>
> A proprietary analytical method was used. A team of staff were trained to describe jobs based on interview and observation. The job descriptions were assessed by a panel of six people, with the personnel department in the chair.
>
> The initial investment costs in the system were high, with overall staff time (planning, training, describing, evaluating, concluding) of around a person day per job, and added costs for external consultants. The system had to be maintained in a similar way, i.e. with analysts describing jobs and a panel of six evaluating them.
>
> The approach to job evaluation and pay, delivered a simple and controllable set of grades and pay levels, with access to external benchmarks.

Exhibit 12.2

Yorkford Financial Services Plc, 1998

Reviewing its management practices after a change of status from mutual to bank and following a recent merger, the company felt its grading and pay system to be inflexible and unsuited to a fast changing organisation. The aim was to establish an approach to jobs and pay which matched the strategy.

The company chose to concentrate on defining the main generic jobs and job groups, starting with customer services in retail banking. An internal project team worked with groups of staff to describe the changing nature of their jobs, identify differences between jobs and the reasons for them. The HR department and line managers matched jobs against these generics, and used the process to set pay within broad bands.

The initial costs were fairly high because of widespread participation, but concentrating on typical or generic characteristics kept total staff time to around half the cost of the organisation's 1978 review. While the generic levels would have to be reviewed from time to time, using them as defined was simple.

Taking in related issues of pay, development and performance, the new system was part of a complete realignment of management processes for a new market.

These 'case studies', while a little caricatured, are intended to express several aspects of change in job evaluation and the way it is used from the 1970s to the 1990s. This coincides with a period of considerable development in the human resources function where ownership of the job evaluation system normally resides. Human resources departments are now far smaller – with less than one HR person to every hundred company employees, compared to the 1:25 ratios of the 1970s – with a richer mix of qualifications and expertise. For them as for their internal customers, system design is important but system maintenance has to be kept as efficient as possible. Their needs and the needs of their business have changed.

The process of change can be seen under a number of headings:

- *Purpose.* At one time, job evaluation was a technical approach used to build grades to support pay. It provided rigour and helped control costs. Now it is more commonly one of a number of management systems and mechanisms which have to match business need. Cost control is still important, but the way evaluation is done and how the results are used vary far more by type and style of business.
- *Method.* In the 1970s there were many in-house points rating schemes for big companies, job classification schemes (both localised and generic), and proprietary analytical schemes. In the past 20 years, some of the big in-house schemes have disappeared, but the market offers a far wider range of methods, supporting a greater diversity in how jobs and pay are managed.
- *Process.* The older approach of large job evaluation panels has diminished. Job evaluation is more often done by smaller groups or by individuals, and/or by agreement between an HR professional and a line manager. An alternative to group debate has been to use computer-assisted job evaluation, which focuses assessment on a single job analyst and therefore again tends to diminish the number of people involved and

the time cost. None of this necessarily makes 1990s job evaluation less comprehensible to staff – much depends on how the system is explained and how outcomes are communicated.

- *Cost.* In keeping with changes in HR and also growing pressures on management time, the continuing cost of maintaining job evaluation systems has been reducing. Some organisations have made reducing bureaucracy and costs around job evaluation one of their main objectives in recent reforms. Even the cost of introducing new approaches has been declining, when internal and external consultancy costs are taken into account.

- *Benefits.* The principal change has been a transition from job evaluation as a major system in its own right and as a support to the pay structure to a far broader and more business-related proposition. While our 1978 example has jobs being described as they are and as discrete entities, the 1998 case shows a process of defining jobs in context, in relation to each other and as they should be rather than as they are now. Today, companies expect processes like job evaluation to fit the strategy, and to provide a value beyond the immediate issue of pay.

These developments are simply a reflection of a number of wider forces for change in the work place. Three of these forces in particular need to be mentioned:

1 The drive for flexibility

Management trends in the past decades have emphasised delayering, devolution or empowerment, and focus on the customer, whether internal or external. Growing competition in all markets for goods and services has forced reductions in overheads, production and decision time and emphasised the need to deliver value to customers. There is less of a sense of hierarchy within functions, and more of collaboration across functions and disciplines. Many jobs are less specific and confined than they were – there are more loosely drawn roles, which allow room for development, involvement and customer response beyond the core set of responsibilities. In reconfiguring job evaluation, organisations have emphasised this flexibility in the method, process and outcomes, including the setting of broader pay levels.

2 The drive for integration

The emphasis on both the internal and external customer has underlined the sense in which all parts of an organisation are interrelated. If one department such as HR has a system or policy, it must be seen to be in the service of the whole. But many businesses have also undertaken major internal reviews which have intensified scrutiny of areas like job evaluation. First, the trend in the 1980s towards strategy clarification posed questions about whether internal systems were aligned to that strategy. Second, process reengineering reviewed the efficiency of the internal workings of the firm, and sought to anchor all processes in the customer. Job evaluation has survived these trends but in a different form – or more accurately, in a far wider variety of forms than it took in the 1970s. There is even a case for saying that job evaluation has been strengthened, inasmuch as its value outside pay and its links to wider issues of organisation design and performance have become clearer.

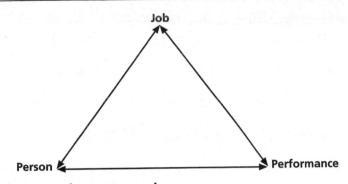

Fig. 12.1 Balancing what to reward

3 The drive to reduce costs

Competitive pressures and changes in management philosophy have reduced staff numbers in management itself and in HR departments and have certainly compressed the time they have available for internal processes like job evaluation. This has combined with increasingly detailed examination of the cost of all processes and systems to force changes in the way job evaluation is done. Whatever the merits of job evaluation panels – and they do have potential advantages of open debate, involvement and informed decision making – many organisations would now say they could not afford them.

These forces have combined not just to change job evaluation, but to broaden its positioning from technical system to business support. This is visible in the link between job evaluation and pay. Organisations looking at reward will among other things ask themselves about what they want to pay for, and in particular how to balance payment for three things (see figure 12.1).

While a small number of organisations and job types reflect an extreme point on this triangle, the majority represent a balance between the extremes. But, within that balance, there has been a shift down the triangle, away from rewards tightly related to jobs and job size and towards more flexibility to recognise personal skills and competencies or performance or both. This has taken the emphasis off job evaluation as the main determinant of pay, but it has also meant that job evaluation has a new role, which it can only perform if it meshes effectively with themes of development, competencies and performance.

Quite where these developments leave much of the private sector in relation to equal value law is unclear. It may be that many organisations are good practitioners of new, flexible systems, but they often do not place the emphasis on detailed examination of the current demands of the job which statute and caselaw seem to ask for.

The public sector

We believe it is important to highlight a very different path of development in the public sector. None the less, it would be wrong to identify a sharp distinction between public-and private-sector experience and to treat the public sector as a single homogeneous group. Several factors point to a more complicated truth:

- In the past 20 years the definition of the public sector has changed enormously. Privatisation has affected major areas of national service provision, notably water, electricity, gas and rail. It has broken up national employers with national bargaining into regional or functional companies. All have found a need for job evaluation during that process of change, and their experience is not dissimilar to that of the private sector, albeit condensed into a shorter period.
- Industries which remain nationalised use job evaluation, though they may employ a mix of matching against defined generic roles for some groups and formal analytical job evaluation for others.
- The break up of civil service pay arrangements in the 1990s has created a diverse group of agencies and departments. Many use a computer assisted points rating job evaluation method designed and developed with Treasury support. Across the agencies, however, a wide range of methods and processes are used, reflecting the variety of organisation types and styles.
- Local government has a long history of involvement in job evaluation – initially with national points rating schemes for different levels or grades of staff, and from the late 1980s with the introduction of proprietary analytical schemes to cover all non-manual staff, as many councils moved to introduce local pay. It is only since the mid 1990s, as local government finances have tightened and 'single status' for manual and non-manual staff has been promoted nationally, that management attention to issues of grading and pay in local government has become more definably public rather than private sector.

In spite of these reservations, there are several clear and distinctive characteristics which affect the view of job evaluation in key parts of the public sector, i.e. the National Health Service (NHS), higher education and to some extent local government. First, national bargaining remains an important feature of pay, and can influence the choice of job evaluation method and process to underpin pay.

Second, the tradition in these sectors is to have grading and pay agreements which cover functional or occupational groups whose work may be similar in level, weight or size in job evaluation terms. For example in the NHS, nurses, various therapy groups and managers have separate national grading and pay systems even though they clearly overlap in job size. Equally, clerical and technician roles in old universities overlap in job size with academic-related grades, but the jobs are graded by different criteria and paid on different scales.

Third, particularly in the NHS and higher education, there is a sense in which job evaluation is a new and still mysterious technique. While since the mid 1990s there has been some introduction of generic (proprietary or home grown) analytical job evaluation schemes, most organisations in these sectors have never established a discipline of assessing all jobs according to common factors. There are job groups which have never been subject to any systematic form of job evaluation. This lack of experience combined with the equal value risks created by functional or occupational pay agreements has established a distinctive context for job evaluation debate.

Recent public discussion of job evaluation and pay against this background has been dominated by equal value – by a growing appreciation of the fact that people doing work which imposes similar levels of demand are paid very differently, and a concern to ensure that new systems introduced to put this right are meticulous in their

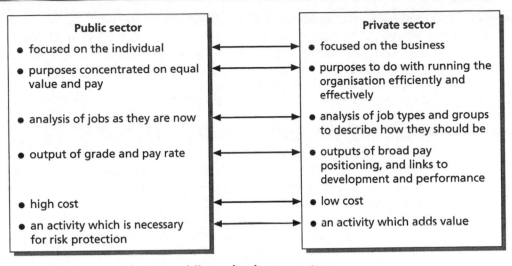

Fig. 12.2 Comparing the public and private sectors

attention to detailed comparison. NHS pay is under scrutiny, and this includes a review of job evaluation. The aim is to test whether a method is available or can be created which is capable of assessing all NHS jobs, from top to bottom and side to side of the service; and whether the process for applying it can uncover job content in sufficient detail. In higher education, the first job evaluation scheme to be specifically designed to cover all job types in universities and colleges is a computer-assisted points rating scheme. It is applied by an analyst conducting a detailed (e.g. two- or three-hour) interview of the jobholder before making an assessment. In local government, a new national job evaluation scheme has been developed to support the introduction of single status for all staff. The method has been carefully designed for the purpose. The process for applying it is detailed description of individual jobs as they are and judgement by a trained panel – the process common in the private sector in the 1970s but no longer so much in fashion.

In all these cases, distinctively public-sector debate has pointed to job evaluation being done in a very different way to the private sector. If what is currently still a debate is played through in practice – and the cost of 1970s style job evaluation may yet preclude this – the UK economy will show a divergence between two approaches to evaluating jobs (see figure 12.2).

The direction of change

This means that the market for job evaluation remains diverse and there is no single and simple trend. None the less, there are three interrelated themes which emerge from recent developments.

1 Method and process will depend on need

Different organisations have different needs, depending on what they do, what they are trying to achieve and their culture and traditions. For some organisations, it may be that an analytical job evaluation method with job evaluation panels is the right approach. For others a similar method but a computer-assisted process would be suitable. Others again may prefer in-house definition of broad job levels, or of generic jobs and levels within 'job families'. There is no need for uniformity. What is critical, however, is that each organisation genuinely selects what is appropriate for them, rather than following the fashionable trend in the market.

2 One organisation may have several approaches

If the choice of job evaluation method and process has to be relevant, there may be several different systems in use at once. This can be illustrated by returning to our example of the financial services company. It has a call centre, in which several hundred people occupy one of three generic jobs: service adviser responding to incoming calls; telemarketing adviser, making outgoing calls; and team leader. Here, and in retail branches, the key issues are clarity of role and service to customers. In addition, the company needs to be able to test external market pay rates. Defining generic roles, matching people into them and using surveys to compare with similar jobs in competitor companies can serve these purposes. In the same company, the management, professional and policy staff at headquarters occupy a wide variety of job types, some of which are one-off jobs while others have a small number of occupants. Categorising these and distinguishing between levels is more difficult and some form of analytical job evaluation may well be needed simply to provide a logical platform for pay. Further up the organisation, the top 100 jobs may be managed differently again. If, for example, rewards are more based on individual contribution at these levels and people are seen as a more mobile, flexible resource, it may be that broader bands would be used for pay. Matching into these could be done using simple generic statements of contribution for each level or band. So in this one organisation, we may have three different approaches to job evaluation, each fit for the purpose but each offering a different kind of output.

3 The wider benefits of job evaluation

Much of this chapter has been about job evaluation as a support to pay, because it establishes relativities, provides a basis for grouping jobs for pay purposes and supports pay benchmarking. But job evaluation has always been concerned also with the design and development of jobs, and with the relationship of individual jobs to the purpose of the organisation. As some of the bureaucracy surrounding job evaluation has fallen away, particularly in the private sector, this wider added value has become clearer.

We began this chapter with comments which showed the strong reactions which job evaluation can provoke. There have been times in the past two decades when commentators have predicted the demise of job evaluation. None the less, in the new millennium it is still with us – evolving, serving many purposes and taking a wide variety of forms. It is valued and used by many, and remains a major source of contention.

LEARNING ACTIVITIES

1 To what extent are the mechanisms in your organisation, job evaluation or other means, successful in aligning pay effectively with market rates? What indicators could you use to assess this issue?

2 Outline how you would present a defence of a job evaluation scheme in an equal value claim?

3 If you were advising on organisation looking to replace an ageing job evaluation scheme, what factors would influence the recommendations made?

4 Discuss the statement that job evaluation has 'no relevance for the lean organisation of the new millennium'.

REFERENCES AND FURTHER READING

Armstrong, M. and Baron, A. (1995) *The Job Evaluation Handbook*. Wiltshire: IPD.

Hillage, J. (1994) *The Role of Job Evaluation*. London Institute of Manpower Studies.

Johnson, C. and Dewberry, C. (1991) *Equal Pay for Equal Value: A guide to the non-discriminatory use of job evaluation*. BPS.

Neathey, F. (1996) *Job Evaluation in the 1990s: a directory schemes and a review of current practice*. London: IRS.

13 Inter-firm comparisons

Steve Flather

INTRODUCTION

The setting of pay, indeed the very basic concepts behind the reward structure of any organisation are not based on science. To argue such would assume that the principles of science would apply – set up a hypothesis, test it by experimentation and based on the results of those experiments, confirm the hypothesis or adjust it and then retest and so forth. With reward and especially in the world of commercial organisations, few, if any, have the luxury of such a clear and defined process. Typically, reward specialists will propose alternative strategies based on a range of parameters and from the combined wealth of their and other professionals' experience. There is then a single opportunity to implement the major elements of that policy, with little or no chance to change any of the fundamental principles. Thus the setting of structures and pay may be regarded not as a science but as more of an art, and, to undertake it, there is a basic need for data on the current and past activities of others in the field to attempt to make the best judgements in all the circumstances. Reward specialists need access to information on other organisations that will be of benefit in a whole range of ways. An indication of the number and variety are shown below:

- to as far as possible effect a 'try before you buy' check on a process or procedure
- to refine their decision-making process,
- to establish their perspective on best practice,
- to assist in competitor intelligence work,
- to support business process re-engineering,
- to clarify any policies on work of equal value issues,
- to support remuneration committees in the setting of the pay of the directors,
- to underpin annual business strategy planning and budgeting,
- to respond to, or initiate negotiations with trade unions,
- to establish and maintain policies on relocation,
- to undertake a benchmarking exercise,
- to respond to enquires and challenges from overseas parent organisations,
- to support and reinforce cultural change within the organisation,
- or to review bonus or benefit policies and systems.

It becomes clear that, interest in the activities of reward specialists in other organisations and the effects of their activities on their organisations, is crucial. Inter-firm comparisons therefore form an essential part of the armoury of any professional reward specialist.

This chapter explores the reasons for making inter-firm comparisons, reviews the type of information that is being compared, considers the methods of comparison, and finally indicates how the information is used.

WHY MAKE INTER-FIRM COMPARISONS?

This section gives an overview of ten important reasons why inter-firm comparisons should be made. They range from establishing best practice to gaining an insight into the cultural norms and working practices of overseas subsidiaries. No one is more important than another, but those relating to pay best practice and process review are the most common.

Best practice

Professionalism apart, it is good business to operate with the best possible practice – 'doing the right things' as well as 'doing things right' (sic). Part of the process of establishing the 'right things' is to research current practice and use that information to decide if the activities and objectives of the organisation are currently being made by those individuals currently undertaking the task. Further, others with similar circumstances may have preferred different solutions, which are equally valid for the circumstances. It is well understood that no one person has a monopoly on wisdom. It follows, therefore, that information from other organisations, matched, or not, with the original, will tend to improve the quality of the final decision. The applicability of the final result will depend on the decision maker, but good, relevant and applicable inter-firm comparisons can only aid the decision and drive towards best practice for the organisation.

Competitor intelligence

In the management of organisations today, understanding the market place is crucial. An organisation must understand a wide range of information about the activities of its competitors if it is to survive and detect market movements – it is possible that they may have detected a market movement that the organisation has not. With regard to reward, the information most likely to be of interest will fall into two levels: strategic, such as income per employee, overall pay bill and reward policy, or tactical, such as the bonus scheme used for salesmen, or specific pay levels. In larger organisations, competitor intelligence is a corporate activity, but proposed changes in pay structures or market positioning on pay are both of considerable interest and may be established through formal or informal routes.

Business process re-engineering

In recent years organisations have had to undertake substantial change to enable them to restructure and reform in the changing market environment. Inevitably, this has resulted in large changes in the structure and focus of those organisations, including the introduction or removal of products and the operating units that produce them. As this has become a more general activity, reward specialists have sought out information from other organisations who have undertaken similar activities to establish any commonalty and therefore applicability to their own activities.

In such circumstances, where substantial change is taking place, reward has an important place to play in the re-enforcement of any changes. The past success or otherwise of various approaches is crucial to establish, in order that mistakes are not made which could impact an the overall success of the business process re-engineering exercise.

Reward structure review

Whether as part of a business process re-engineering or other strategic change or innovation, the re-structuring of reward is likely to take place within an organisation on a five to ten year cycle. It is crucial under any such review that current information on reward strategies in other similar organisations is established to assist in any such review.

Directors' remuneration review

The recommendations of the Cadbury, Greenbury and Hampel Committees deal extensively with corporate governance, and, to the extent that this includes the pay of the directors and their reward packages, recommend that external independent advice is sought on the packages that should be applied to the directors. These recommendations will ultimately lead to a considerable growth in the information being supplied by organisations within their annual reports and accounts. If a stock market quoted organisation is to avoid criticism and also maintain its stated market stance for the packages for its directors, it is essential that information is gleamed from such sources.

Business strategic reviews

The annual review of business strategy has become part of the operation of most organisations to ensure their continued focus and success in the challenging business environment. Part of this process is to review the reward structure and packages of their employees. Whilst this may rightly reflect on the internal structures, information on the external market is equally essential to ensure the competitive nature of the packages and to avoid labour turnover and defections to competitors.

Trade union proposals

Major trade unions are well known for being well informed about the reward policies and practices of the employers for whom their members work. They have a unique opportunity to communicate the policies and practices across a wide range of organisations to their membership to assist in their members' negotiations with the employers. Amongst themselves, employers would probably see this level of communication and the detail as being contrary to commercial good practice, but no such constraints exist for trade union members. Frequently trade union negotiators are far better informed than their employer counterparts about the activities, pay and benefits of organisations similar to those for whom they are negotiating.

Relocation

When an organisation is relocating one or many employees, it is usually the case that they would support the employees in the cost of some or all of the elements of the cost of relocation. Whilst under such circumstances employers would tend to be driven by their own personal views, when an organisation is regularly relocating individuals, such as in the brewery, retail and oil industries, regular information on the relocation policies and practices of their competitors is crucial.

Benchmarking exercises

As a response to the ever-increasing competition, particularly on a global scale, organisations are evermore frequently comparing their performance in certain crucial aspects of their business, with others who they regard as worthy comparators. This is known as benchmarking and usually is undertaken by organisations either clandestinely through competitor intelligence activities, or, within a benchmarking club of hand-picked organisations. Such a club would agree on the information to be shared which could be across all aspects of the organisation, and could include reward strategies.

Requirement of overseas parent

Organisations which are subsidiaries of overseas parents can find themselves challenged on the practices which they propose to undertake within their organisation, especially on reward issues. Within any country, the policies and practices which obtained are based on custom and practice and the legal framework. Often there is disparity between different countries and cultures. This is best illustrated by the British fetish for the company car, which is considerably in excess of that seen on mainland Europe and in the USA. In such circumstances, the local customs and practices of employment policies and strategies within each country are essential information to assist the local organisation to explain to the overseas parent the typical approach to reward. It is self-evident that failure to apply local approaches could prejudice the operation of that business.

WHO MAKES THESE COMPARISONS?

Organisations and individuals would compare any aspect of their reward strategy to that of others if they are undertaking any of the activities listed in the above section. This would particularly be the case where substantial review is taking place in the organisation and confirmation of the proposed course of action is required. It may be that others have undertaken the same activity or applied the proposed policy. In such circumstances, investigation of the consequences is essential to ensure that the required action will achieve the desired result. In many cases, the circumstances under which policies are applied will differ between organisations. However, information on the activities of others is always valuable.

It is also the case that some individuals and organisations would wish to appear to be part of a club, where operations or strategies are seen to fall in line with those which they or others perceive to be good practice. This 'halo' effect can be much sought after when proposing a course of action. Indeed, the ability to be able to point to other similar, often high profile, household name organisations who apply similar approaches will be perceived to improve acceptability considerably. This approach is typical of the case for those in very large organisations – the FTSE 100 or perhaps the top 1,000 companies, where competition for top individuals can be intense and tracking the approaches and strategies of those within the group can be very important.

Similarly, there are some small organisations working at the leading edge of technology, or departments within large organisations, who require special individuals with specialist skills and knowledge, without whom their business would lose profits or might not continue to operate. These could be computer specialists, but equally they could be specialists in science and technology without whom some organisations would have difficulty in developing new products. In such departments and for such individuals, it is essential to have the best possible information on the packages of similar individuals within competing organisations. Whilst it may be the case that such individuals are virtually able to name their price, the loss can be catastrophic and market intelligence on the reward package is therefore crucial.

WHAT IS COMPARED?

Inter-firm comparisons can be undertaken on any particular point or aspect of the reward package or strategies. These will be covered in turn to illustrate the information that is available or it is possible to compare.

There is a large number of organisations who either assist in the comparison of data or provide researched data on their own account. Many of these collect this information to assist in developing their own organisations and typically these will be consultancies. The others research and publish data and are information sources in their own right. Without prejudice to others, such organisations as Industrial Relations Research/ Eclipse, Incomes Data Services, the CBI and the Engineering Employers Federation are well known for supplying information that they have researched independently and published either generally or to their membership. Other organisations specialise in the research and publication of information in specific locations, such as salary survey organisations like The Reward Group. Some information, however is almost impossible to supply on a generalised basis and can only be provided within a benchmarking or consultancy environment. Such information could be the elements within a long-term incentive scheme for directors. The following non-exhaustive list of areas and types of information that may be compared between organisations illustrates the diversity of the reward package and how it might be applied to an organisation.

Pay

The level of pay, the range within which pay might fall and speed with which an individual might rise within a pay structure are all crucial elements of a reward strategy. Organisations build pay structures based on their perspective of internal and external relativities. This may be, and probably should, be in all but the smallest organisations, supported by an analytical job evaluation scheme.

The typical elements of a pay scheme would be:

- level of pay for any particular job,
- the number of pay grades,
- the range of those pay grades,
- the overlap of the pay grades,
- the number of zones within the pay grades,
- the position and range of those zones within each pay grade,
- the method of establishing pay ranges,
- the method of establishing pay increase levels.

These are all areas where organisations would justifiably compare their operation with that of others.

Depending on the availability of staff within the local or national labour market, skill shortages can occur. These will eventually drive through to changes in the pay levels for those individuals affected. The speed with which the pay for those jobs or individuals changes will be of considerable importance to an organisation. Across-the-board pay settlements, overall earning movements, forecasted earning movements by industry, region and size of organisation all become important parameters to be established by those wishing to maintain competitiveness. It must be remembered that it is often cheaper to retain an individual employee even by paying them a substantial pay increase, than to let them leave and then to suffer the consequences to the organisation of not only the costs of recruitment and training but also of the impact to the organisation of the loss of the corporate knowledge and employee's contribution. This will particularly be the case at senior level, but, similarly on the shop floor, the loss of a number of craft specialists can have a devastating effect on an organisation's profitability through loss of production or decreased quality.

Often, responding to changes in the market to provide increased pay for jobs to recruit or retain staff increases tension with internal relativities, but such tensions are regarded as being an appropriate and reasonable problem within an organisation rather than accept the consequences of increased labour turnover.

Benefits

The provision of employee benefit packages has come into focus in recent years. In the 1980s, the period of the 'Lawson boom' saw an explosion in the provision of employee benefits to a wide range of levels within organisations, as competition for employees intensified within the labour market. As the British economy has returned to relatively stable growth, the interest in employee benefit packages has continued.

The range of benefits which might be compared between organisations would typically include:

- contracted hours of work,
- holidays,
- company cars,
- life assurance,

- long-term disability insurance,
- private health insurance,
- health club membership,
- institute membership,
- mobile phones,
- sports and social facilities,
- motor mileage allowances.

Following the explosion in pay and benefits during the Lawson boom, when competition for individuals within locations and across the UK rose dramatically, the benefit levels stabilised, as did pay increases. The last recession at the end of the 1980s and early 1990s saw a retrenching of the provision of benefits, although in reality, once particular benefits had been provided, organisations would have difficulty in removing them and inevitably would have to buy them out. In the current climate at the end of the 1990s, any re-occurrence of skill shortages is likely to result in rises in pay levels and, after a brief respite, benefits would then re-enter the picture as being the battleground between organisations for individuals with scarce skills.

Job evaluation factors

Job evaluation, the method by which organisations establish internal, and sometimes external, relativities falls into two categories being either, 'non-analytical', where the job is considered in its entirety, or 'analytical', using factors and levels to consider the content of each job. In the former category, job ranking, job classification or whole job evaluation are used to take a view on the level of a job with respect to others within the organisation by consideration of the entire job. This is usually undertaken by a panel of staff who are familiar with the jobs and their content. The alternative method of non-analytical job evaluation is paired comparisons, where each job is compared to every other job and scored as to whether it is equal to, above, or below it in its importance to the organisation. The scores for each job are then summed and a rank list created. In both these cases, however, the assessment is based on the entire job and is therefore regarded as less precise than analytical job evaluation. Further, it can only provide a ranked list of the jobs, rather than an indication of the difference in levels between jobs. Non-analytical methods of job evaluation are also regarded as unreliable in avoiding discrimination.

Analytical job evaluation uses a range of factors considered relevant for the organisation, such as, education, experience, knowledge required, job complexities, innovation required, control experienced or exercised and so on. Within each factor a series of levels are created. For each level within each factor a score is allocated. In analytical job evaluation, the evaluator chooses a level within each factor that corresponds to that which the evaluator considers appropriate for the job in question. The scores for all the chosen levels in every factor are then summed to create a total score for the job, in job evaluation points. There are a number of proprietary job evaluation schemes, created and utilised by a range of well-known management consultants.

A further form of analytic job evaluation has recently been introduced – competency-based job evaluation. This focuses on the ability of the individual within the job to produce the required standard of performance ('output'), and operates in a similar fashion to that noted above for an analytical scheme. Organisations using such analytical schemes will usually be assisted by a consultancy in implementing and operating the scheme, which, although generally and almost universally applied by that consultancy, may be specialised to the organisation.

When considering implementing a job evaluation scheme, an organisation may wish to consider schemes as used by others and establish their efficacy and ability to establish meaningfully the relative importance of jobs. Further the scheme must aid the organisation to achieve its business objectives. In such circumstances, particularly when a review is being undertaken of the reward structure, organisations may wish to compare the job evaluation scheme that they are considering with those used by others. Such information would not normally be available on a general basis, but networking usually can enable individuals to establish such details to enable a reasoned judgement to be made.

Grading structure

The grading structure used by an organisation would usually be particular to that organisation alone. It would normally exist, based on job evaluation, by the application of the job evaluation scores to establish logical groups of jobs which might be jointly classified and treated as being equivalents within a grading structure. However organisations would wish to check that their structure roughly matches that of equivalent organisations through a benchmarking or networking exercise.

Pay structure

Once a grading structure has been created, a new pay structure, often the basic background reason for undertaking a reward review, would be created. Typically the number of pay grades would coincide with the number of grades created within the grading structure, with a pay range created for each grade.

However, whereas the grading structure would not have overlapping points levels, it would be typical for organisations to implement a pay structure which has overlapping pay bands. The percentage range of the pay band for each of the pay grades with respect to the mid point or reference salary, is an important factor in constructing a new pay structure. The number of pay bands and the degree of overlap between them would be fundamental issues within an organisation, whether reviewing its structure or not, and comparator data from relevant organisations would be essential. In certain cases, particularly in broad-banding and broad-banded pay structures, it is possible that job families or pay zones may be created. The relative position of these zones needs to be defined.

In this particular case, more than in the case of grading structures, the structure implemented by an organisation needs to be considered with respect to typical structures used by others both locally and nationally within similar industries. Failure to do this can lead to difficulties in recruitment and retention. Whilst this information is not usually published on a general basis, it can be obtained through consultancies, by an organisation undertaking a reward review.

Performance-related pay schemes

Organisations wish to maintain secrecy as to how they are successful, and one of the deemed commercial secrets tends to be incentive schemes, especially those related to the sales operations. Therefore, the details of performance-related pay schemes would be kept private within organisations. Nevertheless, comparison of the targets, performance measures and objectives used, provide powerful comparators between organisations. Similarly, bonus and commission schemes tend to be very particular to an organisation but are also useful information for organisations to use to establish alternative reward strategies. Reward should be directed to assisting the organisation to achieve its mission and strategic objectives. If it does not do so then it will fail in its purposes. Thus, bonus and incentive schemes related to those areas of the business to be developed would be specific to that organisation. However, the levels of payment, and the targets, especially in the case of directors, would benefit from external comparison to ensure that the levels and measures are appropriate and reasonable compared to the market.

In the case of bonus and commission, and some performance-related pay schemes, the information on typical payment levels is readily available. However, the methods of incentivising sales bonuses are typically held secret, and such information would normally only be available through personal contact.

Pensions

The structure of pension schemes can be complicated, especially final salary schemes, where contribution levels, funding and performance are all complex. Nevertheless, once a scheme has been created, it is possible, with specialist advice usually from a consulting actuary, to compare either final salary or money purchase schemes with other schemes with respect to the benefits, particularly in the event of death in service and payments to relatives. Such information is available within reports published by consultancies but often requires specialist interpretation to understand the nuances of the differences between schemes.

HOW IS THE COMPARISON CARRIED OUT?

As information becomes more and more of a commodity, and expectations of the volume and accuracy of that information increases, it is not surprising that many organisations would tend to expect that information of the type noted above should be available freely and easily. Regrettably this is not the case and due to the nature of the information is only available from specialist sources.

Published sources

There are a number of specialist organisations, which research and publish information on reward, typically they would fall into two groups.

Pay review commentators

As noted previously, Industrial Relation Services/Eclipse, Incomes Data Services, CBI and The Engineer's Employers Federation, regularly survey client or member organisations to establish the level of across-the-board agreements that have been reached and the content of those agreements, particularly those related to trade union negotiations. Such organisations will collect information at regular intervals and publish it, usually indicating the name of the organisation. In addition to pay details, they also undertake reviews of terms and conditions of employment and other employment issues such as call-out allowances. Such information is usually timely, relatively cheap and offered on a subscription basis.

Salary survey organisations

Salary survey organisations obtain the actual pay levels from their client companies, together with across-the-board pay increase information and other benefits data. These survey organisations then consolidate the data, and publish it in surveys which are either available to the participants only or to non-participants also. Dependent upon the volume of the data, the quality of such surveys can be excellent, but it should be noted that in the case of some specialist jobs, the samples can be small. This, of itself, may not be detrimental since there may only be a few such individuals or jobs available within the survey universe.

Salary surveys may be specific to a location or region, an industry, a profession or a function. The discussion of salary surveys and their use is substantial and beyond the scope of this chapter. Professionally produced surveys will provide sufficient information to enable the user to apply the results of the survey to their own circumstances. Information, such as job matching methods, outline job description methods, data collection methods, data samples, method of use of the survey, statistical measures and methods, should all be provided within the survey to enable the user to make the comparisons required.

Benchmarking clubs

It has already been noted that increasing global competition and the drive by organisations for 'world-class' standards, has encouraged organisations to come together to form benchmarking clubs to assist them all to reach the standards achieved by the best within the group for each of the parameters to be benchmarked. Benchmarking is an extensive subject and requires further reading. Typically, organisations will come together to decide the parameters or areas of their business that they wish to compare. Then, on a personal basis they exchange, or on a group basis collectively survey, data related to those parameters. With regard to reward, such information exchange would probably be similar to that used and prepared by the publishing survey companies but related only to those organisations within the benchmarking group. Such information is of extremely high quality but made of a limited sample.

Consultancy

When organisations are undertaking a review of their reward structure or replacing it, it is likely that at some point in the exercise they will require external support to obtain both confirmation that their approach is in line with current practice and also to enable them to obtain up-to-date information on pay and benefits or systems. Such information would normally be provided by consulting organisations. Typically, consultants would have considerable experience within the industry or within the subject and would provide advice on current practice in the relevant sector. Consultants operate in all aspects of reward, from job evaluation, job grading, pay banding, pay levels, performance pay to long-service incentive schemes, and are a major source of inter-firm comparison. Experienced consultants should have considerable personal knowledge of many aspects of their subject and would require little or no reference to other sources in giving advice.

Annual accounts

The committees chaired by Cadbury, Greenbury and Hampel have provided a code of practice and framework on corporate governance within organisations, especially in regard to directors' rewards. As the recommendations for those committees begin to be implemented, increasing numbers of annual reports and accounts prepared by companies quoted on the Stock Exchange provide considerable detail on the pay and benefits packages, including pensions, provided to their directors. Progressively this information resource will grow as companies move towards the requirements established by the Stock Exchange following these recommendations. Often, the annual reports and accounts will include a report from the remuneration committee. Such committees are increasingly being staffed by non-executive directors and if the Greenbury and Hampel recommendations are being supported, use independent advice from reward specialists.

Organisations can call for a copy of the annual report and accounts for a publicly quoted company or copies of reports and accounts are available from Companies House. Such information is extremely focused and, as the source develops, reports are likely to name the individuals and their roles, further increasing the quality of the data. For directors, therefore, there is a growing pool of specialist data, but those seeking information may need to do some research.

Local networking groups

Whether through the auspices of the Institute of Personnel and Development, the local Chamber of Commerce, Business Links or other business or professional organisations, managers tend to form self-help networking groups which may ultimately become salary clubs. These are forums for the exchange of pay, benefits and related information. Often their informal nature enables subjects of mutual interest to be discussed, even if these are not strictly reward-related matters. The very nature of these groups usually enables high-quality local information to be exchanged, to enable participants to keep in touch with local and national reward issues.

Data quality

It is important to recognise when undertaking inter-firm comparisons, that the quality of the information needs to be questioned at all points. Quality is often measured by the volume of the data, but, as noted previously, this may by its nature be small, if the sample for a particular job is small also.

The most crucial feature in any survey is to ensure that the matching of the jobs and the organisations has been undertaken correctly. Job matching may be by level and function, job classification or job evaluation method.

As the type of job matching method changes so does the quality and the price of the data. In the use of any published data it is fundamental to establish the basis on which the data have been collected and aggregated to ensure that the correct use is made of the data in their application to the organisation and the particular investigation. It is also essential to establish the date on which the data were collected to ensure that it could be brought up-to-date. Typically, survey and consulting organisations will publish within the survey, the date when the data were current and will provide information on the calculation to bring it up to date to any reasonable point in the future.

Clearly the sample and its relevance to the organisation are crucial and typically survey organisations will supply the names of those who participated in the survey or at least, those who have agreed to be named. As noted previously, one of the prime factors in establishing the quality of data, irrespective of the volume, is the method of matching the jobs. This factor deserves careful consideration in the use of data, no matter the source, to be confident that the eventual use is appropriate and relevant to the organisation.

CONCLUSION

This chapter has set out to discuss the issues of making comparisons of reward strategies and data between organisations. It has detailed a wide range of reasons for making such comparisons, the types of data usually involved or available for comparison, and the sources and methods for making comparisons. Although this chapter has suggested that comparisons of reward data between organisations is beneficial, in reality, it is often the case that the required information is not readily available. It is at this point that the true skills of the compensation and benefits specialist come into play and the setting of the reward strategy can be seen as an art, supported by science, rather than a science in its own right.

LEARNING ACTIVITIES

1 Select those jobs within your organisation for which local comparisons would be useful and identify six local organisations which would provide useful comparative data, giving reasons for your choices.

2 Suggest jobs for which regional or national comparisons, rather than local, might provide more useful data and justify your selection.

3 Suggest the most appropriate method of benchmarking employee benefits for a medium-sized manufacturing organisation based in the Midlands.

4 Using library-based information produce a report on one of the following:
  - computer specialists' pay and conditions
  - working hours
  - holidays
  - supervisor pay in the retail sector

FURTHER READING

For those with IPD Membership, read only copies of some reports by the Reward Group are available (for visitors only) in their library.

Anderson, B. *et al.* (1996) *The Benchmarking Handbook: Step-by-step instructions*. London: Chapman & Hall.

Bramham, J. (1997) *Benchmarking for People Managers*. London: IPD.

Easterby-Smith, M., Thorpe, R. and Lowe, A. (1996) *Management Research: An introduction*. London: Sage.

Zairi, M. (1998) *Effective Management of Benchmarking Projects*. Oxford: Butterworth Heinnemann.

In addition the following regular publications by Incomes Data Services are useful:
- Report
- Studies plus
- Studies
- Focus

PART III

Strategic reward

14 Auditing a remuneration system

Richard Thorpe, Angela Bowey and Mark Goodridge

INTRODUCTION

This chapter considers and advises on strategies for monitoring and auditing remuneration systems. The importance of consultation through steering groups, and of other processes in effective monitoring and decision making, is again stressed. There are three main reasons for conducting an audit of remuneration systems.

The first reason is to test out whether the original objectives of the system are still appropriate, and whether the organisation's current and future priorities for success are being served by the payment system.

The second reason is to test out whether the implementation and operation of the payment system are producing the expected results. Poor performance can result from poor systems or poor implementation. The result of this can be a drift in expected outcomes, or systems that send the wrong messages to employees such that they do not behave in the ways the system was meant to encourage, i.e. to subvert the system.

The third reason for auditing a payment system is that change might be taking place in the organisation or in the environment which necessitates a completely new approach to remuneration and reward.

The effectiveness of a remuneration system in each of these three areas can be undermined by its degeneration over time.

THE PROCESS OF DEGENERATION AND DECAY

A perennial problem facing managers of payment systems is an understanding of the processes by which payment systems degenerate. If payment systems are used in inappropriate circumstances or are poorly maintained, they can drift in such a way as to have serious consequences for the organisation in which they operate. There is a great deal of research evidence on *symptoms* exhibited by decayed or decaying systems, but only little on the *processes* of degeneration which can inflict considerable damage on an organisation. It is, we feel, particularly important to identify the circumstances by which a payment system can succeed (as we have attempted to do in chapter 7) and

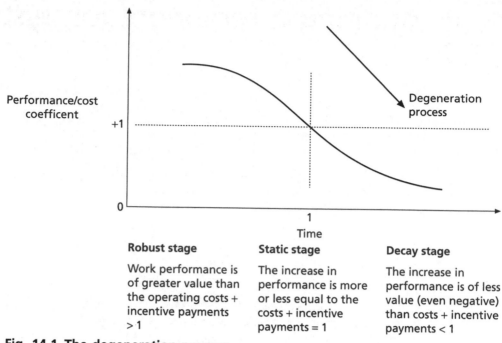

Fig. 14.1 The degeneration process

to contrast these with the circumstances in which degeneration occurs. It is crucial to understand the changes in behaviour through which the process of degeneration comes about. How can these be identified and what might be done about them?

Payment system degeneration is defined here as the process by which the total work (i.e. not just that which is measured or paid for) performance of employees either declines, fails to increase, or is insufficient to gain the remuneration or other rewards offered. If this process remains unchecked, it can result in the payment system reaching a state of decay and the system becoming so debilitated that the performance of the organisation is threatened.

For the purpose of illustration, assume that the real value of the increase in organisational performance per month can be expressed as monetary figure 'V' and that the total monthly costs of operating a payment system (including direct administrative costs which would not otherwise be necessary, plus all payments to staff and employees resulting from any incentive scheme) can be expressed as a sum of money 'C'. Three stages of a based payment system's effectiveness can then be identified by the co-efficient V/C (the ratio of organisational performance to total continuing costs resulting from the system) – *robust* (V/C > 1), *static* (V/C = 1), and *decay* (V/C < 1) (as illustrated in figure 14.1). Note that the calculation for 14.1 does not take account of the initial costs to the organisation of introducing a new payment system. A successful system would need to remain robust for a long enough period to recover at least these initial costs.

Payment system degeneration is then the persistent decline in magnitude of the performance/cost coefficient which, if not overcome, will lead to a state of decay with consequent net losses to the organisation. This may be a continuing process, that occurs in fits and starts, or reflect earlier degeneration which has come to a halt.

The processes by which payment systems degenerate are very subtle and often difficult to detect. Even with no outside influences, the performance of a system and the attitude of employees may 'creep' downwards as people become more familiar with their jobs, or as the product market or technology changes, and so on. Were the degeneration processes more obvious, managerial effort to avoid them might be more successful. It should be recognised that managers who have recently introduced a new and apparently successful performance-based payment system will be unlikely to set out to find evidence of its degeneration as they will refuse to believe that its effectiveness can be adversely affected in such a short time period; and the integration of systems to the performance of managers will make acceptance of degeneration even less likely. It is also unlikely that employees will broadcast information about the work procedures through which a performance-based system may be degenerating. So unless managers are aware of the process and have developed a high degree of openness and trust in an organisation they are unlikely to learn more than a superficial story of how the system is operating. It is only where managers and researchers are in very close contact with the workers that they have been able to identify the process of degeneration.

There have been many studies that have attempted to examine the ways in which the performance of payment systems operate in practice, often illustrating the attitudes and performance of individuals and how they react to different payment systems. Much of the resulting literature, although appearing some time ago, continues to be worth reading today, as there is still much for managers to learn from this work (Roy, 1952; Ditton, 1979; Lupton, 1963; Wilson, 1953; Thorpe, 1980 and Bell, 1999).

To illustrate the rich source of behavioural data that exists in such studies, it is worth examining one of a case study that illustrates the way in which decay manifests itself.

A classic study conducted by Donald Roy in the early 1950s revealed that a payment-by-results system, designed to improve performance, could actually lead to a decrease in productivity (Lupton, 1972). Much of what Roy understood is still relevant today and still relates to a wide range of performance-based payment systems and their practice, not simply to the kind of piecework systems Roy studied.

In the steelworks where Roy worked as an operator/observer, the employees were paid a bonus based on the time saved from the time allowed for a job – the more time saved, the higher the bonus. The time allowed for each job was calculated by work measurement staff who studied each task and then set estimated times for how long an average worker, working at normal pace, would take to complete it. Since work measurement is not a precise science, it was expected that on occasions these estimates would be generous, allowing too much time, and sometimes they would be 'tight', not allowing enough. The assumption Roy made was that if the employees were working at the same pace throughout the week (and during a week they would work on a large number of batches of work, each having a time allowed), a graph drawn depicting the frequency of the different 'effort' ratings would peak roughly at the standard effort rate (normally 100) and be distributed around this mean, tailing away after this point (see figure 14.2). But the recorded frequencies Roy calculated looked nothing like this, as shown in figure 14.3.

The reason for this strange distribution was that, on all the jobs which had been 'tightly' rated, it was difficult for the employee to earn a worthwhile bonus. So, as the workers were paid a 'fall back rate' of 85 cents an hour irrespective of how slowly

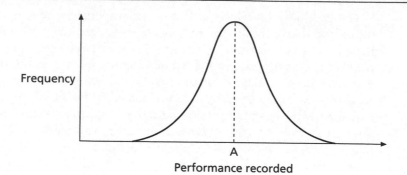

Fig. 14.2 **Expected frequency of different scores (normal distribution of performance)**

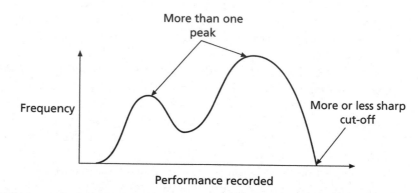

Fig. 14.3 **Actual recorded frequency of different effort scores**

they worked, they could not be bothered to 'bust a gut' only to gain either a small bonus or none at all! On these jobs, the employees therefore coasted, saving their energy and working slowly. Hence, the jobs to the left of the standard effort point became pushed down to an effort rating of about 60 representing less than a day's work (which is normally taken to be 75), appearing as the lower peak of jobs in figure 14.3. The jobs which had loose rates were, on the other hand, easy to complete in the allowed time, and were duly performed at great speeds. Roy found that after six months on the job he could easily earn a bonus on these jobs and, if he so chose, work at effort ratings of more than 300 per cent above standard (that is to have potential to produce up to three times the amount on each job). But Roy found that these high performances were never reported to management, because the machine shop operators believed that if they declared that these work rates were attainable or made a bonus of 45 cents or above, the work measurement officers would be on the shop floor to use the words of one operator, and the work would be re-timed 'so damn quick, your feet wouldn't touch the ground'. This belief may or may not have been true (the company denied that it would do it, but because the employees believed it would, they kept their bonus earnings to a maximum of 44 cents per hour on any job). Although they still continued to save a great deal of time on these easy jobs, the workers only recorded a small proportion of it against the actual jobs, the rest of the saved time being allocated to other jobs (to raise them into the bonus-earning bracket) or wasted in an assortment of ways (cleaning up, tea breaks, chatting, and so on). Roy found that the act of wasting all this surplus time, whilst appearing to be working, was one of the most difficult parts of his job. This finding was borne out in British studies of work in industry, for example by Jason Ditton (1979) in his study of a bakery, and by Richard Thorpe in his participant observation study of an engineering works (1980). Thorpe reported that the most difficult part of the work he had to do was 'learning how to skive'.

If these behavioural consequences which are as alive today in pay-linked appraisal systems, and merit or profit-related schemes as they were in the 1950s are the results of incentive payment schemes designed to motivate hard work and improved performance, then there is something seriously wrong with the principles of the payment systems.

Business objectives and payment systems

One of the reasons why payment systems in general so often decay and deteriorate before any corrective action is taken is the lack of systematic approaches to evaluating their effectiveness on an on-going basis. This may not be as surprising as it seems since there is rarely in organisations a consensus about what the objectives of any particular policy or strategy should be. As payment systems often attempt to buttress particular strategies seen to be important to an organisation (team working, waste reduction, retention of employees, and so on), the choice of payment is no less problematic. It is often assumed that the inherent logic of a system will convey the same messages to all those involved. However, if gaining consensus between individuals working at similar levels within an organisation is difficult, conveying the same message to individuals at different levels in an organisation is even more so.

Payment systems can be viewed from three main perspectives. The first is sometimes called the 'normative' view. This means that the senior managers in an organisation see a specific purpose for a particular kind of payment system, and expect it to operate in a given way and to produce certain outcomes or results. The second perspective can be referred to as the 'perceived' view. This view is based on what those who operate the system believe to be its objectives, which can often be at odds with the views expressed by senior managers and even by other managers. The third perspective can be referred to as the 'operative' view. This view can be ascertained by trying to understand what the individuals who work under the system are trying to achieve.

It is, in our view, very important that managers understand these three sets of views. Only by doing so will they be able to understand fully the operation of the existing system and to optimise any new one. In most organisations, wide differences are apparent between these three perspectives leading to subversion of the system and conflict with resulting poor pay system performance.

Furthermore, it is only through the better alignment of these perspectives that the payment system can be used to its maximum potential as a catalyst for wider organisational change, ensuring the communication tool that it represents can make the link between business strategy, company culture and reward. As the American Productivity Centre has shown, unless changes are made in a range of organisational and workforce dimensions, payment systems will continue to fail to yield the expected benefits.

As we have reported elsewhere in this book, the importance of pay is its use as a policy instrument to make changes and adjustments in an organisation, through rewarding appropriate behaviour. Thought of and used in this way, remuneration systems can become important systems components that should not be seen in isolation from the objectives of the organisation. Again the ways in which payment systems and strategy can be linked have been discussed in more detail in chapter 7 with an emphasis placed on the use of participative methods at both the design and implementation stages.

ESTABLISHING THE HEALTH OF THE CURRENT SYSTEM AND TESTING THE STATE OF THE PAY SYSTEM

In identifying the state of the pay system, information must be established in three important areas. One is the constituents of pay at the various levels throughout the organisation. An understanding must be gained of just how many different ways of remunerating and rewarding individuals there are. For example, what are the variety and levels of reward paid to top management as opposed to middle managers, design staff or operatives? What is the logic behind the differences? In looking at this aspect of reward, you should consider all the elements of pay, such as bonuses, overtime, fringe benefits, merit pay and such things as market supplements. A second level of question might be whether the assumptions behind these different pay practices are consistent, logical and coherent, and whether they link with and support the organisation's strategic priorities.

Figure 14.4 illustrates dramatically the number of pay constituents there may be in a medium-sized organisation.

The second important area is the general level of an organisation's pay in direct comparison to payments made by competitors or those employing individuals with similar skills – in essence, an external benchmarking exercise (see exhibit 14.1). The third is the grading and position of jobs within the company in terms of pay. Exhibit 14.2 sets out questions to ask when encoding job evaluations within an organisation.

A number of simple measures can be used to establish initiatives in these three areas.

Wage levels and surveys

Normally, the wage level would be expressed as an average figure for all jobs through a gross comparison of job rates, for a number of key jobs, with rates for a comparable internal wage structure, which is characteristically established in terms of various grades or levels. Information used to determine a company's wage level is often obtained from wage surveys conducted within the industry or within a geographical locality. Chapter 13 describes how this is achieved. Information used in setting up a wage structure is usually derived from some kind of job evaluation procedure (described in chapter 12).

Wage and salary surveys are particularly useful for organisations which have either a defined compensation and benefits strategy, or have a particular recruitment or retention problem. For the former group, surveys provide the means for ensuring that their overall strategies are maintained, for example that they pay upper quartile salaries for the industry or area. For organisations with a recruitment or retention problem,

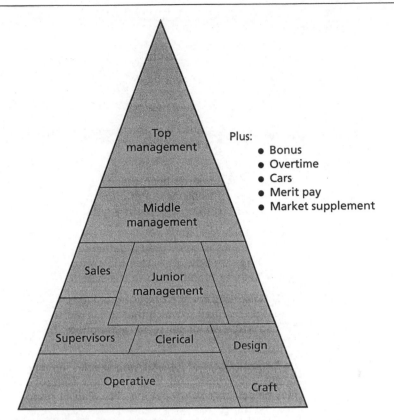

Plus:
- Bonus
- Overtime
- Cars
- Merit pay
- Market supplement

Fig. 14.4 Organisation pay consitiuents

Exhibit 14.1

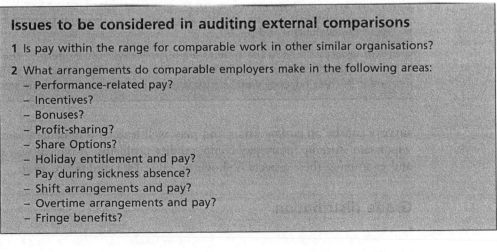

Issues to be considered in auditing external comparisons

1 Is pay within the range for comparable work in other similar organisations?

2 What arrangements do comparable employers make in the following areas:
   - Performance-related pay?
   - Incentives?
   - Bonuses?
   - Profit-sharing?
   - Share Options?
   - Holiday entitlement and pay?
   - Pay during sickness absence?
   - Shift arrangements and pay?
   - Overtime arrangements and pay?
   - Fringe benefits?

Exhibit 14.2

Questions to ask when reviewing a job evaluation system

1 To what extent are the present basic salaries or wages a fair reflection of the difficulty, responsibility and content of the jobs? If they are not, then there may well be a need to introduce a new system for evaluating or grading jobs.

2 Can new jobs be slotted into the structure fairly easily and systematically, or is this often a problem for the management? If it is a problem, then a new system is indicated.

3 Have basic wages and salaries been changed in line with changes in the content of the jobs? If there are problems in this area, they may be solved by modifications to the grades/evaluations using the existing system. In extreme cases a new system may be needed.

4 Is the bulk of the jobs in some grades gathered at the top of the salary bands, with no further progression possible within the grade or band? This would indicate a need for a revision or modification to the system, and re-grading of jobs.

5 Are the principles used for the original grading or evaluation still relevant, or has the organisation changed so much that this is not the case? If the logic behind the current structure no longer seems appropriate, this can be rectified by a new system.

6 Are there large numbers of jobs carrying salaries higher than their job score and pay level indicate, and consequently receiving some form of special payment? In such a case it may be desirable to review the allocation of responsibilities to try to align job scores with payment.

7 Is there any evidence that jobs done by women were graded or evaluated at some time in the past in a manner which perpetuated unfair discrimination in pay? Do the factors in the job evaluation or grading system favour the jobs done by men? Were benchmarks used?

8 Are the job descriptions on which evaluations are based adequate in terms of their consistency and content? If there is considerable variation in length, style, nature of content, language, complexity, etc. they may be an unsound basis for determining grading, evaluation and pay?

9 Do the factors used in the systems adequately cover the content of the full range of jobs, treat all categories of work fairly, and use suitable measuring scales? Are there areas (such as hours of work) which are not covered by the current set of factors?

surveys can be an *ad hoc* affair and may well lead to fragmented salary adjustments which can store up future pay comparability problems. A typical way of approaching and examining these aspects is shown in table 14.1 and figure 14.4.

Grade distribution

In terms of grade distribution, the graph in figure 14.5 shows an example of how the distribution of jobs can change markedly over a relatively short period of time. In this engineering company, it is clear that there are effectively two groups, with a great number of jobs at one end of the graph, in grades 2 and 3, and another group of jobs at

Table 14.1 Wage survey summary report

Job	Company A Average minimum maximum employees	Company B Average minimum maximum employees	Company C Average minimum maximum employees	Company D Average minimum maximum employees	Company E Average minimum maximum employees	Average for all companies (weighted by no. of employees) Average minimum maximum employees
Office jobs File clerk Sorter operator Typist						
Factory jobs Loader Welder Drillpress operator						
Sales jobs Sales trainee Industrial salesman Sales clerk						

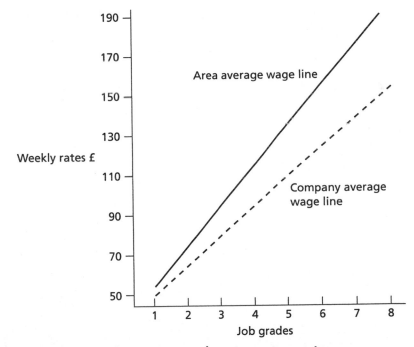

Fig. 14.5 Comparison of company and area average rates

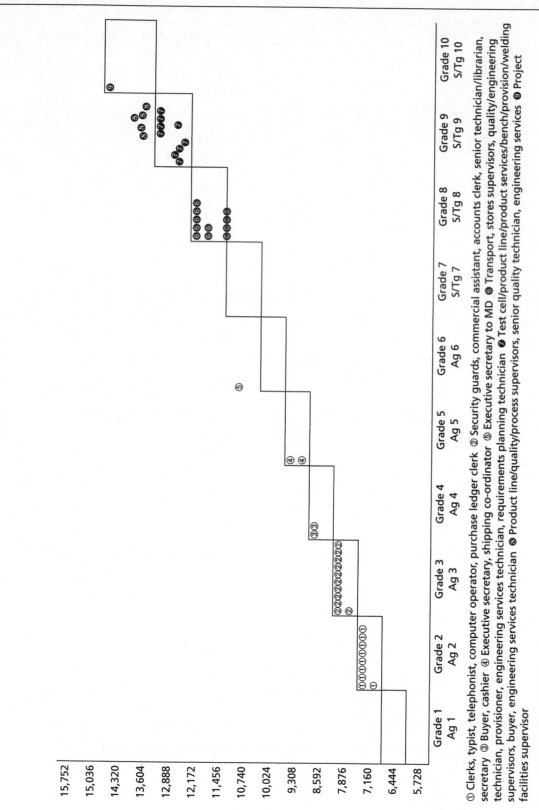

Fig. 14.6 Original structure

① Clerks, typist, telephonist, computer operator, purchase ledger clerk ② Security guards, commercial assistant, accounts clerk, senior technician/librarian, secretary ③ Buyer, cashier ④ Executive secretary, shipping co-ordinator ⑤ Executive secretary to MD ⑥ Transport, stores supervisors, quality/engineering technician, provisioner, engineering services technician, requirements planning technician ❼ Test cell/product line/product services/bench/provision/welding supervisors, buyer, engineering services technician ❽ Product line/quality/process supervisors, senior quality technician, engineering services ❾ Project facilities supervisor the other end of the scale, in grades 8 and 9. There are virtually no jobs in grades 1, 4, 5, 6, 7 or 10! Considerable drift and grade bunching has occurred, which is tending to distort the structure.

Job evaluation as a process is about discriminating (in a 'felt fair' manner) between jobs. Grade bunching would suggest either that jobs are becoming more similar or that regradings are failing to discriminate adequately between the value of different jobs (how this can be rectified is shown in chapter 8). If the former is the case, then it is a sign that the scheme requires review, and that a policy decision needs to be made on the number of grades it is desirable to have. Figure 14.7 shows the redesigned structure in the same organisation with greater progression in fewer grades.

Some other measures that can point to decay are more qualitative, relating, for example to the number of appeals made or even the number of jobs that have been regraded each year:

$$\text{Appeals ratio} = \frac{\text{Number of appeals per annum}}{\text{Total number of jobs in scheme}}$$

$$\text{Regrading ratio} = \frac{\text{Number of jobs regraded per annum}}{\text{Total number of jobs in scheme}}$$

Some level of appeals and regrading will be inevitable in any scheme, especially in a fast-changing organisation. However, major fluctuations in either of these ratios need to be investigated as they could be early indicators of the system being under strain.

Location of individuals within grade

Where progression through merit, achievement or seniority is provided for in a grade structure, then the distribution of individuals within the grade becomes important. This is because once a large proportion of people is at the top of a band or grade, pressure to regrade is likely to increase until it becomes problematic.

Figure 14.6 plotted the salaries and grades of two groups of workers – Ag grades and S/Tg grades. In terms of job distribution we have seen there are two groupings at either end of the salary scale, with grades Ag1, Ag4, Ag5, Ag6, and S/Tg7 and S/Tg10 almost empty. The company was keen to change the system because the differentials and anomalies were causing problems. In terms of the location of individuals within grades, it is easy to see that, because individuals could progress up through the grades, nearly all the occupied grades have people 'stuck' at the top of them, unable to transfer on to the next grade.

Grade pressure

Grade pressure often indicates primary problems with the systems structure. For example, pressure from equal value claims require serious attention. Much literature has gone as far as suggesting that many proprietary schemes are inherently discriminatory through uneven job descriptions, inflated job context size of male jobs, or unreal differences in demand in the factory scales. There is also a very large body of literature relating to equal value and the discriminatory aspects of job evaluation schemes. (Chapter 12 deals with many of these issues under equality and reward.)

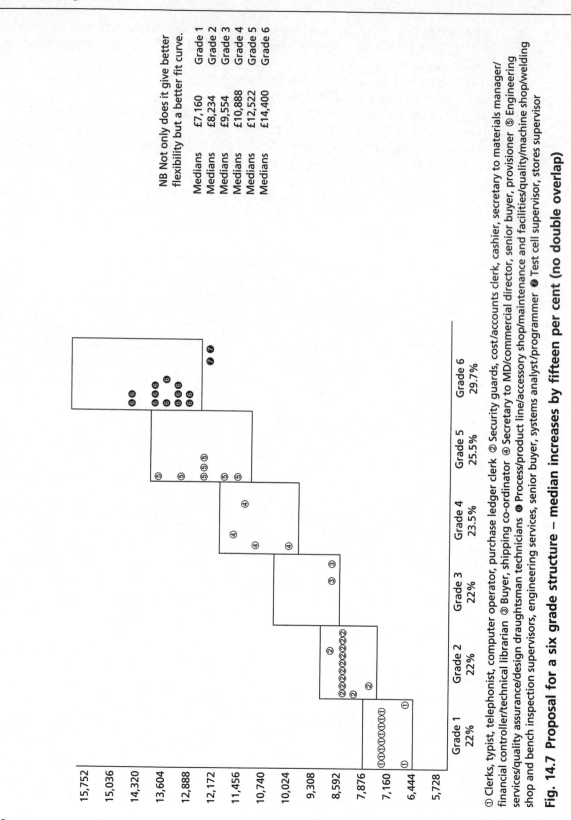

NB Not only does it give better
flexibility but a better fit curve.

Medians	£7,160	Grade 1
Medians	£8,234	Grade 2
Medians	£9,554	Grade 3
Medians	£10,888	Grade 4
Medians	£12,522	Grade 5
Medians	£14,400	Grade 6

Grade 1	Grade 2	Grade 3	Grade 4	Grade 5	Grade 6
22%	22%	22%	23.5%	25.5%	29.7%

Fig. 14.7 Proposal for a six grade structure – median increases by fifteen per cent (no double overlap)

① Clerks, typist, telephonist, computer operator, purchase ledger clerk ② Security guards, cost/accounts clerk, cashier, secretary to materials manager/financial controller/technical librarian ③ Buyer, shipping co-ordinator ④ Secretary to MD/commercial director, senior buyer, provisioner ⑤ Engineering services/quality assurance/design draughtsman technicians ⑥ Process/product line/accessory shop/maintenance and facilities/quality/machine shop/welding shop and bench inspection supervisors, engineering services, senior buyer, systems analyst/programmer ⑦ Test cell supervisor, stores supervisor

The pressure of market forces also operates against the inherent logic of the most carefully thought out and implemented systems. Figure 14.6 shows six jobs outside their grades – one, in grade 6, we can reveal being the secretary to the Managing Director! Unless anomalies are addressed, they will lead to more degeneration and the scheme's credibility will suffer increasingly.

Changes in job content

Job content changes often give rise to the individual perception that a regrading is automatic. Multi-skilling and flexibility are very difficult to recognise on job evaluated criteria. The pay expectation of the individual who has acquired a new skill is often high, but few evaluation schemes fully recognise this. If it is the intention to recognise skill, the scheme will need to reflect such changes in job practice. They should then also be evaluated to ensure that they do.

Auditing total compensation

As shown earlier in table 2.2 in Chapter 2, wage and salary payments comprise only one part of the overall compensation package. As a consequence, benefits should also be included in any comprehensive review of reward. One fairly simple but effective way of auditing these on a comparative basis is to examine at the mix of total direct compensation against non-direct compensation. Figure 14.8 illustrates how this might be done.

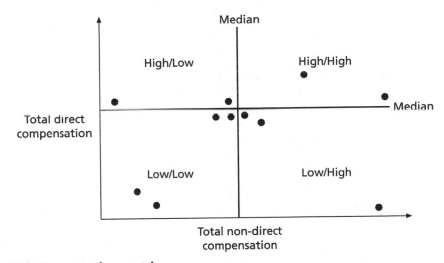

Fig. 14.8 Pay practice matrix

The perceptions of individuals, and internal and external pay relativities

Although this is a difficult dimension to audit, individuals' perception and related views on their job inputs and outputs can be important ingredients of satisfaction with pay. Lawler (1971) offers a model of the determinants of pay satisfaction (see figure 14.9).

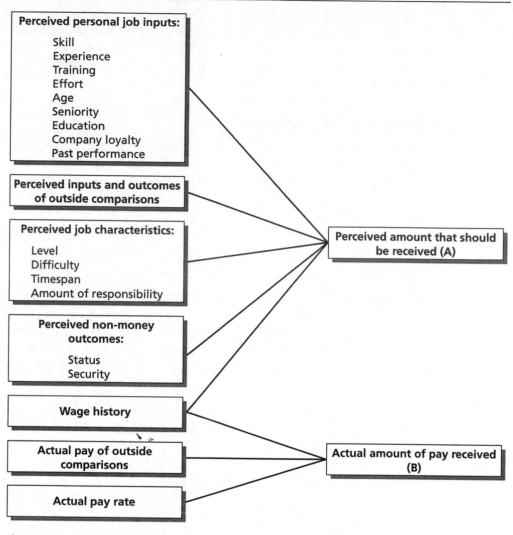

If A = B Pay satisfaction

A > B Pay dissatisfaction

A < B Guilt, inequity, discomfort

Fig. 14.9 Model of the determinants of pay satisfaction

We have stated before that there appear to be few problems with pay that do not have at their root dissatisfaction with differentials; perceptions of these differentials (in terms of job inputs and outputs, and characteristics of the work) are as important as any reality. Failure to address these areas of discontent could quickly lead to more serious problems of motivation or dispute. The internal system of pay relativities is most often based on some form of job evaluation. There is a range of measures which can assist in examining the dynamics of the internal structure in order to ascertain whether there are trends within it which are likely to lead to malfunction and decay. Some of these are not solely in the realm of the rational and objective, but may relate to the constitution of the pay steering committee, the credibility with which a particular job evaluation panel is regarded, whether management and staff consultative committees exist, and so on.

Maintenance costs

The costs of maintaining a payment system are rarely calculated or included in any assessment of its total cost, although some people suggest that they should be, so that changes can be logged and acted upon. We might consider the costs of using consultants; time spent in committees; the process of evaluating jobs and job descriptions; negotiations; and work measurement or bonus staff or others involved in calculating performance-based incentives.

Monitoring variable aspects of pay

Not all payment systems include an incentive or performance-related pay element, and exhibit 14.3 suggests the coverage of an audit of this type of scheme.

Where systems do have a performance element, however, this needs to be evaluated to ensure that output (however measured) is continuing to justify the extra pay or rewards offered. The can be done by plotting the ratio of increase in work performance to operating costs of the scheme plus incentive payments made, as shown earlier in the chapter in figure 14.1.

Exhibit 14.3

Audit coverage in payment systems with no incentive or performance-related pay element

1 How good is productivity/performance, and is it likely that an incentive or performance-related payment system could motivate workers to perform better?

2 Do the managers and supervisors believe that better performance would be achieved if an incentive/performance-related system was introduced? If they do not, then there is a high probability that such a scheme would fail.

3 Do the employees have sufficient control over factors which affect organisation performance to justify performance-related payments? If they do not, then such a scheme may be unwise. If they do, and there is a need for improved performance, then introduce a suitable scheme.

4 Are there government or other incentives (such as tax advantages) which the organisation could be taking advantage of by introducing a performance-related (perhaps measured as profit-related payment system?).

TO MAINTAIN THE SYSTEM, OR TO ALLOW IT TO DECAY?

Having established the health of the current system and tested the extent of decay using the measures described above, you must then decide whether to maintain the scheme, or to allow it to decay. The latter course of action is likely to have a number of effects on the overall effectiveness of the organisation, as illustrated below:

An example: degeneration of a performance-based pay system can have serious consequences for the whole of a company

Undertaking a participant observation study, Richard Thorpe (1980) was able to learn about the wilful manipulation of a payment scheme that nearly brought a large and well-known company to its knees. As a consequence of this manipulation process times increased so much when a new product line was introduced into the factory, the first item produced took 50 hours to complete, against a target time of only 16 hours (which already included an allowance for the extra time needed to produce a new product!).

In this case, one of the main reasons for the decay was the number of disputes that arose over the time allowances. Because the product was new and there were many employees (who had not yet learnt the sophisticated art of negotiation!), an opportunity was spotted to dispute all the times allocated for this product and negotiate each one separately. This proved to be an extremely long and costly exercise.

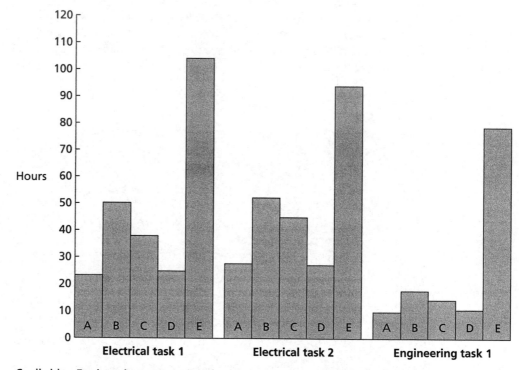

Coalbridge Engineering: comparison between times set by rate fixers (A), times claimed by employees (B), times eventually agreed after dispute (C), times achieved by workforce after agreement (D) and times achieved during period of dispute (E)

Fig. 14.10 Times taken to complete Assembly line tasks

Figure 14.10 shows a typical range of assembly line tasks that were subject to dispute, there were hundreds of these, and their graphs all show the same pattern. The A columns show the times which the company proposed for completing the task, and B columns the times which the workforce claimed were needed (which were always considerably higher than the targets – usually about twice as much). The disputes always resulted in compromise and the C columns show the times which were eventually agreed usually slightly nearer the workforce's claims than the company's targets. When the times had been agreed the workers would settle down to production taking the times indicated by D columns, which were always remarkably similar to the company's original figures as shown in the (A columns). But the really devastating aspect of the situation was that the times taken during the period of disputes were those shown in Columns E – enormously higher than even the claims of the workforce.

Productivity during the dispute period was typically less than one third of the eventual post-dispute rate of working. The delay in settling these time allocations cost the company dearly in terms of orders and reputation.

After six months, only 40 per cent of the assembly piecework times had been agreed and the patterns shown in figure 14.10 were typical of the many jobs which were examined. By the end of a year, only twenty-six items had been delivered as opposed to the seventy planned. Even after taking stock and rescheduling the work, the workforce had become so powerful that only thirty-two items were delivered against a planned 115. Worse still, the company had negotiated strictly fixed price contracts with customers, and the delays in deliveries meant not only lost revenue in a period of high inflation, but also penalty clauses and substantial sums of money tied up in expensive stocks for the targeted production plan. The interest on money tied up in those stocks trebled in only two years. Raw materials were being purchased, but little revenue was being received from sales. Throughout the period, order books for the product were full, yet it was not possible to meet orders. Poor delivery performance, prejudiced future contracts and the final losses amounted to just over £13 million, the first loss the company had ever made (Bowey and Thorpe, 1996).

The original cause of dissatisfaction had been complaints about differentials between different groups of employees, including some managers. During the period of the decay, the performance-based pay for skilled manual workers had increased three fold in only two years, even though performance had declined. This increase occurred entirely through the degeneration of the payment system as opposed to through any annual negotiated increases (these being subject to an incomes policy). Although worrying, the drift in the bonus element itself was not of great concern, although it had risen substantially. It was the effect of this drift on differentials within the organisation that caused tensions, disputes and disruption to production, further adding to costs.

Two important differentials which were eroded by the scheme were those between manual workers and their supervisors, and manual workers and inspectors. Because of a government policy of wage restraint, supervisors and inspectors had their salary increases kept in line with the statutory norms. This led to continual industrial relations problems as they strove to restore their former differentials. Inspectors had traditionally enjoyed staff conditions, along with pay parity with the factory average for skilled workers. In the engineering industry, inspectors are highly trained employees and are conscious of their status. At one stage, a situation was reached where the differential between factory average and inspectors' pay was twice as much as it should have been to be considered 'equitable'. This resulted in a strategy of non-cooperation by the inspectors in order to change the situation.

A performance-based incentive system was then devised to restore the previous differential, but once arranged for inspectors, it was demanded by all other groups in the factory. The inspectors had been an easy group with which to arrange a deal due to low productivity with plenty of scope for improvement. The management was reported to be quite happy that this deal was genuinely self-financing and to have said that it would have withstood the Department of Employment scrutiny of the day. However, the system devised for supervisors to enable them to regain their differential was justified on a more dubious criterion – the number of completed assemblies leaving the factory! When targets set were found not to be attainable, it was changed to the number of sub-assemblies made, and so on – thus removing any real performance element.

Another problem relating to the performance-based incentive system for supervisors and inspectors was that these two groups could connive to increase their bonus payments. For example, inspectors would continually fail work for small faults so that they could re-check it again later, thus claiming two inspections on the same part in order to enhance their bonus earnings. Supervisors would also think of reasons why assemblies would not be ready or could not be done in a particular way so that allowances would be invoked to add to their bonuses.

In addition, whilst all these difficulties lasted, it became more difficult to attract and promote high calibre staff to the supervisor and inspector roles and to other white-collar and technical grades. These were serious problems for a company in which there was a heavy dependence on quality, and technology played a large part.

The escalating incomes of employees at this one site also caused problems for the business group as a whole, causing claims for parity from other sites. Perhaps most significantly was the fact that the new technology was effectively being impeded by the workers in their efforts to negotiate better time allowances for themselves. Improved technology was at the heart of all the markets in which the company operated, and yet when new technologies were required, they were seen by the employees simply as opportunities for gaining more money. There are two schools of thought on this issue, one of which suggests that payment schemes help to overcome resistance to change in technology because of the opportunity given to employees to increase their earnings. However, in this case, where workers were confident of their negotiating strength, changes were welcomed only as opportunities for prolonged negotiations to push up wages.

The degeneration of the incentive payment system described represents a frightening, if not extreme, example of how decayed systems can have a serious effect on a company's health and well being.

From past research into performance-based incentive schemes, it is possible to predict some of the areas where degeneration and decay might occur, together with symptoms to look out for (Bowey and Thorpe, 1996). These symptoms are summarised in exhibit 14.4.

Proliferation of special allowances

These usually take the form of allowances for waiting time and for work for which there is no time allowance or measurement. Deliberate or accidental performance/cost drift can also occur through allowances for shift working, special conditions, training, difficult work and so on. Many such components in pay serve to complicate the pay packet and reflect an over-dependence on pay as a means of achieving control, rather than controlling through better management. Imposing one layer of 'influencing worker behaviour through pay' upon another limits the effectiveness of either by confusing the

Exhibit 14.4

Symptoms of schemes in need of modification or replacement

1 Are the kinds of effort which are encouraged by this scheme going to contribute in the best way to the organisation's main objectives? It is often the case that the kind of effort which is measured and rewarded is not relevant or even runs counter to business aims.

2 Are the supervisors required to take account of the different earnings potential between different tasks when allocating work? If so, the payment system may be placing constraints on management's ability to schedule work efficiently.

3 Is performance low towards the end of the day? If so, this is probably because employees are controlling their rate of work to protect informal or explicit targets.

4 Have the times allowed or rates of pay for particular pieces of work kept pace with changes in methods of technology? If not, there may be discontent among those whose pay has not benefited from such changes, while others may be receiving high payment.

5 Is incentive- or performance-related pay a true reflection of effort? If it is not perceived to be so, there may be considerable discontent among those who believed themselves to be under-rewarded.

6 Is there evidence of discontent about access to high incentive or performance-related pay? If there is, then the systems may be acting more as a disincentive than as a motivator.

7 When performance or productivity is measured by objective indicators (preferably the auditor's own), does it correlate with incentive or performance pay? If not, the systems is not rewarding the right patterns of behaviour.

8 Are accurate records of the labour content of work produced, or is there a tendency for elements to be cross-booked from one job or activity to another? If this is happening, there is a danger that prices to the customer will not reflect costs and will be uncompetitive.

9 Are supervisors or managers sometimes making adjustments to such things as allowances or expenses in order to ensure acceptable or fair pay to individuals? If this is the case, the payment system is unlikely to be respected by those individuals.

10 Do the variations in earnings from week to week and between individuals seem reasonable, or are they a source of discontent?

11 Is management in control of the level of payments (possibly within a range which is acceptable to the organisation)? If not, the scheme may be in danger of costing the organisation more than it can afford.

12 Does the scheme include all the people whose performance is important to the organisation?

supposed motivational message. The result can be increased costs for no improvement in performance. This kind of degeneration can be identified for employees by examining the total cost of these allowances. If either of the first two of these indices plus the last are increasing then the scheme is degenerating through this process.

Manipulation of allowances

The allowances discussed above are very often the source of manipulation to increase incentive or bonus payments. Manipulation can be effected by increasing the period for which an allowance is payable, for example by recording additional time spent waiting or working on tasks for which the average bonus is payable. Less time therefore appears to be spent on the bonus-generating activities, which therefore accrue more bonus by being completed in a supposedly shorter time. By such strategies, it is possible to increase the amount of incentive bonus earned per hour.

This kind of manipulation is done by staff at all levels in the organisational hierarchy and on all kinds of different schemes. It is sometimes also done by managers and supervisors who wish to see a fairer allocation of earnings, or who favour a particularly helpful employee, and by remuneration managers and administrators who wish to see a more acceptable outcome from an incentive scheme than would otherwise be the case. When the manipulation is done by blue-collar workers it usually results in more pay and is referred to very often as 'making bonus with pencil'. When the figures are altered by supervisors, managers or administrators, an individual's (or group's) pay may be increased or decreased, usually with the aim of achieving a better match between effort and reward, but sometimes also to resolve industrial relations or motivational difficulties.

In one memorable example, following a six-month study of the coal industry bonus scheme to see how the miners manipulated this, Richard Thorpe (1980) telephoned the personnel manager of a pit to collect output dates (measured in tonnes of coal) to compare with the bonus figures already collected. When all the figures had been relayed over the telephone, the personnel manager enquired whether the tonnes produced and bonus figures correlated. After a brief check, Richard replied that they did. 'Good', came the answer, 'we spent enough time ensuring they did'. What Richard was being told after six of months focusing on the miners was that the managers were in fact manipulating the scheme almost as much!

Manipulation of allowances can be identified by monitoring the levels of allowance paid month by month (collectively and separately). If these are increasing, or if they intermittently increase and then remain high, the scheme is degenerating through this process – unless some objective and external change (such as a change in market demand) can explain or account for the whole of the increase.

Slackening performance standards

Incentive schemes can also degenerate because the performance standards to which pay is related may become less appropriate over time. This can be caused by a number of factors, from individuals becoming more proficient to a change in the criteria used to establish performance standards. One of the biggest difficulties is 'a' measure becoming 'the' measure, the wider business context becoming lost in the narrow (often slowish) adherence to measurable targets. Recent writers on performance measurement (for example Kaplan and Norton, 1996), have stressed the importance of process, multiple measures and the inclusion of qualitative as well as purely quantitative variables.

Cross-booking and cross-subsidisation between easy and difficult tasks

This type of degeneration has been recognised since the days of Roy's study in the 1950s (Roy, 1952 and 1954). Although schemes where this is possible are on the decline, the practice Roy identified can still be found wherever work-measure schemes are operated. It arises because it is easier to earn a bonus from some tasks than from others, due to the difficulty of setting a uniform performance standard where there are many tasks which an employee can be asked to undertake. Under certain systems, there is a tendency for employees to cross-book time from medium 'bonus' jobs on to slow 'bonus' jobs. This results in a higher incentive payment rate for a shorter period for the medium 'bonus' jobs, and no change in the rate of pay (because it is below the threshold for bonus payment) for the slow jobs, but a longer period of time apparently spent on them. Whether or not this practice increases overall pay depends entirely on the gearing of the bonus curve (the relationship between pay and performance).

Even where employees are not benefiting financially from this cross-booking, they may still choose to manipulate the time spent on jobs in this way in order to protect the easy jobs from being noticed by management.

It should be also noted that, even without a fall-back level of pay, employees can always increase their pay by cross-booking times spent on jobs wherever the relationship between performance and pay is not uniform for all levels of performance. It could apply, for example, if salesmen's commission varied with total sales for a period, resulting in cross-booking sales from one period to the next. In one factory studied by Angela Bowey, which had recently removed a piecework incentive payment system, one of the operatives, Vhari, began to get ready to go home at 3.00 p.m., when the normal finishing time was 4.30 p.m. When asked by the supervisor why this was, she replied, 'I've made my wage for the day – I'm going to go home now!' What this woman was doing was still calculating how many items she would have to do in a day to make her wage (the amount she was comfortable with). Under the new system of a consolidated wage, there was of course no need to stop at 3.00 p.m. as she got the same pay whatever, but Vhari was still counting under the old system and considered she had done enough for the company that day.

This process of degeneration can be identified just as Donald Roy diagnosed it, by plotting the frequency with which tasks completed by a workforce (or section of a workforce) are recorded at each performance level in the appropriate range (usually between 50 and the maximum recorded level). The sample would need to be a large one to cover all the tasks completed by the group in a representative period of time. The performance range should then be divided into equal segments and a tally made of the number of completed tasks falling into each segment. If the segments are small enough and the number of tasks is large enough, a graph or histogram of the results can be drawn. If the histogram approximates to a normal distribution, as shown in 14.2, one can assume that the employees are applying a fairly uniform rate of effort to tasks which vary in their degree of difficulty but tend towards a mean (denoted by A on figure 14.2.

If, however, the pattern is skewed with a higher proportion of jobs at a position above the peak representing standard performance than below it, then it is reasonable to assume that the employees are motivated by the higher bonus payments from easy jobs. They therefore put more effort into those jobs, so raising them into a higher performance category, but are not, it can generally be assumed, manipulating the recording of performance. If, however, the graph is bi-modal as in figure 14.3, then there is strong evidence of cross-booking. The relative size and the number of peaks are not important. The significant indicators are the marked trough between peaks (which does not, however, have to be as low as that indicated) and the more or less sharp cut-off point on the second distribution which may occasionally by exceeded by a few non-conformist individuals – almost always the same ones!

Fixed levels of performance

As performance-based systems are supposed to be designed to reward additional effort and as such performance standards, then one can assume that, in a properly working system, achievement should vary from one period to another, save perhaps only for an upward general trend as competency levels improve. A performance-based system that remains constant at one level of performance (usually the highest level that is acceptable to management) will usually indicate a need for further investigation. Either the system is being manipulated in order to yield a constant income (which may or may not be a problem, depending on the kind of manipulation), or it has so little motivational impact that employees are maintaining a steady but low level of performance.

Loss of managerial control – particularly at the level of supervision

As pay is vitally important to employees, they usually seek to control those factors which they know can affect their bonus/incentive earnings. This may result in employees dictating (directly or indirectly) aspects of their work schedule so that activities which pay well are those they get to do. It may not follow that this is the most rational allocation of work from the company's point of view, and it may well result in the inefficient use of materials, equipment and labour (for example, in manufacturing increasing the number of 'set-ups' by not maximising the batch sizes). Managers and supervisors frequently accede to these pressures in order to avoid other problems which the workforce might create. To find out whether this is a problem, there is no substitute for a detailed knowledge of the department or organisation.

Frequent disputes about pay

Claims for regrading, arguments about differentials and disputes over performance standards could all be indications of a decaying performance-based incentive scheme. These can lead to low company performance, through poor industrial relations.

In a gas depot studied in the early 1990s, it was clear that the single most important priority for the business was customer care. To improve the contribution gas fitters could make to customer care, the company embarked on a huge programme which included training for all staff, and the use of customer service cards (cards the fitters would hand out to customers when the job had been completed). In studying whether or not this was having an effect, we found that there was a very low return of cards and no improvement in customer satisfaction. We considered why this was the case.

Upon further investigation, we found that apart from the fact that many of the gas fitters had 'missed' the 'compulsory' training, they did not feel it was right to try to sell a new fire or appliance when they had just condemned an old one. They were, they told us, gas fitters and not salesmen, and their reluctance was all the greater if they felt the householder could not afford a replacement. But by far the most significant reason for not 'selling on' was that they were on a performance-based incentive bonus scheme in which their weekly wage depended on how many jobs they did each day. What the fitters never knew was whether the next job they would go to would be a good one ('loose') or a bad one ('tight'), so instead of staying around to chat and 'sell', they moved on as quickly as they could. Here we found an incentive scheme that, through the way it was being operated was cutting across the company's most important priority and, in so doing, reducing the organisation's potential profitability.

PROBLEMS ASSOCIATED WITH DEGENERATION

These costs of decay or degeneration in performance-based payment systems can appear in many guises, as shown below:

1 Increased unit costs, incurred as a direct result of paying higher labour costs than in a previous period.
2 Difficulty in scheduling output.
3 Inaccurate pricing as a consequence of the manipulation of performance measures, of wages or of both, possibly resulting in a loss of competitiveness.
4 Poor flexibility, evidenced by poor performance on work which offers less financial reward.
5 Low productivity during periods when wages are being negotiated, for example with the workforce attempting to conceal how quickly certain tasks can be completed.
6 Resistance or slow acceptance of new technology because of its less-attractive incentive/ bonus payments compared to a degenerated scheme.

A NEW APPROACH TO REMUNERATION AND REWARD

The link between consultation and the long-term effectiveness of a payment scheme is, as we have indicated, an important one. Too many payment systems are considered, introduced and then forgotten, left to decay. The need for effective consultation at both the design and the implementation stages has been emphasised, but this is just as important once a scheme has been installed. In order to ensure that a system remains relevant and effective, managers need to communicate not just with each other, but also with trade union representatives and employees. The trust so developed and the communication channels so formed can provide a very important part of the 'early warning system' for detecting signs of degeneration – if the organisation wishes to listen and can develop mechanisms for doing so effectively. Marchington (1977) identified seven factors in the context of industrial relations which appear to have a significant influence in bringing about change. One such change could be the onset of problems related to payment schemes:

1 Product market.
2 Technological environment.
3 Institutional influences external to the plant.
4 Organisation structure.
5 History and nature of unionism.
6 Labour context markets, region and sex.
7 Organisation culture.

Over time, any one of these factors, or a combination of them could change in such a way as to make the payment system less appropriate than it was when it was first introduced.

It is one thing to consider that the payment system may require modification throughout its life; it is another to have such modifications accepted by employees and their trade union representatives. Lack of consultation is likely to produce a situation where the changes proposed are all put forward by management to resolve 'organisational' problems. But payment systems may cause problems for employees and trade union representatives just as much. It would be arrogant to forget that employees may also wish to see changes, but be wary of risking the benefits of an old or decayed system for the uncertainties of something new. Only through continuous consultation can such fears be allayed and fair adjustments made to a payment system to solve the problems for all the parties affected. The important elements in developing a strategy change are summarised below:

1 Extensive consultation with the people involved or affected by the changes.
2 Drawing attention to the factors which make the proposed changes desirable (to managers and also to workers).
3 Identifying the aims for the changes, making sure they are derived from, and contribute towards, the business plan or corporate strategy of the organisation.
4 Identifying the elements in rewards which are to be covered by the changes, and the desired features of any revised systems (from the points of view of all those consulted).
5 Identifying changes in other control procedures which will be needed to support the changes in the reward system, and any new activity which will become necessary.
6 Considering how the proposed changes may affect other groups of employees not directly covered by them.

CONCLUSIONS

This chapter has stressed the importance of auditing systems and shows the problems that can result from drift and decay. As shown in exhibit 14.5, which summarises the stages in auditing a payment system, audits need to begin with the identification of the organisation's goals and objectives, to ensure that the pay policies and structures are designed and operated to meet these.

Exhibit 14.5

Stages in the audit of a payment system

1 Assessing what the organisation needs from its various systems for allocating rewards, in the light of current objectives and priorities.

2 Considering payroll costs relative to added value (or to revenue, profit, sales value or output), over a review period. The same review period would also be used for stages 3 to 13.

Looking at performance levels achieved, and variations in these over time and between sections or individuals.

3 Analysing any time for which performance-related pay is awarded without reference to the actual performance of the employee at that time (e.g. incentive pay during waiting time; in lieu bonuses for unmeasured work, or productivity pay based on work of some other.

4 Examining the distribution of performance-related earnings between individuals and between sections.

5 Measuring performance-related pay as a percentage of total pay.

6 Investigating absenteeism and turnover of staff, by section, grade and sex.

7 Assessing the extent and requirement for overtime working, and its distribution.

8 Studying the extent of and requirement, for shift working, and its pattern, reward and distribution.

9 Measuring pay differentials between various groups, and trends in these (e.g. males versus females, supervisors versus operatives, production versus sales/services/technicians, and grades versus other grades and distribution within grade, etc.

10 Evaluating the consistency and logic of pay differentials.

11 Comparing wages/salaries, fringe benefits and remuneration systems with other competing employers.

Assessing compliance with the law and the extent to which government incentives (e.g. tax advantages) are being taken up.

The outcomes of any payment systems audit should be a report to the board (containing the element and recommendations shown in exhibits 14.6 and 14.7) and an action research project where key organisational members work to make changes as information is collected. It is important that those at the highest level possible are involved (not just the specialist functions), because the recommendations made will affect the whole organisation and action might well need to be taken in a range of areas.

Exhibit 14.6

Contents of payment system audit report

1 An analysis of the figures in the light of the current organisational objectives and priorities.

2 Comment on these figures and trends, with special reference to discrepancies or anomalies and any problems they are creating or aggravating.

3 Current and projected effectiveness of procedures for motivating performance.

4 Current and projected effectiveness of the job evaluation or grading system in use.

5 Issues identified by comparisons with other employers.

6 Employee relations issues pertaining to pay.

7 Issues identified by the audit indicating the need for change in other areas (e.g. in supervisory training, production planning, public relations, etc.).

8 Comments on the effects on the remuneration system of investment policy, market situation/trends, or other expected changes or problems.

Exhibit 14.7

Recommendations in payment system audit reports

1 Introducing incentives where motivation is inadequate.

2 Dealing with a poor incentive scheme which is more trouble than it is worth.

3 Adjusting a faulty incentive scheme.

4 Introducing job evaluation where it is clearly needed.

5 Taking out job evaluation where it is inappropriate.

6 Modifying a job evaluation scheme which is faulty but salvageable.

7 Dealing with underpaid individuals.

8 Dealing with overpaid individuals.

9 Adjusting the structure to respond to external comparisons.

LEARNING ACTIVITIES

1 Select one payment system currently operating in your organisation and assess whether the system is producing the expected results in terms of its objectives at implementation.

2 Establish whether the information systems in your organisation generate sufficient accurate, detailed data to enable the reward systems to be audited.

3 Justify the costs involved in auditing a payment system.

4 Outline the reasons why a payment system consisting of a basic pay determined by job evaluation and a performance-related incentive scheme might decay.

REFERENCES

Bell, E. (1999) 'Changing the Line of Sight on Payment Systems: A Study of Shop Floor workers and managers within the British Chemical Industry', *International Journal of Human Resource Management*, 10(4): 924–940.

Bowey, A.M. and Thorpe, R. with Hellier, P. (1996) *Payment Systems and Productivity*. London Macmillan.

Ditton, J. (1979) 'Baking Time', *The Sociological Review*, 27: 1.

Kaplan, R.S. and Norton, D.P. (1996) 'Using the Balanced Score card as a Strategic Management System', *Harvard Business Review*, pp. 75–85.

Lawler, E.E. (1971) *Pay and Organisational Effectiveness: A psychological view*. New York: McGraw Hill.

Lupton, T. (1963) *On the Shop Floor*. Harmondsworth: Penguin Press.

Lupton, T. (1972) *Management and the Social Sciences*. Harmondsworth: Penguin.

Marchington, M. (1977) 'Worker Participation and Plant-wide Incentive Schemes', *Personnel Review*, 6(3, Summer).

Roy, D. (1952) 'Quota Restriction and Goldbricking in a Machine Shop', *American Journal of Sociology*, 57: 427–42.

Roy, D. (1954) 'Work Satisfaction and Social Reward in Quota Achievement: an Analysis of Piecework Incentives', *American Sociological Review*, 18: 4.

Thorpe, R. (1980) 'The Relationship Between Payment Systems, Productivity and the Organisation of Work', unpublished M.Sc. Thesis, Strathclyde Business School.

Wilson, S. (1953) unpublished Ph.D. Thesis, University of Manchester, Department of Economics and Social Science.

15 Time-based pay

Philip Lynch

INTRODUCTION

Reward systems are exchange mechanisms; employees offer skills, experience, knowledge, effort and time in exchange for money and other benefits. An important component of that exchange is time, sufficiently important to be an explicit part of the contract of employment. The time element of reward systems is on the agenda of collective bargaining, subject to the UK and EC regulations, often forms one of the differentiating factors between blue- and white-collar employees and has recently become the focus of the quest for flexibility. Furthermore, payment for variations in time worked can substantially influence the wage costs of organisations, and it therefore merits closer scrutiny.

This chapter reviews, first, how the time factor is recognised in reward systems and the ways in which organisations seek to achieve flexibility in this element. It then goes on to explore in detail the development of payment systems incorporating annualised hours, the most recent and perhaps fundamental attempt to achieve time-based flexibility since shift systems.

Base wage is the core payment made by the employer for work performed and usually tends to reflect the organisational value of either the work that the employee undertakes or in the case of base pay determined by the skills or competence of the individual undertaking the work. It is base pay that is normally linked to time. This can be directly expressed in a rate per hour or more broadly in a wage per week or month. There are a number of assumptions that underpin the relationship of time to pay. One of these is that time beyond stated hours of work has more exchange value and therefore is paid at premium rates, the most common being time and a quarter, time and a half and double time. The variation in premium rates reflects the differing value placed on different periods of time, so, for example, it might be common to pay time and quarter for hours worked beyond normal finishing time to say 7.00 p.m., whilst hours beyond that time attract time and a half. The value of the additional hours worked at the weekend is recognised by the common rating of hours worked on a Saturday as time and a half, whilst hours worked on Sundays commonly attract double time.

There are two pay systems in organisations and the boundary between them carries problems. Sitting alongside time-based pay systems in organisations are salary systems where no explicit link exists between pay and time worked and no pay accrues for additional hours worked. We refer of course to management-style salary systems. These may apply to managerial, professional and technical staff, who are at a particular hierarchical level in the organisation. The assumption is that these systems already include recognition that the job will overspill normal working time. This can result in first line managers or supervisors receiving substantially less than the staff that they supervise on occasion. Should this become a regular state of affairs it is likely to lead to motivational problems, pay claims for comparability, refusal to work additional hours or difficulties in recruiting to the posts in question.

There are sometimes differences in hours worked between different groups of employees, white-collar workers often working less than their blue-collar equivalents by up to five hours per week (a 35 hour week compared for example with a 40 hour week). However there has been, in recent years, a tendency for hours worked to converge prompted both by attempts to harmonise terms and conditions of employment as a human resource strategy and as a result of negotiation under pressure from unions. The 35 hour working week for all employees remains an explicit target of the trade union movement.

Relativity within time-based pay tends to be determined by either job evaluation or skills and competency-based systems (see chapters 12 and 16). This may be insufficient to reward or motivate all the behaviours required by the organisation and time-based pay may be supplemented by additional forms of pay such as various forms of performance-related pay (see chapter 17) or profit-related pay and employee share options (see chapter 20). These systems may be organisation wide or aimed at some specific group of employees, such as sales representatives. Any one organisation may have several of these additional systems.

Flexibility in time-based systems

Many jobs or roles require flexibility in the number of hours worked or the time of day at which they are worked and a range of approaches have developed over time to accommodate this need for flexibility. Capital-intensive industries tend to require 24 hour seven day week working. A range of shift systems has developed to meet these needs, all of which have different working hours each week. Shift systems on five day week working can be fixed, that is an individual will work a permanent shift of early, late or night hours; here the night shift would attract the highest payment. Alternatively a rolling shift system might be in place; here employees will work successive shifts over a three week period, early, late, night, and so on. In this case the variations in pay are often smoothed so that the employee receives the same wage for each shift. In seven day working, rostering becomes more complex with employees working a complex pattern of varying shifts and days on and off. Again, it is usual for negotiations to establish patterns of work, but the pay to be smoothed to a regular weekly or monthly wage.

Changing social and work patterns have led to a need for increased flexible working in some sectors, such as retailing with the advent of Sunday and 24 hour opening. Here unsociable hours payments are made to part- and full-time staff working before

6.00 a.m. or after 8.00 p.m. within their normal designated hours. These are in addition to premium payments for working hours beyond a full working week or premium rates for Sunday working.

Other jobs such as long-distance driving are unpredictable in their requirement for additional hours working. Routes may be planned to time but roadwork or traffic accidents may add on hours at a time when no member of management is available to sanction the additional cost. To deal with this problem an approach called 'consolidated hours' may be used. In this system, a set number of hours are worked or not and therefore forms a stable part of the income for the individual and a controlled cost for the employer. Should the employee work less or more overtime hours in any one week the payment does not vary, a swings and roundabouts philosophy is applied.

The need for flexibility in time-based systems, together with the need to recognise seasonal or cyclical workflow patterns, has led to a new approach called 'annualised hours'. This approach matches work time to business needs on an annual basis. The opportunity then exists to detach the pay system from an hourly or weekly basis and move to an annual salary. We term these new time-based systems Stable Income Plans, The remainder of this chapter looks at the development and operation of these plans.

Stable income plans are part of major change programmes in organisations. What we are really talking about is the end of basic pay plus overtime as a concept and replacing this with a fixed salary in relation to a working time contract.

We expound the argument that overtime is not motivational in most pay systems and its elimination is a major factor in cultural and motivational shifts in organisations. The growth of 'capped' annualised hours agreements where a salary of £ X is paid for a contract of N hours per annum as the main means of achieving the change is explored.

The reform of premium payments is also discussed since the opportunity can be taken to maximise the use of plain time hours (i.e. non-premium working hours) and to reform non-standard working payments and allowances.

We touch on the theory of 'capped' annual hours contracts and the positive motivation of not having to work all the hours employees have been paid for. Why this is an important and increasingly popular idea, particularly in Britain and Ireland, is discussed.

We trace the connection between this kind of reward strategy and the unit labour costs of organisations and show why stable income plans will nearly always have a major positive impact on the costs and profits of businesses.

We discuss how organisations manage to achieve a plan for change in which employees may suffer income loss through overtime elimination and, at the same time, agree to major work practice and performance changes. We also look at alternative 'buy-in' strategies.

Finally, we examine how time-based pay fits in with other initiatives on organisational change including performance-based pay.

A STABLE INCOME PLAN

Definition

A stable income plan is essentially a fixed salary for a given working hours contract, usually an annual hours contract. Of course, there may be job grades and performance-related pay as with conventional pay plans. The distinguishing element is that there is no mechanism for improving pay as a result of working more hours. In this sense a stable income plan is not unlike a management salary scheme where hours of work could be to some extent undefined and there are no overtime payments.

A major goal of these plans is to eliminate overtime completely, so the main features of a stable income plan are usually (but not invariably):

- An equalised pay arrangement, which gives equal monthly or four weekly amounts for a yearly contract of hours, even though the company might have different requirements for working hours at different times of year.
- No payment for additional hours of work and no mechanism for purchasing additional hours and the elimination of allowances based on overtime. For example, call-outs might have previously been based on a minimum number of 'overtime' hours. Now they need to be re-thought (section 3.2 below).
- Higher guaranteed pay: This might arise because contracts are specified which contain hours beyond the normal basic hours of the contract, e.g. 42 hours rather than 39 hours. The treatment of what we call 'hours plus' contracts and the uses of 'committed' and 'reserve' hours merits a separate description (see below). Higher guaranteed pay often means higher pensionable pay because overtime does not normally count towards pensionable pay in most organisations.
- Rationalisation of unsocial hours payments. It is a feature of modern businesses without stable income plans that unsocial hours payments are based on tradition rather than sound principles. For example, weekend working allowances need to be rethought completely if the weekend hours done under a stable income plan are no longer 'overtime' hours as well.

There are a number of other features of stable income plans which companies may incorporate, for example, broader banding of jobs, competence-based pay, participation bonuses. But these elements are not necessarily common across all organisations. We discuss the relationship with other pay mechanisms later (section 5).

Link with annualised hours

Because of the 'salaried' nature of a stable income plan, particularly the equalisation over a year, the plan is very often associated with annualised hours contracts. These are effectively a yearly contract of working hours rather than an hourly or weekly contract. A 39-hour weekly contract, for example, might translate into a 1,778 hour annual contract and be calculated as follows:

	Calendar year	52.18 weeks	(365.25 days)
Less	Public Holidays	(1.6) weeks equiv.	(8 days)
Less	Annual Holidays	(5.0) weeks equiv.	(25 days)
	Working year	45.58 weeks	
		× 39 hours	
	Annual basic hours	1778 hours	

The normal approach is to have the hours in the contract split into:

1 *Committed hours* which are used for planned work and training. These may be rostered into working patterns for the year or used in a flexible 'time account'. Certain schemes may contain a combination of the two aspects.

2 *Reserve hours* are the second element. These are held in reserve for absence cover, unplanned work, customer rush orders and to make up for performance failure against set criteria. The hours are prepaid but may not all be used in the year. On the contrary, the aim of employees and management is to minimise reserve hour use by 'working smart'.

The most common annual hours contract involving a stable income plan is what we call a 'capped' scheme. Capped schemes have been implemented on basic hours only. Much more common than basic hours is the 'hours plus' version where the committed and reserve add up to a contract of hours in excess of the basic hours. Often the total hours can be quite high, since the risk of using reserve hours can also be high. Typically the reserve can be between 8 per cent and 15 per cent of basic hours, sometimes higher. The following is a real example:

Basic hours	1778	
Additional	160	9%
Hours plus contract	1938	

Depending on the business needs of the organisation, it is not automatic that the basic hours are equal to committed hours, nor is it automatic that the additional hours are equal to the reserve. It is quite common to have some reserve hours as unrostered basic hours. Alternatively, some of the additional hours could be 'committed' to working patterns. These choices are part of the design process. The following exhibits (15.1 and 15.2) are taken from a company which used a capped annual hours scheme to introduce a stable income plan and other changes as part of a total change programme.

Exhibit 15.1

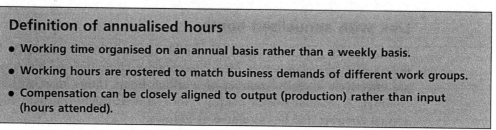

Definition of annualised hours

- Working time organised on an annual basis rather than a weekly basis.
- Working hours are rostered to match business demands of different work groups.
- Compensation can be closely aligned to output (production) rather than input (hours attended).

These exhibits illustrate the essence of the cultural shift that is required, driven by an annualised hours scheme and containing at its heart a reform of the pay/working time bargain.

It is possible to have capped hours contracts at different levels of annual committed and reserve hours to meet the business needs of specific groups within the same organisation. For example, if a group of workers needs to start work earlier than another group but both groups have the same finishing time, it is quite permissible to have a higher number of committed hours for the first group. This means a higher contract

Exhibit 15.2

Annualised hours generates a 'cultural shift'

From	*To*
• All improvements viewed through overtime filter.	⟶ • Improvements evaluated in business terms.
• Inefficiency is rewarded.	⟶ • Energy (and creativity) devoted to work completion.
• Absenteeism is beneficial.	⟶ • Absenteeism penalises others.
• Increased rewards come from clever negotiation demands.	⟶ • Increased rewards come satisfying business.
• Associate mentality is to protect status quo.	⟶ • Associate mentality is to progress.

of hours and of course a higher stable income. But by practising flexibility between job groups the number of discrete levels can be minimised.

The growth of these kinds of deals in Great Britain and Ireland has been very significant amongst leading-edge manufacturing companies in their moves towards world-class manufacturing. There have also been a number of deals in transport and distribution businesses and in companies within the services sectors, such as financial services. In fact, it would be fair to say that we know of no large manufacturing or services sector that does not have a significant annual hours deal linked to a stable income plan as a central plank of an overall change programme. Ten years ago you might have been able to count the number of deals on the fingers of one hand. It is also significant that most deals require trade union agreement and this has been secured, since the philosophy and approach of stable income plans is something the trade unions feel able to back. Indeed, I have consulted in companies where the request for such a deal has come from the trade union side.

THE IMPORTANCE OF OVERTIME ELIMINATION

The realities of overtime within a conventional pay system

Why should companies want to get rid of overtime from their pay systems? Why should they go to considerable lengths in terms of time, effort and money to overturn a conventional system which may have been in existence since the company's foundation? The reasons are not hard to find. So let us consider for a moment just what the impact of overtime really is on company pay plans and the disadvantages that it brings. By contrast, let us also look at what the stable income plan alternative would be:

1 The first element is the cost. The use of overtime will increase labour costs much more than it will increase output. If as a company, we want to expand volume and we do so using overtime, it will often increase our labour costs by 50 per cent or 100 per cent because we are paying premium time. Under stable income plans expected

volume increases are met with modular working patterns, which come into play once the volume increase is signalled.

2 The cover for absence by overtime can become widely abused. In some organisations I have come across sophisticated overtime abuses where shift employees deliberately take 'sick leave' in order to trigger overtime and shift payments to day workers. Both the absence itself and the overtime used to cover the absence are examples of what is termed ineffective time. They are 'repaid' by workers at some future time as they rotate from shifts on to days. A stable income plan uses reserve hours to cover absence. So one person's absence is another person's reserve hour working for which no extra pay is earned.

3 Overtime bolsters inefficiency. In effect we say to someone who is inefficient . . . 'here are some extra hours to do the work in and what's more we will pay you a premium rate of pay to do it'. Again a stable income plan will use reserve hour working in the event of productivity failure. Both absence and inefficiency are therefore discouraged and 'working smart' is rewarded.

4 Overtime encourages earnings protectionism. Employees will not impart training or skills to other people if their overtime opportunity thereby diminishes. For example, a craftsman is not encouraged to teach line operators about elementary machine fault identification if his 'out of hours' overtime opportunity is going to be reduced. Under a stable income plan the incentive works in the opposite direction.

The pay impact of overtime elimination

What does it mean to operate in an overtime-free environment from the point of view of pay strategy? First, the elimination of overtime allows pay differentials to be based on the relevant factors in organisations, such as responsibility, skill and performance. Below are three charts showing the spread of earnings differences due to overtime in administration, operational areas and support areas in one company in 1997. The charts are in the form of 'winners and losers' in relation to a new stable income plan. In each case the effects of differences in grade, service pay and shift pay have been taken out, so one can easily see the distorting effects of overtime on income. Once the new stable income is implemented there would of course be only one single bar on each chart at the zero mark!

The second aspect of an overtime-free environment is that premium payments need to be reviewed. If unsocial hours are worked as part of the standard week what revised premiums should apply? For example, what is the correct premium for week-end unsocial hours allowances once the overtime element is stripped out? Should this allowance be set at a higher rate for Sundays? One company with a significant amount of seven day working and a stable income plan put in place the broad banding of premium categories as below:

Group 1   Annual rostered 3 cycle × 5/7 shift pattern with other rostered patterns as required.

Group 2   Rostered shift patterns (other than Group 1) and 5/7 daywork patterns with other patterns as required.

Group 3   Basic Monday – Friday work pattern: could be a small requirement for work outside this pattern.

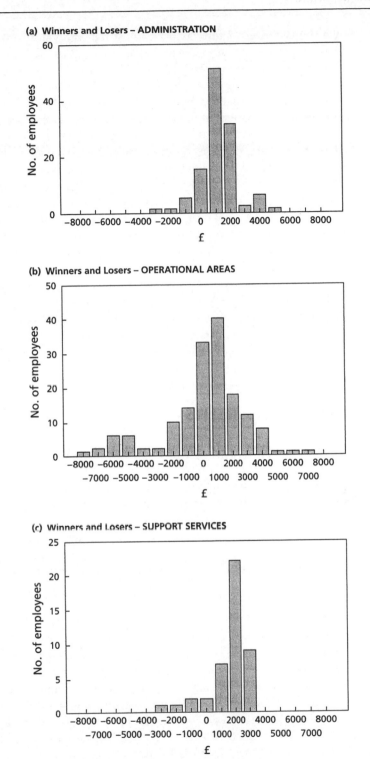

Fig. 15.1 Earnings differences due to overtime

Once the overtime factor has been extracted, the value and logic of having rational premuim payments will emerge. The broad-banding of premium categories as part of the stable income has to facilitate job flexibility and this is a really vital aspect of the total system.

The third aspect is what value to put on additional hours. There is no doubt that these are actually 'overtime' hours, since by definition they are additional to basic hours. If we make the working assumption for the moment that all additional hours are in fact *reserve* hours, then we do not expect the employee to work all of them. In fact we want him to work as few as possible. So where does that leave us with valuing additional hours? We could certainly justify giving a low premium loading to these hours. There is the option of holding the value of the additional hours apart from the new stable income. However, in most applications the experience is that the value is consolidated, thus enhancing guaranteed pay and pensionable pay. It might be a very necessary aspect of the buy-in process to make the guaranteed pay as attractive as possible and not just rely on a one-off payment.

Pitching the right level of contract and package is very important to the acceptability of the deal to employees and the establishment of a stable income plan. There are going to be winners and losers, particularly in a company with an endemic overtime culture. In this context it should be borne in mind that overtime is still very common in the UK (30 per cent of full-time employees work more than 46 hours per week compared with an EU average of 11 per cent).

COSTS AND BENEFITS

Consolidating part of the pay that used to be earned on overtime (as in the figures above) and increasing guaranteed salaries looks like a recipe for increasing payroll costs. Equally, reducing the number of available hours to the business looks like a formula for increasing headcount. So why should a stable income plan linked to an annualised hours deal be such a good bet for the organisation? The key is in the productive use of working time and a reduction in the added costs of premium time. Let us for a moment consider how this can be so. Our starting point is the measure everyone in business uses to measure productive performance, namely unit labour cost.

$$\text{unit labour cost} = \text{labour cost} / \text{output}$$

Senior managers of businesses refer to this simple ratio as a means of judging competitive performance. Multinational companies will often use an international version of this ratio. For example, oil companies might compare performance in terms of $ labour cost per barrel, converting local currencies into a common yardstick. Within the UK, companies comparing manufacturing costs might use £ of labour cost per tonne. In distribution it might be £ cost per case or container. So this measure is understood universally. How does working time and pay fit into this formula, since on the surface it has nothing to do with either? To find the answer we need to break the formula down to its constituent parts as below:

$$\text{Output} = \text{productive time} \times \text{average output rate}$$

$$\text{Labour cost} = \text{paid time} \times \text{average labour cost}$$

It follows from the above, by simple extension that:

$$\text{Unit labour cost} = \frac{\text{paid time}}{\text{productive time}} \times \frac{\text{average output}}{\text{average labour cost}}$$

So now we discover the underlying factors which really influence productivity and we can begin to see the connection between working time, pay and productivity. There are two really crucial factors:

1 by increasing productive hours in relation to paid hours we can improve the ratio on the left-hand side of the equation,
2 by reducing the proportion of labour hours paid as premium time we will reduce the average labour cost and improve the ratio on the right-hand side of the equation.

Of course the other factor is that the two sides of the equation are multiplied together. For example, if we raised our productive time from 75 per cent to 85 per cent and reduced our average labour cost from £15 per hour to £14, then we would reduce unit labour cost by 18 per cent.

This is the fundamental reason why stable income plans work effectively, since they reduce ineffective time and make more use of plain time hours (For more detailed analysis of these issues, see Lynch 1991). As a result the organisation can operate with fewer working hours and can operate without hours that carry an overtime premium. The benefits for the employee are higher guaranteed pay and access to more leisure time. The benefits for the company are reduced unit labour costs, greater profitability and a more demand-responsive organisation. The platform is there to build major cultural and organisational change, if required. Some organisations are prepared to break even on the introduction of the stable income in order to achieve the other major changes needed. Others may choose to make a buy-in payment and take the savings from year two. Whatever method chosen, it is likely that the benefits will far outweigh the costs in the future.

OTHER INITIATIVES

We have seen that the stable income plan linked to annual hours is not only justifiable in its own right on cost/benefit grounds, but is also the vehicle of cultural and organisational change. Many organisations I consult with consider the change programmes will only begin at the point of implementation of the stable income plan.

Let us consider for a moment what *future state* position many companies are aiming at and we can then see the pivotal position of the stable income plan. To illustrate this point I quote below from the American management writer E.E Lawler (in Lawler, 1982) regarding the design features for a participative system:

Organisational structure	Flat
	Lean
	Mini-enterprise oriented
	Team-based
	Participative council or structure

Job design	Individually enriched
	Self-managing teams
Information systems	Open
	Inclusive
	Tied to jobs
	Decentralised – team based
	Participatively set goals and standards
Career system	Tracks and counselling available
	Open job posting
Selection	Realistic job preview
	Team based
	Potential and process skill oriented
Training	Heavy commitment
	Peer training
	Economic education
	Interpersonal skills
Reward system	Open
	Skill based
	Gain-sharing and/or employee share ownership
	Flexible benefits
	All salary
	Egalitarian
Personnel policies	Stability of employment
	Participatively established through representative group
Physical layout	Around organisational structure
	Egalitarian
	Safe and pleasant

We can interpret the stable income plan therefore as the facilitator of a participative system. Lawler links *all salary* with other specific features, in particular skill-based pay and gain sharing or employee share ownership. The importance of other features such as self-managing teams, indicates the need to take a wide-ranging view of the impact of a stable income plan.

Our experience mirrors the Lawler model in the UK and Ireland, particularly amongst multinationals and other leading-edge businesses.

So how does a stable income plan linked with annual hours make it easier to implement these other changes? Two specific aspects come to mind: first, a skill-based pay plan which gives more pay to those who are prepared to acquire and practise more job-related skills. The aim is greater job flexibility. Under conventional pay systems, earnings protectionism (see p. 280) will tend to inhibit this flexibility mechanism. Under a stable income plan the barriers are removed.

Second, the heavy commitment to training can be accommodated under annual hours in the following way:

1 hours are specifically set aside for training in the scheme design and these are set apart from planned work,
2 the training is then linked to skills acquisition and teamworking.

We find the good intentions of companies cannot be realised under conventional pay systems not only because of earnings protectionism, but also due to differences in over-time earning opportunity attaching to different jobs. One multinational I worked with found its highest trained and highest graded process operators applying to be fork lift truck drivers in the warehouse because of big differences in overtime opportunity.

These examples serve to illustrate the importance of getting the reward structure right at the outset, through the mechanism of a stable income plan. The plan can then be developed in relation to other initiatives which are in tune with the *future state* position of the company. In reality, the plan unblocks the current situation and allows the organisation to move towards continuous improvement.

CONCLUSION

There is no doubt that the growing popularity of stable income plans is well justified. It is likely that they will become the basis of reward systems in the future and in my experience will work well in businesses with at least some of these factors:

- in a seasonal and/or a volatile business position
- in a stable or growth market situation
- where benchmarking indicates an inadequate competitive position
- with average to high levels of paid overtime [beyond 10 per cent of worked hours]
- employing either full-time or part-time employees and with significant use of peripheral workers
- with absenteeism at 5 per cent or above
- with below adequate performance and motivation
- where a change programme is a business imperative.

The main disadvantage of a stable income plan initiative is that it requires a significant amount of organisational time and effort to put into place. But the payoff to the organisation can be assessed at the design stage prior to implementation and this will include an assessment of risks and costs.

I believe that those responsible for remuneration strategy in organisations will need to have stable income plans at the forefront of their thinking and planning in the future. Internal pressures for change will be reinforced by the external impact of EU regulations over working time in the next few years.

LEARNING ACTIVITIES

1 Review the cost of premium hours worked in your organisation and express them as a percentage of the total wage bill.

2 Analyse the number of premium hours worked in your organisation by occupational group or broad job grade and identify those groups or grades which work premium hours in excess of 10 per cent of total hours worked.

3 Develop a presentation for the senior management team putting forward a case for introducing annualised hours into an international airline for both professional and support staff.

4 Identify the factors which might indicate that the introduction of annualised hours would be inappropriate.

5 Review the demand profile in your organisation and determine how far out of alignment the worked hours are from the demand pattern.

REFERENCES

Lawler, E.E. (1982) 'Increasing Worker Involvement to Enhance Organisational Effectiveness', in P. Goodman (ed.), *Change in Organisations*. San Francisco: Jossey-Bass.

Lynch, P.H. (1991) 'Making Time for Productivity', *Personnel Management*. March, pp. 30–5.

FURTHER READING

Casey, B., Metcalfe, H. *et al.* (1997) *Employers use of Flexible Labour*. London Policy Studies Institute.

Pasfield, J. (1999) *Annual Hours Contracts and Working Time Transformation*. J.P. Associates.

Pitt, G. (1998) *Blackstone's Guide to Working Time*. Fairhurst, J. London: Blackstone.

16 Skills- and competency-based pay

Gill Homan

INTRODUCTION

Skills- and competency-based pay offers a different approach to the design of reward systems. Most payment systems are job based and concerned with outputs from the job, whether quality, productivity or some other measure. Skills- and competency-based pay is concerned with the person performing that job and the range of skills and competencies that the individual brings to their work. This approach to payment is not particularly new, as there have long been payment systems which place value on the acquisition of skills and experience over time (Mahoney, 1989). The old craft apprenticeship system awarded pay increases which recognised both the attainment of certified skill levels and the additional value offered by the building of practical experience and know-how gained, on the job, over time. Pay spines for teaching staff are a further example. Entry level to the 'spine' is normally based on qualification levels and years of experience. Progression up the 'spine' is by the acquisition of further qualifications or the perceived added value of additional years of experience, or both. Both of these examples can lead to two or more individuals carrying out the same job but being paid very different amounts, and moreover that situation being regarded as acceptable and the norm by those concerned.

Why then is skills- and competency-based pay regarded as something new and different in terms of its approach to the development of payment systems? The answer must be that it allows a wider range of organisations to build payment structures that enable the application of this form of payment system to much broader sections of the workforce or indeed the whole workforce, rather than just very specific groups or professions.

This chapter first explores the context in which skills- and competency-based pay has gained wider usage and the objectives of organisations adopting this approach to reward strategy. Second, the options for implementation, from simple to complex, are reviewed and assessed together with some of the issues and problems encountered in their introduction. Finally, current research on the extent to which this approach is utilised and the degree of success with which skills- and competency-based pay has achieved its objectives is surveyed, and its long-term future discussed.

DEFINING THE TERMS

For the purposes of this chapter the terms competency-based pay and skills-based pay are used synonymously, however, there are differences between the two both in terms of their definition and in the ways which they are derived, developed and utilised. Skills-based pay can be defined as 'person based and structured means of rewarding an individual for the acquisition, development, effective usage and upkeep of skills on a continuing basis' (Cross, 1994). Lawler (1996), records skills-based pay as having its origins in manufacturing industry in the 1960s particularly in start-up situations on greenfield sites. Mahoney (1989) sees skills-based pay as useful where 'variable task performance is dependent on skill level and career paths are based upon skill'.

Competency-based pay is more difficult to define because of the controversy surrounding the concept of competencies themselves (Ledford, 1995; Lawler, 1996). Ledford (1995) refers to competency-based pay as simply a re-labelling of skills-based pay to make it more acceptable to managers and knowledge workers. This debate extends to the ways in which the word itself is used, 'competency' generally being used where a behavioural approach is taken, whilst 'competence' tends to be used when defining standards to be achieved (IDS, 1997b). Lawler (1996) also questions the inclusion of personality traits as competencies, emphasising the difficulties of defining some of the 'softer' and the more 'intellectual' skills and behaviours that underpin performance (Brown and Armstrong, 1997, Sparrow, 1992). Finally, there is the issue of what constitutes competent performance. Does it refer to effective behaviour or excellent behaviour (Klein, 1996) . Many of these debates have yet to be resolved but for our purposes the definition of competencies is taken from the Income Data Services in IDS Study 639 (1997b). Competencies are 'the skills, knowledge, experience, attributes and behaviours that an individual needs to perform a job effectively'. Competency-based pay is a system which rewards individuals for the acquisition, development and effective use of these competencies.

THE CONTEXT FOR SKILLS- AND COMPETENCY-BASED PAY

The emergence of competency- and skills-based pay has been enabled by the interplay of a number of complex factors. These can be grouped under four main headings. They are the direction of structural and cultural change within organisations; the rise of human resource management and the notion of the strategic integration of human resource policies; both of these leading to the requirement for greater flexibility within core groups of employees; and an increasing focus on the individual as the unit of significance in human resource terms.

The increasing globalisation of markets (Lawler, 1991; White, 1991; Crouch, 1997) and the difficult economic and competitive climate of the 1980s and 1990s together with the impact of increased technological innovation (Claman, 1998) in the work place has resulted in significant changes to the structures of organisations (IDS 639, 1997b). The organisations of today are leaner, have fewer layers in the hierarchy and have adopted changed forms of operation, such as just-in-time production, team working, project-based working and matrix-based forms of management. These changes require a more flexible approach to working, one in which job boundaries are more fluid, and tightly defined job descriptions seem inappropriate and counter productive. Wider spans of control within these delayered organisations require individuals capable of working within much wider frames of reference and able to address problems creatively, without constant reference to higher management. Changes in structures and processes have been matched by changes in culture, most commonly attempts by organisations to become more quality focused and customer oriented. These developments are, in the main, employee led, thus it is the individual employee's ability to become more responsive to customer requirements and more aware of quality standards and techniques that enable these changes to be achieved.

The rise of strategic human resource management and its relationship to corporate strategy has been charted extensively in the literature. One of the major tenets of that literature has been the notion of strategic integration, both vertical, that is that human resource strategy should both support and feed into corporate strategy (Lengnick-Hall and Lengnick-Hall, 1988; Schuler and Jackson, 1987), and horizontal. Horizontal integration implies that the various components of a human resource strategy, for example, recruitment and retention, development, reward, performance management, communications and employee relations strategies should support and reinforce each other (Guest, 1987). This level of synergy between policies is difficult to achieve not least because each of the components tends to have a different cycle of decay and therefore to be reviewed on divergent time scales but also because organisations have a varying range of factors to be considered in the design and renewal of each component. For example, it is likely that an organisation may have to consider more constraints in the design and a greater level of consultation and negotiation in the introduction of a new reward system, that of a training and development strategy. Any concept that seems to offer a framework for the integration of the components of human resource strategy is therefore going to generate a good deal of interest. Such has been the case with the competence approach to human resources (Hooghiemstra, 1992). Croner (1996) sees competencies as 'providing the ideal medium to translate corporate values into tangible indicators for every job holder . . . using a common everyday language'.

Atkinson's (1984) original model of the flexible firm describes a central core of permanent employees, highly trained, multi-skilled and rewarded in line with their value to the organisation. From a perspective over 15 years further on we can add further dimensions to Atkinson's vision of the core employee. For many organisations it is not sufficient that their employees are multi-skilled, those skills need to be constantly reviewed in the light of changing task demands and their reward policy must ensure that it supports this need and that the acquisition and updating of skills is perceived by employees as valued and rewarded by the organisation. The changing structures of organisations call for flexibility in other ways, not least of which is that of employee career paths (Crouch, 1997).

The reduction in the number of levels in the hierarchy of organisations has resulted in the loss of clearly defined career paths for many individuals. Organisations too have struggled to find ways, within traditional job-evaluation-based structures, to reward those whose value remains within a specialist field, but who may not exercise responsibility for staff or financial resources which usually carry heavy weighting in such systems. Competency-based systems address both of these concerns to some degree (Lawler, 1991; Ledford, 1995).

All of the issues discussed in this section have highlighted the increasing focus on the individual as the unit of significance within organisations today. Many carry within their mission statement a recognition of this factor. Barham (1988 in Legge, 1995) quotes, amongst others BMW. 'At BMW there is a new concentration on the individual. We have got to achieve as far as we can a self-organising company and this means that there has to be more individual responsibility.' Individuals too have a greater need to focus on their own development and skills profile to equip themselves for a job market in which there is far less security and greater competition than before.

Given these developments organisations have looked to find a reward system that can encourage the behaviours that can gain and sustain commitment to these developments. Significant numbers have found that answer to varying degrees of success within skills- and competency-based pay systems.

THE OBJECTIVES OF SKILLS- AND COMPETENCY-BASED PAY

The literature provides a wealth of practical case studies detailing the reasons given by organisations for their move to skills- or competency-based pay. By far the most frequently quoted objectives that organisations are seeking to achieve by the introduction of skills- or competency-based pay are the support of some form of change initiative, the pursuit of flexibility or the need to build a broader skills base within the organisation.

The change initiatives in the areas of culture included those focused around quality (Lawler, 1992), developing a customer-oriented culture (White, 1991; Olorenshaw, 1994; Armstrong and Murlis, 1994; McNerney, 1995; Falconer, 1992; CEPU, 1996) and the desire to build a high commitment, high involvement learning culture (Armstrong and Murlis, 1994; Falconer, 1992; IDS, 1995a; Klein, 1998; Lawler, 1992). The need to support or reinforce structural change, particularly delayering, featured strongly (Olorenshaw, 1994; Falconer, 1992; IDS, 1998; Klein, 1998), as do changes to work systems, such as the introduction of team working (Armstrong and Murlis, 1994; McNerney, 1995; Falconer, 1992; Lawler, 1992). The need for flexibility provided by a wider skills base and the elimination or reduction of job boundaries and demarcation was seen as a key objective by many organisations (White, 1991; Armstrong and Murlis, 1994; McNerney, 1995; Falconer, 1992; Wagel, 1989; IDS, 1996; IDS, 1995a; IDS, 1995b; IDS, 1998; CEPU, 1996; Klein, 1998; Ledford, 1991; Lawler, 1992). Flexibility is seen to offer the organisation the opportunity to work leaner, enable problem solving at lower levels and give better coverage during absence.

Introducing a skills- or competency-based payment system was seen as a way of signalling to employees the value that the organisation places upon what the individual brings to the job (Cascio, 1995; IDS, 1995b; Klein, 1998; Brown and Armstrong, 1997) with a view to aiding retention (White, 1991; IDS, 1995b; CEPU, 1996; Ledford, 1991), raising levels of job satisfaction and self-esteem and the ability to minimise lay-offs by moving people to other jobs within a wider range of capability (Klein, 1998; Lawler, Chang and Ledford, 1993).

Additional objectives stated included the opportunity to manage out poor performers, marginalise union influence and to reinforce the devolution of pay and performance management decisions to line management within the context of a changing role for the human resources function (Olorenshaw, 1994).

There was also recognition that competency- and skills-based pay systems could offer a partial response to the problems of the changing psychological contract. Whilst organisations cannot offer a 'job for life' or in many cases the traditional upward career paths, they can offer the opportunity to develop an increased range of skills and therefore increased marketability and the opportunity to increase earnings by lateral development (White, 1991; Armstrong and Murlis, 1994; Falconer, 1992; IDS, 1998; Klein, 1998; Lawler, 1992).

Competency- and skills-based pay systems were also seen as a means to deal with the managerial/technical divide. Highly skilled knowledge or technical workers often do not score highly under the old job evaluation schemes because they tend not to have high levels of responsibility for finance or staffing, both of which tend to carry heavy weightings (Lawler, 1992), these can be recognised and rewarded within these systems.

Finally, competency- and skills-based payment systems were seen as transparent and passing the 'felt fair' test (Wagel, 1989; Klein, 1998; Lawler, Chang and Ledford, 1993; Olorenshaw, 1994), to offer opportunities for harmonisation of payment systems and to reduce existing complexities (IDS, 1995b).

SKILLS- AND COMPETENCY-BASED REWARD SYSTEMS – ISSUES IN DEVELOPMENT AND DESIGN

There are a number of writers on reward that describe the process of developing a skills- or competency-based pay system (Armstrong and Murlis, 1994; Milkovitch and Newman, 1996). There is broad agreement about the process involved in the design of a skills- and competency-based system (Ledford, 1991; Bunning, 1992) though there are differences expressed about the most appropriate initial step. Armstrong and Murlis (1994)) advocate starting with the identification of the jobs or tasks to be included in the system, whereas Lawler (1991) begins with the establishment of a core principle, and Bunning (1992) favours a review of the appropriate models available to establish the steps to be undertaken.

All recognise the importance of the analysis of the jobs or tasks and their component skills or competencies. Many organisations that have completed this process emphasise the importance of including a wide range of stakeholders at this stage in the process. These include line management, whose involvement is seen as critical (Ledford, 1991), the appropriate trade unions (IDS, 1996) and the workforce involved. In addition, useful information and guidance can be gained from external sources, such as industry lead bodies and the study of other companies that have already been through the process.

Milkovich and Newman (1996) define skills analysis as 'a systematic process to identify and collect information about the skills required to perform work in an organisation'. They define competency analysis as 'a systematic process to identify and collect information about the competencies required for a person and organisation to be successful'. One can see from these definitions that a competency-based system has a much wider remit and a closer linkage to broad organisation strategy. The definition of the competencies must begin with a consensus about what constitutes organisational success and the contribution of the individual to that success. This is the point at which the diversity of options becomes apparent (Milkovich and Newman, 1996; Ledford, 1995). A number of choices have to be made which will profoundly influence the design of the system. For example, are the component skills and competencies to be expressed in a generic form or as narrow tightly defined competencies? Should they emphasise depth or breadth? Will the statement cover just the skills and competencies in current use or will new skills be included, what is the balance between current work competencies and those seen as desirable or necessary for the future? What will be their predicted stability over time? Another issue concerns whether the statements will identify and provide a framework for differing levels of competence. This can form the basis for a performance or merit element to the scheme (Lawler, 1992). In writing up the skills and competence statements, most writers emphasise the importance of achieving transparency by avoiding complexity and aiming to express them in a common and easily understood language, which avoids jargon. Having identified the skills and competencies the next stage in the process is to form them into skills blocks or levels. Many writers see this as the most difficult stage in the design process. Most advocate trying to keep the system simple with six to eight headings for the skills blocks. The blocks themselves should be of equal weight with a mixture of repetitive and complex skills or competencies. This will ensure that some blocks are not easier to attain than others and make for ease of allocating monetary value. An uneven construction of the skills blocks may result in pathways developing through the system where 'difficult' blocks are avoided or seen as providing poor value for the assigned award.

There also needs to be a strategy linking the blocks to meet the organisation's need for flexibility. Lawler, Chang and Ledford (1993) propose following the steps in the production process or differentiating prescribed routes between different job families. The route for progression through the blocks and levels must be clear, with the degree of choice in progression spelt out, together with any time required to be spent at one level before progression to the next can take place. Any 'gates' designed to manage the flow of employees to the highest levels of the scheme will have to be clearly identified (Lawler, Chang and Ledford, 1993).

A number of models are available to help with the task of linking the skills blocks (see Cross, 1994; Roberts, 1996; Cofsky, 1993; Milkovitch, 1995 amongst others). The most common forms are the ladder-based systems which arrange skills blocks vertically and generally offer a straightforward sequential progression. Variations on this model include a common base ladder for core skills blocks diverging into two or more specialised routes, and the skills blocks arranged in order that trainees can vary the order in which they undertake the training for each block. Ladder models can also be designed to give an amount of overlap, that is, the point of entry for the second and subsequent blocks is one or two blocks lower than the highest block of the previous level (see figure 16.1). This allows for entry into the system at a higher level for those with higher qualifications but lacking experience.

More complex matrix systems allow for the application of skills- and competency-based pay systems to greater numbers of or the whole workforce. They also allow the integration of external qualifications, internal training and planned experience (see figure 16.2).

Training for the system is a major element of the design (Lawler, Chang and Ledford, 1993). The training programmes for each block will have to be designed and decisions

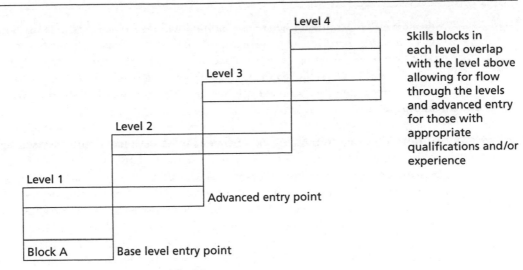

Skills blocks in each level overlap with the level above allowing for flow through the levels and advanced entry for those with appropriate qualifications and/or experience

Fig. 16.1 An integrated ladder system

Job families	Technical	Management	Engineering	Sales	Quality
Entry points		Internal Skills Blocks			Level 4
Degree or equiv.					Level 3
HNC/D or equiv.					Level 2
ONC/D or equiv. Base level					Level 1

Each level contains skills blocks which must be completed to achieve a complete level.

The achievement of external qualifications and time in each block may be designated before progression can take place.

Each level will normally have an entry and maximum pay level. Progress between the two is by successful completion of the designated skills block, external qualification and experience level.

Jobs within the organisation may specify different routes i.e. appropriate blocks from different job families and levels.

Fig. 16.2 A matrix system

about who will train and where the training will take place. Trainers can include peers and team members, line management, internal and external specialists and educational establishments. Training can take place off the job, off site, or on the job. Most organisations tend towards the majority of training taking place on the job. This then requires a large investment in trainer skills for those in the work place that will be undertaking this role.

The skill or competence may not be accredited purely on the training alone, a length of time allocated to building experience may be designated and assessed by means of a log detailing the time spent on or practise of the component skills or competencies. Assessment and accreditation systems also need to be established at this stage in the design process, particularly any links to externally certificated schemes, such as National Vocational Qualifications. Assessors will have to be designated and trained and a robust recording system set up, failure to give these issues sufficient attention can damage the credibility of the scheme lead to accusations of bias and lack of consistency and result in the scheme losing its 'felt fair' standing. There will also have to be policies relating to the upkeep and re-test of skills and competencies to ensure their currency, the regular review of the competencies and skills themselves to ensure that training in redundant skills is not taking place and, finally, a policy for dealing with those who fail assessments.

It is likely that any organisations with trade unions will find that these systems will generate an interest in training issues (Crouch, 1997) that, perhaps, has not been in evidence previously. Their concerns are likely to centre on the selection for and progression through training, the organisation's ability to provide the resources to meet the demand for training, the fairness and consistency of the assessment process and the treatment of those who fail. Organisations may find themselves pressured to have an appeals process for these issues (CPRE, 1995; CEPU, 1996).

The next stage of the system design is to develop the monetary framework. Issues to be dealt with include the establishment of the minimum and the range to any maximum remuneration levels. Market data are usually the means of establishing these though organisations will find bench marking these systems more difficult (Ledford, 1991). Determining what constitutes a payment block and how much each block should receive is the next key stage, here internal equity is important, that is that the payment blocks are relatively equal to each other and that any overlaps in the payment of each level are established.

At what stage payment for each block is made also needs to be defined: is this to be after the training has been accredited, after competence has been established on the job or after a specific length or breadth of experience attained?

Finally a system of monitoring and evaluation needs to be designed into the system to measure whether it is achieving its objectives for the organisation and meeting the needs of the workforce for whom it is designed.

THE PROBLEMS AND ISSUES IN INTRODUCTION

The introduction of a skills- or competency-based payment system involves a major change and therefore attracts all the difficulties inherent in changing any part of the reward package. It is not an easy task to establish the basic principle of exactly what an organisation wants their payment system to achieve (Fierman, 1994;

Heyes, 1996). Change often involves eliminating long-standing practices, such as overtime payments and commission that is likely to meet with substantial resistance from the workforce (Heyes, 1996) and if any system is to be effective it must ensure that it embodies the 'felt fair' principle and engages the commitment of the target groups.

Skills- and competency-based payment systems, however, also have particular difficulties associated with their introduction. These difficulties relate to all phases of the system, design, introduction, transition, operation, maintenance and decay, as well as broader difficulties, such as equality, the role of trade unions, the impact on the management hierarchy and the change in organisational culture and climate that the move to an individually based system from a job-based system entails. The difficulties associated with the design of a system have been discussed fully earlier in this chapter. It is worth repeating, however, that the design phase is crucial to the effectiveness of the system and that it is resource intensive in terms of both cost and time and requires the involvement of all levels of the organisation in the definition of the skills/competencies on which the system is to be based (Ledford, 1991). Achieving this involvement may require substantial investment in communication to overcome the resistance to the idea of change and the move away from a familiar and understood system of wage and salary determination.

Implementation inevitably brings with it the first and probably most intrusive period of training. In the transition period this may leave work teams weaker (Fierman, 1994) and creat tensions between the need to manage both the training and the maintenance of work flows at the same time (Falconer, 1992) and may even generate conflict within work teams if team members resent the absence of colleagues at this time (Fierman, 1994). The organisation also has to develop a policy to deal with failure (Lawler, Chang and Ledford, 1993). Do those that fail to achieve the required level of competency have the opportunity to retrain, if so, how many opportunities do they receive, and what action is taken.

The organisation may have within it those who have not undertaken training of any sort for some considerable time and who express fear and insecurity now that, effectively, their pay will be linked to their ability to learn. This may require the organisation to introduce some 'returning to learning' or 'learning to learn' training prior to the system-based training.

Many problems in the transition phase relate to fears expressed by the workforce that the new system is designed to deliver savings by cutting pay. These can often be calmed by issuing definite statements that no one will receive a pay cut. Dewey (1994), identifies three major transition issues relating to pay. The first of these concerns the assessment for initial placement within the system. This can take a long period of time where there are large numbers of staff involved. Dewey advocates placing people initially at the most appropriate place for their current wage and adjusting at a later stage, then ensuring that all initial assessments take place as soon as possible. Alignment is a further concern raised by Dewey. What action to take with those who are under-paid or overpaid for their skill level following initial assessment. For those overpaid Dewey suggests isolating the amount of the over-payment on the payslip and negotiating a time frame within which the employee will have to 'catch up' their skills or lose the over-payment remaining at the end of the period. Under-payment, especially if large numbers are involved can be expensive for the organisation to deal with at the initial assessment stage. Here Dewey recommends negotiating a phased schedule for catching up, which sets a definite time frame for completion. These points are obviously going to be major concerns of any unions involved.

Once the system is implemented the successful operation of the system can also generate problems and issues. Administratively, competency- and skills-based systems are complex, though in different ways than, for example, job-evaluation-based systems. With this type of system each employee is administered as an individual, therefore there are few of the volume advantages offered by job-based systems (Lawler, 1991; Armstrong and Murlis, 1994). The training systems involved must also be robust enough to deliver the required monitoring and progression information to the payroll system accurately and on time. These records will almost inevitably be more complex (Cascio, 1995; Armstrong and Murlis, 1994) and require input from more sources than those previously used to service the training and personnel functions alone.

The introduction of a competency- or skills-based pay system may have the effect of dramatically increasing the demand for training, creating bottlenecks at various stages. This can be addressed by ensuring that the definition of training is sufficiently wide, and establishing contracts with each individual or team which offers a realistic framework for access to training (Dewey, 1994). Managers behaviour can often contribute to these blockages (Falconer, 1992), if they lack commitment, are inconsistent or have time pressures which prevent them providing sufficient training time.

Utilisation of the range of skills developed both to ensure effectiveness and to keep the skills current requires continual attention to the organisation and management of the workforce, failure to achieve this can lead to a substantially over-skilled workforce and an inflated payroll (Olorenshaw, 1994; Cascio, 1995; Armstrong and Murlis, 1994). Certain aspects of a scheme need to be carefully managed to avoid conflict, particularly the application of 'gates' or quotas to control the upward push towards the top level or grade.

Equality and organisational politics are issues with all payment systems, and skills- and competency-based systems are no exception. It is possible for bias to be designed in at the development stage inhibiting the assessment stage and affecting its operation (Strebler, Thompson and Heron, 1997; Hay et al., 1996; Heyes, 1996; Klein, 1996; Gupta and Jenkins, 1996). Klein, calls for special care to be taken at the analysis and development stage of the competency statements and assessments and that testing for validity, reliability and bias in these takes place. Others (Gupta and Jenkins, 1996) suggest keeping records of access and progression of all employees in case of claims.

Lawler, Chang and Ledford (1993), Klein (1998) and Fierman (1994) all point out that the initial design of the pay system is likely to be flawed and that there has to be recognition that the original skills and competencies on which the system is based will inevitably have to be amended and allowed to evolve within the system as it matures, Ledford (1991) refers to these as 'course corrections'. Too rigid an approach can lead to the system achieving a poor fit with the organisation's needs and losing credibility quickly.

Introducing skills- and competency-based pay is a costly process, as is the updating and maintenance of the system. These costs may be considered a fair price for the flexibility and other advantages that the system offers. Competency- and skills-based pay systems do not offer financial flexibility. That is the ability to vary the payroll costs in relation to the changing financial performance of the organisation. This can be a real disadvantage which may affect considerably the numbers of organisations willing to adopt this form of payment system.

THE EXTENT TO WHICH COMPETENCY- AND SKILLS-BASED PAY HAS BEEN ADOPTED

There is evidence, building over the last ten years, of a gradual increase in the numbers of organisations using skills- and competency-based pay for all or part of their workforce. The extent of the evidence would seem to suggest that skills- and competency-based pay is now an established means of determining base pay for a significant number of organisations both in the USA and the UK.

In 1983 some 40 per cent of companies in the Fortune top 1,000 index used this form of pay for all or some of their workforce (Bunning, 1992). By 1993 that had increased to 60 per cent (Ledford, 1995) covering approximately 20 per cent of the working population. In the UK and Europe there have been two very recent studies which have reviewed the current situation. A 1997 survey by Towers Perrin (Learning From the Past; Changing for the Future) looked at 300 multi-national companies operating in Europe. It reported that 20 per cent were linking skills and competencies to pay, whilst a further 50 per cent saw it as one of their top three reward priorities over the next three years.

An Industrial Society survey of 1998 (Managing Best Practice Series No. 43; Competency Based Pay), covered 344 human resource specialists from a range of organisations. Their findings showed that a third of companies either already had a competency-based pay system in place or would do so within the next 12 months. It also found that of employers with competency-based pay systems 53 per cent believed that they were popular with employees as opposed to 5 per cent who thought that they were unpopular.

Anyone wishing to look, in detail, at organisations moving to skills- and competency-based pay can find case studies regularly within the Income Data Services Reports, a number of which feature in the reference section of this chapter and their studies, for example 610 (1996) Paying for Multi-Skilling and 500 (1992) Skill Based Pay. There is, therefore evidence of the take-up of this form of determining pay. There is less evidence of its success or failure. Perhaps because of the relative newness of these systems there is very little research reported of a long-term nature which would give firm evidence of the extent to which skills- and competency-based pay systems achieve their many and varied objectives.

Such evidence that there is tends to be favourable. Sun Alliance (Olorenshaw, 1994) reports improvements and target achievement in the areas of productivity, skills acquisition and cost reduction. Parent and Weber (1994) studied two Canadian plants over a period of ten months and found that the plant operating a skills-based pay system showed significant advantage in skills acquisition, quality, employee involvement, lower staff turnover, lower accident rates and improved cost reduction. It showed, however, a poorer record of productivity, though they point out that this may have been due to significant differences in the age of the operating plant. Murray and Gerhart (1998) conducted a study of two comparable companies, one using skills- and competency-based pay and one not. Their study, however, took place over 37 months. They examined productivity levels, labour costs and quality outcomes. Results indicated 58 per cent greater productivity, 16 per cent lower labour costs and 82 per cent improved scrap reduction at the organisation using skills- and competency-based pay. These are extremely impressive results, but it would be difficult to give an unqualified endorsement to skills- and competency-based pay without further evidence preferably from the UK and, or Europe. What it does indicate is a very substantial research gap in this field.

Nevertheless what can be said is that such evidence that there is points to skills- and competency-based pay having the potential to offer real opportunities for competitive advantage in hard financial terms. At the same time it appears to be favourably received by employees and to impact favourably on their approach to and satisfaction with their work.

THE FUTURE FOR SKILLS- AND COMPETENCY-BASED PAY

It would seem that in terms of added value skills- and competency-based pay has a lot to offer organisations. This is particularly true when the organisation is restructuring and attempting to change. It fits well with the current notions of lifelong learning and with human capital theory (Milkovich and Newman, 1996) and would seem to offer a way forward for the knowledge-based and flexible workers of the future. Why then has the take up of this form of payment system not been even greater than current evidence shows. Payment systems are notoriously difficult to change and with its relatively new and difficult to understand concepts organisations may well shy away from a system where the design process is both crucial and extremely complex or they may not possess, internally, the expertise to progress it.

It is also difficult and requires a large commitment of resources to the training, assessment and certification of skills and competencies. This may well prove a barrier to many organisations. Additionally the fact that the system offers little ability to vary payroll costs with the fortunes of the organisation, unlike, for example, some performance-based systems, may also limit its spread.

Nevertheless the skills- and competency-based pay systems would seem to offer a real opportunity to reinforce effective cultures and achieve effective performance for many organisations. Whether this advantage is of a temporary nature, useful whilst the organisation is in transition or over periods of sustained change and less useful during more stable periods, is yet to be determined. Further research is needed here. Additionally it will be interesting to observe whether these systems remain popular during differing financial circumstances. Again more research is required.

Its impact on and seeming popularity with those employees that have experienced these systems can also not be ignored. Any payment system has to satisfy all parties if it is to sustain its purposes of attracting, retaining and delivering the human resources needed by the organisation. Skills- and competency-based payment systems appear on current evidence to offer one means of achieving this.

LEARNING ACTIVITIES

1 To what extent do competencies underpin the human resource processes in your organisation.

2 Assess the extent to which role flexibility is essential, desirable or non-essential in the different functions of your organisation. Express this as a table.

3 To what extent can the introduction of skills- and competency-based pay support the development of a learning culture?

4 What support and review mechanisms need to be established to ensure that a skills- or competency-based pay system remains effective?

REFERENCES

Armstrong, M. and Brown, D. (1998) 'Relating Competencies to Pay: The UK experience', *Compensation and Benefits Review*, 30(3): 28–39.

Armstrong, M. and Murlis, H. (1994) *Reward Management: A handbook of remuneration strategy and practice*. Third edition, London: Kogan Page/IPD.

Atkinson, J. (1984) 'Manpower Strategies for Flexible Organisations', *Personnel Management*, 16(8): 28–31.

Brown, D. and Armstrong, M. (1997) 'Terms of Enrichment', *People Management*, 11 September, 36–8.

Bunning, R.L. (1992) 'Models for Skill-Based Pay Plans', *Human Resources Magazine*, February.

Cascio, W.F. (1995) *Managing Human Resources: Productivity, quality of working life, profits*. Fourth edition, New York and London: McGraw Hill.

Claman, P.H. (1998) 'Work Has Changed, But Our Compensation Programs Have Not', *Compensation and Benefits Management*, Winter, 1–6.

Cofsky, K.M. (1993) 'Critical Keys to Competency Based Pay', *Compensation and Benefits Review*, 25(6): 46–52.

Communication, Electrical and Plumbing Union (1996) 'Competency Based Training and Pay Structure Agreement (Telstra Corporation Ltd.)', CEPU Internet Database, July.

CPRE (1995) 'Reinventing Teacher Compensation Plans', *Financial Briefs Series*, September.

Croner (1996) *Pay and Benefits Sourcebook*. Southampton: Croner Publications Limited, pp. 6–8.

Cross, M. (1994) 'Competence Based Approaches to Pay', Paper to IPD National Conference, Harrogate.

Crouch, C. (1997) 'Skills Based Full Employment: The latest philosopher's stone', *British Journal of Industrial Relations*, 35(3): 367–91.

Dewey, B.J. (1994) 'Changing to Skill-based Pay: Disarming the transition land mines', *Compensation and Benefits Review*, 26(1): 38–43.

Falconer, H. (1992) 'Learning to Climb the Wages Ladder', *Personnel Today*, 23 February, 25.

Fierman, J. (1994) 'The Perilous New World of Fair Pay', *Fortune*, 129(12): 57–61.

Guest, D.E. (1987) 'Human Resource Management and Industrial Relations', *Journal of Management Sudies*, 24(5): 503–21.

Gupta, N. and Jenkins, G.D. Jr. (1996) 'The Politics of Pay', *Compensation and Benefits Review*, 28(2): 23–30.

Hay Group, Hewitt Associates LLC, Towers Perrin and William Mercer Inc. (1996) 'Raising the Bar: Using competencies to enhance employee performance', ACA Research Reports.

Heyes, J. (1996) 'A Formula for Success? Training, Reward and Commitment in a Chemicals Plant', *British Journal of Industrial Relations*, 34(3): 351–69.

Hofrichter, D.A. and Spencer, L.M. Jr. (1996) 'Competencies: The right foundation for effective human resources management', *Compensation and Benefits Review*, 8(6): 21–4.

Hooghiemstra, T. (1992) 'Integrated Management of Human Resources', in A. Mitrani, M. Dalziel and D. Fitt (eds), *Competency Based Human Resource Management*. Guildford: Kogan Page.

Income Data Services (1992) 'Skill Based Pay', IDS Study 500, February.

Income Data Services (1995a) 'Case Study: TWR Steering Systems', IDS Report 692, July, 28–29.

Income Data Services (1995b) 'Case Study: Skills Based Pay', IDS Report 698, October, 28–29.

Income Data Services (1996) 'Case Study: SKF (UK)', IDS Report 720, September, 29–31.

Income Data Services (1996) 'Paying For Multi-Skilling', IDS Study 610, September.

Income Data Services (1997a) IDS Report 741, July, 12–13.

Income Data Services (1997b) 'Developing Competency Frameworks', IDS Study 639, December.

Income Data Services (1998) 'Case Study: Motorola', IDS Report 762, June, 29–31.

Industrial Society (1998) 'Competency Based Pay', Managing Best Practice Series No. 43, London, Industrial Society.

Klein, G.D. (1996) 'Validity and Reliability for Competency Based Systems: Reducing litigation risks', *Compensation and Benefits Review*, 28(4): 31–7.

Klein, G.D. (1998) 'A Pay for Knowledge Compensation Program That Works', *Compensation and Benefits Review*, 30(2): 69–75.

Lawler, E.E. III (1991) 'Paying the Person: A better approach to management?', *Human Resource Management Review*, 1(2): 145–54.

Lawler, E.E. III (1992) 'Pay the Person, Not the Job', *Industry Week*, 241(23): 18–22.

Lawler, E.E. III, Chang, L. and Ledford, G.E. Jr. (1993) 'Who Uses Skill-based Pay and Why', *Compensation and Benefits Review*, 25(2): 22–26.

Lawler, E.E. III (1996) 'Competencies: A poor performance for the new pay', *Compensation and Benefits Review*, 28(6): 20–25.

Ledford, G.E. Jr. (1991) 'Three Case Studies on Skill-based Pay': An overview, *Compensation and Benefits Review*, 23(2): 11–23.

Ledford, G.E. Jr. (1995) 'Paying for the Skills, Knowledge and Competencies of Knowledge Workers', *Compensation and Benefits Review*, 27(4): 55–62.

Legge, K. (1995) *Human Resource Management: Rhetoric and realities*. Chippenham: Macmillan.

Lengnick-Hall, C.A. and Lengnick-Hall, M.L. (1988) 'Strategic Human Resources Management: A review of the literature and a proposed typology', *Academy of Management Review*, 13(3): 454–70.

Mahoney, T.A. (1989) 'Multiple Pay Contingencies: The strategic design of compensation', *Human Resource Management*, 28(3): 337–347.

McNerney, D.J. (1995) 'Compensation Case Study: Rewarding team performance and individual skill building', *HR Focus*, 72(1): 1–3.

Milkovich, G.T. and Newman, J.M. (1996) *Compensation*. Fifth edition, USA: Irwin.

Murray, B. and Gerhart, B. (1998) 'An Empirical Analysis of a Skill-based Program and Plant Performance Outcomes', *Academy of Management Journal*, 41(1): 68–78.

Olorenshaw, R. (1994) IPD National Conference Paper, 25–8 October.

Parent, K.J. and Weber, C.L. (1994) 'Case Study: Does paying for knowledge pay off?', *Compensation and Benefits Review*, 26(5): 44–50.

Perrin, T. (1997) 'Learning from the Past: Changing for the Future', A Research Study of Pay and Reward Challenges and Changes in Europe.

Roberts, G. (1996) *Pay: Strategy, design and negotiation*. England, Technical Communications Publications Ltd.

Schuler, R.S. and Jackson, S.E. (1987) 'Linking Competitive Strategies with Human Resource Management Practices', *Academy of Management Executive*, 1(3): 209–13.

Sparrow, P. (1992) 'Building Human Resource Strategies Around Competencies: A life cycle model', *Manchester Practices*, Academy of Management Executives, 1(3): 209–13.

Strebler, M. Thompson, M. and Heron, P. (1997) 'Skills, Competencies and Gender: Issues for pay and training', Southampton, Institute for Employment Studies/Equal Opportunities Commission.

Wagel, W.H. (1989) 'At Sola Opthalmics, Paying for Skills Pays Off', *Personnel*, March, 20–24.

White, M. (1991) 'Linking Compensation to Knowledge Will Pay Off in the 1990s', *Planning Review*, 15–17.

FURTHER READING

Armstrong, M. and Murlis, H. (1994) *Reward Management: A handbook of remuneration strategy and practice*. Third edition, London: Kogan Page IPD.

Cascio, W.F. (1995) *Managing Human Resources: Productivity, quality of working life, profits*. Fourth edition, New York and London: McGraw Hill.

Income Data Services (1996) 'Paying for Multi-Skilling', IDS Study 610, September.

Income Data Services (1997) 'Developing Competency Frameworks', IDS Study 639, December, IDS.

Industrial Society (1998) Competency Based Pay, Managing Best Practice Series No. 43, London, Industrial Society.

17 Performance-related pay

Peter Lawson

INTRODUCTION

Whilst there has been a long tradition of relating performance to pay in the blue-collar jobs in the UK it was only in the late 1970s that performance-related pay started to replace fixed incremental systems in white-collar work. Relating performance to pay is now commonplace in jobs from the board-room to the shop floor.

This chapter concentrates on performance-related pay as it is used to reward all those from the boardroom to the shop floor – both professional and manual employees.

The chapter begins by looking at various definitions of performance-related pay before identifying its defining characteristics. It is then described in some detail and particular examples of different applications are briefly summarised. The variety of purposes which organisations claim from the introduction of a performance-related pay system indicates their importance as systems of performance management.

The theory which underpins performance-related pay and the way that managers use that theory to develop explanations and strategies for improving individual and organisational performance are dealt with before we look at the research evidence concerning perceptions of and the outcomes from performance-related pay. Much of this research evidence is critical about the impact of performance-related pay. The difficulties experienced in practice by users are also examined.

The chapter concludes with a brief summary of claimed good practice in the area and also looks forward to the future development of performance-related pay.

PERFORMANCE-RELATED PAY DEFINED

The term performance-related pay is often used generically to refer to all the many ways in which performance and pay have been linked in order to motivate people at work to improve their performance.

For example, the 1990 definition set out below acknowledges the breadth and depth of the links which have been made between pay and performance. However the definition quickly begins to limit its scope and also to identify two categories of performance-related pay, the distinction between the two being seen in terms of the mechanism by which the levels of performance-related pay are determined and the measures by which performance is assessed.

> Theoretically, performance related pay could include all types of incentive schemes outside direct payments by results, hence it would include Profit Sharing, as well as Employee Share Ownership . . . We must further distinguish two basic types of performance related pay. First those that relate to some quantifiable index of performance such as 'added value' which essentially refers to the value added by the production process to raw materials and production costs or to an index of output quality, or to a combination of both. Second, those that seek to enhance individual performance against specifiable criteria as well as taking individual characteristics into account. Sometimes referred to as merit pay the rationale of this type of scheme is to introduce non output related performance standards by providing goals for individual workers (often a manager or white collar employee) to strive for. Examples may be found in both the public and private sectors. (University of Strathclyde, 1990)

It is the second category identified above which is of interest to us in this chapter although the former Institute of Personnel Management, also in 1990, offered a definition which is so wide in its scope and so brief in its explanation that it rules practically everything in and nothing out.

> Performance of related pay is the explicit link of financial reward to individual, group or company performance (or any combination of the three). (Personnel Management, 1990)

The Institute of Management is much more helpful by confirming the link between pay and performance but also indicating briefly how this link may be made and also what is paid and also how it is paid.

> Performance-related pay links additional payments, over and above basic salary and cost of living increases, to an assessment of an individual's performance. Each employee is set targets or objectives at the beginning of the year and is then assessed on them at the end. Depending on how well they have done, they are awarded a sum of money which is paid on top of next year's salary. Performance-related pay is appropriate for both individuals and teams. (Institute of Management, C.I., 43)

Armstrong and Murlis (1994) add an additional consideration by widening the concept of performance to include both competence and pay progression. Competence we may understand as work related behaviours and pay progression embraces the notion of both increases in pay and of the movement of pay across and up pay bands and scales.

> Performance-related pay links pay progression to a performance and/or competence rating. The rating could be carried out during a performance review or it could be conducted at different times specifically for PRP purposes . . . it normally provides for an increase in base pay which is governed by a rating against such criteria as performance and contribution outputs and skill and competence inputs. There may be provision, however, in some schemes for achievement bonuses to be paid in certain circumstances which are also determined on the basis of ratings carried out by managers on the individual's performance etc.

In summary then, rather than attempting a tight, comprehensive definition of performance-related pay, it is, perhaps, more useful to identify the defining characteristics of performance-related pay schemes. Thus, the diversity of schemes that might be called performance-related can be as follows:

- where individual performance criteria are established so that actual individual performance can be judged or assessed against the performance criteria established
- where links are established between the level of individual performance as assessed and the level of reward received by the individual
- where the actual relationship between pay and performance is established by a managerial assessment of performance which may be based on either objective or subjective criteria
- where it is assumed that these links will lead to increased organisational performance through improved individual performance which arises from higher rewards for improved performance
- where a formal performance management system is used to establish the linkage between the performance of the individual and the performance of the organisation

PERFORMANCE-RELATED PAY DESCRIBED

Therefore a performance-related pay scheme is one which provides for payments to individuals at work which are related to their performance. In some schemes performance-related payment is also linked to an individual's position in the pay range. Performance-related pay schemes are bespoke designed for specific applications so that the performance assessment ratings and the payments associated with them will vary from application to application and will depend upon circumstances, including the competitive position of the organisation involved.

The rationale for performance-related pay is to improve the performance of the organisation through motivating individuals to improve their performance. It is argued that performance-related pay achieves its objectives by motivating all people in the organisation; by focusing attention on the key areas which will improve overall performance. The literature also makes a number of other significant claims for performance-related pay: such as, it communicates information about the performance expectations of the organisation; it helps the organisation become more results or performance focused or it supports existing cultures or values which are already characterised by high performance, innovation, quality and teamwork; it can also emphasise the importance of teamwork as well as individual effort; it can improve recruitment and retention of high-quality employees who will expect that their high performance will be appropriately rewarded; it ensures that the pay bill varies in line with performance. It is difficult to see how all these claims can be met and indeed how individual schemes are designed to ensure that only the desired outcomes are achieved.

Very often performance-related pay is related to a formal performance management system in which individuals agree work targets or objectives and their performance is assessed in the light of their achievement in relation to those targets. Indeed it may be argued that the quality of the links established between performance-related pay and formal performance management systems are crucial to the issue of raising organisational performance and therefore crucial to the success or otherwise of performance-related pay systems if their declared objective is to improve organisational performance.

Issues related to the robustness of the links between higher-level business plans, divisional and departmental plans and the targets or objectives agreed between managers and their subordinates are key to improving business performance. Clearly in these circumstances the link between the targets and performance of the individual and the performance of the organisation as a whole is critical. For individual performance to impact positively on organisational performance the link between the two needs to be direct and self-evidently so. If the wrong individual performance measures or targets are chosen the impact on overall performance will be affected; also equally critical will be the judgements that managers make about individual performance – if those judgements are inaccurate the relationship between performance and the overall pay bill will be distorted as will the motivation of employees.

Also important are the skills which individual managers bring to the performance appraisal/assessment aspects of the performance management process. Later in this chapter we refer to research which cites the quality of the manager–employee relationship as a factor which positively impacts upon the perceived fairness of performance-related pay schemes. Such perceptions are closely related to levels of motivation to be derived from such schemes.

Another critical aspect of performance related pay is the size of individual performance-related pay increases related to their assessed level of performance, and also the limits of what is affordable in particular organisations. Some writers have suggested that increases of the order of 10–15 per cent are required to have a positive impact on individual performance. This suggests that increases of 4 or 5 per cent are insufficient to change individual behaviour. Armstrong and Murlis (1994) suggest that:

> those whose performance is outstanding may deserve and expect rewards of at least 10 per cent . . . people whose level of performance and rate of development is well above average may merit increases of 8 to 10 per cent, while those who are progressing well at expected rates towards the fully competent level may warrant an increase of 5 to 7 per cent . . . performance related increases of less than 3 per cent are hardly worth giving.

Three examples of individual performance-related pay schemes are outlined below (Income Data Services, 1997).

A major utility company

The company wanted to put a new emphasis on a closer link between individual and company performance.

Merit pay was underpinned by a company wide performance appraisal scheme. The annual performance cycle begins with the agreement of key performance areas (KPAs). On the basis of these KPAs an individual and their boss agree individual objectives for the coming year. Objectives describe specific results to be achieved within the performance cycle. It was also regarded as important that objectives should be the product of a dialogue and mutual agreement rather than being imposed by a manager. It is not regarded as essential that every KPA has a related objective. Integral to the appraisal is the agreement of a personal development plan used for employee development, team building and business focusing.

Formal performance review takes place twice annually, but employees are coached continually. At the formal reviews individuals receive feedback on their performance and objectives may be revised in the light of changing priorities. Individual achievement is measured against five performance ratings ranging from 'outstanding' to 'unacceptable progress'. A process is in place to check the consistency of ratings. When developing this scheme the company and the trade unions agreed that the whole process should be open and transparent. Employees were made aware of the performance criteria and the standards they had to meet. All documentation is made available to individual members of staff concerning their appraisal and final performance ratings. Training was given to both appraising managers and their staff.

When the company has decided the amount of money available for performance awards, a pay matrix is developed which links performance rating to a range of increases in pay. Pay is also linked to position in the salary range. Merit increases are highest where salaries are below mid point of the grade whilst those at the top of a grade receive no increase at all. Special arrangements are made for people in this position in the form of a possible non-consolidated bonus.

A major government department

A variation on the approach of the utility company above has been adopted by the Foreign and Commonwealth Office who after 80 years of centralised pay bargaining for the civil service took advantage of the opportunities provided by full decentralised bargaining to devise a new approach to pay. This involves a system of 'equity shares' which are allocated to employees according to their position in the salary scale and their appraisal rating based on a three-point scale. Equity shares were chosen because they guaranteed that the exact amount available for pay awards would be spent. Whilst at the outset the pay award included an across the board increase it is hoped in the future to move to a situation where the entire budget for pay review will be distributed through equity shares and the merit grid.

A major financial institution

The pay arrangements for 40,000 clerical staff were changed to a system which links performance through an appraisal system based on basic annual increases and additional merit awards. This system allows the differentiation of performance levels with a wide spread of salary awards whilst at the same time controlling pay costs and creates a consistent approach to reward for all grades.

A new performance management system defines job standards in terms of the required skills and competencies for each job, which could be situated in one of five grades. The clear definition of skill and competencies with an emphasis on customer service was intended to minimise subjectivity in performance appraisal and also to give employees a clear idea of how their behaviour and how they apply their skills are translated into pay. Performance levels are assessed on a five-point scale ranging from 'unacceptable' to 'outstanding'.

Increases in basic pay are intended to ensure that basic salary rates remain competitive with market rates for set levels of skill and competency. How each employee uses those skills and competencies earns them what is called 'variable pay' which add up to substantial additions to pay.

The distinctive aspects of performance-related pay schemes have been identified as (Kessler and Purcell, 1992):

- the nature of the performance measures
- how performance against such criteria is assessed
- and, how this assessment is linked to pay

Relating pay to performance is not new; piecework and incentive schemes which link the performance, or more specifically units of output, of individuals and groups to their pay, very often in the most direct and explicit way, have been part of the industrial landscape for many years. Whilst they are not in as widespread use as they once were they remain a significant element in the industrial pay scene.

What is new is relating pay to the performance of non-industrial, white-collar, professional, managerial and executive staff. This change, which has been evident since the late 1970s or early 1980s, seems to have been prompted by the increasing competitive pressure which has forced managements to consider payments systems which relate pay to company or individual performance.

Performance-related pay schemes have linked pay and individual performance where performance may be defined in terms of subjective criteria or 'soft' criteria as well as 'harder' more objective measures. The performance criteria in such schemes can be based on inputs: the skills, competencies, qualifications and other attributes, which an employee brings to the job. Output-based criteria are usually defined in terms of objectives related to broader company plans or to an individual's job description.

An individual employee's boss (the immediate line manager) usually makes the assessment of performance but the extent to which other managers are involved in the process varies. In some organisations, for example, more senior managers may wish to sanction the performance assessment made by more junior managers. Furthermore the number of levels of performance may vary from organisation to organisation; also the definition of these levels may be clearly specified in some whilst in others it is not specified at all.

Similarly the link between performance assessment and pay can be made in a number of different ways; for example, a percentage increase in pay, a lump sum or an incremental progression on a salary scale; or, perhaps the link is made in a combination of these ways.

Given these variations it is useful to consider the objectives which companies have in mind when selecting a particular performance-related pay scheme. A key aim is to improve performance or productivity. Performance-related pay is based on an underlying assumption that employee performance is improved by a clear link between effort and reward. A further aim of some is the use of individual performance-related pay as a means of facilitating change in organisational terms. In these circumstances the very concept of individual performance-related pay is seen as encouraging a change in values.

The processes and procedures which underpin many performance-related pay schemes change the nature of the relationship between manager and employee; the relationship is individualised and is probably intended to give managers greater control in the work place. The individual, their work and its evaluation are separated from the work group.

In addition whilst many performance management systems are based on participation, discussion and agreement in the end the assessment and evaluation of performance is in the hands of managers.

This individualisation of the employment relationship can also be linked to strategies for changing the role of the union in the workplace particularly with reference to pay bargaining. The introduction of performance-related pay is often part of a number of measures which are designed to encourage the view that employee benefits are not solely dependent upon union action. A further aspect of the employment relationship, which the introduction of performance-related pay seeks to influence, is the relationship between a manager and his subordinates. Performance-related pay focuses powerfully on this relationship thrusting the manager and the employee into a one to one, face-to-face relationship. Furthermore a manager may be forced to make difficult decisions about performance and pay and may be called upon to defend and to justify those decisions. Lastly performance-related pay is seen as a way of exercising greater financial control, targeting pay where it can be most effective; it is seen as providing better value for money than the general more global increases related, for example, to cost of living or length of service. The total pay bill comes to be regarded as an investment on which an adequate return must be earned rather than a cost to be recovered.

PERFORMANCE-RELATED PAY: THE THEORY

Managers, when they implement performance-related pay schemes, are seeking to change the way people behave at work. They are trying to motivate people to improve their work performance and, in so doing, to improve the performance of the organisation in which they work.

Self evidently, actions such as these embrace a number of assumptions as follows:

- that the performance of people at work is measurable
- that differences in performance between individuals are discernible
- that the relationship between differences in performance and the associated differences in pay will be experienced as being related
- that the prospect of increased pay will motivate changes in behaviour which will improve performance
- that there is a link, which can be established, between individual and organisational performance so that as individual performance improves so does organisational performance

The ideas or concepts, about motivation and goal setting, which support these assumptions have been the subject of considerable academic attention, and managers have used this theory as the basis for action when approaching problems associated with the performance of people at work.

However there is no over-arching theory of motivation. The body of theory, which does exist, has been divided into two groups – content theories and process theories. (Steers, Porter and Bigley, 1996). Content theories assume that factors internal to individuals activate, focus and sustain behaviour; included in these theories are Maslow's hierarchy of needs, Alderfer's existence–relatedness-growth model and Herzberg's motivator–hygiene model. Process theories of motivation seek to describe how behaviour is activated, focused and sustained. The most important and relevant of these is expectancy theory which was originally developed by Tolman and Lewis in the 1930s. Their work was adapted to the work place setting by Vroom in the 1960s and later in that decade it was elaborated and extended by the work of Porter and Lawler.

Goal setting theory is also relevant to the behaviour of people at work. Just as theory has developed over time so has the way that managers have used this theory to inform their actions in the workplace when dealing with issues relating to the performance of people at work. Managerial approaches have been categorised as traditional, human relations and human resources models (Steers, Porter and Bigley, 1996).

Traditional model

As industrialisation developed so the requirement for an ever-increasingly efficient work force grew. People at work were seen as pursuing their own economic self-interest and new models of motivation were required to link this perceived economic self-interest to the requirements for efficiency and high levels of return on investment.

Perhaps the best expression of the new model of motivation is to be found in the work of Frederick Taylor in which he explained the concept of scientific management. Taylor placed the responsibility for the efficient organisation of production at the door of managers. It was a management responsibility to recruit good quality people and to train them in the most effective and efficient methods of accomplishing their work. After training the workforce Taylor argued that it was a management responsibility to design and install an incentive payment system through which it was possible for people at work to maximise their economic advantage by implementing the methods in which they had been trained to do their work.

The ideas of scientific management were underpinned by some very specific ideas about human nature. The stereotype worker was seen as inherently lazy and dishonest. In order to attract this stereotypical worker into the factory where hours were long and conditions often arduous and dangerous, a competitive wage had to be on offer. Once in the factory the worker then had to be persuaded to produce efficiently in circumstances in which the work was often short cycle and highly repetitive and monotonous. In these conditions it was argued that efficient production could be achieved by setting output targets which when exceeded attracted an additional payment in the form of a bonus. The manager's role was to supervise the worker to ensure that they adhered to the methods of working specified and also that they met or exceeded their production targets. The underlying assumption to this approach to motivation was that workers would tolerate the highly specified, tiring and tedious working methods for an acceptable level of economic reward.

However, over time, in the constant quest for an increasing return on their investment, managers, began to modify their approach. As the division of labour became more sophisticated the work of individuals became more routine, more short cycle and repetitive. Limits were placed on the amounts workers were able to earn; earnings did not keep pace with output; furthermore new methods of working required fewer people causing fears for the security of jobs to arise. The response of people at work to the changes was to develop complex and sophisticated methods which maximised their earnings whilst restricting their output. A further component of this situation was the growth in trade unionism in the work place.

Human relations model

Such developments as these led to a re-appraisal of the underlying assumptions about the motivation of people at work in order that a new impetus could be put behind the drive for increased output and the retention of a skilled workforce. Furthermore, whilst money has remained central to approaches to motivation and is still regarded as a prime motivational force, more complex assumptions are made when compared to the rather crude motivational assumptions of scientific management.

For example the 'human relations' model of motivation, which had its origins in the work of Mayo and Roethlisburger and Dickson from the late 1920s onwards, argued that it was necessary to consider the 'whole person' at work. It was thought that the increased simplification of work diminished the possibility of the work itself being satisfying. Therefore, satisfaction at work had to come from elsewhere. And, the failure to treat people at work as 'human beings' came to be seen as the cause of low morale and poor performance.

Management responsibility for people involved making employees feel useful and important, to recognise their achievements and to ensure the satisfaction of the social needs of employees. The emphasis shifted to developing greater understanding of interpersonal and group relationships at work. Research into behaviours at work were initiated and attempts were made to measure morale and job satisfaction. However the ways that work was designed and organised did not change. The new approaches to motivation, which emerged, from such assumptions were:

- Management felt it had to make workers feel important
- Vertical communication channels were opened up so that employees could express their views and also learn more about the organisation
- Routine decision making was devolved
- Group-incentive schemes were designed as understanding developed about informal groups with their own culture and norms

As motivation came to be seen as a social process so the training of supervisors was modified away from the role of taskmaster to that of facilitator. However it should be stressed that their purpose remained that of securing employee compliance.

Human resources model

In time the theoretical perspectives underpinning the human relations model were criticised as being both incomplete in their understanding of human behaviour and also as manipulative as the scientific management approaches (for example, McGregor, 1960; Likert, 1967; Schein, 1972; Miles, 1965). The term 'human resources' has been used to describe these modified perspectives.

Thus human resource models see human behaviour and its motivations as both complex and complicated. The argument is that a complex of interrelated factors such as the need for affiliation, the need for achievement, the desire for meaning and, of course, money, underpins behaviour. Furthermore it is argued that the extent to which these variables affect individual behaviour will be different from one person to another.

Such ideas as this demand a modified managerial response. Managers must first of all understand in general terms the extent of the pool of human talent that resides in its workforce before considering how best to use this resource. In using this resource the manager will consider how to allow employees to meet some of their personal goals whilst at work. Furthermore implicit in this concept is the idea of creating opportunities for people to participate more fully in the work place taking decisions and exercising autonomy at an appropriate level.

The human resources model implies a very different role for managers, that of creating the circumstances in which people at work can satisfy their own needs and meet their own goals whilst simultaneously meeting the requirements of the organisation.

Finally it should not be thought that managerial thinking in this area has been a serene process from one approach to another. Indeed it would be fair say, that, in the late 1990s, all three models of human behaviour at work may co-exist in the same organisation at the same time. This strategy, based on the nature of the organisation, its technology, its people and its aims and objectives has been called the 'contingency approach' to management. Such an approach allows managers to decide, in the light of their own circumstances, which way of working is most appropriate for them and how best pay and performance may be linked. Such circumstances beg the question about the contradiction between the complexity of the theory and the apparent simplicity of many performance-related pay schemes in practice.

PERFORMANCE-RELATED PAY: THE OUTCOMES

A recent survey (IPD, 1998a) of over 1100 organisations covering 1.5 million employees indicated that 40 per cent of management and 25 per cent of non-management employees were subject to individual performance-related pay schemes. The survey reported an average annual attrition rate of about 3 per cent for all types of performance-related pay schemes since 1990. The finding that 59 per cent of all individual performance-related pay schemes have been introduced in the last five years counterbalances this. The survey argues that the importance of performance-related pay schemes within an organisation could be judged by the proportion of employees covered and also the size of pay awards arising from such schemes. As far as individual performance-related pay is concerned the indications are that the percentage of employees covered by individual performance-related pay schemes are in the range 70–80 per cent and that the median value of awards for senior managers is 11 per cent and the mean value is 5 per cent. For other groups of employees these values are a percentage point lower in each case.

Employers perceive that individual performance-related pay has a beneficial effect on employee performance (74 per cent) and also that it 'delivers a clear message about the importance of organisational performance' (69 per cent). The survey also reports a large improvement in the behaviour of high performers in 21 per cent of respondent organisations whilst this impact is reduced to only 4 per cent for average or poor performers. Significantly the survey does not report on the perceived impact of individual performance related pay on organisational performance. Furthermore it is reported that only 28 per cent of organisations carry out any formal evaluation of the effectiveness of their individual performance-related pay arrangements. However 'significant and serious problems' have been experienced as follows: individual performance-related payments too small to act as a motivator; concerns about the accuracy of management judgements; favouritism; inadequate management training to operate such schemes; and poor communications.

A considerable amount of research has been conducted in recent years into the effectiveness of performance-related pay. A recent survey and study (Thompson, 1992) suggests that this research 'fails to provide convincing evidence of a link between individual performance-related pay schemes and improvements in productivity'. However this empirical evidence is often contradicted by personnel professionals who often evaluate their own schemes as effective even when there is no hard evidence to support such a view.

The research indicates that the employee perspective on performance-related pay is unequivocal as follows:

● Performance-related pay fails to motivate (even those with high performance ratings) and may do more to de-motivate employees
● Employees are negative or at best broadly neutral about the impact of performance-related pay on organisational culture
● Employees are unclear about whether or not performance-related pay rewards fairly
● Employees involved in the design of performance-related pay schemes are more likely to perceive such a scheme as fair and thus to be motivated by it
● The line manager – subordinate relationship is crucial to the success of performance-related pay; when this relationship is good and positive (which is rare) employees were likely to react more positively towards performance-related pay
● The issue of fairness is strongly linked to the role of the line manager in performance-related pay
● Employees generally regard performance-related pay systems as unfair in practice

Furthermore trade union perceptions of performance-related pay strongly reject that it improves employee performance or that it is a fair system; rather the perception is that performance-related pay leads to favouritism and unfairness and that employees are more likely to be de-motivated by it (Heery and Warhurst, 1994).

Performance-related pay often dismantles collective procedures to expose the essentially individualistic nature of the employment relationship and in doing so has provided the opportunity for greater managerial control (Kessler and Purcell, 1992). Although this control may be mitigated by the procedures and processes attached to particular performance-related pay schemes, in the end managerial prerogative reigns as follows.

Performance criteria

Problems may be experienced in establishing performance criteria for particular jobs. For example it may not be easy to establish performance measures for journalists or research scientists. At higher levels in organisations the link between organisational goals and objectives and the performance criteria for managers may be straightforward whilst for lower levels in the hierarchy the link becomes less direct, and also at this lower level in the organisation jobholders may have less scope to improve their own performance. As a result softer performance targets have been used for professional groups of employees. In addition, some organisations have used both input and output criteria suggesting that it is important to encourage individual development as well as the achievement of specified targets: for example, a grading structure, which relates incremental progression to performance as measured by growth or capability within the job coupled with a system which also rewarded the achievement of specific targets. Another example is a salary matrix in which movement across levels within a grade was dependent upon the acquisition of skills, whilst movement through the grades was based on output performance in the job.

Furthermore managerial perceptions of what a performance criteria or measure is and also how such measures or criteria can be established can vary quite widely. Within a single organisation definitions of performance criteria could vary about how long it would take to achieve and how measurable it was.

Examples also exist of managers using performance criteria to pursue their own agendas. One manager always included a health and safety objective as well as an objective related to the management of people. Whilst the encouragement of managerial development may be laudable the question must be asked how such approaches fitted in with what was intended at a strategic level.

Performance assessment

This stage in the process provides, perhaps, the greatest opportunity for distortion. These opportunities arise both from the pressure, which may be put on the process, and also the degree of subjectivity, which enters the process at this stage. There may be pressure not to assess employees realistically, in practice too harshly. Very often managers take the soft option, assessing employees at an average level or even making inflated judgements thus inflating their reward. In some organisations managerial choice is constrained in some way, for example through statistical means or quality control procedures to avoid this problem. Assigning labels to particular levels of performance can also be problematical. The effect on individual employees and their careers of not being labelled 'a high flyer' or being called 'average' should not be under-estimated.

Careful and considered performance assessment takes time. With many demands competing for managerial time it may be that any perceptions that a manager has that a performance management process can increase the level of control exercised, or can allow the pursuit of sophisticated strategic objectives, may simply be overridden by the need to get the job done somehow. Managers may experience a tension between the need to facilitate the achievement of strategic management objectives and therefore giving it the attention it deserves and seeing performance-related pay and performance management as yet another 'personnel' initiative.

Also, subjectivity can be a factor in a number of ways. Performance targets or measures may degrade over a relatively short period of time and may therefore require frequent revision. When to do this and the extent by which targets should be revised is a matter for subjective judgement. Another moment of subjectivity is at the overall assessment stage. Some attempt to create spurious objectivity by use of scoring schemes which do not always offer appraising or assessing managers guidance about how to come to an overall assessment.

The link with pay

The link of performance with pay is the defining characteristic of performance-related pay. At the most simplistic level such schemes are based on the premise that the perception of a direct link between pay and performance will motivate employees to higher levels of performance. As we have seen such a view flies in the face of research which emphasises the importance of a whole complex of factors when understanding motivation. Furthermore, even if this perception of a direct link between pay and performance were valid it is doubtful that it would remain unaffected by the influence of work place pressures, both social, economic and political.

However, where the performance link with pay does exist, it may itself give rise to other difficulties. The setting of particular performance objectives may lead to concentration on those targets at the expense of other aspects of the job. Similarly as individuals pursue their own individual self-interest, the interest of the work group or the team may be overridden.

The financial constraints under which schemes operate can also cause difficulties. The amount of money available may be limited particularly if an across-the-board cost-of-living increase is also part of the arrangements, so reducing the amount of money available for performance-related increases. This issue may be acute during periods of high inflation. Such a situation may lead to discontinuity between performance assessment and financial reward. Any expectations raised by positive feedback about performance, which are not supported by an appropriate level of financial reward, will lead to de-motivation. Similar levels of dissatisfaction may be caused when managers are able to use a pay budget to deal with structural defects in the pay system thus diverting money, which could have been used for rewarding performance.

Although individual performance goals are often subject to discussion and agreement they are in the end determined by the manager as is the subjective assessment of individual performance.

PERFORMANCE-RELATED PAY: GOOD PRACTICE

The literature related to performance-related pay schemes is full of experience-based descriptions by managers or consultants suggesting best practice concerning the design, implementation and management of performance-related pay. These are summarised as follows:

- Full senior management commitment to the scheme
- Introduced top–down rather than bottom–up
- Employee involvement in the design and implementation of schemes
- Existence of a competitive base salary structure
- A valid job evaluation system
- A well-designed, accurate performance appraisal system which is held in high regard by most employees
- Introduced at a pace which is appropriate to the organisational culture
- Systematic and regular training for managers in performance review and feedback
- Effective quality control mechanisms for both performance management and performance-related pay systems

The same literature suggests that performance-related pay should not be introduced:

- Where the level of trust between managers and employees is low
- When individual performance is difficult to measure
- When performance must be measured subjectively
- When inclusive measures of performance that cover all the activities of the job cannot be developed
- When large pay awards cannot be given to good performers

PERFORMANCE-RELATED PAY: THE FUTURE

The amount of work being undertaken in organisations to modify, change and improve individual performance-pay schemes indicates a level of unhappiness with them. Particular concern has been expressed about the closeness of the link between pay and organisational objectives. However very few employers suggest that their concerns are sufficient to discontinue their use.

Employers appear most concerned about their performance management systems and also with the design of their bonus and incentive plans. And, worryingly, the majority of employers intend to involve neither their employees nor their trade union representatives in any re-design or improvement processes.

As indicated the human resources model of management embraces the notion that individual employees should be able to attain personal goals though their work; that idea has now been developed to the extent to which it is suggested that an individual human life be seen as an 'enterprise of self' in which individuals continuously engage in the 'continuous business of living to make adequate provision for the preservation, reproduction and reconstruction of one's own human capital' (Gordon, 1991: 44).

Others have argued that the idea of 'an entrepreneur of self' suggests that work becomes the vehicle for self-development rather than a purely, rather tiresome or even painful economic activity. In the future the success of organisations may become in part at least dependent upon the extent to which they are able to harness the impulse to self-development that exists on the part of their employees. It seems likely that approaches to performance-related pay need to adapt to embrace even further the development of particular competencies and skills which the organisation defines as necessary for development of self (Du Gay, Salaman, Rees, 1996).

LEARNING ACTIVITIES

1 Analyse the extent of use of performance-related pay in your organisation by occupational group or grade. Compare your results to the results of national research given in section 5 of this chapter.

2 Using the data from question 1 establish the percentage of total pay generated by performance-related pay. Is this consistent throughout the organisation?

3 Taking a stakeholder perspective on performance-related pay, identify the key stakeholders and outline their different perspectives on this form of payment system.

4 Given the lack of corroborative research evidence on the positive benefits of performance-related pay, why do so many UK organisations persist in its use?

REFERENCES

Armstrong, M. and Murlis, H. (1994) *Reward Management*. Third edition, London: Kogan Page/IPD.

Du Gay, P., Salaman, G. and Rees, B. (1996) 'The Conduct of Management and the Management of Conduct: Contemporary managerial discourse and the constitution of the "Competent Manager"', *Journal of Management Studies*, May, Oxford: Blackwell.

Gordon, C. (1991) 'Governmental Rationality: An introduction in The Foucault Effect', Burchell, G. Brighton: Harvester Wheatsheaf.

Heery, E. and Warhurst, J. (1994) *Performance Related Pay and Trade Unions: Impact and Response*. Kingston, Kingston University.

Income Data Services (1997) 'Pay and Benefits Bulletin', IDS Study 416, January.

Institute of Management Foundation Continuing Professional Development Checklist 143 'Setting up a Performance-related pay' scheme.

IPD (1998a) Performance Pay Survey, Institute of Personnel and Development.

IPD (1998b) Performance Pay Survey, Institute of Personnel and Development.

Kessler, I. and Purcell, J. (1992) 'Performance Related Pay: Objectives and Application', *Human Resource Management Journal*, 2: 3.

Likert, R. (1967) *The Human Organisation*. New York: McGraw Hill.

McGregor, D. (1960) *The Human Side of the Enterprise*. New York: McGraw Hill.

Miles, R.E. (1965) 'Human Relations or Human Resources?', *Harvard Business Review*, 43: 148–63.

Personnel Management (1990) 'Performance Related Pay', Personnel Management Fact Sheet No. 30, June.

Schein, E. (1972) *Organizational Psychology*. Englewood Cliffs NJ: Prentice-Hall.

Steers, R.M., Porter, L.W., Bigley, G.A. (1996) *Motivation and Leadership at Work*. New York: McGraw Hill.

Thompson, M. (1992) 'Pay and Performance: The employer experience', Brighton, Institute of Manpower Studies.

University of Strathclyde (1990) 'Trends in Incentive Payment Schemes into the 1990s', The Department of Organisation, Management and Employment Relations.

FURTHER READING

Bowey, A., Thorpe, R., Gosnold, D., Mitchell, F. and Nichols, G. (1982) 'Effects of Incentive Payment Systems, United Kingdom 1977–1980', Research Paper No. 36 Department of Employment.

Dowling, B. and Richardson, R. (1977) 'Evaluating Performance Related Pay in the National Health Service', *The International Journal of Human Resource Management*, June.

Heery, E. and Warhurst, J. (1994) *Performance Related Pay and Trade Unions: Impact and Response*. Kingston, Kingston University.

Kerr, S. (1997) Ultimate Rewards – What really motivates people to achieve? Harvard Business Review.

Kessler, I. and Purcell, J. (1994) 'Performance Related Pay: Objectives and application', *Human Resource Management Journal*, 2: 3.

Lawler, E. III (1990) *Strategic Pay*. Jossey Bass.

Marsden, D. and Richardson, R. (1994) 'Performing for Pay? The effects of merit pay on motivation in the public sector', *British Journal of Industrial Relations*, June.

Randle, K. (1996) 'Rewarding Failure: Performance related pay in a pharmaceutical research and development company', University of Hertfordshire, Working Paper Series, 1996: 1.

Steers, R.M., Porter, L.W. and Bigley, G.A. (1996) *Motivation and Leadership at Work*. New York: McGraw Hill.

Thompson, M. (1992) *Pay and Performance: The employer experience*. Brighton, Institute of Manpower Studies.

Walters, M. (1995) *The Performance Management Handbook*, Brighton: Institute of Personnel and Development.

18 Team-based pay

Jim Harrington

INTRODUCTION – A MEANS TO ORGANISATIONAL SUCCESS

The constant need to improve organisational performance has led many organisations to consider team working as a solution. This has gathered momentum, in recent years, partly because of the emphasis placed upon quality assurance, customer service and productivity. Departments and whole companies have been restructured to provide a customer-focused service or to introduce the concept of process ownership, i.e. encouraging the team to accept ownership of the production or service delivery process.

The importance of aligning reward strategies with business objectives has been covered in earlier chapters. This chapter is based on a number of premises the overarching one being that it is not sufficient to introduce teamwork per se as a good practice. Organisations require collaboration by all employees, rather than simply teamwork. Ineffective and inappropriate team-based recognition and pay strategies occur because there is a failure to analyse the requirements for collaboration and the effective behaviours that lead to it.

Premise one, drawing upon reinforcement theory, is that organisations seeking to achieve the corporate goals above would tend to reinforce effective team-working practices through team recognition and/or reward strategies. However, surveys indicate that very few organisations have team-based pay, although the interest in such rewards is high. In a survey by the Institute of Employment Studies, of those companies with team working, only one in ten had a team-based reward. In another survey, 58 per cent of the participants were actively exploring team-based rewards (ER Consultants, 1995). As great interest is shown in team working, the small uptake in team-based pay needs exploration.

Key issues for discussion

Interest in employee involvement and group working has been evident for many years as indicated in the results of a survey of 1,598 firms shown in table 18.1 (O'Dell and McAdam, 1987).

The concept of involving employees in overcoming performance problems, discussing organisational policies and direction is well documented but organisations have

Table 18.1 The interest in employee involvement and group working

Employee involvement practice	(N)	%*
Small problem-solving groups	364	23
Quality circles	354	22
Team or group suggestions	335	21
Cross-functional employee task forces	314	20
Other employee involvement efforts	194	12
Labour/management participation teams	159	10
Quality of work life programmes	133	8
Self-directed, self-managed, or autonomous work teams	128	8
Total using at least one E.I. practice	795	50%

*Sums to more than 100% due to multiple responses.

grown in complexity and so has the nature of teams and team working. These and other factors suggest that, despite the increased interest shown in team-based rewards, this will not be carried through into aligning reward strategies with the business objectives. The reasons give rise to a second premise, which is that team-based pay strategies bring together many issues for which the conclusions of underpinning theories and concepts are divided and compounded by perceptions about team working.

The issues to be discussed are:

- the nature of teams and the need for collaboration within organisations
- reinforcing effective team behaviour and outcomes
- selecting a team-based pay option
- team-based recognition and pay options
- further research to point the way forward.

THE NATURE OF TEAMS

Widespread references to team working

Various factors have combined to give rise to the perception that team working is widespread, for example:

- flatter organisation structures
- project working
- The common and loose use of the term 'team'.

Flatter organisation structures have led to the notion that team working is widespread. Placing people in the same band or grade does not produce a team, although the effect of such delayering is spoken of as fostering a team spirit. This will be pursued in a later section.

Project teams have become more common. Such teams may have a temporary or long life, e.g. new product development teams charged with taking the product from conception to birth in the market place. Membership of successive project teams has become the normal role for an increasing number of employees.

The drive to produce a seamless customer service has led to more interest in the empowerment of staff. Information technology has facilitated this, for example, in customer call centres. Such customer-focused staff are often referred to as 'the customer services team'. The aim of providing a seamless service requires greater collaboration between employees both within and across business units. Team members are expected to resolve problems by contacting, for example, the warehouse and distribution centre to respond to a query on availability and delivery. Such examples highlight the issue of where to draw the team boundary.

The above challenges the notion of discrete teams and introduces premise three. The greater interdependence of systems within organisations requires an emphasis upon organisation-wide collaboration rather than discrete teams. To expand this we need to discuss the nature of teams and which characteristics of team work it is desired to reinforce.

The nature of teams and team work

The reality is that many people work with other individuals every day but they are not necessarily teams. They may be quite independent in the way they work, only meeting together occasionally to review progress, etc. Such groups enable members to opt in and out of commitment to collaboration.

Various commentators (for example, Moxon, 1993) have distilled the criteria of a team as:

(a) a common purpose
(b) acknowledgement by each individual that he/she is part of a team
(c) interdependent roles, i.e. necessitating collaboration
(d) agreed norms and values which affect the behaviour of team members.

A fifth criterion for many teams would be:

(e) acceptance of accountability for parts of the process within their control and influencing those parts outside their control.

There are different types of team which would arguably meet the above criteria. For example, management consultants may be thought of as a group of independent traders selling their personal skills and knowledge but operating under the brand and brand values of their chosen company. Such individuals are encouraged to display high individual performance coupled with collaboration. The balance of individual strengths and subordination to the team goals presents a tension for team-based pay as many managers and employees believe that individual performance should not be subsumed by a team culture. Premise four is that, although difficult to manage, there is not a contradiction in encouraging individual growth and nurturing collaboration to ensure the success of the organisation.

Peter Drucker (1995) uses the analogy of sports teams to illustrate that teams have different characteristics both in terms of their flexibility and the roles demanded of the members. He uses the example, amongst others, of a tennis doubles team to show how the players need to train and work together so as to understand each others' strengths and weaknesses, to anticipate these when playing and thus support and complement each other to win. Other teams do not necessarily require such close working of the players.

The analogy highlights a critical point in reward theory – the need for clarity about the behaviour and results to be reinforced. The nature of the work may be such that it is desirable to reinforce the outputs of a discrete team but in other cases it may require everybody (teams and independent workers) to collaborate in ensuring the success of the company, i.e. to reinforce the desirable behaviours in the whole organisation – the team of teams. At times it becomes difficult to distinguish where the team stops or whether one is creating inflexibility by emphasising discrete team working. For instance, if discrete teams are rewarded on the basis of their performance, resistance may be encountered in transferring staff from a high performance, well-paid team, to a lower performance team unless some protection is agreed.

The extent to which collaboration is required will also be determined by the interdependence of business systems, such as technology, key processes, work flow and managerial structures. The internal customer concept helps in understanding the chain of interdependence and other factors which affect the outputs of the 'team'. Figure 18.1 illustrates the concept.

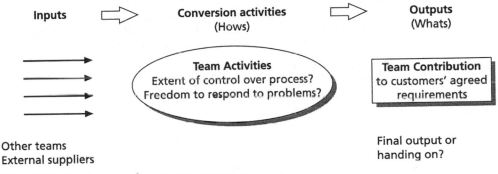

Fig. 18.1 The internal customer process

The concept illustrates the idea that a team is part of an internal supplier and customer chain. At the input end the team is dependent on the various 'suppliers' which may comprise other internal teams and external contractors. The output end sets out what the team is required to produce to meet the customer's agreed requirements. The middle conversion activity is how the team will fulfil the outputs. This includes the effective behaviours to be adopted. Reinforcement theories show that if team working is important to the output, reward or recognition should be directed at the effective behaviours required and not just the outputs. However, in practice, many reward systems only reward the outputs and do not reinforce the need to develop and maintain effective behaviours that will lead to the outputs. The issue of reinforcement will be discussed in the next section.

BEHAVIOURS AND OUTCOMES TO BE REINFORCED

Team working comprises various behaviours which need to be understood to ensure that the critical elements are reinforced. Such an analysis also provides an insight into what methods of reinforcement are appropriate. Pay alone may be insufficient, as explained later.

Figure 18.2 depicts the key dimensions to be analysed, in the context of each organisation, to determine:

- which behaviours are to be developed and reinforced to produce the required outcomes
- the balance between individualism and teamwork
- whether team work is applicable generally or only to particular groups or areas

The dimensions approach provides a means of understanding whether collaboration is essential or peripheral to the desired outputs. Then, those behaviours which are important in producing the outcomes can be identified. Figure 18.2 lists a few behaviours as the full range is well documented in texts.

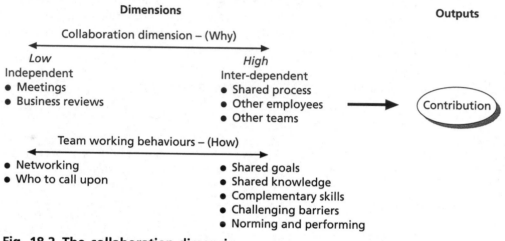

Fig. 18.2 The collaboration dimension

The collaboration dimension partly explains the hesitation by managers towards team-based pay. The existence of discrete teams makes it relatively easy to introduce rewards in some areas. This, it is feared, will give rise to perceptions of injustice when internal comparisons are made by various teams. Internal equity is a strong influence as to whether employees will be satisfied with their pay (Lawler, 1971) but its influence can be overstated as much depends on the organisation's labour markets and employee relations culture.

Reward systems both reinforce and legitimise certain behaviours. Bonus schemes designed in the 1960s and 1970s attracted criticism because volume was interpreted as the source of earnings and not quality even though productivity and quality were espoused. The work of Bowey and Thorpe (1986) has illustrated the need to both design the pay system to fulfil the business objectives and to ensure that those objectives and the link with the pay system are effectively communicated to both employees and managers.

Inconsistent messages and reinforcement actions are seen too often. Team working is espoused but individualism is given prominence. For example, senior managers often applaud individual actions and play down team performance in the way they reward and recognise employees. This is symptomatic of the belief that role models and individuals are needed who will take the initiative to turn situations around or to grasp opportunities whether that be in sales, development or service delivery. The success of some organisations is due to the presence of that spirit.

Reflecting the over-arching premise, we have emphasised the need to understand the organisational context, the collaboration dimension and the behaviours that are critical to the required outcomes. The next section outlines the options for team-based pay.

SELECTING A TEAM-BASED PAY OPTION

Focusing on the reward objectives

The analysis above will enable us to see more clearly whether and what type of team-based pay options are appropriate. There are many ways to reinforce team working and collaboration: for example, team building, team recognition. Pay is only one method and the selected option will send out signals as to what is acceptable behaviour and performance for the future.

Three basic design choices arise:

1 to reward the development of the behaviours to produce the outcomes
2 to reward the behaviours and outcomes
3 to reward the outcomes

Reward structures should not be viewed as permanent fixtures but more as transitional schemes, just as organisations continuously change. The choices provide flexibility to align the reward system with a particular change phase. For example, if a significant change in behaviour is required to ensure the fruits of team working, choice (a) may be selected as this will emphasise the development and maintenance of the behaviours. When those behaviours are demonstrated routinely, then a pay scheme based on choice (b) would be more appropriate.

Team-based pay and recognition options

These can be summarised as below:

- recognition of team achievements
- competency-based pay
- gain sharing
- group and individual bonuses
- team factor job evaluation approaches
- profit sharing

The options can be narrowed down, for a particular context. Table 18.2 lists the options according to:

- how well the option reinforces team-working behaviour
- the relative risk involved in the option in terms of the cost and effect

The options are expanded in the next section.

Table 18.2 Effectiveness of team-based pay options

Option	Reinforcement Effect		Risk
	High	Low	
Team recognition	X		Low
Competency-based pay	X		Low
Gain sharing	X		Med
Group bonus		X	High
Individual bonus		X	Med
Team factor job evaluation		X	High
Profit sharing		X	Low

CRITIQUE OF THE OPTIONS

General design considerations

When considering the options in this section, the following points should be borne in mind. These can promote the involvement of the team and members' understanding of which behaviours and outcomes are important:

- Will the team members be involved in agreeing the indicators of success for their team?
- Will the team as a whole be rewarded or will individual contributions also be recognised?
- Will payment be based upon an equal sum for all, the same percentage or variable amounts? Equity theories indicate that rewarding each member with the same sum will be more powerful in reinforcing the common purpose of the team.
- How will the contribution required of the team and individual members be made explicit so that there are no surprises during subsequent reviews?
- Will the team be given regular and relevant performance data to review their own performance?
- Will the team be given sufficient authority to correct performance problems and access to expert help, internal and external customers?

Recognition strategy

Debate surrounds the relevance to today of some motivation theories, such as Maslow's hierarchy of needs (Maslow, 1954). However, they still provide an insight into the various needs that individuals seek from life. Maslow's theory should be thought of as a staircase of needs upon which individuals travel up and down according to their changing circumstances. The criticism that the lower needs are no longer appropriate in our society ignores the constant changes in personal circumstances, e.g. job security; these cause us to go up or down the hierarchy of needs. Such theories indicate that recognition is a key need.

Premise five is that a recognition strategy should be a cornerstone of encouraging team work. Such a strategy seeks to reinforce desired behaviours by celebrating and awarding both achievements and progress towards them. Recognition strategies are relatively low cost and low risk and enable imaginative practices to be adopted which nurture co-operation. The practices may include:

- teams provided with a cheque to donate to their named charity; team arranges publicity and presentation
- trophy for coming first in quality assurance/customer satisfaction and an award also for the team showing the greatest improvement in the same period irrespective of their position in the league table
- outing to a show, theatre, sports event
- visit to other sites/suppliers/customers
- giving a team a small budget to implement improvements or to pilot ideas.

Recognition strategies offer flexibility as the nature of the award can be aligned to the significance of the contribution/behaviour and can be given soon or immediately after the event. The latter is an important part of reinforcement theory as the link is made with the desired behaviour while it is still fresh in the mind of employees.

Individual recognition strategies are often criticised because only a few employees benefit and the size of awards is small. Team awards recognise the achievement of the team and, with innovative application, become coveted by employees as they strive for recognition. They remain a positive talking point long after the event compared to a pay award.

Competency-based pay

The term competency needs to be understood as identifying the expected behaviours and values that are to be displayed for the effective performance of a job. The behaviours comprising effective team working can be identified and a short but clear picture in words developed so that all employees are aware of what team working means within the company.

Competency descriptions can be developed to reflect the different types of team working situations. Users discover that team working is the result of a variety of behaviours and that a competency approach can capture general collaboration behaviour and the individual team member's behaviour, thus addressing the individual versus team tension noted earlier.

Pay is usually determined via a traditional individual performance review system – the percentage increase being determined by effectiveness at the critical competencies. These can be weighted to stress their importance. A few firms have experimented with linking pay reviews to the effectiveness of the team and not just individuals. Whether this has any benefit over the more traditional individual approach is as yet unknown.

Surveys show that the main use of competencies has been as a development tool for individual employees. Team development is a lower priority, and its use for reward the lowest (Coverdale Organisation, 1995). Competencies are a useful process for clarifying and defining the team or collaborative behaviours that should be observable. These can then be incorporated into performance reviews, succession planning, promotion interviews. In that way the desired behaviours are reinforced as employees see colleagues progressing who demonstrate the desired behaviours. This type of approach provides a safe route for those organisations that are not sure about linking desired team-working behaviour to pay.

One criticism of competencies is that they can take a lot of time to develop. Today there are core sets of competencies that can be adapted to the needs of an organisation and methods to streamline the development and piloting process. Compared to the time invested in a job evaluation project, competencies offer a more useful output for the time invested.

Gainsharing

Gainsharing has moved on from the complex formulae systems of Rucker and Scanlon. Schemes are now firmly based upon sharing the gains from improving productivity and maintaining quality assurance. The principles promote problem solving and co-operation between employees and managers and emphasise organisational realities as payment is directly linked to actual improvements. Schemes use simple but realistic measures of productivity and can be coupled with waste reduction. Gains are shared equitably between employees and the company.

Team working is necessitated by the principles behind such schemes – the need to collaborate to overcome the cause of the performance or service problems in order to secure higher earnings. Studies indicate that it can be successfully applied to many hundreds of employees across a location.

The success of a gainsharing option will depend upon effective communication of the principles and realities upon which the scheme is based. Managers and employees must see it as a means of focusing upon solving problems rather than merely another bonus scheme. Because of the principles underpinning the schemes, employees realise that collaboration is a key means to succeed and the barriers of discrete teams begin to recede.

In common with many bonus schemes, there comes a time when a performance plateau appears and earnings stabilise. At this stage the risk is that performance will decline as employees become demotivated by the ceiling they have reached. The problem solving and co-operation philosophy underlying the scheme tends to give the schemes that extra impetus compared to the life of group bonus schemes.

Group and individual bonus

Group bonus schemes can be a means of reinforcing a result-orientated team culture. However, because they are not underpinned by co-operation and problem-solving principles, many bonus schemes fall into disrepute. The assumption can be that by placing employees in a group payment scheme, team working will be an outcome. Much effort is spent on developing the performance measures and rules to the detriment of considering the interdependence of systems and teams. The practical result is friction between included and excluded groups. The inclusion of non-productive staff may lead to tension if the earnings are diluted considerably. These type of consequences run counter to the spirit of team working and need to be considered when designing such schemes.

Nevertheless, group bonus schemes can be effective for encouraging small discrete teams to work more effectively together. Team work can be reinforced by involving the team in agreeing performance measures and using performance feedback. To emphasise the importance of the team's contribution, the bonus may be linked to the results of a performance review of the team by its members. Although some studies indicate that there is a reticence for members to criticise each other, this can be partially overcome by focusing on the team contribution. Another approach is to link group earnings into an index, such as customer satisfaction, thus emphasising a key goal. Such schemes tend to be designed as an add-on feature and the reaction of employees is similar, i.e. that it is seen as a bolt on and not a key reinforcer of behaviour.

Individual bonus plans can be used to reinforce collaboration. By linking the bonus payment to the extent to which the individual collaborated effectively, the desired behaviour can be stressed. Surveys indicate that the focus of directors' bonuses are changing – more are dependent upon contribution to the team rather than just individual performance (ER Consultants, 1995). However, the link is often weak as, despite the bonus plan, the underlying message is for a strong performance in the profit/revenue objectives – the team-working link being desirable. This illustrates the need to be clear about the degree to which collaboration rather than team working is essential.

Profit sharing

Profit or related measures are used to focus on the 'team of teams'. Reflecting the theory that employee involvement will raise commitment and performance, profit sharing, in its many forms, is one means of building a co-operative culture. Employees become more interested in the company's plans and financial success as they receive share allocations or cash. Anecdotal evidence suggests that individuals may change their behaviour to save costs and to satisfy customers. There is a lack of sound evidence to indicate that improved team working is sustained through the adoption solely of such an option although some studies suggest that profit sharing is one of a range of means which appear to encourage a sense of oneness within a company.

Flatter grading structures

Job evaluation systems and pay differentials have been strained by flatter structures. To encourage team working, attempts have been made to reduce the number of roles, grades and pay differentials within a team. Many approaches over-estimated the flexibility required of team members and costs rose.

Such an approach can work for teams comprised of the same roles, for example, operators or clerks, but in mixed teams it ignores market-rate pressures which eventually lead to inflation of the salary structure and internal dissension. Research studies indicate that differentials tend to re-emerge as employees seek to restore the gap. This suggests that structural attempts to create team working will not survive as employees compare levels of skill, decisions, etc.

The interest in team working has also led to developments in the use of team factors within job evaluation. Two approaches are emerging. The first in which the individual role is analysed against factors which include team demands and the score reflects the relative value of the job. The second in which individual roles are analysed against a business unit or company team profile and assigned to a team score. The individual is assigned to a pay grade on the basis of the team contribution rather than individual inputs. The effects of such developments may be short term. Anecdotal evidence suggests that, while the approach is being introduced, the method helps to change attitudes but the effect tails off.

Another variant has been the use of skill- or knowledge-based pay to produce a team salary structure. The process managed by a team is analysed to identify the specific skill and knowledge modules which are deemed necessary for possession between the team. Team members are then rewarded as they acquire skills/knowledge from a predetermined matrix to ensure that there is a sufficient number of developed employees to ensure ownership of the process at all times. This is an effective way to build cover in a team but does not necessarily produce team work. To remedy this, team working skills can be included amongst the list of skills in the matrix.

Such schemes have been seen as personal pay plans – the aim of employees being to increase earnings by acquiring the modules as quickly as practical. Dissatisfaction creeps in when the ceiling on pay progression is hit. Attempts are then made to extend the qualifying skills/knowledge. This is an issue but should not stop innovative attempts to align rewards with business needs.

THE WAY FORWARD

As reward structures send out strong signals as to what behaviour and outcomes are legitimate, analysis should be undertaken, as discussed earlier, to take account of the nature of the collaboration and associated behaviours required.

There is a need for more focused research into the effectiveness of reinforcing team behaviour and team-based pay and, in particular, which behaviours are best reinforced through which options. Meanwhile, a low risk approach is to introduce a team-based recognition strategy because of its strong reinforcement capability. This will enable organisations to reap the benefits of collaboration now and to assess whether the benefits would be better reinforced, at a later stage, by team-based pay.

LEARNING ACTIVITIES

1 Using the practices detailed in table 18.1 audit your organisation to establish the extent of employee involvement and group working.

2 To what extent does the current reward support system work against these employee involvement initiatives?

3 List the arguments for and against the premise that rewarding both the team and the individuals within that team is incompatible with a coherent approach to reward strategy.

REFERENCES

Bowey, A.M., Thorpe, R., Gosnold, D., Mitchell, F. and Nichols, G. (1982) 'Effects of Incentive Payment Systems: United Kingdom, 1977–1980', Research Paper No 36, Department of Employment.

Drucker, P. (1995) *Managing In A Time Of Great Change*. Oxford: Butterworth-Heinemann Ltd.

Lawler, E.E. (1971) *Pay and Organisational Effectiveness: A psychological view*. New York: McGraw Hill.

Maslow, A.H. (1954) *Motivation and Personality*. New York: Harper Bros.

Moxon, P. (1993) *Building A Better Team*. Hampshire: Gower.

FURTHER READING

The first of these books provides a useful overview of the issues and processes involved in building and utilising teams in organisations, whilst the latter two offer further insights and case studies illustrating the use of team based pay in organisations.

Armstrong, M. and Ryden (1996) *The IPD Guide on Team Reward*. London: Institute of Personnel and Development.

Moxon, P. (1993) *Building A Better Team*. Hampshire: Gower.

Thompson, M. (1995) *Teamworking and Pay*. Brighton: Institute of Employment Studies.

19 Gainsharing

Angela Bowey

INTRODUCTION

The philosophy behind gainsharing is basically that of trying to make 'work' into a 'win–win' situation, where both employees and the employing organisation derive direct financial benefits from the success of the operation. This method of reward differentiates gainsharing from other 'motivational' programmes, such as total quality management (TQM), self-directed work teams, quality circles, job enrichment and so forth, where there is no link to remuneration and no financial benefit to the employees.

The importance of process

Gainsharing relies on a process of activity where groups of employees and their managers meet regularly to review performance and plan how to improve it, leading to enhanced company performance. When measurable improvements in performance are achieved and maintained, these fund regular payments to employees. The organisation and workers thus share the gains from making improvements and develop a shared interest in company success. The magic of gainsharing lies in this process of managers and employees coming together with the shared purpose of improving organisational performance and a shared determination to succeed. It is quite common for people to confuse the process of gainsharing with the formulae that are used for calculating the gains and the shares. These formulae are not gainsharing; they are only a part of it. Whilst they have to be right in the sense of being appropriate to the circumstances, they are not in themselves sufficient to ensure success.

An organisation that is running sweetly and that has no real problems could introduce gainsharing formulae for the purpose of sharing the benefits of success with its employees. But where gainsharing is being introduced to create benefits for the organisation as well as the employees, then a focus on process is required.

There are no magic formulae for gainsharing. Fortunes have been made promoting particular methods of calculating the gainshare but, at the end of the day, even if the formulae are slightly wrong, a good gainsharing process will allow the system to succeed anyway. This chapter addresses the design of both formulae and process.

Origins of gainsharing

Gainsharing started in the United States of America in the 1930s with simple 'Scanlon plans'. Joe Scanlon, a union organiser in a steel works, put a proposal to the owners aimed at saving the jobs of his members. The steelworkers agreed to work in a more efficient way in return for an equal share of the savings that this generated. The plan was so successful that it was copied in numerous other companies. Since that time, generations of managers, consultants and researchers have experimented with gainsharing, studying the results and making improvements. Consequently, behind the latest developments in gainsharing are 60 years of gradual improvement.

Gainsharing is today used throughout the world, especially in the USA, the United Kingdom, Australia and New Zealand. As a recent US publication (Hattiangadi, 1998) stated,

> In fact, gainsharing seems to be the most effective incentive reward scheme. Through gainsharing and employee involvement, firms are able to achieve significant and sustained productivity gains, raise the real wages of workers, and improve firm performance. Research documents the significant productivity and real wage effects of gainsharing in firm case studies. Gainsharing's popularity is growing, and it is expected to increasingly be adopted in the service sector over time.

Applicability of gainsharing

Gainsharing has proved itself to be suited to virtually all situations. It has saved and revived declining companies, and it has strengthened thriving companies, enabling them to share the benefits of success with their employees. It has made private-sector companies more profitable, and it has made public-sector organisations more efficient and effective.

Sometimes people mistakenly believe that gainsharing is inappropriate for employees working in not-for-profit organisations. In contrast to profit sharing, however, the gains to be shared result from improved performance measured by indicators tailored to the particular organisation. These can include, for example, greater efficiency or costs saved, which are just as appropriate for non-profit organisations as for commercial ones.

TYPES OF GAINSHARING

There are three types of gainsharing, differentiated by the kind of measures used. The first type uses a financial measure only (for example, Scanlon and Rucker plans). Exhibit 19.1 provides an example of a fairly typical Scanlon plan. The only factor is 'costs saved' and this is calculated from the ratio of sales to labour costs.

This kind of system, which in the 1930s saved more than one inefficient steel plant in the USA from going bankrupt, is very crude, making no allowance for factors beyond the control of the employees. Although they have limited suitability for organisations today, even simple Scanlon Plans have a good track record for reducing costs.

Rucker plans came later than Scanlon plans, but they also take a very simple one-factor approach, as illustrated in exhibit 19.2.

Exhibit 19.1

Example of a one-factor Scanlon plan calculation

1 Calculate average monthly sales over a base period, usually the previous year or 18 months. (Let us suppose, for the purposes of our example, that this is £1 million.)

2 Also calculate average monthly wage costs over the same base period. (Suppose these are £200,000).

3 Work out the 'normal' ratio of wage costs to sales as derived from these base period figures. (In this example, this would be 20 per cent.)

4 If sales in the first month of the gainsharing scheme are then £1.2 million, application of the normal ratio would produce wage costs of £240,000.

5 If actual wage costs are £210,000, then there has been a £30,000 saving, to be shared 50:50 between the company and the employees.

Exhibit 19.2

Example of a one-factor Rucker plan calculation

1 Using a base period of the previous 12 or 18 months, calculate the normal monthly sales, cost of bought-in materials and services, added value, and wages. (Suppose that these are £1 million, £500,000, £500,000 and £200,000 respectively.)

2 Work out the ratio of wages to added value. (In this example, this would be 40 per cent.)

3 If, in the first month of operation, sales are £1.2 million and the cost of bought-in items £600,000, the added value is £600,000. This is an improvement of £100,000 on the normal added value of £500,000).

4 This improvement would be shared out, with the employees receiving a 40 per cent share (in line with the ratio of wages to added value).

Whilst considering these simple early systems helps the acquisition of a basic understanding of the principles underlying gainsharing, such one-factor systems do have many disadvantages.

The second type of gainsharing uses a single measure of productivity. Basing the calculation of gains on a formula for productivity improvement is a more recent development in gainsharing. The most well-known scheme of this type is the 'Improved Productivity through Sharing' plan – or 'Improshare'. In this, the improvement in employees' productivity is estimated from the number of work hours saved for a given number of units produced. The value of the savings is then shared between company and employees.

The disadvantage of this kind of system is that it is again based on one factor and, as such, does not take account of changes in prices, revenue volume, client satisfaction, client loyalty and a range of other elements which may be very important in a particular organisation.

The third type of gainsharing uses a 'family of measures', taking a multi-factor approach. This is the most recently developed and the most successful form of gainsharing, usually involving a mixture of short-term measures (for example reduction in unit costs) and long-term indicators (e.g. client loyalty). Multi-factor plans also mix financial indicators (for instance revenue per head) and non-financial measures (such as reduction in lost time from injuries). Factors like safety improvement emphasise common interests of the organisation and its employees.

SUCCESS CRITERIA FOR GAINSHARING

Research in the UK (Bowey et al., 1982), supported by findings in the USA, shows that the best results are obtained from gainsharing when it is introduced and operated in a consultative way. To quote a recent US study (Hattiangadi, 1998),

> productivity gains resulting from employee involvement alone range from 18 to 25 per cent, with an additional 3 to 26 per cent gains when used in combination with an incentive reward system such as gainsharing.

In the late 1970s, a major study conducted at Strathclyde University looked at 63 organisations that all introduced a new incentive reward system at about the same time. This is the only large-scale comparative longitudinal study of the effects of incentive remuneration systems in the UK.

The aim was to find out what systems or what features of systems were most successful. There were only four factors that were significantly associated with good results. These were: clear and tight job specifications (meaning that gainsharing works best when the employees know what is expected); group basis for payment (systems based on group performance being more effective than individual incentives); the variation of payments to reflect level of performance (with pro-rata payments for partial performance, as opposed to 'all-or-nothing' schemes); and extensive consultation (which the most successful systems always involved).

It is a pity that we still come across companies that have introduced what they call 'gainsharing' using outmoded designs and principles, with insufficient consultation and management support. We strongly recommend that gainsharing should incorporate a number of key principles:

1 Extensive consultation
2 Mixture of short- and long-term measures
3 Mixture of financial and non-financial measures
4 Design that ensures there is always some payment if there is measurable performance improvement
5 Regular meetings between employees and managers about performance improvement
6 Regular feedback on the results of measuring performance
7 Strong support from senior executives

Gainsharing is essentially a process of activity, not just a method of working out and sharing gains. It is the activity of working in groups to identify ways of improving performance, that is the key to major success with gainsharing plans the world over.

These groups should consist of a cross-section of employees and managers. Meeting regularly, they plan and implement the changes that produce improvements in financial performance of the company. The resultant gains are shared with employees, provided they reach the agreed targets.

DESIGNING THE GAINSHARING PROCESS

Gainsharing is a term which covers a wide range of collective performance-related reward systems. However, there are two types of remuneration scheme that should never be called gainsharing because their design principles are at odds with its philosophy. The first of these is any remuneration system based on individual incentives; gainsharing meanwhile is essentially a collective form of reward (although individual targets may be superimposed on gainsharing for senior executives). The second is profit sharing. Whilst gainsharing motivates and rewards employees for improving their contribution to organisation performance and results, profit is influenced by many factors that are beyond the control of employees. Profitability can be one of the factors in gainsharing, but it cannot be the sole measure.

There are five key steps involved in introducing a gainsharing system – consideration of policy issues; consultation at all levels; tailoring the system to suit the particular organisation; training; and implementation and monitoring. This section describes each of these steps.

Consideration of policy issues

The employer must first consider some key policy issues that are fundamental to the design of gainsharing. The first issue to consider is the level of commitment that the organisation is prepared to put into gainsharing. It is vital that the senior executives understand what is involved and are prepared to invest the necessary resources. Other issues which must be addressed are shown as follows.

1 Objectives that the organisation is seeking to achieve by introducing gainsharing
2 Which employees should be included
3 How frequently payments can realistically be made
4 Whether or not gainsharing will be part of the formal contract of employment
5 Basis of calculating payments (e.g. the same sum for all employees or a percentage of salary)
6 Division of gains between the organisation and the employees
7 What to call the system
8 How to ensure maximum commitment to the programme

It is no use consulting with employees before these policy positions have been considered, although consultation may produce modifications. The aim of this part of the process is to prepare the organisation's preferred outcome in respect of these policy issues, and to identify any areas where those at the top organisational levels have very strong views. In other words, what is fixed and what is open for consultation?

Consultation

Sometimes there are shareholders or board members whose permission will be needed before gainsharing can proceed. Certainly, the organisation's own managers need to be committed to gainsharing and must be consulted at an early stage to secure this commitment. If there are union representatives who speak on behalf of the employees, they also need to be consulted, as of course do the employees themselves. It is particularly important to consult with supervisory levels, as they will be an essential element in the success of gainsharing.

The purposes of this consultation are to explain about gainsharing and make sure that everyone understands what is involved; listen to points of view and adapt the gainsharing system to suit the particular organisation; convince people of the benefits of gainsharing; win commitment to making a success of the project; and plan the next stages together.

It is valuable to have an experienced consultant to contribute to the presentations which start off the consultation process, suggest suitable measures, advise against known pitfalls and generally provide guidance on keeping the process on track.

Tailoring the scheme to the organisation

It is necessary to design indicators and performance improvement factors which can be measured, which the employees can contribute towards, and which will lead to better performance for the organisation.

In setting targets for gainsharing, areas must be identified where some aspect of organisational performance needs to be improved. It is a common error to look for targets that are easily measured, or commonly used elsewhere, and not to give enough attention to finding the issues that are really important to the particular organisation. At the end of the day, gainsharing will only be worthwhile to the organisation if it contributes to goals or aims that were high on its list of priorities.

Another key feature of the proposed targets is that they must be something the employees can influence (though not necessarily control). They also need to be measurable and relate to realistic comparisons. Comparative information for improvement may be historical records of performance in this organisation, or benchmark indicators from other comparable organisations. Exhibit 19.3 describes a good way to set a target, designing links between the targets, the organisational improvements and the payments to employees.

A very important part of gainsharing is to set up consultative groups to discuss and make improvements. These groups are drawn from the employees and their supervisors and managers, and meet regularly (usually every fortnight or month). Their purpose is to review the performance achievements to date, identify ways of improving performance and achieving the targets and plan and implement ways of making improvements.

Training

Once details of the scheme have been designed and agreed, the success of gainsharing then depends on adequate training for managers, supervisors and those employees who will take part in the consultative process of improving performance. There are three kinds of training that will be needed – training in understanding how gainsharing will work in the organisation, training in the skills needed to make gainsharing successful and training in performance improvement skills and knowledge. Training is probably the most expensive phase of introducing gainsharing, but it is also one of the most important.

Exhibit 19.3

Setting a gainsharing target

1 Draw a line on a graph from where you are now to the performance level that is desired, using a timescale that is acceptable and achievable. From that point onwards, level off the line to horizontal. This line can be your upper target, for which 100 per cent of the money available for this target is earned. (Note that this is a moving target up to the point where a satisfactory/good level is achieved. The reason for continuing with the target even after this performance level has been achieved is that the organisation will continue to reap the benefits of this higher performance level so long as it is maintained.)

2 Draw a parallel line below the target line, which represents the level below which no payment will be made from gainsharing for that target. Common sense should be used in setting achievable targets whilst providing a level of challenge or 'stretch', and it is important that the employees are prepared to work towards achieving the targets.

3 Design about four or five targets, each counting equally towards the payment and each having an upper and lower limit for performance and payment.

4 Work out how improvements in these performance areas could be measured. What records are already available? What new information gathering procedures would be needed? Gathering measurement data and providing feedback to the employees should use existing reporting procedures where possible. This feedback is very important, and large charts showing progress are recommended. These should be placed in a prominent position, such as at the entrance or in the canteen.

5 Develop a formula to calculate the financial gains that would be generated if target levels of improvement in the key areas were achieved. How much is a 3 per cent improvement in this factor worth to the company, for example? This is then the sum of money that would be available for sharing between the organisation and the employees if a 3 per cent target is fully achieved. It can be reduced pro rata back to zero for no improvement beyond current levels of achievement.

6 It is important to ensure that the sums of money that can be earned for 100 per cent performance target achievement are sufficiently large to generate enthusiasm from employees, but not so large that the organisation might refuse to pay them!

Implementation and monitoring

This stage involves holding consultative meetings, measuring performance and giving feedback on this, making sure the figures are being collected accurately, displaying the results in prominent places, checking that the initial assumptions were valid, making the payments and monitoring to see when changes are needed to the performance indicators. An important part of implementation is making sure that the necessary resources and management support are provided.

It is essential for a consultative group to review the system when it has been operating for about six months, to identify any anomalies, errors in calculation or data collection, or unexpected factors. It is important that everyone understands that gain-sharing is a flexible system, and that changes can be made at this stage if mistakes are identified. No system is ever perfect however well it is originally designed.

Some 18 months after implementation, it will be time for a major review, to assess the results and plan improvements. This can help gainsharing to be kept alive in people's minds. Experience shows that greater benefits often follow 're-launching' a modified version of gainsharing after 18 to 24 months than are obtained from the original introduction.

RESULTS OF GAINSHARING

There have been several studies of gainsharing in the USA, all showing favourable results. The Puckett study in 1958 (reported in Lesieur, 1958) showed that in the first year of operation of gainsharing, the mean improvement in productivity was 22.5 per cent, with a further increase in the second year of 23.7 per cent on average.

Another study of 54 firms across the USA in 1981 included 36 firms with gainsharing (17 Scanlon plans, eight Rucker plans, and 11 Improshare plans). This study, by the General Accounting Office, showed that the labour cost savings attributed to gainsharing plans averaged 17 per cent. The longer the gainsharing system had been in place, the greater the gains.

In 1988, Roger Kaufman obtained data from 104 US organisations that had introduced Improshare plans. These showed a median productivity growth in the first three months of 4.17 per cent, with 5.9 per cent during the first six months and 8.31 per cent over the first year. Median increases over the first three years ranged from 5 per cent to 15 per cent during a period when there was an annual growth rate of just 2 per cent for all manufacturing industries (Kaufman, 1992).

The American Compensation Association carried out a study in 1992 of 663 variable pay plans, which included 348 gainsharing plans in one form or another. Of these plans, 68 per cent were introduced with the aim of improving productivity. The 55 per cent of plans which provided information on the dollar value resulting from their productivity gains showed an average 129 per cent return on their investment in gainsharing. The average gain per employee was over 2,200 US dollars per year.

Anita Hattiangadi reports on these and several other studies of gainsharing in the USA in her booklet published in 1998. In her conclusions, she writes,

> The evidence presented here shows that through gainsharing and employee involvement, firms are able to achieve significant and sustained productivity gains and raise the real wages of workers. Although gainsharing may not be for every firm, when properly implemented, it can significantly improve firm performance.

Evidence from the USA is overwhelmingly in favour of gainsharing. It may not be so widely used in other countries, but the results can be just as dramatic, as the case study of Stagecoach Auckland (formerly the Yellow Bus Company), New Zealand illustrates.

Gainsharing was introduced to Auckland's metropolitan transport company in December 1995 after an extensive period of consultation throughout the organisation. At the time, the company operated a fleet of just under 500 buses in the city of Auckland, New Zealand. It carried people on 25 million passenger trips each year, covering a total distance of around 22 million kilometres annually. There were close to 900 employees, all of whom were included in the gainsharing system except the top management team of four people.

Exhibit 19.4

Features of the gainsharing system at Stagecoach Auckland

1 Everyone except top management is included.

2 There is a gainshare team at each site.

3 A central consultative group monitors results and advises on changes.

4 All workers can earn the same money for 100 per cent performance at their depots.

5 Payments are made quarterly.

6 Each depot is measured on three separate targets, plus two company-wide targets.

7 There was an extensive training programme.

8 In 1997 gainsharing was relaunched with one new measure and some changes to the basis of calculation, in order to localise it.

9 Consistent support was given for gainsharing, most especially from the top.

Table 19.1 Original targets and current performance at Stagecoach Auckland

Factor	Original target	Current performance
Missed trips	0.1%	0.05–0.1%
Attendance	97.5%	97–98%
Lost time due to injuries (per 100,000 hours)	5.3 hours	2 hours
Bus changeovers (on road)	7.5% fewer	35% fewer

Gainsharing was a major part of the company's strategy for integrating its team and achieving a common set of aims, which, by 1998, has brought it from a conflict-ridden, bureaucratic loss-maker to a highly successful organisation. Exhibit 19.4 shows particular features of the gainsharing system employed.

Before gainsharing, this company had an entrenched public service culture, with many employees openly expressing their hostility to the very idea of seeking a profit from running buses. Operating costs were extraordinarily high, and the company was losing some 51 million New Zealand dollars per year, this loss being subsidised from local taxes. There was strong resistance to change, a very poor attitude towards customers, and a tradition of hostile bargaining over wages and annual strikes at negotiation times.

Over a period of three years, this culture was turned around. There was greatly increased commitment to the company; an enhanced customer focus; better contract negotiations with acceptable outcomes; excellent improvements in performance target results; and valuable savings initiated by employees. The company was sold in 1998 as a profitable enterprise to Stagecoach for a sum in excess of 100 million New Zealand dollars. Gainsharing was a cornerstone of the management policies which brought about these changes.

Table 19.1 shows the specific targets and the initial standard required for each, along with the performance levels being achieved in 1998.

Exhibit 19.5

> **New Zealand Can**
>
> This Auckland company, which manufactures drinks cans, introduced gainsharing based on five factors:
>
> - percentage of metal spoilage
> - number of cans produced per hour
> - accident rate
> - customer satisfaction
> - level of involvement
>
> Over the first 18 months, there was a 25 per cent reduction in metal spoilage and a 23 per cent improvement in the number of cans produced per hour. Following the implementation of a programme for the prevention of hazards, accidents became very rare. Workplace cleanliness also improved dramatically. The company was recognised as a first-class supplier by its major client.

Exhibit 19.6

> **City Design**
>
> City Design, a professional consultancy organisation in Auckland, introduced gainsharing based on three factors:
>
> - revenue from external clients
> - profitability
> - customer satisfaction
>
> Over the trial period of 12 months, the following results were achieved:
>
> - the revenue from external work doubled to over $1.6 million.
> - revenue per head increased by over 7 per cent.
> - controllable overhead costs were reduced substantially.
> - customers expressed an 80 per cent loyalty factor.
> - substantially better ratings from customers were achieved on a wide range of indicators.
>
> There were problems with profitability due to factors beyond the organisation's control. However, the multi-factor nature of the gainsharing system motivated excellent results, rewarding staff for the performance improvements which were achieved.

Exhibits 19.5 and 19.6 give examples of two further New Zealand organisations with successful gainsharing schemes.

CONCLUSIONS AND RECOMMENDATIONS

Gainsharing has many potential benefits, including the organisation and its employees making gains and developing a shared interest in the success of the concern. Improvements are generated in key areas, leading to enhanced productivity and profitability, and reduced unit costs, whilst employees learn how the organisation works financially. The process can greatly improve communications, strengthen involvement and help all employees to work together as a team. The steps involved in developing a draft plan are summarised below:

1 Explain gainsharing to those who will be involved.
2 Set up a consultative steering group.
3 Design the detail of gainsharing.
4 Identify the improvement targets.
5 Check the amount of potential gains (in pounds).
6 Set up the project groups.
7 Train the managers and the employees.
8 Get all those involved to work out how to make improvements.
9 Measure performance, give feedback and calculate gains.
10 Share the gains.
11 Monitor and review the process.

Gainsharing should include all working together to improve the organisation, reduce costs and increase revenue. In this way, gains can be made and the benefits shared.

LEARNING ACTIVITIES

1 Assess the reward systems in your organisation that are linked to performance. What form do they take and what behaviours do they encourage?

2 Does your organisation actively pursue any Employee Involvement strategies? Are any of these strategies directly linked to the organisation's reward systems?

3 Identify the advantages to both employer and employee of successful gainsharing plans.

4 To what extent is organisational culture a key factor in the success of gainsharing plans?

REFERENCES AND FURTHER READING

Bowey, A.M., Thorpe, R., Gosnold, D., Mitchell, F. and Nichols, G. (1982) 'Effects of Incentive Payment Systems. United Kingdom, 1977–1980', Research Paper No. 36, Department of Employment.

Hattiangadi, Anita (1998) 'Raising Productivity and Real Wages: Through gainsharing', Employment Policy Foundation, Washington DC.

Kaufman, R. (1982) 'The Effects of Improshare on Productivity', *Industrial and Labour Relations Review*, 45 (2, January).

Lesieur, F.G. (ed.) (1958) The Scanlon Plan: A frontier in labour management cooperation. MT Press.

20 Profit sharing and employee share ownership

Andrew Pendleton

INTRODUCTION

Profit sharing and employee share ownership have become widespread in the UK over the last 20 years. A high proportion of large firms now have arrangements for employees to participate in the profits of the enterprise, and financial participation forms an important component of the remuneration package for many employees, especially managers. Since the late 1970s around 3.5 million employees have received shares in their companies, whilst 3.6 million have participated in profit-related pay schemes since 1987 (Inland Revenue, 1997). In fact employee financial participation is more widespread in the UK than in any other country in the European Union except France. The most important factor stimulating this development has been the raft of legislation since 1978 which provides a set of tax benefits to employees and to firms participating in profit sharing or share ownership.

In this chapter we will outline each major type of financial participation scheme in the UK and provide details on the development and incidence of each. We then explore the possible benefits of profit-sharing and share-ownership schemes by considering the reasons that may influence firms' decisions to adopt these schemes. Following Kruse (1996) we discuss four sets of objectives for financial participation schemes: increasing productivity, enhancing flexibility, discouraging unionisation and securing tax concessions. We critically evaluate the efficacy of financial participation in each of these respects by scrutinising the main features of the schemes in use in the UK. Finally, we briefly survey the research evidence on the extent to which financial participation schemes bring about changes in employee attitudes, behaviour and performance.

PROFIT-SHARING AND SHARE-OWNERSHIP SCHEMES IN THE UK

In the UK, as elsewhere in Europe, it is possible to identify two main types of financial participation. The first involves cash payments to employees based on the performance of the firm in the current or preceding period which are financed by profits (profit sharing) or cost savings (gainsharing). Here, the link between company performance and employee rewards is direct. These schemes reward employees for more or less their existing behaviour, possibly with the intention of influencing work behaviour in the immediate future. The second type of schemes embodies indirect links between performance and remuneration. In this second type, rewards are share-based, with employees typically being provided with the opportunity to purchase shares in the future at current prices. Here the benefit from profitability is derived from dividends and/or from the growth in share value between taking out and exercising the share option. The assumption is that improvements in work performance will lead to greater profitability which in turn will be reflected in the positive effects on dividends and share value. The reward is therefore based on future behaviour and is secured several years in the future. It is possible to identify variants on both types of scheme. In the UK, as in some other European countries such as Germany, share-based profit sharing stands midway between the two types: share acquisition is financed by current profits but shares are not actually received until some point in the future and part of the benefit resides in movements in share value.

In the following sections we outline the main features of each type of scheme in the UK, on the basis of the chronological order in which they were introduced.

Cash profit sharing

The simplest form of profit sharing is where employees receive a bonus at the end of a period based on collective performance during the period. The basis of the payment might be profits earned or reductions in costs achieved (gainsharing). These schemes might be relatively *ad hoc*, with the employer deciding year by year what amount (if any) should be passed on to employees, or may be more systematic with a set formula for allocating profit shares each year. This relatively simple form of financial participation, where reward is directly linked to some measure of performance, has been used throughout the industrial period though its appeal has ebbed and flowed over time. Cash-based profit sharing rarely attracts any legislative or fiscal support from governments since tax concessions could encourage firms to use 'cosmetic' schemes whereby part of core remuneration is falsely portrayed as a profit share. However, this situation was to change dramatically in the UK with the introduction of profit-related pay (PRP) in the late 1980s (see p. 345). Gainsharing schemes, where bonuses are based on reductions in costs have not been popular in the UK but they have had wider appeal in the US. The attraction of this type of scheme is that it can provide bonuses in not-for-profit and public-service organisations.

Share-based profit sharing

Until the introduction of profit-related pay, most new profit-sharing schemes in the UK during the 1980s took the form of 'approved profit sharing' (APS) schemes, first introduced in 1978. These schemes can be viewed as an intermediary form since they incorporate features of direct and indirect financial participation. Part of profits (up to 5 per cent) are used to purchase shares in the employing company on behalf of employees. These are placed in trust for two years, and if the employee holds them in trust for a further year (three years before 1995) he/she is exempt from income tax on the value of the shares as a benefit from employment. Instead, they are liable to capital gains tax on the growth in value over the period when the shares are sold. This benefit is within the tax allowance for most employees so no tax is due. Employees receive dividends on the shares from the outset and voting rights can be passed through. Employees may elect to receive a cash profit share in place of shares but no tax benefits are secured. Some companies operate a variant known as BOGOF (Buy One Get One Free) whereby a share purchase scheme and deferred profit share scheme are operated in tandem.

The portion of profits allocated to the scheme may be decided by the company each year but it is common for large firms to operate a pre-set formula, such as a proportion of pre-tax profits, a function of the rate of profitability profits (i.e. profits in relation to sales), a function of actual to forecast profits or a function of the extent of change in profitability (see Incomes Data Services, 1995). Some firms also require a minimum level of profits or related measure to be achieved before the scheme is triggered. The tax benefits to the company are that the part of profits set aside to buy shares and the direct administrative costs of operating the scheme may be set against corporation tax. Furthermore, if a new share issue is used to resource the share distribution the company may benefit from a cash injection based on the tax relief. This type of scheme therefore can be a highly cash efficient method of providing additional rewards to employees.

Since the scheme was started in the late 1970s about 1,200 schemes have been approved by the Inland Revenue. Of these about three-quarters are thought to be still 'live'. The number of employees benefiting from share allocations during the 1990s has ranged from just over 600,000 to nearly 900,000, and the average value of shares distributed has been between £400 and £500 (Inland Revenue, 1997). Not surprisingly this form of profit sharing is found in firms with issued share capital, and therefore tends to be found in larger firms. In fact, this type of scheme is especially found in the finance sector: one survey conducted in the mid 1980s found that 50 per cent of finance-sector firms had such a scheme (Poole, 1989). Share-based profit-sharing schemes are also quite common in Europe, and similar schemes can be found in Denmark, Germany, France, Ireland and the Netherlands (Commission of the European Communities, 1996).

Share option schemes

The current approved share option schemes were introduced by the Conservative governments in the early 1980s, and amended in the mid 1990s. The first scheme, introduced in 1980, is known as a Save As You Earn share options scheme. Employees decide to purchase shares in three, five or seven years time at current market prices or up to 80 per cent below. Meanwhile they accumulate the cash to realise the option using an income tax exempt Save As you Earn savings scheme. When the period is up employees can choose whether or not to exercise the option, and this decision will be influenced by movements in share value during the period between taking out and exercising the option. In addition to the tax benefits of the SAYE contract, employees are exempt from income tax on the benefit of receiving shares at discounted rates and on any growth in value during the savings period. They may be liable to capital gains tax (CGT) if they sell the shares but most employees will not exceed their CGT allowance and so no tax is paid. Since 1992 shares acquired under SAYE (and APS) schemes are exempt from capital gains tax if they are transferred into an Individual Savings Account (ISA).

SAYE share option schemes are required to be open to all employees with five years service. By contrast, Discretionary Share Option schemes, introduced in 1984, could be restricted to employees of firms' choosing. The core mechanism was similar to that of SAYE schemes. Selected employees could take out options, at up to four times current salary or £100,000 (whichever was greater), to purchase shares in the future (three to ten years) at current prices. SAYE contracts were not available to raise the funds necessary to exercise the option but some firms provided 'soft' loans to assist the purchase. The option price could be as low as 85 per cent of market value as long as an all-employee ADST or SAYE scheme was also in operation. Like SAYE schemes the option need not be realised when the option period expires. The tax benefits are similar with the exception of those emanating from the SAYE contract. These schemes tended to be restricted to top executives in most cases. By the mid 1990s discretionary option schemes had become highly controversial since they provided tax subsidies to high-income earners at no risk to these employees. Coupled with more generalised concerns about corporate governance, as reflected in the Greenbury Report, they appeared to give many top managers the capacity to award themselves large rises in remuneration at the tax-payers expense. In 1995 discretionary option schemes were replaced by Company Share Option Plans (CSOP). Although the discretionary element remained, the top limit for options was reduced to £30,000 and discounts on current market value were withdrawn.

Comparison of the growth rates of the two main types of scheme provide interesting insights into company priorities in remuneration policy. In all but one year, the number of new SAYE schemes has ranged between 80 and 115 since the mid 1980s. By the mid 1990s 1,500 schemes had been introduced in total, of which just under 1,200 were thought to be 'live'. They are therefore more common than deferred profit-sharing schemes but the pattern of development is not substantially different. By contrast, discretionary schemes have grown at a much higher rate. Over 6,500 schemes have been introduced since 1984, an average of over 540 new schemes each year. The average initial value of discretionary options has been much higher. In most years this figure has exceeded £20,000 compared with 2,000–3,000 in SAYE schemes. The participation rates of eligible employees is much higher in discretionary schemes: over 90 per cent compared with 20 per cent (see Pendleton and Robinson, 2000). However, the proportion of eligible employees is much smaller in discretionary schemes: 9 per cent compared with over 80 per cent in SAYE schemes. The inference that might be gained from this comparison is that many companies have attached rather more importance to executive reward packages than developing broad-based employee share ownership schemes.

The characteristics of firms with SAYE option schemes are clear. Besides having a share capital, they tend to be large, multi-site, UK-owned firms and to have strong positions in their product markets (Poole and Whitfield, 1994). They also tend to be more participative than firms without stock option schemes, and have a variety of mechanisms for employee involvement (Pendleton, 1997; also Poole, 1988). SAYE schemes tend to be more evenly distributed between sectors than deferred profit sharing, though they are especially common in financial services. Less is known about the distribution of discretionary schemes since research interest has focused upon all-employee schemes. However, the distribution between size of company seems to be similar to all-employee share-based schemes (see Baddon, Hunter, Hyman, Leopold and Ramsay, 1989).

Profit-related pay

Profit-related pay was introduced in 1987 and is one of the few cash profit-sharing schemes anywhere in the world to attract tax concessions. It was introduced primarily to bring about greater flexibility in pay and in the hope that employees would be prepared to see part of their current 'base' pay as profit related. The implication of this is that after a bad year for the firm, employees' pay would be reduced. Unlike most profit-sharing and employee share ownership schemes which are designed to supplement 'base wages', profit-related pay has been aimed at wage substitution. To overcome understandable reluctance on the part of employees to make this concession, generous tax benefits were an integral part of the scheme. Initially income tax exemption was allowable on half of the employee's PRP payment, which could be up to 20 per cent of salary (or £3,000, whichever was lower) but, in response to lack of employer interest, income tax exemption was extended to the full PRP payment in 1991. For employees on average incomes in the mid 1990s this could lead to an increase in actual take home pay of about £750 each year. In most firms using PRP in the mid 1990s the PRP element of pay was 10 per cent or under, and between 10 and 20 per cent in about one-third of cases (Industrial Relations Services, 1994).

There are two main approaches to linking the PRP 'pool' to profits: one expresses it as a simple percentage of actual profits ('method A'), the other calculates it as a function of the extent of change in profits in relation to profits in the baseline period ('method B'). In practice the employer can limit the degree of change in individuals' PRP payment each year by using method B with a dampening factor on the percentage change, by registering new PRP schemes each year, or even suspending the scheme should profits be running under forecast levels. A small number of employers even undertake to make good any reduction in employee pay resulting from the operation of the PRP scheme. The evidence to date suggests that firms have used PRP in three sets of ways. One, is to provide a profit share to supplement existing levels of remuneration. Most early PRP schemes took this form, and involved conversions of prior-existing profit-sharing schemes. PRP therefore made little impact on the overall incidence of profit sharing in the UK in the early years. The second use of PRP has been as a substitute for an annual pay increase. Net employee pay may be increased at no cost to the firm. The third, known as 'salary sacrifice', substitutes PRP for part of current pay whilst maintaining net take-home pay at pre-scheme levels. In effect the firm rather than the employee benefits from the tax concessions. In practice the benefits tend to be shared, with employees receiving a net increase in take-home pay and firms a reduction in wage costs. The use of the various dampening measures mentioned above means that employee pay can be maintained at stable levels whatever the movements in profits.

In the 1990s PRP became a very popular scheme indeed. Once the tax breaks were improved in 1991 the number of new schemes increased by several thousand each year. By March 1996 there were nearly 13,000 live schemes in operation in the UK, with just over 3.5 million employees participating. Surprisingly there has been little academic research into profit-related pay, and hard evidence on the characteristics of firms with

PRP is hard to come by. Calculations using Inland Revenue data indicate that the average number of employees participating in PRP schemes is smaller than share schemes, suggesting that PRP is more evenly distributed between size categories of firm than share-based schemes (Pendleton and Robinson, 2000). Initially most schemes took the form of profit bonus schemes but after the improvement in tax concessions 'salary sacrifice' became the most popular. Since the degree of risk and flexibility in employee salaries in these types of schemes was minimal in practice, PRP functioned as a blanket tax subsidy for any firm which cared to set up a scheme. At around the same time as public criticism of executive share option schemes mounted, PRP schemes came to be seen as an expensive tax 'dodge'. By the late 1990s PRP was forecast to lose the Exchequer around a billion pounds each year in lost tax revenues, and in November 1996 it was announced that PRP would be phased out from 1998. The size of the PRP payment attracting tax relief was to be reduced in £1,000 steps so that by the millenium no tax relief would be allowable.

THE REASONS FOR USING PROFIT-SHARING AND EMPLOYEE SHARE OWNERSHIP

The discussion of the features of the main profit-sharing and employee share ownership schemes in the UK has indicated that firms may have a variety of objectives for financial participation schemes and that these may differ between schemes. Advocates of financial participation often refer to a range of possible benefits to firms but these are not always subject to critical scrutiny. Theoretical benefits (and costs) may not be secured in practice because of the particular features of the scheme adopted.

Kruse (1996) has recently identified four sets of reasons for firms to adopt profit-sharing and share ownership schemes: productivity-related reasons, flexibility-related reasons, a concern to tackle trade unionism, and a desire to take advantage of tax and social security concessions. We consider each of these in turn, and attempt to critically consider UK schemes in relation to these.

Productivity

The most common explanation for the introduction of financial participation is to provide an incentive for employees to work harder and/or more productively. Thus profit-sharing and employee share ownership might be a means to induce changes in work attitudes and behaviour. At its simplest the potential to earn additional rewards provides a simple incentive to devote additional effort. Moreover, the promise of additional rewards might be used to secure employee compliance to changes in work organisation designed to improve productivity. Clearly profit sharing and other forms of simple collective performance-based bonuses are more likely to serve these functions than stock option plans since the remuneration-performance link is more direct.

Even so, this argument is based on two major assumptions about employees which may not be tenable in practice. One is that the potential to secure additional rewards is important to the employee. Yet it has long been established in pay research that individuals make a tradeoff between wages and effort (see Baldamus, 1961). Additional remuneration may not be a priority for some employees or the size of the additional benefits on offer may be insufficient to bring about greater levels of effort. The second assumption is that individual employees will both perceive a link between personal effort and remuneration, and want to base their own behaviour on this. The problem is that employees may believe that their own work performance has little impact on collective performance, and therefore that it is not worth expending additional effort. They may decide to 'free-ride' on the efforts of others. Once some employees are perceived to be free-riding, this may become the group norm since there will be a powerful disincentive for others to work harder. Thus all employees might come to share an interest in not working harder. All things being equal, the size of the firm is likely to have a significant bearing on these processes: the larger the firm, the weaker the link between individual effort and collective performance, and the greater the opportunity to free-ride on the efforts of others.

Another variant of the motivation perspective sees a key benefit of financial participation as the encouragement of co-operation both between employees and between employees and management. This co-operation might take the form of sharing information with others, thereby reducing those information asymmetries between managers and workers which inhibit managements' capacity to organise work effectively in all but the smallest firms and work places. Drawing on game theory, Kruse and Weitzman (1990) argue that employees will see the benefit of co-operating, and that in a repeated-games scenario will change their behaviour towards greater co-operation. A less 'altruistic' view emphasises the potential for financial participation schemes to encourage employees to ensure that *others* co-operate or work harder. The basis of this argument is that without financial participation most employees will not be sufficiently concerned to take action to rectify sub-optimal performance by others. Group norms may not actively promote the restriction of output but they do not favour peer group action to enhance it. Financial participation may provide an incentive for employees to monitor the work performance of their colleagues and to take action to raise effort levels. It has been suggested therefore that financial participation will be especially attractive in work situations where individual output is hard to monitor, as in many non-manual occupations and where automated technology is in use. The evidence so far, however, provides mixed support as profit sharing is not significantly more prevalent in firms with a high proportion of white-collar staff, high capital intensity and advanced technology (Pendleton, 1997; Heywood, Siebert and Wei, 1997).

Information asymmetries and employee monitoring may become more problematic as firm size increases, so that financial participation may be more attractive to larger firms. This of course contradicts the suggestion derived from the free-rider problem that financial participation offers more to smaller firms. In fact, the UK evidence finds that cash profit sharing is fairly evenly distributed between categories of firm (see Poole, 1989) and work place size (Pendleton, 1997). By contrast, all-employee share option schemes are concentrated in larger firms, though this may be explained as much by administrative reasons and the presence of share capital as much as by these theoretically derived arguments (see Poole, 1989). It may also be that share schemes have different attractions to cash profit share schemes, and are adopted for different reasons.

Share option schemes clearly embody a less direct link between personal effort, collective performance and remuneration than cash-based forms of profit sharing. The financial benefits are based on dividends and increases in share value which are only contingently related to company productivity and profitability performance. They are, however, more focused on future rather than past performance since financial benefits will be related to performance improvements secured after the options are taken out. Even so it seems unlikely that they will make a major contribution to productivity improvements in most cases as participation is voluntary and typically only a minority of employees will take out options. The main exception is executive share option schemes where the potential size of the reward may be sufficient to ensure executives secure improvements in company performance. However, perverse outcomes are possible since the incentive is to focus on actions which lead to improvements in short-term shareholder value (which may only be loosely related to productivity improvements) rather than the long-term productivity and health of the company. For this reason, alongside criticism of the 'tax dodge' element in many executive schemes, Long-Term Incentive Plans (LTIPs) have become more common in the latter years of the 1990s.

Top executives aside, the main function of share option schemes may be to promote a perceived identity of interests between employees and the firm rather than to secure immediate changes in task behaviour. Advocates argue that options will encourage employees to take an active interest in the fortunes of the firm and especially in movements in share value. Certainly the survey evidence suggests that promoting an identity of interest between employee and the firm tends to be more important for share option and deferred share-based profit sharing than cash profit-share schemes (see Smith, 1993). The productivity benefits of this might be more diffuse than in the simple incentive model associated with cash profit sharing but may be especially important in organisations where work is hard to measure and where knowledge, creativity and initiative are vital for successful completion of work tasks.

One indirect productivity benefit of all types of financial participation scheme, but perhaps especially of those with a more long-term focus such as share option schemes, is encouragement to employees to remain with the firm. In this way the stock of knowledge and skills can be built up and maintained at high levels. Profit sharing and share ownership schemes may function, therefore, to raise remuneration above market levels to deter employees from quitting or behaving in a manner which might lead to them being dismissed. These 'efficiency wages' may be useful where knowledge and skills are highly firm specific, where training costs are particularly high, and perhaps where investment programmes have recently been initiated. Besides this use of financial participation to retain productive employees, it might also be used as a tool for attracting the best-quality recruits to the firm in the first place. Certainly, this seems to be an important function of executive option schemes in labour markets for top managers, and many managers argue that these benefits outweigh the negative, tax evasion characteristics of these schemes.

Flexibility and risk sharing

A further function of financial participation is to provide the firm with greater flexibility. In principle, it should allow total labour costs to fluctuate in line with the fortunes of the firm. This function may be especially important in firms facing high levels of uncertainty in their product markets and/or profit streams (e.g. because of currency fluctuations) or who have just embarked upon an investment programme where employee co-operation is required and the benefits of the investment are uncertain. In other words, the firm transfers a degree of its risk on to its employees. There is indeed a certain amount of evidence that firms facing greater than average uncertainty in these respects are more likely than others to use financial participation (see Pendleton, 1997; Kruse, 1993).

However, the capacity of financial participation schemes to bring about flexibility can only be judged by reference to specific schemes. The evidence shows that most cash profit-sharing schemes provide bonuses in addition to wages rather than functioning as a substitute for part of base wages (Bhargava, 1994; Whadhwani and Wall, 1990). They therefore boost total remuneration, and hence total labour costs, though they do in theory provide for downwards flexibility should company fortunes deteriorate. As Kruse puts it, 'for risk-averse employees, the higher financial risk in these plans may be mitigated by higher average levels of compensation' (1996: 517). The problem, however, is that if bonuses at similar levels are generally paid from year to year, they can assume a quasi-fixed character and it can be difficult for the firm to revise bonuses downwards to the extent required, especially if it is arguable that the downturn in profits has little to do with employee performance (i.e. because of adverse currency movements).

Profit-related pay is particularly interesting here since it was explicitly designed to promote pay flexibility. Drawing explicitly on the ideas of Harvard economist Martin Weitzman (1984), the Conservative government aimed to combat 'wage stickiness' in the UK economy. The problem here is that when company profitability declines firms adjust by shedding labour rather than by revising pay downwards. The scheme therefore was aimed to making pay more flexible so that the pressures for labour shedding would be diminished. At the same time, the reduction in the marginal cost of labour would encourage firms to hire more labour when times are good. In this model profit sharing needs to substitute for part of current remuneration rather than adding 'gravy' to it. Initially profit-related pay did not function in this way: most schemes were conversions of existing bonus schemes. More recently, however, profit-related pay has substituted for part of base pay.

Has profit-related pay therefore succeeded in shifting risk to employees? The answer must surely be no. As seen earlier, the risk to employees from profit-related pay schemes has been minimal or non-existent. To iron-out salary fluctuations, schemes can be registered on an annual basis, a dampening factor can be used and some firms undertake to make good any shortfalls after bad years. Schemes can be suspended if profits are bad and salaries based on pre-scheme salaries can be paid instead. Pension contributions may be based on pre-scheme pay (adjusted to take account of movements in the cost of living). The reason that these safeguards have been necessary is that firms have to gain the agreement of their employees to pay substitution schemes as they involve a material change to contracts of employment. In practice, as pay research has shown over the years, most employees tend to be risk averse in relation to pay, preferring a sub-optimal but stable level of pay in the medium and long term rather than optimal levels in the short term. To secure employee consent, therefore, firms have had to minimise the risk of adverse wage movements. What really happened with PRP is that firms transferred risk on to the taxpayer not their employees.

Share schemes appear to be quite successful in promoting pay flexibility since they can boost total remuneration without commiting firms to additions to the pay bill. Indeed share-based profit sharing can make a slight positive addition to cash flow via corporation tax injections. This is because they are usually 'financed' by additions to share capital. Other shareholders bear the costs of the scheme through dilution of their claims on ownership and on residual profits. For this reason, financial institutions can be ambivalent towards employee share schemes. Whilst they welcome their apparent benefits on employee attitudes and behaviour, they are wary of their capacity to dilute potential dividend flows and share value. In fact there are Stock Exchange and insurance limits on the issue of new shares for employee share schemes to counter this dilution effect. Increasingly large firms are setting up Employee Benefit Trusts to purchase existing shares on the open market so as not to be constrained by these limits.

Whatever the flexibility of share option schemes, though, it should be clear that there is minimal risk transfer to employees as they can choose not to exercise the option should share value have fallen.

Discouraging unionisation

A concern to discourage unionisation and promote attitudinal change may also lie behind the adoption of financial participation. It may weaken unionisation in two main ways. One, it can weaken union influence over pay outcomes if some part of remuneration is linked to profits or some other measure of performance. Two, if these schemes promote a sense of identification with the firm they may weaken employee attachment to unions. There is some historical evidence that firms have used financial participation as part of strategies to weaken the influence of unions. The influential 'cycles of control' thesis developed by Harvay Ramsay (1977) suggests that firms turned to devices like profit sharing at times when unions were powerful, and there is evidence that adoption of this type of scheme has been higher at times when labour markets are taut and union power is increasing. This argument is less compelling for the 1980s when union power was seen to be declining (Ackers, Marchington, Wilkinson and Goodman, 1992).

Each argument should, however, be considered critically. On the first point, although unions might lose some degree of detailed control of pay outcomes, they can retain a substantial measure of influence on outcomes in so far as they influence or negotiate the formula that is used to allocate profits. In practice, however, there is substantial evidence that in the past in the UK the implementation of financial participation, especially share option schemes, has occurred independently of collective bargaining. To some extent this has reflected union disinterest in financial participation or concern to maintain a distance from schemes which may be associated with reductions in remuneration, as much as managerial intentions to marginalise unions. However, the use of profit-related pay has been split fairly evenly between firms using collective bargaining to set pay and those who do not, and approximately half of profit-related pay firms with unions negotiated the introduction of profit-related pay with them (Industrial Relations Services, 1994). Although substantial numbers of firms with some form of sharing do not negotiate them with unions, it is clear from the 1990 Workplace Industrial Relations Survey that work places belonging to firms with share option schemes tend to recognise unions (see Pendleton, 1997). They also tend to be more participative in other respects, and most writers in the area view share-based financial participation as a strategy to deepen participation in already relatively participative firms rather than as a strategy to weaken union-based forms of representation and participation (e.g. Poole, 1989).

A key assumption behind the second argument – that closer identification with the firm will lead to a decline in attachment to unions – is that attachment to the firm and to unions have a zero-sum relationship with each other. However, there is evidence from the (mainly American) 'dual commitment' literature that employees can identify with both their employer and unions, and indeed that those most committed to unions are also those who identify most with the firm.

Legislation and tax concessions

The final factor that may influence a firm's decision to introduce sharing is the presence of external pressures and benefits, such as tax concessions. That the overwhelming majority of financial participation schemes in the UK are 'approved' for tax concessions shows how important this reason can be. The rapid growth in various types of scheme once tax breaks are introduced shows that tax concessions can be a highly effective policy instrument in promoting the use of financial participation. They appear to shift the frontier of decision making about whether to introduce schemes. Without tax concessions, the firms that are most likely to use financial participation are the better performing ones, in part because they have something to share. Introducing tax concessions can widen the appeal of financial participation to firms with a less-impressive record of performance.

This observation suggests that tax concessions can achieve important public policy goals. As well as promoting redistribution of wealth (if that is judged to be important), the promotion of sharing amongst less-productive firms may bring about performance improvements in those firms. Unfortunately it is difficult to set the tax breaks at appropriate levels: set them too small, as with PRP prior to 1991, and firms display disinterest; set them too large and firms introduce cosmetic schemes to take advantage of the concession, as with PRP after 1991. There is a further danger that where schemes are judged to make excessive demands on the public purse, as has been the case with PRP, the tax benefits will be reduced or withdrawn and firms will have to undergo a potentially painful adjustment process.

OUTCOMES

A key issue for policy makers and managers is whether profit-sharing and share ownership schemes have the beneficial impact claimed by their advocates. The claims made for these schemes usually rest upon a three-stage argument. First, it is argued that schemes will lead to a change in employee attitudes in the direction of a more favourable orientation towards their work and the firm. Second, this will lead to a change in behaviour, as manifested by greater work effort, co-operation, and reduced propensity to quit. Third, this will lead to improvements in collective performance, such as improvements in productivity. In the case of cash profit share schemes though, it is often suggested that the beneficial effects occur at stage 2 since it is assumed that employees are already responsive to incentives. In the remainder of the chapter we briefly survey the evidence on each of these stages.

Employee attitudes

This is a complex area with conflicting results from research investigations (for a survey of the literature see Pendleton, Wilson and Wright, 1998). By and large studies on this topic concentrate on employee share schemes because they are more orientated towards changing attitudes than cash profit share schemes. Some studies (e.g. Bell and Hanson, 1984) have uncovered evidence of more positive attitudes towards the firms, such as greater identification and commitment, after share schemes are implemented, but typically these studies have relied on employee perceptions of attitudinal change as their main source, and hence may be subject to respondent biases. There is also the problem that participants in voluntary share option schemes may be those with more favourable attitudes to the firm anyway. There is some evidence, though, from cross-sectional comparisons of shareholders and non-shareholders that these differences are slight. More ambitious studies have attempted to compare attitudes over time to see whether share ownership makes a difference. The main UK study here, that by Dunn, Richardson and Dewe (1991), indicates that attitudes of shareholders and most non-shareholders do not change very much over time.

Extrapolating useful and valid lessons from the mass of often conflicting evidence is not at all easy but some generalisations can be drawn. The first is that participation in decision making needs to accompany financial participation schemes to bring about attitudinal change. Second, the size of the rewards may well have an influence on the extent of change: share ownership per se is not sufficient. Third, the extent of attitudinal change seems to be dependent on the extent to which employee shareholders feel like owners (see Pendleton, Wilson and Wright, 1998).

Behaviour

There are very few studies on the extent to which profit sharing and share ownership bring about behavioural change. This is because it is extremely difficult to develop and operationalise objective measures of work effort. Other measures such as absenteeism and turnover are also fraught with measurement problems, first, because employees obviously attempt to conceal absenteeism and, second, because labour turnover is subject to a range of influences (the state of the labour market for instance) whose intensity varies over time. The indicators that tend to be used, therefore, are employee perceptions of their own behaviour, such as their propensity to quit rather than actual behaviour. The little evidence available suggests that share schemes lead to a lower liklihood of quitting but that the factors listed above may be necessary to achieve this. Even with this proviso, however, it cannot be assumed that attitudinal change will necessarily lead to behaviour modification.

Performance

There have been a large number of studies into the effects of financial participation on company performance in recent years since this provides the acid test for evaluating these schemes. Most studies have focused on profit sharing rather than share option schemes since performance effects are most likely to be witnessed in relation to these schemes. Most have used productivity as the outcome measure as this is less subject to extraneous influences than other measures of performance.

Summarising the US evidence, Kruse and Weitzman (1990) suggest that profit sharing has a mildly positive effect on productivity, and this finding has been reflected in studies in the UK and Europe (see OECD, 1995). The difficulty with many studies is that they examine performance at some point after sharing is introduced. Whilst it can be shown that sharing firms perform better, it is less easy to demonstrate that sharing leads to superior levels of performance. It is possible, and there is a fair degree of evidence to support this, that better-performing firms are more likely to adopt sharing. After all, they are more likely to have something to share. Ideally longitudinal studies should be undertaken so that performance can be tracked over time, and preferably before and after the adoption of sharing. The few studies that do this, such as Kruse (1993), find positive productivity effects which, to quote Kruse and Weitzman's comments, 'are neither small enough to be negligible nor so large as to be implausible' (1990: 138–9). Even then, a note of caution has to be entered. As Kruse remarks, unseen biases in sample selection (e.g. that firms adopting sharing were about to improve performance anyway) may influence the results. Overall, it seems likely that profit sharing can have positive productivity effects but having observed the potentially 'cosmetic' nature of some sharing schemes, these effects will not always be present.

SUMMARY

A variety of theoretical arguments have been developed over the years to argue that profit sharing and employee share ownership are a good thing, and by and large the objectives of policy makers and managers reflect this. The suggestion in this chapter, however, has been that these hypothesised benefits may not be achieved in practice. The institutional characteristics of financial participation schemes and the context in which they are introduced may mean that few benefits are achieved or that they may be outweighed by their costs at either the company or societal level. An extreme case in point is profit related pay which created massive costs to the public at large whilst failing to bring about pay flexibility or transfer risk from firms to employees. Part of the problem here was that employees do not respond directly and straightforwardly to pay incentives. Other factors such as stable levels of remuneration may be just as important. The lesson here is that employees have complex sets of attitudes and desires, and financial participation schemes have to recognise these if they are to be successful. It is probably unrealistic to expect that any one participation scheme can have a transformational effect on employees or upon the firm in which it is introduced. They have to be used in conjunction with other human resource management instruments and, if well designed, may have mildly positive effects on firm performance.

LEARNING ACTIVITIES

1 Examine any profit-sharing or employee share option plans offered by your organisation and identify the objectives for their introduction.

2 Based on the evidence from question 1 assess the extent to which the objectives are evaluated and achieved.

3 Discuss the role of profit-sharing schemes and employee share option plan in reward strategy.

4 Identify the impact and assess the implications of the removal of tax advantage for profit-sharing schemes.

REFERENCES

Ackers, P., Marchington, M., Wilkinson, A. and Goodman, J. (1992) 'The Use of Cycles: Explaining employee involvement in the 1990s', *Industrial Relations Journal*, 23: 286–83.

Baddon, L., Hunter, L., Hyman, J., Leopold, J. and Ramsey, H. (1989) *People's Capitalism: A critical analysis of profit-sharing and employee share ownership*. London: Routledge.

Baldamus, W. (1961) *Efficiency and Effort: An analysis of industrial Administration*. London: Tavistock.

Bell, D. and Hanson, C. (1984) *Profit Sharing and Employee Share-Holding Attitude Survey*. London: Industrial Participation Association.

Bhargava, S. (1994) 'Profit Sharing and the Financial Performance of Firms: Evidence from UK panel data', *Economic Journal*, 104: 1044–56.

Commission of the European Communities (CEC) (1996) 'Report from the Commission: Pepper II: Promotion of participation by employed persons in profits and enterprise results (including equity participation) in member states', Brussels: Commission of the European Communities, Com (96) 697.

Dunn, S., Richardson, R. and Dewe, P. (1991) 'The Impact of Employee Share Ownership on Worker Attitudes: A longitudinal case study', *Human Resource Management Journal*, 1: 1–17.

Heywood, J., Siebert, W. and Wei, X. (1997) 'Payment by Results Systems: British evidence', *British Journal of Industrial Relations*, 35: 1–22.

Incomes Data Services (1995) 'Profit Sharing and Share Options', Incomes Data Services, Study 583, London.

Industrial Relations Services (1994) 'PRP in the 1990s: A survey of 333 employers', *Pay and Benefits Bulletin*, September, 2–11.

Inland Revenue (1997) *Inland Revenue Annual Report*, London: HMSO.

Kruse, D. (1993) *Profit Sharing: Does it make a difference?* Kalamazoo: Upjohn Institute.

Kruse, D. (1996) 'Why Do Firms Adopt Profit Sharing and Employee Ownership Plans', *British Journal of Industrial Relations*, 34: 515–38.

Kruse, D. and Weitzman, M. (1990) 'Profit Sharing and Productivity,' in A. Blinder (ed.), *Paying for Productivity*. Washington: Brookings Institution.

Organization of Economic Cooperation and Development (OECD) (1995) 'Profit Sharing in OECD Countries', *Employment Outlook*, chapter 4

Pendleton, A. (1997) 'Characteristics of Workplaces with Financial Participation: Evidence from the Workplace Industrial Relations Survey', *Industrial Relations Journal*, 28: 103–19.

Pendleton, A. and Robinson, A. (2000) 'Profit Sharing in the United Kingdom', in A. Pendleton and V. Perotin (eds), *Profit Sharing in Europe: The characteristics and impact of profit sharing in France, Germany, Italy and the United Kingdom*. Cheltenham: Edward Elgar.

Pendleton, A., Wilson, N. and Wright, M. (1998) 'The Perception and Effects of Share Ownership: Empirical evidence from employee buy-outs', *British Journal of Industrial Relations*, 36: 99–124.

Poole, M. (1988) 'Factors Influencing the Development of Employee Financial Participation in Contemporary Britain', *British Journal of Industrial Relations*, 26: 21–36.

Poole, M. (1989) *The Origins of Economic Democracy*. London: Routledge.

Poole, M. and Whitfield, K. (1994) 'Theories and Evidence on the Growth and Distribution of Profit Sharing and Employee Shareholding Schemes', *Human Systems Management*, 13: 209–20.

Ramsay, H. (1977) 'Cycles of Control: Worker participation in sociological and historical perspective', *Sociology*, 11: 481–506.

Smith, G. (1993) 'Employee Share Schemes in Britain', *Employment Gazette*, April, 149–54.

Weitzman, M. (1984) *The Share Economy*. Cambridge, MA: Harvard University Press.

Whadhwani, S. and Wall, M. (1990) 'The Effects of Profit Sharing on Employment, Wages, Stock Returns and Productivity: Evidence from UK micro-data', *Economic Journal*, 100(399): 1–17.

FURTHER READING

Baddon, L., Hunter, L., Hyman, J., Leopold, J. and Ramsey, H. (1989) *People's Capitalism: A critical analysis of profit sharing and employee share ownership*. London: Routledge.

Income Data Services (1995) 'Profit Sharing and Share Options', IDS Study 583, London.

Kruse, D. (1993) *Profit Sharing: Does it make a difference?* Kalamazoo: Upjohn Institute.

Pendleton, A. (1997) Characteristics of Workplaces with Financial Participation: Evidence from the Workplace Industrial Relations Survey, *Industrial Relations Journal*, 28: 103–19.

21 Occupational pensions

Stephen Taylor

INTRODUCTION

According to the most recent Government Actuary's statistics, 10.7 million people in the UK are members of 128,000 occupational pension schemes – approximately 57 per cent of working men and 37 per cent of working women (Goode, 1993: 78). A further 7 million retired people currently benefit from pensions provided in this fashion. They thus provide income, in addition to the state pension for a clear majority of individuals over retirement age (Dilnot *et al.*, 1994: 1). Estimates of the total value of UK pension fund assets vary but are in excess of £500 billion (Ward, 1995: ix). Their cost to employers varies too, depending on the extent of fund surpluses or deficits. According to the 1993 annual National Association of Pension Funds Survey, the average cost of a contributory scheme to which employer contributions were currently being made was equal to 10 per cent of the total corporate wage bill (IRS, 1994: 3). Often employers are required to pay considerably more so as to ensure that fund assets are sufficient to meet actuarial estimates of liabilities. It can thus be safely concluded that UK occupational pension funds are highly significant institutions in terms of their contribution to retirement income, their actual and potential cost to employers, and their influence in international equity and bond markets.

The importance of occupational pension funds, whilst widely accepted, has rarely been reflected in the reward management literature. Far more attention has traditionally been given to collective bargaining processes despite the fact that many more people are members of pension schemes than trade unions, and to performance-related incentives of one kind or another despite the fact that pensions typically cost employers a great deal more to provide. Why this should be the case is something of a mystery. In part, it probably arises from the technical complexities of pension scheme management and the perception that the topic is both dry and too highly specialised to be of great interest to a general management readership. Another possible explanation is the notion that occupational pensions are provided simply to take advantage of tax concessions and not because they have a meaningful role to play in the achievement of management objectives. Whatever the reason, this chapter is an attempt to redress the balance somewhat and to assess the occupational pension scheme from the perspective of the human resource management function. It starts with an introduction to the main varieties of scheme design before summarising and assessing the impact of the vast body of new legislation concerning their operation that has come on to the statute books in recent years. The second half of the chapter considers what objectives sponsoring employers intend their occupational schemes to meet and how far in fact they do so. This discussion draws on the results of 20 interviews with company pension managers carried out by the author in 1996 and 1997. The chapter concludes with a look at likely future trends and recommendations for further reading.

FORMS OF OCCUPATIONAL PENSION SCHEME

An occupational pension scheme is an arrangement set up by an employer as a tax efficient means of providing retirement income for employees. In the UK, tax concessions are only given where a fund has been granted exempt approved status. In practice this means that it must be set up as an 'irrevocable trust' for the purpose of providing retirement benefits. It must also operate within a variety of other Inland Revenue rules which limit the level of contributions that can be made and the value of pensions that can ultimately be paid. In terms of design, schemes fall into three broad categories; the defined benefit, defined contribution and hybrid forms. In addition employers can sponsor group personal pension arrangements, which, while not strictly speaking occupational pension schemes, share a number of similar features.

Defined benefit schemes

In the UK at present, the defined benefit form of occupational pension is the most common, with 80 per cent of private-sector schemes together with all public sector schemes taking this form (NTC, 1997: 11). Here contributions are made by employers and employees into a single organisation-wide fund. Retired employees are then paid pensions according to defined formulae. In most cases these are related to the final salary (i.e. the salary at the date of retirement or in the few years immediately prior to retirement), but can also be based on other calculations such as average salary levels over a longer period of time. While some such schemes are termed 'non-contributory' because they do not require employees to make any contribution to the pension fund, over 75 per cent are 'contributory' and compel members to contribute a fixed percentage of their salaries each year.

In the private sector the most common arrangements are 'sixtieths' final salary schemes. Here retirees are paid an annual pension equivalent to 1/60th (1.67 per cent) of their final salaries multiplied by the number of years' pensionable service they have completed with the employer concerned. Hence 40 years' service produces a pension that is equivalent to two thirds of the final salary (the maximum pension permitted by the Inland Revenue). In practice, of course, few employees complete 40 years' service while being a member of a pension scheme, so pensions equivalent to half the final salary or less are more commonly paid. By contrast, public-sector schemes have traditionally operated on an eightieths basis, whereby the annual pension paid is equivalent to the number of years' service multiplied by 1/80 (1.25 per cent) of the final salary. Retirees are then compensated for the lower level of pension by being paid an additional tax free lump sum on retirement.

The key feature of a defined benefit scheme, at least in theory, is that it is the employer who bears the investment risk. In other words, where, in the opinion of an organisation's actuary, the assets of the pension fund are insufficient to meet its liabilities, the employer is obliged to make up the difference by committing additional resources to the fund. As a result, however, the investments that are made with the fund's assets ensure, the retired employee will receive the pension benefit expected. Conversely of course, as matters currently stand, when a fund is in surplus (i.e. when its assets are more than sufficient to meet its liabilities), it is the employer and not the employee or pensioner who benefits. In such circumstances, unless the employer wishes to improve benefit levels, the level of pension provided remains the same. Such a situation has been very common in recent years leading for calls on the part of trade unions for surpluses to be used to improve benefit levels. In practice, most employers have simply taken 'contribution holidays' whereby they suspend their own contributions to the fund either wholly or partially (NTC, 1997: 18).

Defined contribution schemes

Also known as 'money purchase' arrangements, defined contribution pension schemes are rather more straightforward and have grown in number over recent years. In 1997 15 per cent of UK schemes took this form, compared to only 6 per cent five year's earlier (NAPF, 1992 and 1997). Here, instead of the level of pension being linked to final earnings, it is simply determined by the value of the investments made at the time of retirement. Employers therefore pay into the fund a fixed contribution on behalf of each employee (e.g. a figure equivalent to 5 per cent of the annual salary). Employees also make a fixed minimum contribution, but are also generally able to increase this if they so wish. The combined sum is then invested, in a similar manner to a building society savings account, until the individual reaches retirement age. Whatever sum has then accrued is then used to purchase an annuity from an insurance company from which a lifetime pension is paid. The level of the annual pension thus depends on the amount of contributions made, on the investment performance of the fund and on the value of annuity that is ultimately purchased.

For the employer, the advantages of money purchase arrangements are the lack of long-term investment risks and predictability in terms of the contribution levels that will be paid. Whereas in a defined benefit scheme the level of contribution that employers have to make can vary from year to year depending on actuarial estimates of fund assets and liabilities, in a defined contribution scheme the only commitment is to pay a fixed percentage of the salary bill into funds annually. Furthermore, because the payment of pensions is handled by the provider of the annuity and not by the employer, defined contribution arrangements are usually less costly in terms of administration than their defined benefit counterparts.

That having been said, there are those who argue that defined contribution schemes compare unfavourably with defined benefit plans when viewed from the employer's point of view. The case here relies on the latter's perceived value for money. It is argued that while defined benefit plans may be less predictable and may cost employers more over the long term, they nevertheless provide more per pound invested by way of pension because they permit a greater portion of the fund to be invested in high-yeiding equities than is usually possible in a defined contribution scheme. Moreover, it is argued that they benefit employers more than defined contribution schemes because of their positive effect on labour markets – a subject we will return to later in the chapter.

From the employee's perspective an advantage of a defined contribution scheme, aside from ease of comprehension, is the value of pension that can be transferred when taking up a job with a new employer. For many younger employees who intend to move from job to job, the amount of pension that they can take with them to invest in a new employer's scheme will be higher in the case of a defined contribution scheme than with a defined benefit scheme. The discrepancy arises from the methods used to calculate transfer values in each type of scheme. However, that said, it is generally agreed that the defined contribution scheme is inferior to the defined benefit variety for most employees because of the level of risk that they have to carry. While it is possible to envisage circumstances in which the balance of financial advantage favours a defined contribution scheme (e.g. low wage inflation combined with high investment returns for a prolonged period), such conditions have not prevailed in recent years.

Hybrid schemes

A third type of pension scheme contains elements of both the above forms. The aim is to combine the best features of defined benefit and defined contribution arrangements so as to ensure that the maximum gain accrues to each employee. The security of having a guaranteed pension linked to final earnings and associated with defined benefit schemes is thus combined with the flexibility and portability of a money purchase scheme.

Hybrids themselves take several different forms. First there are those that are basic-ally defined benefit schemes but which provide what is known as a 'money purchase underpin'. Here, for most retirees, the pension is calculated with reference to the final salary level and the number of years of pensionable service completed. However, where the level of pension would be higher if calculated on a defined contribution basis, this method is used and an annuity purchased accordingly. Furthermore, because this requires fund assets to be accounted for in terms of contributions made by or on behalf of each individual employee (as in a defined contribution scheme) it means that trans-fer values can also be calculated in the same way. As a result it is possible to ensure that relatively young employees moving to other employers can take with them a sum calculated on defined contribution principles where that is higher.

Another form of hybrid for the most part operates like a defined contribution scheme but is also underpinned by features of defined benefit arrangements. Here, in situations where the accrued value of an individual's pension is insufficent to provide a pension that is equal to one which a final salary pension would have provided, it is topped up by the employer to ensure that it does. In practice such schemes are most associated with executive pension provision and result in accrued funds being amelior-ated so that an annuity providing a two-thirds pension can be purchased. A third form of hybrid scheme is more rigid in its structure. Here younger employees (e.g. those under the age of 40) are given a money purchase arrangement on the grounds that they are likely to move to new employers and will thus benefit from transfer values calculated accordingly. However, after the age of 40 a defined benefit formula takes over so that a greater measure of security is provided in the years immediately prior to retirement. A variation on this kind of scheme is one which allows employees a measure of choice as to which method of calculation is used. Employees, on joining an organisation, can thus opt for defined contribution benefits but then switch over to the defined benefit formula if they later decide to remain employed by the company concerned through to retirement.

Group personal pensions (GPPs)

Many smaller companies, but also one or two larger ones, do not offer an occupational pension scheme but have instead set up a group personal pension arrangement to be run by a financial services company. From a legal and taxation perspective these are no different from the kind of personal pension plan that any individual might be set up. However, because the arrangement has been made on a bulk basis by the employer, the level of commission paid per plan is usually considerably lower. In addition, of course, employer contributions are made in addition to those the employee chooses to make.

The advantage of such an arrangement for the employer is clearly the absence of any of the administration costs associated with running an independent pension fund. There is also a very high degree of portability for leavers. However, as Harrison (1995: 160–1) shows there are considerable potential disadvantages for employees too – particularly if they later wish to take up employment with an organisation that offers a bone fide occupational scheme.

ADDITIONAL BENEFITS

In addition to providing income in retirement for employees, most occupational pension schemes also offer a range of other benefits to members. These differ greatly in terms of their nature and generosity, but typically include the following:

- a widow's or dependent's pension
- a lump sum paid on retirement
- death in service/life insurance benefits
- early retirement options
- ill health/disability pensions

THE REGULATORY REVOLUTION

Prior to 1985, subject to Inland Revenue rules and the principles of the law of trusts, employers had a wide degree of discretion as to how they ran their occupational funds. If they so pleased they were able to compel employees to become scheme members; they were also able to exclude specific groups from membership (e.g. part-timers) and could refuse to transfer funds from the pension scheme when an employee resigned to join another employer. There was little requirement to communicate details about the scheme or its investments to employees and there were no restrictions on employers who wished to invest their pension funds in their own businesses. Furthermore, there was very little supervision of scheme trustees on the part of government agencies.

Since 1985 this situation has changed radically. As it would be impossible in a short chapter to deal in any detail with the plethora of new regulations that have been introduced, a brief summary of the most important measures is provided here. The main instruments by which legislation has been introduced are as follows:

- The Social Security Act 1985
- The Social Security Act 1986
- The Finance Act 1986
- The Social Security Act 1989
- The Finance Act 1989
- The Social Security Act 1990
- The Finance Act 1990
- The Pension Schemes Act 1994
- The Pensions Act 1995
- The Finance Act 1997

In addition a number of judgements made by the European Court of Justice have had a significant effect. Among the most important are the following:

- *Bilka-Kaufhaus v Weber von Hartz* (1986)
- *Barber v Guardian Royal Exchange* (1990)
- *Coloroll Pension Trustees Ltd v Russell* (1994)

Rights for early leavers

Some of the main changes introduced in the Social Security Acts of the late 1980s concerned the rights of those with short service – i.e. those who are members of an employer's pension scheme but who leave to take up different employment prior to the retirement age. Until 1986 employees in this position had only two options, both of which were widely seen as being unsatisfactory. They could ask for a return of their own contributions or they could request that their pension was frozen for them to claim at the normal retirement date for the pension scheme in question. In the latter case the level of pension would then be calculated according to the earnings level at the time of leaving (often many years before the date at which it would actually be paid). The result, especially in times of relatively high inflation, was a hefty financial penalty for those who switched employers. Moreover, only those over the age of 25 and who had completed five years' service had the right to a deferred pension.

The situation is now much changed. The age limitation has been removed and the vesting period reduced from five to two years. Employees who have completed two years' service now have the option of transferring their accrued pensions across to another occupational pension scheme or to a personal pension if they so wish, with the transfer value calculated according to standard conventions. Alternatively they may leave their pensions in the original employer's scheme where their value will be 'preserved' or revalued in line with inflation (to a maximum of 5 per cent per annum). As a result, the pension they then draw on retirement will at least to some extent reflect the cost of living at that time.

Voluntary scheme membership

Before April 1988 it was lawful for employers to force all eligible employees to join their occupational pension schemes, and this frequently happened in practice. Since then employees have been given freedom of choice in this regard. It is also now possible for an employee to leave a pension scheme while remaining employed in the organisation and to request that it be preserved or transferred to a personal pension plan. The right to take this course of action led to what has become known as the 'pensions mis-selling scandal' whereby providers of personal pensions or agents acting on their behalf persuaded people who were members of occupational schemes to transfer into inferior personal pension plans.

Disclosure of information

Trustees of occupational pension funds are now required to disclose a substantial body of information concerning their schemes to members, potential members and recognised trade unions, as well as fund beneficiaries and their spouses. Disclosure regulations were first introduced in 1986 and have subsequently been expanded further. Broadly speaking, the information concerned can be divided into two categories: that which must be disclosed to these parties if requested and that which must be provided in writing automatically. Information that must be disclosed on request includes the following:

- relevant trust deeds
- scheme rules and any documents amending the rules
- trustees' annual report
- most recent actuarial valuation
- the level of benefits earned to date and likely future pension
- rights and options available in case of the death of a member or beneficiary
- the schedule of contributions/payment schedule for employers' contributions
- a statement of investment principles

Information that must be provided automatically includes the following:

- categories of persons eligible for scheme membership
- contribution levels
- basic information concerning the scheme's tax approved status and whether it is contracted out of SERPS (the state earnings related pension scheme).
- the normal pension age
- details of benefits payable under the scheme
- methods used for the calculation of preserved and transferred pensions
- details of the internal disputes procedure
- notice of the proposed use of fund surpluses

Self-investment

A further significant regulatory change that has occurred in recent years is new restrictions on 'self-investment', namely the investment of pension fund assets in property, companies or other ventures controlled by the sponsoring organisation. The whole issue of the protection of scheme assets became a matter of great public concern in 1992 following the collapse of the Maxwell Group of Companies and the subsequent discovery that £248 million of pension fund assets had been used to secure loans to failing private Maxwell companies. Concern was compounded when similar occurrences were found to have taken place, albeit on a smaller scale, in other companies taken into receivership in 1992 (Goode, 1993: 361–2). However, prior to these events steps had already been taken to limit the extent to which self-investment was to be permitted. These culminated with the introduction in March 1992 of new regulations restricting pension fund trustees from investing any more than 5 per cent of a scheme's total assets in employer-related shares or property. The Pensions Act 1995 went further in banning altogether the practice of funds giving loans or loan guarantees to the sponsoring employer.

Sex discrimination

One of the most difficult tasks faced by scheme administrators and legislators over the past decade has been the question of how to equalise pension rights for men and women. Among the many issues that have had to be tackled in this field three stand out as being particularly significant. The first is the established tradition of different 'normal' retirement ages – 65 for men and 60 for women. The second arises from the fact that, on average, women in the UK live for seven years longer than men and thus require additional funding if they are to enjoy pensions of equal value. The third concerns equalisation of access to pension scheme membership for predominantly female groups, such as part-time workers, who have often been excluded in the past. The cost implications associated with equalising pensions are considerable when all three of these issues are considered.

The unlawfulness of unequal pension ages was effectively established in 1990 when the European Court of Justice decided in favour of the plaintiff in the case of *Barber* v *Guardian Royal Exchange*. The issue at stake was whether or not pensions should be legally defined as forming part of an employee's pay or whether they could be treated differently. In deciding that they should be treated in the same way as other forms of pay, the court brought them within the ambit of equal pay law with immediate effect. Hence from May 1990, despite the fact that the state pension age for those born prior to 1950 remains discriminatory, it has been unlawful to set different pension ages for men and women or to discriminate between them in any way in the funding or management of an occupational pension scheme. Later cases established that the Barber principles were not to be applied retrospectively (*Coloroll Pension Trustees* v *Russell*, 1995) and that it was lawful for employers to introduce equality by raising the female pension age to that set for male employees (*Smith & others* v *Avdel Systems Ltd*, 1994).

Different principles were established by the court in respect of discriminatory actuarial assumptions about male and female life expectancy. In *Neath* v *Hugh Steeper Ltd* (1995) the ECJ decided that it was lawful for an employer to pay additional contributions into a pension scheme on behalf of female employees on the grounds that they could be expected to live longer than their male colleagues. Moreover, it was decided that this was permissible even where it resulted in women receiving higher lump sums on retirement or higher transfer values when changing employers. In the view of the court it would thus seem that transfers and lump sums, unlike pensions in payment, are not defined as forming part of an employee's pay.

The third field in which major changes have occurred concerns rights of access to occupational pension schemes. For a variety of reasons part-time workers were often excluded from membership of an employer's occupational pension scheme in the past. This was partly because of perceived high turnover among part-time workers which placed a heavy burden on scheme administrators, partly because the flexible hours worked by many part timers made pension calculations difficult and partly because of established prejudices concerning the position of 'second income earners'. The practice of denying access to part timers who wished to join occuptional schemes was held by the ECJ to amount to indirect sex discrimination in 1987 (*Bilka-Kaufhaus GmbH* v *Weber von Hartz*). However, it was not until the Pensions Act 1995 that the ruling was specifically incorporated into UK law.

Minimum funding

Among a raft of different measures designed to protect the interests of final salary pension scheme members, the Pensions Act 1995 included strict regulations requiring employers to ensure that their schemes were solvent. The new minimum funding standard requires that trustees obtain actuarial valuations at set intervals to establish whether or not a fund's assets are sufficient to meet its liabilities (defined as the minimum funding level). In practice this requires an actuary to calculate what assets the scheme would need to have were the employer to become insolvent (What would be the cost of purchasing annuities on behalf of existing beneficiaries? What would be the value of transfers to other schemes on behalf of existing employees?). Where assets fall below this minimum funding level employers now have five years to restore the level of assets. Where assets are judged to have fallen below 90 per cent of the minimum funding level, they must be restored to the 90 per cent level in one year.

New regulatory bodies

The Pensions Act 1995 also provided for the establishment of two new regulatory bodies to oversee the provision of occupational pensions. The first of these, the Occupational Pensions Regulatory Authority, consisting of members appointed by the Secretary of State, has the power to investigate complaints, fine trustees and employers found to be breaching the rules, dismiss or suspend trustees, wind up pension schemes and initiate criminal proceedings. A second body, the Pensions Compensation Board, has been set up to provide financial assistance when an organisation becomes insolvent and cannot meet its pension liabilities. The aim is to provide for situations such as those experienced by members of the Mirror Group pension funds in 1992. The board is financed via a levy charged on all pension schemes. In addition to these two bodies, there has been since 1991 a Pensions Ombudsman appointed to investigate formal grievances on behalf of scheme members who feel that they have been treated unjustly. The Ombudsman's office is also funded via a levy on pension schemes.

The abolition of tax credits

The Finance Act 1997 abolished what were known as 'tax credits' on advanced corporation tax paid to pension funds. In effect these were devices whereby pension funds could reclaim a rebate from the Inland Revenue for most of the tax automatically paid on the share dividends they receive. The aim was to encourage more long-term investment on the part of companies by reducing the incentive for pension fund managers to demand high dividend payments. The result was the removal of a huge portion of existing tax relief on pension fund investments. Estimates have varied as to the long-term effects, but most analysts agree that in the immediate future it will result in pension funds paying £5 billion of additional taxation per year (*Financial Times* 3 July 1997, *Economist* 5 July 1997).

There are two major consequences of the new legislation described above. First its combined effect, over a period of time, has been to increase considerably the costs associated with the provision of occupational pensions. The precise effect on any one employer will clearly vary depending on its workforce profile, its position as regards sex equality and pension-related communication prior to the changes and the extent of any fund surplus. Moreover, the additional long-term costs on the provision of defined benefit schemes are significantly higher than is the case for defined contribution schemes. Second, the measures taken to protect the interests of early leavers have significantly reduced the ability of employers to use their pension schemes as a means of limiting staff turnover. The overall effect is thus to discourage employers from setting up or continuing to sponsor occupational funds, and in particular, to inhibit the survival of the defined benefit form of scheme design. The extent to which trends in this direction are occurring as a result of regulatory changes is a question of debate. The answer depends in large part on the view that is taken of employers' purposes in providing occupational pensions and the value they perceive them to have. It is to this issue that we now turn.

OBJECTIVES OF OCCUPATIONAL PENSION FUNDS

When asked by researchers why they continue to sponsor occupational pension funds, employers have tended to draw attention to a variety of different reasons (e.g. Goode, 1993; Casey, 1993; Alexander Consulting Group, 1993; Confederation of British Industry, 1994; Taylor and Earnshaw, 1995). In terms of clear management objectives, the major categories are as follows:

- to assist in the attraction of new staff
- to assist in the retention of existing staff
- to assist in funding redundancy by providing for early retirements
- as a general tool in improving employee relations

Such responses are unsurprising given their status as received wisdom among pensions managers, the pensions industry, trade unions, independent commentators and government ministers. However, it is interesting to note that a good proportion of employers also claim to provide occupational pensions primarily for paternalistic reasons. Both qualitative and quantitative studies have suggested this to be the case. As many as 63 per cent of respondents to the Alexander Consulting Group survey gave 'employee welfare' as their first preference from a list of possible objectives, while 28 per cent of the senior directors surveyed by the Confederation of British Industry identified 'paternalism' as the most important reason for having a pension scheme.

The number of possible explanations for occupational provision grows when the views of academics and other commentators are included in addition to the results of surveys. Of particular interest is the work of economists such as Ellwood (1985), Wise (1986) and Handa (1994) who have shown how defined benefit schemes act as an incentive encouraging employees to retire at a time chosen by the employer. Others, such as Olian, Carroll and Schneier (1985) have argued that the provision of an occupational pension may also have a positive motivational effect and thus enhance employee performance. Drawing on Herzberg's (1966) two-factor theory of intrinsic and extrinsic forms of motivation, they suggest that, while an amelioration of pension benefits may not lead to improved employee motivation, their reduction or withdrawal will in all likelihood have a negative effect on motivation levels and job satisfaction. However, they also suggest that where the level of pension benefits is in some way performance-based (i.e. where employer contribution levels increase either to reward good performance or as part of a promotion package), a considerable motivational effect can be created. In the UK bonuses and incentive payments are not usually pensionable (although there is no reason why this should not be the case in a defined contribution scheme), but a number of companies do provide more generous levels of benefit for more senior staff (e.g. 50ths or 30ths instead of 60ths). In such circumstances pensions could thus be claimed to have a motivational effect as well as a more general retentive effect for staff with serious prospects of promotion.

A different school of thought argues that in many cases employers do not in fact have any specific, positive reason for sponsoring an occupational pension. Ward (1995), for example, includes the following 'accidental' explanations in her list of reasons:

● Because one (i.e. a pension scheme) is already in operation, and, although you might not choose to set one up from scratch, getting rid of it would cause too many problems.
● Because your company has acquired a business, or a group of workers, and continuation of pension provision was laid down in the sale terms.

Others, in arguing that employer-sponsored provision is both the most efficient and risk-free form of retirement saving available (e.g. Bodie, 1990) have simply argued that the principal reason for their provision is their tax sheltered status. The implication is that there is no need to look for employer objectives in seeking to explain occupational pension provision; instead it is sufficient to show that society in the form of employers, employees, employee representatives and governments has evolved a system for providing income in retirement that is cost-effective for all parties. It can be plausibly argued that this is indeed the major reason for the establishment of pension schemes in the public sector in the first decades of the twentieth century.

It can therefore be concluded that there is no clear, straightforward answer to the question 'Why do employers provide occupational schemes?' and that a number of factors may have operated at different times and in different organisations to establish the form and scope of pension arrangements that now exist.

The evidence is also somewhat varied when it comes to exploring the effectiveness of occupational pension schemes at achieving employer objectives. Only a limited amount of research has been carried out in the field, and much of what has been published has either been based on questionable assumptions or has drawn on evidence gathered against the backdrop of a far looser regulatory regime than now exists in the UK. For example, there is a great deal of published research examining the theoretical effects of pension schemes on employee behaviour. The vast majority of this work has been undertaken in the USA, much of it during the 1980s under the auspices of The National Bureau of Economic Research (e.g. Lazear, 1983, 1985 and 1990; Ellwood, 1985; Viscusi, 1985; Kotlikoff and Wise, 1987; Lazear and Moore, 1988). Among its many conclusions, the following stand out as being particularly significant:

- It can be shown that in theory pension schemes can reduce employee turnover for all classes of employee, but that the effect is particularly strong in the case of long-serving employees over the age of 40.
- It can be shown that pensions can influence the age at which employees retire by giving them a disincentive either to retire before or after the date chosen by the employer.
- It can be shown that in theory pension schemes should act as an incentive for older employees to work harder up to the set age of retirement because in so doing they maximise the value of their pensions.

The extent to which these findings hold true for the UK at the end of the twentieth century is questionable for a number of reasons. First, it must be pointed out that the vast majority of this research is based on pensions within the final salary design. Consequently they cannot be said to apply to defined contribution schemes, hybrid plans or defined benefit schemes which calculate pensions on a different basis. The second reason for caution arises from the fact that this research was carried out against the background of the US regulatory framework. Minimum vesting standards were introduced in the USA in the Tax Reform Act (1986), but even now they are far less restrictive than is the case in the UK. How far the above conclusions apply to a regime which requires full vesting after two years of employment is thus doubtful.

Finally, of course, there is the more general question of how far in practice the results of theoretical studies reflect the way employees behave. The problem here is the extent to which people act in an economically rational manner when making decisions about whether to leave an employer, retire or work harder in the years prior to retirement, or even whether they have the information available to make such judgements. Surveys undertaken in the UK strongly suggest that ignorance about pension schemes and apathy towards them is widespread (Towers Perrin Foster and Crosby, 1986; Goode, 1993: 118), so there are serious grounds for questioning the contribution that this body of American research can make to the current British debate.

A further stream of research has used large data sets detailing individual work histories to analyse how far in practice pension scheme membership affects job mobility. The results of these are consistent with the findings of the theoretical work described above in so far as they have invariably found a significant positive association between pension scheme membership and job tenure. This is as true for the American studies (e.g. Schiller and Weiss, 1979; Mitchell, 1983; Ippolito, 1991) as it is for those conducted in the UK (McCormick and Hughes, 1984; Maelli and Pudney, 1993). They thus provide evidence to suggest that, in practice, employees who join an employer's scheme are more likely to remain with the employer for longer than colleagues who refuse the offer of membership. However, there are problems here in so far as correlation is found to be evidence of causation. It could be the case that the correlation is explained not by the retentive effects of the pension scheme but by employees who intend to remain in the employ of one organisation for some years choosing to join the pension scheme. Maelli and Pudney (1993: 30) state that they found little evidence of this alternative possibility, but accept that such an interpretation of their data is possible. The five studies cited here, like the theoretical work, were all conducted using data gathered either at a time or in a place in which very different regulatory arrangements were in operation. Where the employer is under no obligation to transfer a pension, or revalue it after someone has left, it is not surprising that there should be evidence found of employees choosing not to seek work elsewhere. The extent to which the same considerations apply now that employers do not have this freedom of manouevre is, at the very least, questionable.

The author's own recent research interviews with 20 pensions managers in private-sector firms suggest that the impact of occupational pensions may vary considerably between different groups of employees. When asked what they believe their pension schemes achieve, discussion with the managers invariably revolved around their role in attracting staff to the organisation, retaining them and in retiring them at a time of the company's choosing. However, the effects were perceived to vary depending both on age and the type of work being undertaken. In terms of attracting new staff, a clear majority of interviewees expressed the view that their pension schemes had only limited value. The reason was held to be widespread ignorance and general disinterest in pensions among employees. However, a distinction was often drawn between, on the one hand, the attitudes of graduates and higher-earning employees, and, on the other, of those who are less well-educated and more poorly paid. In the case of the retailers there appears to be great difficulty in persuading store-based, weekly paid employees to join pension schemes at all, whatever efforts are made to do so. For this group, as for some shopfloor workers and warehouse staff employed in manufacturing and distribution companies, there appear to be no grounds for believing pensions to have any significant impact on recruitment.

A rather different picture emerges in companies employing a higher proportion of professionally qualified staff. Here there is less of a problem persuading people to join, although the view is expressed that for most the type of pension scheme is largely irrelevant. There may thus, as yet, be no great advantage in labour market terms in offering a particularly generous scheme or one that is especially flexible in its design. What is important is that some kind of pension arrangement is offered. Pensions are judged to be one of several benefits that prospective employees looked for, but were by no means the most important. Two exceptions to this general picture are senior managers and financial specialists, who appear to be the only groups to take a serious interest in their pension arrangements and who routinely take account of the benefits on offer when deciding whether or not to take up a position.

Opinion is also divided on the extent to which membership of an occupational pension scheme deters employees from seeking alternative employment. Again, in the case of relatively low-skilled employees, the effect is perceived to be limited. The question of pensions provision does not appear to weigh highly in employees' minds when they are deciding whether or not to resign – it is well down the list below salary and career prospects. Again, for these groups, there is perceived to be a lack of appreciation of the true value of an occupational pension scheme. According to the pension managers of two large retail companies, staff discounts on company merchandise were far more effective tools for reducing turnover than pensions. In the case of more highly skilled employees, graduates and senior managers the ability of a pension scheme to retain staff increases with age. This is partly seen as resulting from longer serving employees building up substantial pension rights, but also because among these groups, knowledge about pension provision also increases with age. In the case of younger professional staff, the same considerations appear to apply as for lower-skilled staff. Pensions tend to be well down the list of priorities and are not believed to have a serious retentive effect, however generous the scheme in question may be.

A subject on which all interviewees in the author's sample agree is the usefulness of final salary schemes in easing the process by which people are retired early or made redundant after the age of 50. The use of pension scheme assets to enhance redundancy terms is not only a means by which the costs associated with redundancy are reduced; it also provides a valuable means by which an unpleasant management decision can be somewhat 'sweetened'. This latter point is significant from an organisational perspective as it implies that were such an option not available, poor performers in their 50s and early 60s would remain in post longer than is currently the case. It may also go some way to explaining why so little organised resistance was offered in the face of so many redundancies during the recessions of the 1980s and 1990s.

It can thus be concluded that, given the current legal environment and workforce perceptions of the value of occupational pension schemes, there are grounds for doubting that they have a significant effect on employee behaviour. At the very least, there is sufficient evidence to call into question the argument that they are provided by employers principally to attract and retain staff (see Davies, 1992 and 1993). While this might have been the case some years ago and may thus explain the growth in pension scheme coverage in the post-war era, it cannot be relied upon as an explanation of their continued existence.

FUTURE TRENDS

In recent years there has been a pronounced and steady trend away from the provision of defined benefit schemes towards the defined contribution and hybrid forms. Furthermore, there are good reasons for anticipating an acceleration of this trend in the early years of the twenty-first century. First, there is the impact of the regulatory changes described above and the additional costs and workload they have imposed on employers providing defined benefit plans. In the author's view the trend would have occurred faster and sooner had it not been for the presence in the 1990s of large fund surpluses built up in the 1980s. These have served to protect employers from the cost increases imposed via new regulation and have tended to ensure that the attention of finance directors has been turned elsewhere. For many companies surpluses have reduced sharply in the late 1990s, leading some to make employer contributions again for the first time in a number of years. Inevitably this has led to a reassessment of pension provision and to consideration of offering only defined contribution forms of pension to new members of staff. In some cases there may be labour market reasons for taking this course of action too, particularly where a young workforce is to be recruited without expectation of more than a few years' service. In most cases, however, the motives for change appear to be financial rather than HR oriented – a course of action that is entirely rational when viewed in the light of the research evidence described above.

If this prediction is correct it raises interesting possibilities as regards the effects of pension schemes in labour markets. Foremost among these is the prospect of a far greater variety of pension scheme provision on the part of companies than is currently the case, with a substantial proportion offering money purchase plans to new starters and a further group looking to offer 'Rolls Royce' hybrid schemes. If such were the case there are grounds for arguing that pensions might play a far greater role in the attraction and retention of staff than occurs currently. In many cases this would simply arise because employees in well-funded defined benefit schemes stand to lose from resigning to join a new employer offering a defined contribution scheme. The more success the government has in communicating the importance of building up private retirement income, the more potent such labour market effects are likely to be.

We can thus conclude by arguing that, while pension schemes appear to achieve only limited objectives for employers in the current environment (i.e. the attraction and retention of certain groups and the management of early retirements), it is easy to envisage their playing a more central role in future employer reward strategies.

LEARNING ACTIVITIES

1 Identify the type and coverage of pension schemes within your organisation.

2 Assess the impact of the Pensions Act 1995 on your organisation's pension scheme(s).

3 What role should the human resources function adopt in the management and communication of pension schemes?

4 What factors are likely to impact on the role of pension schemes in the reward package of the future?

REFERENCES

Alexander Consulting Group (1993) *Occupational Pension Funds: An uncertain future. A survey of pension scheme trends*. London: Alexander Consulting Group.

Blake, D. (1995) *Pension Funds and Pension Schemes in the UK*. Oxford. Clarendon.

Bodie, Z. (1990) 'Pensions as Retirement Income Insurance', *Journal of Economic Literature*, March.

Casey, B. (1993) *Employers Choice of Pension Schemes: Report of a qualitative study*. London. HMSO.

Confederation of British Industry (1994) *A View from the Top: Senior executives' attitudes to pension provision*. London: CBI.

Davies, B. (1992) *Locking The Stable Door*. London: Institute of Public policy Research.

Davies, B. (1993) *Better Pensions for All*. London: Institute of Public Policy Research.

Dilnot, A., Disney, R., Johnson, P. and Whitehouse, E. (1994) *Pensions Policy in the UK: An economic analysis*. London: Institute of Fiscal Studies.

Economist, (1997) 'Investment brown-out', 5 July 23.

Ellwood, D. (1985) 'Pensions and the Labour Market: A starting point (The mouse can roar)', in D. Wise (ed.), *Pensions, Labor and Individual Choice*. University of Chicago Press.

Financial Times, (1997) 'Brown's First Budget: Act', 3 July 6.

Goode, R. (1993) *Pension Law Reform: The report of the pension law review committee*, 1(2), London: HMSO.

Handa, J. (1994) *Discrimination, Retirement and Pensions*. Aldershot: Avebury.

Harrison, D. (1995) *Pension Power: Understand and control your most valuable asset*. Chichester: Wiley.

Herzberg, F. (1966) *Work and the Nature of Man*. Cleveland: World.

Industrial Relations Services (1994) 'Pay and Benefits Bulletin' (356).

Ippolito, R.A. (1991) 'Encouraging Long Term Tenure: Wage Tilt or Pensions?', *Industrial and Labor Relations Review*, 44: 3.

Kotlikoff, L.J. and Wise, D. (1987) 'The Incentive Effects of Private Pension Plans' in Z. Bodie *et al.* (ed.), *Issues in Pension Economics*. University of Chicago Press.

Lazear, E.P. (1983) 'Pensions as Severence Pay', in Z. Bodie and J. Shoven (ed.), *Financial Aspects of the US Pensions System*. University of Chicago Press.

Lazear, E.P. (1985) 'Incentive Effects of Pensions', in D. Wise (ed.), *Pensions, Labor and Individual Choice*. University of Chicago Press.

Lazear, E.P. (1990) 'Pensions and Deferred Benefits as Strategic Compensation', in D. Mitchell and M. Zaidi (ed.), *The Economics of Human Resource Management*. Oxford: Blackwell.

Lazear, E.P. and Moore, R.L. (1988) 'Pensions and Turnover', in Z. Bodie *et al.* (ed.), *Pensions in the US Economy*. University of Chicago Press.

Maelli, F. and Pudney, S. (1993) 'Occupational Pensions and Job Mobility in Britain: Estimation of a random effects competing risks model', University of Leicester Discussion Paper in Economics.

McCaffery, R. (1992) *Employee Benefit Programs: A total compensation perspective*. Boston, PWS-Kent.

McCormick, B. and Hughes, G. (1984) 'The Influence of Pensions on Job Mobility', *Journal of Public Economics*, 23.

Milkovich, G.T. and Newman, J.M. (1996) *Compensation*. Chicago: Irwin.

Mitchell, O.S. (1983) 'Fringe Benefits and the Cost of Changing Jobs', *Industrial and Labor Relations Review*, 37: 1.

Mortensen, J. (ed.) (1992) *The Future of Pensions in the European Community*. Centre for European Policy Studies.

NAPF (National Association of Pension Funds) (1992) 'Seventeenth Annual Survey of Occupational Pension Schemes', London: NAPF.

NAPF (National Association of Pension Funds) (1997) Twenty-Second Annual Survey of Occupational Pension Schemes, London: NAPF.

NTC (1997) *Pensions Pocket Book 1998*. Henley on Thames: NTC Publications Ltd.

Olian, J., Carroll, S.J. and Schneier, C.E. (1985) *Pension Plans: The human resource perspective*. Cornell University, New York: ILR Press.

Schiller, B. and Weiss, R.D. (1979) 'The Impact of Private Pensions on Firm Attachment', *Review of Economics and Statistics*, 61.

Taylor, S.J. and Earnshaw, J.M. (1995) 'An Exploration of Employer Objectives in the Provision of Occupational Pensions in the 1990s', *Employee Relations*, 17.2.

Towers Perrin Foster and Crosby (1986) *Survey Into Pension Perception*, London: Towers Perrin Foster and Crosby.

Viscusi, W.K. (1985) 'The Structure of Uncertainty and the Use of Non-Transferable Pensions as a Mobility-Reduction Device', in D. Wise (ed.), *Pensions, Labor and Individual Choice*. University of Chicago Press.

Ward, S. (1995) *Managing the Pensions Revolution*. London: Nicholas Brealey.

Wise, D.A. (1986) 'Overview', in D. Wise (ed.), *Pensions, Labor and Individual Choice*. University of Chicago Press.

FURTHER READING

There are currently relatively few publications in print on the subject of occupational pensions which are both accessible and written from a management perspective. Much of what is available is either highly technical or very basic in terms of its content. However, the following texts include material that takes forward what has been introduced above:

Blake, D. (1995) *Pension Funds and Pension Schemes in the United Kingdom*. Oxford: Clarendon Press.

Casey, B. (1993) 'Employers Choice of Pension Schemes: Report of a qualitative study', London: HMSO.

Goode, R. (1993) 'Pension Law Reform: The report of the pension law review Committee', London: HMSO.

McCaffery, R. (1992) *Employee Benefit Programs: A total compensation Perspective*. Boston: PWS-Kent.

Milkovich, G. and Newman, J. (1996) *Compensation*. Fifth edition, Chicago: Irwin.

Mortensen, J. (ed.) (1992) 'The Future of Pensions in the European Community', Centre for European Policy Studies.

Ward, S. (1995) *Managing the Pensions Revolution: A practical guide to pension schemes*. London: Nicholas Brealey.

In addition, Incomes Data Services (IDS) and Industrial Relations Services (IRS) regularly report pensions issues in their management publications.

22 Flexible plans for pay and benefits

Ian Smith

INTRODUCTION

Flexible plans in remuneration relate to the 'mix' of various cash and non-cash elements in an individual employee's reward package. The method is variously described as cafeteria remuneration, flex plans and life cycle flex plans; at one time 'key player rewards' was a term used to describe the provision of flexibility. In their most developed form, and to date this means American applications, such plans offer employees a variety of 'mixes' for cash and benefits in order to meet different employee needs even at different points in their career. Meeting employee need is at least theoretically a key objective for this flexibility; an emphasis on cash may help a young employee to purchase pre-school child care; an emphasis on pension contributions may help a mature employee to build up a more comfortable pension plan. That such flexibility may enhance retention and motivation, particularly for key staff, is one major reason which might persuade employers to consider the introduction of flexible remuneration practices. Yet flexible remuneration has not proved popular in the United Kingdom. In the United States, where it originated in the late 1970s growth has been considerable in the past ten to 15 years. Difficult administration, and fear of the unknown are some of the reasons for sluggishness in Britain. In this chapter we identify the main elements of flexible remuneration, their place within recent developments in reward management and assess the problems and solutions associated with flexibility together with its value to employers and employees.

FLEXIBLE PLANS

We can consider flexibility in remuneration on three levels as follows:

1 flexible cash and benefits
2 flexible benefits
3 life-cycle flexible benefits

The few organisations in the United Kingdom adopting flexibility have largely embraced cash and benefits while in the United States flexible plans have progressed from straightforward cash and benefits to life-cycle methods for benefits only.

Cash and benefits

A typical example of the cash and benefits approach in the United Kingdom is that being developed in the Birmingham Midshires Building Society reported by Arkin in *People Management*, March 1997. Details quoted by Arkin include an employee option to exchange cash for life assurance; an option to exchange cash for extra holidays or vice versa; and options to exchange cash for dental insurance, health screening and critical illness insurance cover. Those not automatically receiving them in the basic package are able to trade cash for private medical insurance and leased cars. These exchanges between cash and benefits are provided for by a 'flex fund' which accounts for 20 per cent of salary. This flexible scheme also embraces a move to reduce status-based benefit provision and is, untypically for the UK, available to all employees of the building society; it is more usual for flexible schemes to be offered to senior managers and 'key players' only. In the United States flexible plans are normally available to all employees in the organisation.

Flexible benefits

Flexible benefit plans allow employees to choose from a menu of benefit options. Originally limited to health care, these benefit plans in American companies now allow employees choice of benefit provision including the opportunity to drop certain benefits from their personal flexible plan. Thus benefits can be exchanged for benefits with the aim of controlling employer costs through increasing employee awareness of the costs of benefits and leaving them to decide how much they want to pay for benefits out of total salary. Usually employees choose the least-expensive options or are encouraged to share benefits costs with the employer, hence the enhanced control of payroll costs. It is the case, however, that such control sometimes comes at the expense of an extra 'cost' to the employee which may involve some sacrifice of other benefits.

Life-cycle flexible benefits

Life-cycle benefit plans represent a significant step forward. Whereas basic flexible benefit plans are implemented to provide variety at a point in time and at a particular point in the employees' career, life-cycle plans are aimed at meeting changing employee requirements through the length of their career. Allowances are provided to employees from which they 'buy' such benefits as child care, care for the elderly, tuition and school fees, down payments on property, legal services as well as the more normal benefit provisions. This American approach covers a much wider range of provision than is customary in the United Kingdom and is designed to help employees better cope with the costs associated with life's' developments. In some companies the allowances are aimed at a specific type of provision; for example the Xerox Corporation in America provides each employee with a life-time allowance of $10K to spend on the required elements of the flexible life-cycle plan, which include child care, elderly dependent care and educational fees (Grant, 1995).

It is clear that American companies tend to view benefits plans as THE means to simultaneously distribute employee income in the interests of meeting employee requirements and reducing costs to the employer, despite the complexity involved. Against the background of ongoing developments and ever-increasing applications of flexible plans in the United States, take up in the United Kingdom is probably limited to less than 60 such plans.[1] Nor are UK plans developed to the same level of sophistication as their American equivalents. The reason for this may lie in the less than dynamic approach to remuneration which persists in the UK Despite the presence of 'hard' and 'soft' human resource management and reward management, the remuneration methodologies practised in the UK tend toward short-term cost reductions rather than long-term improvement. Unfortunately flexible remuneration is a more likely development under long-term strategies; the current preoccupation with reward management in this country may be closer to a short-term approach in application at least.

DETERMINING THE MIX

The development of a 'flexible package' requires decisions on the *price* for the job, the *cash* and *non-cash elements* and where deemed appropriate *tax effectiveness*. Price for the job means the total amount of cash and non-cash elements given to the employee. In this context, price will normally relate to ability and contribution; future development and therefore improvement of the employee; prices (or pay levels) provided by competitors in the labour market; and the need to avoid disturbing the existing internal pay structure and differentials. It is appropriate to note that a problem can arise here: some applications have benefited significantly from the presence of well-structured and equitable pay systems, but such structures may not exist in many organisations in the first place (Smith, 1998). On the reverse side of the problem, where they do exist they may be disturbed by the complex pattern of individual employee remuneration packages arising from the many elements to be considered for flexible plans and which are influenced by employee choice. Such elements include core and non-core items as follows:

- Core
  - basic salary;
  - basic pension cover;
  - basic death in service insurance cover;
  - basic sickness and disability insurance;
  - basic company car entitlement or cash equivalent;

- Non-core
  - incentive payments;
  - any supplementary retirement benefit;
  - medical insurance;
  - share allocations or stock options;
  - low or interest free loans;
  - housing/moving assistance;

– any additional perquisites such as season ticket loans;
– benefits in kind.

Core items are normally limited in terms of flexibility to ensure minimum provision and security for the employees, or may not allow for any flexibility at all. Non-core items have greater flexibility and in benefit plans are sometimes the only remuneration elements treated flexibly.

Tax effectiveness has become less of a priority in the UK since the introduction of lower marginal rates in 1988, making an assessment of the expectations of the recipient necessary before embarking on the sometimes considerable work involved in preparing a flexible package which is specifically tax efficient. Tax efficiency is not proved to be a major objective for employers and employees involved in flexible plans anyway, but the provision of cash alternatives and non-cash alternatives of remuneration will require some evaluation in the light of tax law and accounting conventions which requires some work by management. Finally, non-cash elements do not normally replace a sacrificed 'cash right' and are not regarded as convertible to cash as a right.

Example of a flexible remuneration package

An example of how core and non-core remuneration can be arranged in a flexible package to enhance financial benefits for the employee and lower costs to the employer is provided in tables 22.1 and 22.2 below. The figures are appropriate to a middle management position. The normal approach to determining remuneration is in table 22.1 followed by a possible flexible package in table 22.2. Of note in this example is

Table 22.1 Example to show traditional method for remuneration package assuming £6,000 allowable tax deductions

	Gross value to employee	Net value to employee		Cost to company	
Base pay	£38,500	£25,486	(66.20%)	£42,523	(110.45%)
Perquisites:					
Company car (Lease)	£6,000	£5,435	(90.58%)	£6,480	(108%)
Security benefits: Pension	£5,775	£5,775			
Insurances: Death-in-service	£270	£270			
Sickness and disability	£150	£150			
Accidental death and disablement	£70	£70			
Medical expenses	£350	£157			
Total pay and benefit	£51,115	£37,343	(73.06%)	£55,618	(108.81%)
Incentive pay	£10,500	£4,562	(43.45%)	£11,597	(110.45%)
Total pay	£61,615	£41,905	(68.00%)	£67,215	(109%)

Table 22.2 Example to show flexible plan method for the same remuneration package presented in table 22.1

	Gross value to employee	Net value to employee		Cost to company	
Core pay	£38,500	£25,486	(66.20%)	£42,523	(110.45%)
Company car	£6,000	£5,435	(90.58%)	£6,480	(108%)
Core benefits	£6,615	£6,422	(97.08%)	£6,615	(100%)
TOTAL CORE	£51,115	£37,243	(73.06%)	£55,618	(108.81%)
Flexible or non-core					
Private petrol	£1,500	£1,005		£1,005	
Second car	£3,000	£2,422		£3,850	
Qualified stock	£3,850	£3,850		£3,850	
Augmented pension	£1,150	£1,150		£1,500	
Cash	£1,000	£450			
Total core and non-core	£61,615	£46,120	(74.85%)	£66,448	(108%)
Increase/decrease (compared with traditional method)	Nil	£4,215	(10.06%)	–£767	(1.24%)

the way in which the flexible approach actually increases the net value of a fixed gross level of remuneration by £4,215 or 10.06 per cent while decreasing the cost to the employers by £767 or 1.24 per cent. Thus gain to the employee is far greater than that enjoyed by the employer. Readers should note that this case is not strictly based on UK practice and assumes a marginal tax rate of 60 per cent which is more typical of European countries.

USER–CHOOSER ISSUES

Although employee choice is important, complete flexibility within schemes has not proved practical on the ground and it is common for employers to 'drive' the provision of a nucleus of benefits (Hewitt Associates, 1991). For example, a minimum amount of pension may be offered, which cannot be traded for cash. Those benefits which are taken instead of cash will normally offer a tax advantage of greater value to the recipient compared with his or her own cash purchase of the benefit. The serious in-depth decision making required of the employee in choosing the right balance of elements can be beyond them however, and, because of this, flexibility in the UK is often limited to executives and professionals with a proved ability in terms of judgement (Income Data Services, 1991). Even with these employee groups the degree of flexibility is often seen to require defined limits, specified by the employer, coupled to the provision of sound advice from the personnel department. In these terms employee take up may be contingent upon professional administration and effective communication of flexible plans.

Where benefits are related to individual circumstances and are reviewed year by year, then costs can be planned on an annual basis, improving payroll cost control. In this way those benefits which become unacceptably costly (e.g. private health care) can be withdrawn from the package, or modified or removed from employer to employee purchase or *vice versa*. Employer contributions which are proportionately related to employee contributions may also ease the cost burden to employer and employee alike, although this may have a limiting influence on benefit provision (Woodley, 1990).

Where employers are concerned about 'rogue' employee decisions some intervention may be justified; in particular ensuring that the basic salary remains the dominant element in the core rewards, coupled to core benefits which are only reduced to a level consistent with the need for minimum security. One conundrum which arises in this connection is the need to maximise choice and ensure that core elements are not reduced to the point where they do not positively influence retention and motivation; consistent with this the non-core cash benefits and perquisites can be expanded or contracted in terms of their presence within the reward package as evidenced at the Birmingham Midshires Building Society. They can be maximised in non-cash terms or converted into equivalent cash payments, but as mentioned above many companies take great care to emphasise that non-cash compensation should not be offered to an employee in exchange for a loss or deferral of a right to cash payments (Income Data Services, 1988). In allowing the individual to select his or her own ideal mix of cash and benefits, it is usually recommended that the company can ensure that employees most valuable to the enterprise are provided with rewards and a degree of status and influence unique to them (Stoneburger, 1988).

OVERSEAS EXPERIENCE

These 'cafeteria' approaches were first used for flexible remuneration in America, and the method was used there particularly to meet the different needs of young and old people, thus putting cash and non-cash provisions to maximum use in influencing retention and motivation at different ages. Section 125 of the US Tax Code introduced as the Tax Reform Act of 1978, allows employees to participate in the process of determining how employee earnings are to be allocated between pay and benefits. In 1983 50 cafeteria systems were in operation in the US. In 1991, the number had exceeded 1,000 including 155 of the Fortune 500 companies, and by 1993 some 53 per cent of US full-time employees were estimated to be working in companies which made them eligible for flexible benefits (US Department of Labour, 1987, 1994). The spread of these schemes is across all sections of the American economy and a significant number of companies are high performers. The following advantages for flexible pay have been identified by US human resource managers (Barber, Dunham and Formisano, 1992; Income Data Services, 1991; Hewitt Associates, 1988; Micelli and Lane, 1991):

(a) companies discover which benefits are popular and which are not;
(b) companies can manage benefit costs more effectively;

(c) companies can communicate the real cost of benefits to their labour force;

(d) companies can use one strategic approach to meet diverse employee requirements;

(e) cost effective improvements in staff retention.

For employees in America the reported benefits come under three headings. First is the improved understanding of benefit costs and variety and the satisfaction deriving from that improved understanding; coupled to this is a greater knowledge of the value of the costs and benefits. Using flexibility to give some 'control' of the benefits package is a second gain for employees leading to enhanced satisfaction. And, third, the needs of new employee groupings including single parents, unmarried employees and individuals in childless dual career relationships can be appropriately responded to with flexibility. The evidence from across the Atlantic underpins the way in which flexibility can better meet the new expectations and needs of the workforces of the next milennium. Certainly the experiences with American flexible plans underline their use as a key strategy for meeting the needs of a changing and more diverse labour force.[2]

Furthermore, flexible methods in America are claimed to have helped streamline payroll administration and improve the quality of management decisions for remuneration. In New Zealand, where flexibility has been similarly popular, cost control and wider choice have been reported as the main benefits. The experiences of American employers and employees in particular appear to be positive. Based on this overseas experience we could perhaps note that flexible benefits may be one (perhaps the only one) potentially 'worthy' element of 'reward management'. As yet the potential is far from realised in the UK.

Flexible plans are also rare in Europe, perhaps rarer than in the UK, but a 1992 Towers Perrin Survey revealed that companies reported projected changes to benefits provision for the year 2,000 including the 'introduction' of flexible benefit plans. It is probably unwise to expect any radical 'departures' on this issue. The 1995 Price Waterhouse Cranfield Survey concluded – 'organisations with innovative and imaginative . . . schemes which make use of a broad range of information to give employees and managers the broadest possible feedback . . . continue to be rare everywhere'. This situation could not be more different to the American use of flexible plans employing sound communications and feedback in the pursuit of change in labour force characteristics.

FOR UNCLE SAM BUT NOT FOR BRITANNIA

Reported examples of flexible remuneration in American companies give evidence that management have positively viewed benefits plans as a key method for simultaneously achieving three desirable objectives; the distribution of remuneration to better meet the needs of employees, improved control of payroll costs, and improvements in the quality of the management of remuneration (Hewitt Associates, 1988). Against the background of on-going developments and increasing applications of flexible plans in the United States, interest and take up in Britain remains low. The reason for this may lie in the less than dynamic approach to remuneration so traditional in the UK, and which persists. Despite the presence of 'hard' and 'soft' human resource management and reward management, the remuneration methodologies practised in the UK tend toward short-term cost reductions rather than long-term improvement. Unfortunately flexible methods are a more likely development within long-term strategies, as discussed later in the chapter. The on-going pre-occupation with reward management in the UK is probably much closer to short termism in the management of remuneration practices (Smith, 1993).

REWARD MANAGEMENT AND ALL THAT

It is worth noting that the principle of flexibility in pay systems is not new for the UK. The linking of an element of remuneration to individual employee characteristics, particularly their performance or contribution, has underpinned various forms of performance-related pay throughout this century from simple piecework to the latter day and more visionary use of core competencies as determinants of reward. Traditionally these approaches have been 'defensive' measures designed to contain labour costs in competitive environments. Since the early 1980s debate and theory (but not necessarily practice) have turned to a more 'offensive' indeed almost strategic role for remuneration in pursuit of long-term sustainable improvements in the effectiveness and adaptability of the organisation's human resources. This debate has flourished under the heading of reward management (Armstrong and Murlis, 1994). The interpretation of these developments requires us to exercise some caution, however. There may not be any 'new age' here in the management of remuneration in the UK. Instead we may have interesting images which soon 'shade to grey' in application and outputs.

The way in which the term 'reward management' has become popularised in the UK within a manager's vocabulary and because of the 'enterprise culture' has meant that it has embraced many practices in the field of performance-related pay. Yet simultaneously, and under the reward management umbrella, flexible remuneration began to rise in prominence as reward management became the 'in' phrase to legitimise innovation in pay systems. Depressingly, the protagonists for reward management have experienced little if any kind of challenge to their claims that this term describes and represents a serious revolution in the management of remuneration which is both strategic and the basis for moving organisational performance forwards. These claims are certainly open to debate and on the evidence it is arguable that there has been no swing to strategic methods; rather developments have been ad hoc reactions to labour market pressures; reliance on money as a motivator has been a continuation of what has gone before in the 'muddling through' so characteristic of traditional wage and salary administration in the UK (Smith, 1992). Thus much of the flexibility (certainly the early attempts) in UK companies tended to be simple and short term in nature, in order to find a quick fix for retention problems among key staff under the heading of 'key player rewards'.

SIMPLE BUT GLAMOROUS ORIGINS

The way in which the patchy development of flexible remuneration has moved in Britain over the past decade or so has been less systematic than in the USA. In the competitive labour market conditions of the 1980s organisations experiencing growth faced difficulties with certain groups of employees, particularly in terms of retention. This problem was most acute in the finance, information technology and leisure sectors and with specialist skills, such as computer programmers, financial analysts, key executive personnel, electronics and electrical engineers. Such employees became popularly known as 'key players' in the late 1980s because of the importance and value of their contribution to the company. Dealing with these so-called key players witnessed solutions ranging from some addition to pay to (exceptionally) a total revision of the remuneration packages for these employees which was originally called 'key player rewards' thus bringing flexible plans into UK practice, but in simple and costly form (Smith, 1989). The over-enthusiastic and *ad hoc* approach of early years with glittering prizes given to a few high flyers in cash-rich companies has given way to a more restrained emphasis in the 1990s accompanied by a name change to 'flexible remuneration' or 'cafeteria remuneration', with the priority placed on benefits. The more 'sober' times of the 1990s, therefore, have caused a few UK organisations to use flexibility in reward systems to underpin employee retention and contributions to company performance and not just for 'key' employees.

The origins of UK methods were dubious forms of rewarding employees who were exposed to competitive demand in the labour market rather than strategic attempts to underpin long-term improvements in employee performance and control of payroll costs. Flexible remuneration was thus tied up with telephone number salaries, expensive company cars, and a glamorous all-expenses-paid life style usually enjoyed by people between 21 and 35 years of age. The City in particular indulged in such generous provisions. Some of these organisations have felt some regret in recent times for the 'over-the-top' approach originally taken, in which some key players were retained by a policy almost akin to allowing employees to 'write their own salary cheques'. Of course these instances were few and limited to people whose potential contribution to operations and profit could be substantial; but they were a bad example and a bad start for flexibility and for the companies concerned a chastening experience, at least in hindsight. Furthermore, many employees provided with flexibility did not enjoy long-term security in jobs normally filled by people under the age of 40; maximising cash earnings 'now' (between ages 25 and 35) was sometimes seen as essential to provide for some financial security in later life, and key player flexible packages were designed to allow such people the opportunity to choose between cash and non-cash alternatives according to their circumstances and expectations, in support of future financial security outside the organisation (Smith, 1995). This scramble for cash could be described as a 'knee-jerk' reaction by managements looking for a 'quick fix' to deal with problems of retention. This was not a complex, administratively smooth development requiring much time and effort by managements. In contrast a serious and balanced approach to flexible plans demands the acceptance of change and much work; the effort required in coping with change has to date represented a step too far for the vast majority of employing organisations in Britain.

DIFFICULTIES AND COMPLEXITY

The complexity and change involved with flexibility derive from the essential characteristic of allowing elements of remuneration to receive differential emphasis based on individual employee choice, even when choice is constrained within a total amount of cash determined by management from which the employees' combination of elements is funded. Each employee determines a potentially 'unique' remuneration package influencing to a limited (controlled) degree his or her desired balance of cash payments, benefits and perquisites within the overall amount for their total remuneration. The perceived complexity and difficulty associated with such choice is compounded in the minds of managers because any existing degree of standardisation in pay structures at company or unit level inevitably gives way to some variability based on individual employee preferences. Flexibility can thereby increase complexity in organisation remuneration structures at two levels: the flexible method itself and the resultant variability in remuneration packages. In addition to the complexity which the core and non-core elements represent, management will need to work hard at achieving the right balance for the two groupings to ensure their cost effectiveness, acceptability to staff and the financial security of different employee groupings. This too involves difficulty which managements may wish to avoid.

Management control of rewards may at first sight appear to be diluted by allowing employee preferences in flexible plans, again making adoption difficult to accept. Employee resistance to the change and complexity involved with flexibility is also reported coupled to 'shyness' when it comes to making choices. But employee acceptance of flexible remuneration is not helped by employer attitudes often ranging from indifference to hostility. Evidence indicates that managers often under-rate employee capabilities in making decisions, a false assumption which can re-enforce management resistance to flexible plans (Fragner, 1995; Hewitt Associates, 1988).

A STRATEGIC PERSPECTIVE

The role of a strategic framework for the management of remuneration has been repeatedly presented as a key feature or requirement for effective reward management practices at least in the literature (Smith, 1991a). Corporate policy and strategies may therefore be a legitimate and consistent starting point to allow for business objectives to influence the assessment and design of flexible plans. This would be of real use to management as they consider the adoption of flexible plans. Further value could derive from coupling a strategic approach to an analysis of labour market conditions which influence employee attraction but more importantly retention. There are no clear examples of how a strategic dimension is used for flexible plans, although American reports claim their existence and emphasise the long-term nature of flexibility. Nonetheless, strategy could provide a useful context in which to evaluate the ouputs of flexibility and the following detailed evaluations reported in UK and US applications (Smith, 1991b).

(a) An assessment of the competitiveness and motivational effects for the recipient deriving from flexible plans; not an easy task but one which management could very usefully evaluate to their advantage.

(b) Some assessment of the ambitions and preferences (now and in the future) of the recipients.

(c) Some margin in the flexible plans to cope with changing company conditions over time.

(d) Greater choice to reflect seniority and higher levels of remuneration.

(e) The balancing of cash and non-cash remuneration, and short-term incentives and long-term capital accumulation (through share options and profit sharing) to provide for maximum financial benefit and value of the package to the recipient.

(f) The value of the reward to the employee being assured if he or she believes there is certainty and longevity for the flexible package.

The use of strategy coupled to and driving the evaluation of the above six issues may show the way forward for flexibility by providing a clear path through some of the complexities and a systematic approach to the management of remuneration. But this systematic approach is not yet finished, for flexible plans need a carefully managed introduction to the company.

FITTING A FLEXIBLE APPROACH INTO THE ORGANISATION

The evaluation, adoption and design of flexible plans must fit the remuneration system. Reconciling remuneration with the corporate policy and objectives of the company has been seen as a possible and useful first step in introducing flexibility. But many companies lack strategic plans and even those which forecast the future rarely relate the corporate plan into a workable human resource plan, and translating a human resource plan into a remuneration strategy is by no means common (Smith, 1983). Where a plan exists however there may be many detail issues which need to be considered under the heading of human resource management if flexible plans or packages are to fit into the organisation culture, human resource management policies and methods. To help obtain this 'fit', policy decisions may be required in the three following areas:

(a) the organisation's requirements for cost effective remuneration and performance targets;

(b) the need to maximise performance in pursuit of financial and non-financial targets;

(c) external and internal constraints on pay and performance.

Following on from such policy decisions management will need to consider the six detailed issues presented below.

(a) the job skills required for flexible remuneration recipients;

(b) the positioning of these employees in the organisation structure;

(c) the status of their jobs within the organisation;

(d) pay relativities – external and internal;

(e) the relationship between flexible compensation and the traditional reward systems;

(f) the relationship of flexible compensation to any performance measurement system such as appraisal.

In the above areas of human resource management and remuneration, management will be searching for and achieving a best-fit between current characteristics which are significant for remuneration and the characteristics of flexible plans. It might be argued that the work involved in this is easily justified because it is sound human resource management practice anyway.

OVERCOMING OBSTACLES AND RESISTANCE

We have seen that, in the United Kingdom, there appear to be real problems in accepting fully flexible plans in remuneration. Objections include difficult administration; problems connected with handling individual employee choices; the requirement for complex costing and records; difficulty in getting employees to make effective choices; employees making mistakes (and for example leaving themselves with inadequate pension cover); employee's circumstances changing over time leaving his or her package inappropriate and giving the employer the costly headache of re-designing the package; and finally the possible hiring of expensive specialist or consultant skills and financial counselling to support the move to flexibility. Changing legislation and the uncertainty for benefits and developments in benefit provision, are further recent and on-going problems which have convinced British companies they were right to stay clear of flexible remuneration; the future of company pension provisions and company car provision looks particularly 'muddy' at present. The major 'voiced' worries about flexibility however remain the difficulty of fitting the plans into current human resource management and remuneration policies and practices and the possible knock-on effect on company-wide differentials. The latter worry is well founded; maintaining differentials and comparability has historically been a headache for UK companies. Managements may therefore feel that a full flexible approach is beyond their administrative capability, may not work and is not justified. The means to justifying flexibility to employees may be seen as adding to complexity, as the following examples show.

1. Changes in taxation can be taken care of by structuring the components of remuneration in a way which allows them to be amended on an annual basis or withdrawn without detriment to the employee or company, but this will require considerable on-going administration.
2. Effective high-order communication skills will be required if management are to convince employees of the benefits deriving from flexible plans.
3. Regular benefit statements may be necessary to maintain awareness of the value of the total package and, where applicable, choices made, as well as how the company has sought to structure the package tax efficiently.
4. Pay statements may be changed to show net and gross salary equivalents to highlight the taxable elements of the package which result in substantial savings; indeed comparison of this with the true potential cost when met personally out of net income may be the only way to prove the true value of relatively highly taxed benefits, such as cars or beneficial loans.
5. Employee subjective responses to particular remuneration items should be monitored to ensure their positive impact (or otherwise) on retention and motivation.

A degree of complexity in the management of flexible remuneration is therefore inevitable, even necessary. Ensuring the attraction, retention and motivation of staff has long been at the core of human resource management in the UK; the question is whether flexible plans can better achieve these goals than simpler methods, including performance-related pay, which have to date enjoyed 'patchy' success at best. Arkin's report on the flexible scheme at Birmingham Midshires Building Society suggests that the change and complexity involved can only be justified if there are irrefutable reasons and arguments for change and an appropriate and receptive organisation culture. At Midshires that culture has been changed through the empowerment of staff in support of employee decisions on pay. Interestingly this type of culture change characterises those American companies which have successfully adopted flexible plans (Rabin, 1995).

CONCLUSION

There is presently little, if any, prospect of flexible plans for pay and or benefits increasing in application in the UK. This contrasts starkly with the situation in the United States where reports reveal high levels of interest among management and staff. A preoccupation with simplicity and performance-related pay in Britain seems to act as a barrier to the lateral thinking required as a first step to a more positive evaluation of flexible plans. Additionally, the introduction of this flexibility requires a management commitment to the long term; flexible plans are no 'flash in the pan' and their success depends on their durability and positive influence on employee behaviour over a significant time period which in the case of life-cycle plans means the whole career of an employee. If British employers are not ready for this sort of long-term commitment it says little for the impact of Human Resource Management and Reward Management on the move to more strategic long-term management of remuneration, and on the empowerment of their employees to allow them a sensible involvement in determining their remuneration packages. In remuneration as in other organisation matters culture is a defining characteristic which currently bars flexible plans.

NOTES

1 This figure is provided by P. Murray of Hewitt Associates and is reported in Arkin (1997).
2 For evidence of the reported advantages for employees deriving from flexible plans in US companies see Harris and Fink (1994) and Rabin (1994).

LEARNING ACTIVITIES

1 Assess the extent and means by which benefits are harmonised or differentiated within your organisation.

2 Outline the benefits offered by your organisation and assess the extent to which they could be offered on a flexible basis in their current form.

3 Identify the benefits and costs to both the individual and the organisation of adopting a flexible benefits package.

4 How might current government economic and social policy impact on the operation and take-up of a flexible scheme in the UK?

REFERENCES

Arkin, A. (1996) 'Mutually Inclusive', *People Management*, 3(6), Institute of Personnel and Development.

Armstrong, M. and Murlis, H. (1994) *Reward Management: A handbook of salary administration*. Fourth edition, London: Kogan Page.

Barber, A., Dunham, R.B., Formisano, R.A. (1992) 'The Impact of Flexible Benefits on Employee Satisfaction: A field study', *Personnel Psychology*, 45.

Fragner, B.N. 'Employees' Cafeteria Offers Insurance Options', *Harvard Business Review*, 53: 2–4.

Grant, D.B. (1995) 'Life-Cycle Flex Plans: The future of flexible benefits', *American Compensation Association Journal*, 4(2).

Harris, M. and Fink, L. (1994) 'Employee Benefit Programmes and Attitudinal and Behavioural Outcomes: A preliminary model', *Human Resource Management Review*, 4(2).

Hewitt Associates (1988) *Fundamentals of Flexible Compensation*. New York: Wiley.

Hewitt Associates (1991) *Total Compensation Management for the 1990s*, Oxford: Blackwell, Chapter 7.

Incomes Data Services (1988) European Report No. 311, April.

Incomes Data Services (1991) Study 481, DIY Benefits for the 1990s.

Micelli M. and Lane, M.C. (1991) 'Antecedents of Pay Satisfaction: A review and extension', *Research in Personnel and Human Resource Management*, 9.

Perrin, Towers (1992) 'Learning from the Past: Changing for the Future', A Research Study of Pay and Reward Challenges and Changes in Europe.

The Price Waterhouse Cranfield Project (1995) International Strategic HRM, Joint Survey.

Rabin, B.R. (1994) 'Benefits Communication: Its impact on employee benefits satisfaction under flexible programmes', *Benefits Quarterly*, 10(4).

Rabin, B.R. (1995) 'Employee Satisfaction Within A Managed Flex Programme: Strategic Design Implications', *American Compensation Association Journal*, 4(2).

Smith, I.G. (1983) *The Management of Remuneration*, Institute of Personnel Management.

Smith, I.G. (1989) *Incentive Schemes: People and profits*. First edition, Kingston-Upon-Thames: Croner Publications.

Smith, I.G. (1991a) *Reward Management: An appraisal*. Kingston-Upon-Thames: Croner Special Report.

Smith, I.G. (1991b) *Incentive Schemes: People and Profits*. Second edition, Kingston-Upon-Thames: Croner.

Smith, I.G. (1992) 'Reward Management and H-R-M', in P. Blyton and P. Turnbull, *Reassessing Human Resource Management*. London: Sage.

Smith, I.G. (1993) 'Reward Management: A retrospective assessment', *Employee Relations*, 15(3).

Smith, I.G. (1995) '*Key Player Rewards and Flexible Compensation*'. Kingston-Upon-Thames: Croner Publications.

Smith, I.G. (1998) 'Reward Management and the Loss of Equity', *British Personnel Management*, 2(12), CCH Editions.

Stoneburger, P.W. (1988) 'Flexible and Incentive Benefits: A guide to programme development', *Compensation and Benefits Review*, 17(2).

United States Department of Labour, Bureau of Labour Statistics (1987, 1994) *Employee Benefits in Medium and Large Private Establishments*.

Woodley, C. (1990) 'The Cafeteria Route to Compensation', *Personnel Management*, May.

FURTHER READING

Armstrong, M. and Murlis, H. (1994) *Reward Management: A handbook of salary Administration*. Fourth edition, London: Kogan Page.

Grant, D.B. (1995) 'Life-Cycle Flex Plan: The Future of Flexible Benefits', *American Compensation Association Journal*, 4(2).

Incomes Data Services (1991) Study No. 481, DIY Benefits for the 1990s, IDS.

Smith, I.G. (1995) *Key Player Rewards and Flexible Compensation*. Kingston Upon Thames: Croner Publications.

Index